The Decline of Carlism

The Basque Series

JEREMY MacCLANCY

The Decline of Carlism

University of Nevada Press ▲▲ Reno & Las Vegas

The Basque Series

Series Editor: William A. Douglass

University of Nevada Press,

Reno, Nevada 89557 USA

First Printing

09 08 07 06 05 04 03 02 01 00 5 4 3 2 1

Library of Congress

Cataloging-in-Publication Data

MacClancy, Jeremy.

The decline of Carlism / Jeremy

MacClancy.

p. cm.—(The Basque series)

ISBN 0-87417-344-2 (hardcover)

1. Navarre (Spain)—Politics and

government—20th century.

2. Carlism—Spain—Navarre—

History—20th century.   3. Oral history.

I. Title.   II. Series.

DP302.N33 M33 2000

946'.5207—dc21   00-009887

To Marí, her family,

and all the people of Cirauqui

Contents

List of Illustrations   ix

Preface   xiii

Chapter One: Introduction   1

Chapter Two: Representing the *Requetés*   15

Chapter Three: Village Carlism   34

Chapter Four: Postwar Carlism   74

Chapter Five: The Rise of the Progressives   89

Chapter Six: Kings and Common Phrases   102

Chapter Seven: Past Masters   116

Chapter Eight: Montejurra   127

Chapter Nine: The Establishment of the Progressives   157

Chapter Ten: Montejurra 1976   169

Chapter Eleven: The Decline of Carlism   186

Chapter Twelve: Village Carlism: 1939–1987   203

Chapter Thirteen: The Legacies of Carlism to Basque Nationalism   233

Epilogue: Montejurra 1986   243

Appendix I: Computer Analysis of the 1897 Cadastral Survey

    of Cirauqui   247

Appendix II: Approximate Numbers Attending Montejurra,

    1939–1989   275

Notes   277

Bibliography   319

Index   339

Illustrations

Following page 156

1. Paco, 1987

2. Marí and the author, 1987

3. Milu and his son Marco, 1999

4. Javi, 1999

5. La Txus Laita and Marí-José Dallo, Cirauqui fiestas, 1999

6. "Requetés," Carlos Saénz de Tejada, late 1930s

7. *Con este signo vencerás*, Gustavo de Maetzu, ca. 1938

8. Dome of the Monument to the Fallen, Pamplona, Ramón Stolz Viciano, 1950

9. Cirauqui, view from the east, 1998

10. Annual village fiestas, 1911

11. Village band at fiesta time, 1912

12. El Cojo de Cirauqui, 1870s

13. *Cirauqui Todo por los Fueros* banner, 1870s

14. Don Javier and Carlos Hugo, early 1960s

15. Pope Paul VI, Carlos Hugo, and Princess Irene, 1964

16. Carlos Hugo and María-Teresa, early 1960s

17. Princesses Cecilia and María-Teresa, Montejurra, mid-1960s

18. Princesses Irene and María-Teresa, late 1960s

19. Princess María-Teresa, mid-1960s

20. The ascent of Montejurra, mid-1960s

21. Mass on the summit of Montejurra, mid-1960s

22. Plaza de los Fueros, Estella, mid-1960s

23. Attack outside the monastery of Irache, 1976

24. Wounded at Irache, 1976

25. Traditional Basque dancers, Cirauqui, 1998

26. *Zezensuko* fireworks, 1998

27. Village name change from Castilian to Basque, 1998

28. Lithograph of General Zumulacárregui by Gustavo de Maeztu, 1940s

MAP

The seven Basque provinces   xx

FIGURES

1. The Development of Cirauqui's Population, 1450–1990   36

2. Political Parties by Tax Group   53

3. Distribution of Total Tax Paid Per Individual   249

4. Tax Paid on Tilled Land, First Class   249

5. Tax Paid on Tilled Land, Second Class   250

6. Tax Paid on Tilled Land, Third Class   250

7. Tax Paid on Tilled Land, Fourth Class   251

8. Tax Paid on Tilled Land, Sixth Class   251

9. Tax Paid on Market Gardens   252

10. Tax Paid on Vineyards, First Class   252

11. Tax Paid on Vineyards, Second Class   253

12. Tax Paid on Vineyards, Third Class   253

13. Tax Paid on Vineyards, Fourth Class   254

14. Tax Paid on Vineyards, Fifth Class   254

15. Tax Paid on Vineyards, Sixth Class   255

16. Tax Paid on Olive Groves, First Class   255

17. Tax Paid on Olive Groves, Second Class   256

18. Tax Paid on Olive Groves, Third Class   256

19. Tax Paid on Olive Groves, Fourth Class   257

20. Tax Paid on Olive Groves, Fifth Class   257

21. Tax Paid on Olive Groves, Sixth Class   258

22. Tax Paid on Mixed Vineyards and Olive Groves, First Class   258

23. Tax Paid on Mixed Vineyards and Olive Groves, Second Class   259

24. Tax Paid on Mixed Vineyards and Olive Groves, Third Class   259

25. Tax Paid on Mixed Vineyards and Olive Groves, Fourth Class   260

26. Tax Paid on Mixed Vineyards and Olive Groves, Fifth Class   260

27. Tax Paid on Mixed Vineyards and Olive Groves, Sixth Class   261

28. Tax Paid on Houses   261

29. Tax Paid on Barns   262

30. Tax Paid on Yards Within the Village   262

31. Tax Paid on Yards Outside the Village   263

32. Tax Paid on Working Horses   263

33. Tax Paid on Working Mules   264

34. Tax Paid on Asses   264

35. Tax Paid on Mares   265

36. Tax Paid on Bovines Aged 1–3 Years   265

37. Tax Paid on Bovines, Native Species   266

38. Tax Paid on Bovines, Swiss and Breton Species   266

39. Tax Paid on Bovines, Working and Breeding   267

40. Tax Paid on Business   267

41. Tax Paid by Taxable Goods, Decile 1   268

42. Tax Paid by Taxable Goods, Decile 2   268

43. Tax Paid by Taxable Goods, Decile 3   269

44. Tax Paid by Taxable Goods, Decile 4   269

45. Tax Paid by Taxable Goods, Decile 5   270

46. Tax Paid by Taxable Goods, Decile 6   270

47. Tax Paid by Taxable Goods, Decile 7   271

48. Tax Paid by Taxable Goods, Decile 8   271

49. Tax Paid by Taxable Goods, Decile 9   272

50. Tax Paid by Taxable Goods, Decile 10   272

Preface

This book is an analysis of the development of a political movement over the course of five decades. It is a sustained attempt to examine, in a rounded manner, the complex reality of an evolving, multifaceted process. Although it is based on information gathered during fieldwork and from a variety of archives, this book is neither a standard political history nor a conventional ethnography. It does not fulfill the usual criteria for a historical account of a political organization because it is not concerned primarily with detailing and explaining the political reasons why the successive elites of a particular movement acted in the way they did. At the same time, it cannot be considered an ethnography in the traditional mold because it does not concentrate on analyzing the social and cultural life of a small face-to-face community.

I have chosen to adopt this approach because a purely political history of the movement, one focused on its leadership, would fail to take sufficient account of the way its rank and file conceived of it and why they continued to support it. When dealing with a movement such as Carlism, whose members have consistently prided themselves on the fact that they have maintained, over generations, their political allegiance and associated traditions, any history that did not take them into account in a fully integrated manner would have to be regarded as partial. Yet an orthodox ethnography of Carlist villagers would have to be considered similarly impoverished and lopsided, for the national Carlist context is almost as important as the local if one is to attempt to comprehend the actions and attitudes of the Carlists. Historians may consider the resultant text historical anthropology; anthropologists may regard it as anthropological history. Its ultimate classification I leave to others. It seems more important to get on with the job of reconciling the two disciplines than to agonize over where to site this book on the academic terrain.

There is no unified history of Carlism, except that provided discursively by historiographers, whether professional or partisan. But the accounts they have produced tend to portray the movement only from the top down, and not also from the bottom up. From a lack of information rather than of effort, historiographers have usually concerned themselves with the machinations of the movement's leaders, the programs they elaborated, and the courses of the wars they initiated. Quite simply, the normal sources are not available that would enable historiographers to discern, except indirectly, what was going on in particular villages, why people joined up, and exactly what conceptions of Carlism villagers held to.

One possible way out of this apparent impasse is to interview Carlist veterans and their fellow villagers about their personal memories and the stories their parents and grandparents told them. My repeated discussions with these veterans and with their neighbors revealed, as one might expect, that there is no single history to Carlism, that Carlists occupying different structural positions within their movement do not hold the same conceptions of the Carlist past. Members of its elites and of its rank and file have related, but identifiably distinct, notions of what it means to be Carlist and of what the Carlists had done. Their accounts, organized in narrative form, are in some aspects complementary to each other, in other aspects conflicting. In this sense, there is no one history of Carlism, but a plurality of histories.

But Carlists' sense of history may be different not simply because of the structural positions they occupy. Lisón Tolosana (1966), drawing on the ideas of Ortega y Gasset, has already demonstrated in his ethnography of an Aragonese village that people's conceptions of their history may differ because of the particular social generations to which they belong. Similarly for Carlists, their perception of the historical time within which they live may color their vision of Carlism and lead them to interpret it in a way distinct to members of earlier, still extant generations. The youthful Carlist progressives who emerged as a political force in the late 1950s and early 1960s were too young to have experienced the war but were old enough to comprehend the effects of Franquism in Spain and to be able to compare it with the rapidly developing economies and social life of other Western European states. Their ideas of Carlism and of what its past signified and of how it should be understood were, to an important extent, a consequence of the time in which they lived. Thus, in order to reveal the varieties of Carlist histories, we need to look at the groups within the movement in both social and generational terms.

The histories produced by these different Carlist groups—members of the elites and of the ranks, conservatives and progressives—are couched in overlapping discourses. *Discourse* I take to be a usefully vague term, one that Sherzer[1] characterizes as "an imprecise and emergent interface between language and culture. . . . It is discourse which creates, modifies, and fine tunes both culture and language and their intersection." Since much of my analysis is concerned with the production of histories, I have to examine that fluid interface. Since there is no simple, stable relation between discourses and the social activities through which they are produced, I have to look, in a sustained fashion, at the *practice* of discourse over time: how, where, and when it was produced, and for what reasons; what can be said, and what cannot be said, at what times, at what places, and by whom. Both discourses and their associated social activities may change, as may the relations between them. Key terms may remain the same, though their content alters. Key terms, and the narratives that they constitute, may change in step with the development of the social activities that produce discourse. Holders of, or aspirants to, power may utilize certain discourses in order to legitimate their positions. Others may use their position to legitimate their discourse. There is no fixed, prescriptive set of connections between discourse and power. We have to follow the course of their varying interrelations wherever Carlist chronology takes us.

History is uttered through discourse. It may also be performed through ritual. Though much of ritual can be regarded as a form of statement, it is at the same time a form of act, a set of embodied routines carried out in time. The central, annual ritual of Carlism, the "pilgrimage" to Montejurra, may be analyzed in this dual way: as a memorial and celebration of the Carlist past, one that is constituted both discursively (by speeches, prayers, shouts, discussions, newspaper articles, and books) and physically (by the symbolic regrouping of participants into battle units and by their experiencing a sense of sacrifice comparable to those who gave up their lives for the cause). Here again we cannot prescribe the relations between discourse and power. The ritual can at turns, or at one and the same time, be both legitimatory of, and legitimized by, those who attempt to control its performance. Carlist villagers, members of its elites, conservatives, and progressives may all interpret its history and historical significance in their own ways, and may try (as they have, with varying degrees of success) to express their interpretation of it. Once again, we have no recourse but to trace Carlist chronology, the historical record of its performances, in order to observe the evolution of these interrelations.

In this book, I wish to portray the plurality of Carlist histories, yet at the same time I have included a unified history of postwar Carlism myself. I have written those sections of this account both because that period has not been analyzed until recently except in a somewhat cursory manner, and because it provides contexts within which the Carlist histories may be placed, however provisionally. I do not regard my interpretation of postwar Carlism as either definitive or exhaustive. Although I have listened to a large number of people who participated in the events of this history, and although I have spent months in a wide variety of archives, I do not doubt that others, with ends similar to mine, might wish, at the end of their scholastic labors, to tell a rather different tale. My account is by no means the final one, merely the latest in the continuing, much-debated story of Carlist historiography. Within this context, it is worth quoting the comments made by one of the University of Nevada Press readers of this book:

> At times I have felt somewhat uncomfortable with the portrayal of Carlist absurdity and Carlist bloodthirsty folly. It is obviously a surreal history, this "most lost of all lost causes." It might be worth considering, however, what a true believer in Carlism might reply to this representation. I can well imagine he or she replying: "Well, you anthropologist, you liberal, you European, you humanist, where is the intellectual ground of your moral and political authority? Aren't you and your country and your discipline and your culture as bloodthirsty and horrendous as mine? Why do you depict my past as this irredentist criminal folly as if this were some exception to your wonderful European history of imperialism and fascism? Where is your ground for political innocence, intellectual distance and ethical judgement to represent me in such terms? Okay, my past, my 'sacramentalism' is atrocious, but doesn't my atrociousness have something to do with your atrociousness, your liberal state, your modernity, your science? Aren't you forgetting the big picture of European history as history of crime, of which we small marginal groups are the victims, the fools, the losers?"

I take the point. In this book, I have tried hard not to cast moral judgment, but to translate from one set of cultures (the Carlist) to another set (those of Western academe). I have interpreted but have endeavored not to overinterpret. Throughout the text, I have let divergent voices be heard and have attempted to provide enough material to let readers construct their own versions. To that end, I have not insisted on inserting a phenomenon as diverse and many-faced as Carlism as a particular example of a certain type of movement (whether that be legitimist, populist, millenarian, or protofascist) within European history. At present, bodies such as the European Commission are keen to propagate ideologically skewed versions of the continent's past, creating a continuous course from classical Athens through the Renaissance and the Enlightenment up to today. Given these aims of the EC and like-minded bodies, it is of contemporary relevance to provide case studies that may be considered counter to historical threads made to run "from Plato to NATO." But exactly where, and how, Carlist histories may be placed within the wider contexts of European chronology is a task I leave to readers, who will have their own agendas.

The first chapter of my account summarizes the work done on Carlism by historians. It outlines the chronology, the social composition, the geographical spread, and the political beliefs of the movement from its inception in the 1830s up to the outbreak of Civil War in 1936. Chapter 2 delineates the historically grounded conception of Carlist culture portrayed by its literary officer elite in the years of, and following, the Civil War. Chapter 3 analyzes the conceptions of Carlism held by village veterans of that war, and contextualizes their words within the moral universe of their hometown, Cirauqui, an ancient settlement of several hundred persons in the northern Spanish province of Navarre. These two chapters may be seen as palimpsets, ones that provide a pair of different, but complementary, historical visions of Carlism.

Chapters 4 and 5 detail the development of Carlism at the national level, from the worst years of its suppression in the immediate postwar period to its reorganization in the 1950s and its rejuvenation, under the aegis of Prince Carlos Hugo de Borbón-Parma, in the 1960s. The factional infighting described in these chapters may at times seem Byzantine and may weary many readers, but they are necessary precursors to understanding the later evolution of Carlism. Chapters 6 and 7 look at the ways progressives tried to propagate their particular vision of the movement by reinterpreting its history, reasserting the centrality of monarchy within it, and by retaining common Carlist terms while simultaneously changing their meaning. Chapter 8 analyzes the development of the annual ritual of Montejurra, the discourses within which the ceremony was couched, and the way the ritual was used by different Carlists to further their ends.

Chapters 9 and 10 detail how the Partido Carlista was moved progressively toward the Left and how those extreme conservatives who felt they had no place within the renovated organization formed their own groups, some of which in 1976 made an armed assault on the ritual performance of Montejurra. The following chapter investigates why the party failed at the polls in postfranquist Spain; the penultimate one examines how the recent evolution of Carlism was perceived and expressed by the villagers of Cirauqui. The final chapter looks at the different, possible legacies of Carlism to Basque nationalism. The book closes with an account of the Montejurra of 1986.

I first went to the northern Spanish province of Navarre in February 1984, in order to improve my rudimentary Castilian and to learn more about my then primary topic of study, the cultural consequences of the political confrontation between left-wing Basque nationalism and right-wing Navarran regionalism. I stayed for ten months, living in the Old Quarter of Pamplona, the provincial capital. Fortified with the funds of a postdoctoral fellowship, I returned in September the next year. During the ensuing three months, which I mainly spent attending an intensive course in the Basque language, I slowly worked out which Navarran village might be a suitable place in which I could base myself. In December, I was introduced to a poet from a village that interested me greatly.

His name is Milu, and his hometown, Cirauqui, is a medium-sized village in what is known as the "Middle Zone" of Navarre. Milu persuaded a neighbor to let me rent the unoccupied part of his second house, the basement of which he filled with cows, and in the attics of which he and his wife hung out to dry hams, sausages, herbs, and clothes. I stayed there for twenty-two months and have since been back every year for at least a few weeks, sometimes for a few months. My landlords, his parents, and their daughter provided me with lunch daily and offered me friendship constantly. Milu was similarly accommodating and had me immediately made a member of his *cuadrilla* (age group) within the village. As I gradually learned more about Cirauqui from all these people and from the other villagers I started to know, I became more and more interested in the Carlism of the area, traditionally the heartland of the movement.

I attended the ceremony at Montejurra in 1986 and 1987, as well as certain Carlist social events. Besides discussing matters Carlist with the people of Cirauqui and neighboring villages, I also interviewed former Carlist militants and Carlist politicians, both veteran and younger, in Pamplona and Madrid. Many of these people I talked with several times, in order to clarify points that had subsequently arisen and to discuss the significance of documents I consulted in the several archives I visited. I took drafts of the chapters about Cirauqui back to the village and read abbreviated translations of them to select villagers, who were kind enough to pass comment.

I am sincerely grateful to all those who helped, in whatever way. But since I do not want my list of acknowledgments to read like a telephone directory, I have to be selective. First on my list must come my landlords, Francisco Arraiza, his parents Luis and Jesusa (both since deceased), his daughter Pili, her husband Gustavo, and especially Paco's wife, Maria Jesús Goldaráz, who spent much time teaching me about Cirauqui and its inhabitants. Milu, his brother Chuchin, and our friend Javier were a constant source of support, friendship, and information. Their *cuadrilla, Los Tajudos* (Navarran dialect, The Badgers), accepted me as a full participant in their weekly dinners and in their collective entry to the fancy-dress competition in the village's annual fiestas. (We usually won.) I am also particularly grateful for the help of Maria José Dallo, Belen Gurrucharri, Josefina, and La Txus Laita. All of the above, and almost all the other villagers, extended to me a degree of hospitality that I do not know how to repay. In a gift of equal importance and equally hard to repay, they showed me another way of life, and how to enjoy it.

In Pamplona, I shared the flat of the long-suffering Juan Luis Ainciburu, who patiently put up with my frustrating Castilian, and who introduced me to his circle of friends. The Navarran historians Angel Pascual and Angel García-Sanz assisted me constantly with my academic inquiries and suggested avenues of inquiry I had not thought of traveling. In Tolosa, where I consulted the Archivo del Partido Carlista, Yon Iglesias Zufeldia and Juan José Zabala Ijurco were as helpful as archivists could be. In Bilbao, Joseba Agirreazkuenaga and Concepción de la Rua were exemplars of academic fraternity, sharing ideas, providing assistance, and offering hospitality. In Britain, I must thank Charles Powell and Steven Roberts for their suggestions, and Glenn Bowman and Elaine Genders for their comments on sections of the manuscript. The funds that enabled me to do fieldwork were generously provided by the ESRC Postdoctoral Research Fellowship Committee; Wolfson College, Oxford University; the Ministerio de Asuntos Exteriores of the Spanish Government; the Nuffield Foundation; and the School of Social Sciences, Oxford Brookes University. Much of the manuscript was written and developed while I gave hourly paid classes in six different departments in three universities. On two occasions during this difficult period, when I thought I might sink, my parents threw me a financial lifeline. I am deeply grateful for their unsolicited generosity and well aware of my privilege. To my sorrow, my father died a few months before the publication of this book, which is the product of his beneficence.

For granting permission to reproduce photos, I am grateful to Antonio Laita, Carlos Sáenz de Tejada, Cayetano Sánchez de Muniain, the Museo Gustavo de Maeztu, Estella, the Museo de Navarra, Pamplona, and *El Diario de Navarra*.

As always, my thanks to Rodney Needham for his unwavering support, intellectual example, and provocative nature.

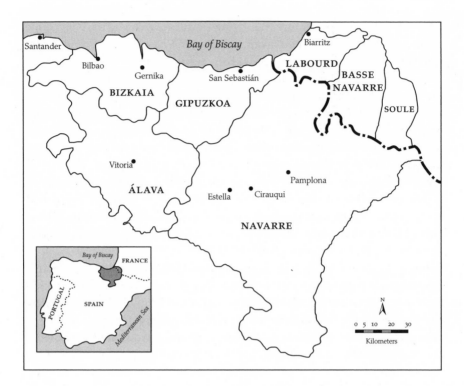

The seven Basque provinces

The Decline of Carlism

Chapter One

Introduction

On 15 June 1977, for the first time in forty years, adult Spaniards had the opportunity to vote in a free, nationwide election. Francisco Franco, dictator since 1936, had died less than nineteen months before, and a democratically elected assembly was needed to decide the constitutional structure of the system that would replace his totalitarian regime. While voters were allowed to choose from a political spectrum that ranged from neofascist parties on the extreme Right to groups of former terrorists on the far Left, there was one organization the government continued to regard as too threatening to legalize: the Partido Carlista.

It might seem strange that in the late twentieth century the leaders of a country in Western Europe could yet view a movement that married legitimism and populism as potentially so subversive. But what is perhaps even stranger is that Carlism was still alive at all. Although its disappearance from the political scene has been prematurely prophesied several times in the last one hundred and fifty years, Carlists have always managed, sometimes almost miraculously, to revive the fortunes of their party and restore it to strength. Never able to achieve its aims, Carlism is Europe's "most enduring lost cause." The reasons for and the nature of its latest (and perhaps, this time, its last) revival, in the latter years of the Franquist regime, are the subjects of this book.

Carlism: Its Social Nature and Geography

The origins of Carlism can best be found in the reaction of Spanish conservatives to the modernizing reforms put forward by their liberal compatriots in the late eighteenth and early nineteenth centuries. Influenced by the ideas of the Enlightenment and the example of the French Revolution, liberals wished to have done with the ancien régime and to bring their backward country up to date. In the constitution enacted by the liberal Cortes in 1812 and in the Triennium of liberal government between 1820 and 1823, they proposed to centralize the state, abolish the *fueros* (rights, laws, and privileges held by villages, towns, or provinces), end the right of entail, sell off the commons, introduce conscription throughout the country, and dissolve the already dying system of guilds. They wanted to create a new Spain of greater social equality and run on the lines of "reason," rather than retain the old Spain organized according to the dictates of customary practice.

Certain nobles and others who saw their interests endangered by the proposed changes fought back by propounding a traditionalism based on a vision of Spain's golden age. In contrast to liberals who put forward rationalizing measures, they wanted the country ruled by a responsive monarch who would be answerable to his Cortes, would swear to respect the *fueros*, and would uphold the central position of the Church. Scared by the proclivity of the king, Ferdinand VII, to associate with liberals when it was expedient, these *apostólicos* looked to his brother, Don Carlos de Borbón, as their figurehead. As a devout Catholic and inflexible politician, as well as being the heir presumptive, Don Carlos was the obvious candidate to bear their banner of "THRONE AND ALTAR," of counterrevolution and religious intransigence. Although some reactionary militias tried to advance their cause in the mid-1820s by staging a number of unsuccessful, localized risings, many conservatives did not feel it yet necessary to join what was in effect an armed Carlism *avant la lettre*, because the major obstacle to Don Carlos's accession—the incumbent king—was clearly ailing. They would not have to wait long.

In 1829, however, the childless Ferdinand confounded his courtiers and critics by marrying for a fourth time and producing two daughters in the following two years. Since the Salic Law of 1713 decreed that only male offspring could succeed to the throne, the king swiftly promulgated the Pragmatic Sanction, which his forebear Carlos IV had formulated in 1789 but had never put into effect. Conservatives denied the validity of this hasty promulgation and advanced the claim of his brother, while the queen promoted the cause of her elder child, Isabella. When Ferdinand died in 1833, his daughter was proclaimed monarch. In the meantime, Don Carlos had been pushed into exile, and many of those partisan to his claim had been removed from office. Since Carlists now thought themselves unable to pursue their cause pacifically, groups throughout the country took up arms to defend their backward-looking ideals. The First Carlist War had begun.

Nineteenth-century Carlism was a complex, labile phenomenon whose social composition may be roughly characterized as a heterogeneous coalition of rural notables, peasants, and artisans. Although they all marched behind the same flag, members of these disparate social groups were united more by their opposition to the rising ranks of the financial bourgeoisie and the mercantile classes than by common adherence to all the particulars of an agreed political program. In their different ways they all wished to retain aspects of the old order: minor nobles did not want to lose their residual privileges; villagers wished to safeguard their livelihood by retaining the municipal commons; and artisans did not wish to have to compete against foreign, more developed industries. Divided traditionally by estate, these different social groups were brought together by their shared antipathy for the newly enriched.

While this summary characterization holds good as a countrywide generalization, the differing types of land tenure systems and of administrative structures, plus the varying extent of liberal reform in different parts of Spain, meant that the political complexion of early Carlism was not uniform across the land and that support for the movement was not equally spread, even within the same region. Although the Carlist platform was at first simply support of the royal pretender and the defense of Catholicism, in many areas the movement was used by disgruntled peasants, who had already taken up arms a number of times against the liberal reforms, as merely the latest vehicle of social protest. Since the War of Independence, laborers in many areas, often living in miserable conditions, had had to pay a constantly increasing level of taxation and, in the early 1830s, had also to shoulder the consequences of a recent and grave economic crisis. In Old Castile, Extremadura, Asturias, and Cantabria, most of those who fought under the Carlist banner were impoverished peasants; in Aragón and Murcia, the majority were artisans, landless day laborers, and men with such small landholdings that they were sometimes forced to work for others. In Cataluña, Valencia, and La Mancha, the affluent peasantry cleaved to liberalism; those who rallied to the Carlist cause tended to be members of the rural oligarchy, urban laborers, artisans, and the poor. In Galicia, the bulk of those who joined the cause were rural notables, minor aristocrats, and above all the clergy; the majority of Galician peasants thought the proposed liberal changes would improve, not endanger, their living conditions, and since they tended to regard the local landowners not as the beneficial leaders of their communities but as their exploiters, very few of them rose up in the name of Don Carlos.[1]

Carlist leaders may have presented their movement as one in support of Catholicism, but the response of the Church was not uniformly positive. Those in the higher reaches of the Spanish ecclesiastical hierarchy were strongly opposed to the anticlerical measures of the liberals, but most of them did not openly come out in favor of Don Carlos. Like some of the major landowning aristocrats, who stood to lose their estates if they strongly supported the losing side, these senior ecclesiastics chose merely to sympathize with rather than to agitate for the Carlists. Similarly, while many monks were against the forced closing of the monasteries, relatively few actively supported Carlism. While parish priests importantly assisted the cause in areas such as Galicia, Cataluña, Valencia, and the Basque Country, elsewhere few members of the "secular clergy" lent their support to the party of the pretender. Indeed, some of them were so anti-Carlist that they adhered to the liberal cause, even leading their own bands of soldiers.

If support for the Carlist cause was only partial in some regions and practically nonexistent in others, in the Basque Provinces it came closer to being a true mass movement. From the last decades of the eighteenth century on, the fiscal privileges of the still largely extant Basque *fueros* had been progressively reduced by both liberals and absolutists who saw them as antiquated regional privileges hindering the construction of a modern state. Liberals wanted to abolish the *fueros,* sell off the very extensive commons of Basque villages, and shift the customs posts from their position along the Ebro River (the southern border of Álava and Navarre) to the frontier with France. Since so many minor nobles and peasants in the area had sought to defend their imperiled interests, the Basque Provinces had by the early 1820s already become a center of armed agitation against the liberals.[2]

Within Navarre, the areas of greatest support for the cause were the northwest and the broad "Middle Zone" of the province. These two regions contained a particularly high concentration of minor nobles who acted as local leaders for the peasants they employed and even led off to war. Those members of the rural nobility who did not become petty warlords set up and ran the administrative structure of Carlism in the area. The local rally to the Carlist banner was greatly stimulated by the efforts of local priests, especially benefice priests whose livings were threatened by liberal reforms. Although there was a very high number of clergy in Navarre, this was not a distinguishing feature of the region, since several other provinces had comparable sacerdotal populations. What marked the Navarrese priesthood was the fact that many came from the parish they tended or from the surrounding area, and traditionally they had very close ties with their parishioners. Moreover, and unique to Navarre, many priests were voted into their position by the parishioners themselves, rather than appointed to the post by their bishop.[3] While it is easy to exaggerate the role of the clergy as privileged mediators between their flocks and the outside world, it is undebatable that parish priests importantly assisted the cause of the pretender by preaching its virtues from the pulpit and in the confessional. Some granted indulgences to those who managed to kill liberals or to extort money from them. Many Navarrese and Basque priests and once-cloistered monks physically joined the movement, serving as chaplains, soldiers, or even, in several notorious cases, as leaders of bloodthirsty bands.

When Ferdinand VII died, there were uprisings throughout the country, but most were uncoordinated local events that were soon dealt with by troops of the liberal government. In Cataluña and Valencia, for instance, Carlism did not become a significant military force until 1835, when the generals Guergue and Cabrera, respectively, began to organize the irregulars of each area and to recruit local sympathizers. One important reason why the cause was so successful in the Basque area from the very outbreak of hostilities was the high level of organization among Carlists there. In many parts of Spain, supporters of the cause of Don Carlos had already been removed from office by 1833. In the Basque Provinces, however, they had managed to retain control of the provincial administrations. Furthermore, since the end of the liberal Triennium, these local bureaucracies had created and maintained their own militias. Within weeks of the king's death, the most powerful of these groups, the Bilbao-based Brigadas de Paisanos Armados (Brigades of Armed Peasants), had asserted its presence in much of the province of Bizkaia and then marched on to Gipuzkoa to assist the rebellion there. Once Carlist forces such as the brigade had won control of an area, they could consolidate their position by recruiting, and later enlisting, the local able-bodied men. That these conscripts were not all committed to the cause is strongly suggested by the number of desertions and of appeals brought by parents against the enlistment of their sons.[4]

To a certain extent, therefore, we can speak of "geographical Carlists," of men who bore the pretender's colors only *because* the movement came to be so well entrenched in their area. During the Republic and the Franquist period, Carlist writers and propagandists tried to portray Navarre as solidly and traditionally Carlist. But looking at a map of the Carlist dominions in the first two Carlist wars does not necessarily give an accurate idea of the strength of support for the movement at that time. Many Basques and many of those living in the northern and central region of Navarre were coerced into the movement. In the south of Navarre, few openly proclaimed their support of Don Carlos: since the titled aristocrats who controlled much of the area did not come out on either side of the conflict, neither did their landless employees, whatever their true sympathies may have been.

Carlist writers, who saw their movement as part of the Spanish resistance to modernization, extolled the purity and virtues of the countryside against the sinfulness they associated with towns. In their portrayals, village life was simple, tranquil, and stable, while in towns the contiguity of ostentatious luxury and shameful poverty constituted a continuing challenge to national and Christian morals. Many historians, confusing rhetoric with reality, have taken the movement's praise of the rural life and its damnation of urban ways as an indicator of the movement's geographical support. In fact, a significant number of Carlists were city dwellers who had to leave their hometowns in order to join up. Carlism became so strongly associated with the countryside only because of its ideological preference for rural traditions, and for a sound strategic reason: the safest bases from which to launch its offensives were mountainous or hilly areas.

An additional reason why Carlism remained confined to the countryside was the inability of its forces to take any major urban center. The only Basque towns of any significance occupied by Carlist forces for any length of time were the relatively small ones of Estella and Tolosa, while Morella, Cabrera's capital in the Maestrazgo, was, according to Raymond Carr, merely a "second-rate" fortress town with a decaying textile industry.[5] This incapacity to impose their military might on urban areas and to extend the rebellion much beyond the original foci of insurrection meant that though the Carlists were able to start a war, they were unable to win one. At the same time they were very difficult to defeat, as the liberal regiments found when trying to dislodge them from their mountainous strongholds, whose terrain the Carlists, unlike their enemies, knew well. The liberal armies might occasionally battle against their massed Carlist counterparts, but it was much harder for them to combat the guerrilla style of warfare practiced by the numerous bands of rural irregulars. At times, the activity of these groups came very close to banditry; indeed some of them were old bands of thieves who had adopted the cause for their own safety and for the sake of a reasonably steady salary.[6]

For all these reasons, armed conflict could stagger on for several years without either side being capable of bringing it to a satisfactory conclusion. Rafael Maroto, the leader of the Carlist forces in the Basque area, managed to end the war in his region only by shooting those seven of his generals who were most opposed to appeasement and by conducting lengthy, secret negotiations with the enemy. To many Carlists this underhand way of making the peace did not signify moral defeat. To them, the First Carlist War would remain a glorious chronicle of battles fought against an army three times the size of theirs and significantly aided, unlike theirs, by supply of foreign troops and material.[7]

Maroto's action may have made sound military sense, but those die-hard Carlist guerrillas who claimed they were prepared to keep up the fight indefinitely from their hilltop redoubts regarded him forever as a traitor. In rural Cataluña, Carlist bands continued to operate, albeit sporadically, until the mid-1860s. From 1846 to 1849, their armed activity rose to such a level and extent that Carlists have dubbed this period the Second Carlist War, though it is now generally known as the War of the Early Risers *(Matiners)*.[8] Intermittent outbreaks like these and other, lesser events did not seriously threaten the ruling monarchy, but they did lend substance to the rising myth of military violence as integral to the Carlist cause.

The Ideologies of Carlism

Because of an apparent lack of documentary sources, modern historians of this period have not yet carried out any systematic study of the attitudes held by villagers and ordinary townsfolk toward Carlism. Quite simply, these people—small landowners, peasants, artisans, and day laborers—are the unvoiced, those whose opinions we can only infer or guess at. The only material that has been studied—newspapers, tracts, speeches—was produced by the literary elite of Carlism. However, despite these limitations, this sort of material can still be illuminating, for it reveals how a certain section of Carlism wished to present the ideals of the movement, both to their opponents and to their followers.

Prophets of the past, Carlist writers damned industrialization and centralization as threats to the rural way of life. In place of such evils they advocated a traditionalist form of Roman Christianity, and the maximum degree of local autonomy (based on the idea of the antique *fueros*) while remaining within the frame of the Spanish state. Some even regarded *fueros* and religion as intimately and indissolubly united. To them, devolution equaled return to a mythically idyllic past, and maintenance of the *fueros* guaranteed the survival of traditional society against pernicious change. Carlist writers saw their brand of Catholicism as a purified form of Christianity, one meant to stand as an exemplar for non-Carlist members of the Church. This refined form of religiosity both sanctified their political ideals and provided them with Christian models of hierarchy, leadership, and association. They emphasized the moral aspect of their doctrines, contrasting it with the corruption of the liberals and, later, the atheism of the socialists. Claiming to despise politics as such, they liked to stress that their movement was one of abnegation and sacrifice, of martyrs and heroes. To some, it did not matter if their cause did not immediately succeed for, as one of the faithful put it, "Our kingdom is not of this world." According to the demonology of these diehards, God was the first Carlist, Lucifer was the first liberal, and the Carlists were the elect of Christ.[9]

For members of the Carlist elite, religious unity, Spanish patriotism, and some form of right-wing politics all went together. To criticize Catholicism was to subvert conservative ideals and to question the very nature of Spain itself. To import foreign ideas was to strike at church, country, and way of life simultaneously. This particular set of irreconcilable opposites was shared with integrists, a faction so intransigent it was later to split from the main body of Carlism. Integrists wished to establish a theocratic nation with Christ the King as monarch. They believed that the state, under the sway of rationalism and liberalism, had secularized Spain. It was therefore necessary for a renovated state to re-Catholicize society and to "divinize" humankind. This doctrine of reconnecting Spaniards with God was a revealed, absolute truth that could not be changed by anybody or anything.[10] Some integrists were so obdurate in their theological attitudes that they would even include in their daily rosary, said *en famille,* a few prayers "for the conversion of the Pope." A similar rigidity in attitude was generated from within the Church itself, for priests were trained, from the 1870s till the days of the Second Vatican Council, to regard Thomism as the only true and acceptable philosophy. Constructive dialogue outside the terms of this scholastic discourse was not countenanced. These intransigent, self-righteous traditionalists and integrists crudely divided the world with Manichaean clarity into the good and the bad. For them, there was no negotiable middle ground.[11] They were the "whites" and the liberals the "blacks." The Carlists called the liberals *guiris* (foreigners), and their opponents returned the rebuke by dubbing them *carca* (old-fashioned, out of date). This dichotomous enmity was also transmitted in song, as shown by one example that, until very recently, was still chanted by Navarrese children as part of a skipping game:

> The liberals are made of grease
> And their rifles are made of dry shit
> And the Carlists are made of bacon
> And their rifles are of fine steel.[12]

The Carlists were renowned, or notorious, as combative characters who championed their creed by exalting violence, in the form of a crusade, to defend the absolute truth. Since one could not compromise with error, all means were justified, including a "holy war." War was a logical outcome of this scheme of things, a cultural predisposition blessed by Carlist tradition. Thus Carlism, as an all-embracing collection of interpretive practices constituting the ontology of its adherents, was meant to engage the passions and orient them toward aggressive defense and propagation of their faith. Carlist politicians and journalists liked to describe themselves and their fellow believers in virile terms: strength, firmness, and readiness to fight.[13] Combining sacred power and secular might, they were proud to be known as the "Civil Guard" of the Church, as bellicose defenders of Catholic values.

As the defense of a particular rural way of life, Carlism politicized villagers' conceptions of their own world and set those conceptions in a wider, national context. This traditionalism exploited the normative prescriptiveness of local tradition in order to intensify the urgency of its own message: since the village way of life was to be maintained, the Carlists had to be supported in their struggle. Thus the movement mobilized rather than invented tradition. Or more exactly, it took advantage of a previously invented literary form of tradition for its own political ends, for the arcadia of Carlist dreams had been created earlier by those Basque politicians of the 1820s who had not wanted to see their *fueros* done away with. In other words, in the discourse of nineteenth-century Spanish politicians, the term *tradition* was not a neutral, descriptive term but the appropriated slogan of a political movement. For the Carlist leaders, traditionality was not a natural given but a strategy to be employed in a partisan fashion.

The most coherent formulation of Carlist doctrine was progressively developed between the 1880s and the mid-1920s by the Carlist leader and ideologue Juan Vázquez de Mella. In contrast to what he saw as the individualist bent of liberalism, Mella propounded a philosophy we can call "organic traditionalism," based on two principles: (1) that people, because born and brought up in groups, are social products; and (2) that these groups, because they have already been formed by "history," are constituted by tradition. Within any one particular country, the totality of these groups formed a hierarchical but harmonious whole, in which the autonomy of each group at each level was respected to the utmost. Thus, for Spain, Mella looked forward to a united state headed by a "traditional" but not absolute monarch advised by a corporative parliament. This body would be composed of members elected from the six "natural orders" of society: agriculture, industry and commerce, the clergy, the armed forces, the aristocracy, and the intelligentsia. In recognition of the historical particularity of different areas of the country, the powers of central government were to be strictly limited for the sake of regional and lesser bodies. The Church was to have total "religious freedom": in other words, it would be free to manage its own affairs, to monopolize education, and to denounce all those whose thought strayed from the orthodox. The presence and work of the king would guarantee political unity; the Catholic confessionality of the state would ensure doctrinal unity; the maintenance of the monarchy, the Church, and other institutions hallowed by tradition would bind all Spaniards, irrespective of class, socially and spiritually into a national, harmonious whole. The state would not need to coerce its members, since people would not exploit one another economically, but would work together, inspired by the same elevated ideals.[14]

Vázquez de Mella's traditionalism may have been much more evolved and somewhat more relevant to the contemporary condition of the country than that of his predecessors, but his program still left unclear how the Carlist utopia was to be achieved and, once achieved, maintained. Any critical thought would have shown the extreme unlikelihood of establishing a corporative state that did not rely on a stern authoritarianism. Pious hopes alone were not going to do away with the brutal culture of laissez-faire capitalism already developed in certain centers around the land, where agnostic proletarians were pitted against greedy industrialists. The harmonious society Carlists dreamed of would have been destroyed by the violent means needed to bring it about.[15]

From the Second Carlist War to Civil War

Carlism, as an ultraorthodox movement bent on instituting a new form of the state, thrived during periods of collective insecurity—when the throne was either empty or occupied by an incompetent. By the same token, during times of political peace, when the incumbent monarch was securely in place, the fortunes of Carlism waned. Thus Carlism languished during the 1840s and 1850s, when Isabella's queendom was never seriously endangered. But in the 1860s Carlism began to reorganize, adapting its program in the process, swapping its main priority of king for that of Church. Thus, instead of campaigning for a return to an absolutist regime, in which religion would play a part, Carlist leaders now argued for the constitution of a Catholic state, headed by a king but based on the principles of Catholicism. They also supported popular criticisms of the liberal regime, arguing strongly for the maintenance of the *fueros* and the commons. Their hopes were strengthened by the progressive weakening of Isabella's monarchy during this period and the inheritance of the Carlist crown by Carlos VII, the grandson of Carlos V.

After the Isabelline monarchy fell in 1868, replaced first by a foreign king and later by a republic, these self-styled guardians of traditional morals felt their chance had come once again. The Second Carlist War followed much the same course as that of the first, and it failed for much the same reasons: the rebellion was restricted to certain rural areas, and the insurgents were unable to take any cities. In 1876, after almost four years of fighting, Carlos VII was forced to follow the example of his grandfather by fleeing across the Pyrenean border.

Spain's republican experiment lasted only a year. In 1875 the monarchy, headed by Isabella's son, Alfonso XII, had been restored, and once the war had finished, the country embarked on a protracted period of relatively stable government. The Alfonsine monarchy, unlike some of its predecessors, did not antagonize the Spanish Church but actively, and successfully, sought its support, thus undermining somewhat the Carlist claim to be national protector of the faith. The fortunes of Carlism, in consequence, declined. It could not win much support under the new system of conservative, Catholic rule led by a politically adept king.[16] The Carlism of the postwar period was further weakened by the disinterest of the disappointed Carlos VII and by schism, with persistent infighting between integrists and those Carlists who wished to pursue a politically more pragmatic line. In 1888 the integrists finally broke away from "official" Carlism and formed their own party. This split had less to do with ideological differences than with personal ones, since the leaders of both camps were resistant to compromise, preferring to exaggerate mutual differences. Although support for integrists was restricted mainly to the rural clergy and to the more fervent of Carlist Catholics, the new party had a certain political weight because of the great number of Carlist periodicals it controlled. Even this limited degree of support gradually declined, however, because of squabbling within the integrist ranks and the opposition of senior ecclesiastics.

The departure of the integrists allowed those remaining within the Carlist elite to restructure the movement, giving it something akin to a proper party organization. Vázquez de Mella developed his modern doctrine for Carlism while he and Carlos VII's delegate-general, the Marqués de Cerralbo, tried to propagate Carlist ideas, revive support, and win new converts by boosting the partisan press and by touring the regions, where they would hold mass meetings followed by banquets and after-dinner speeches. Carlists may have often been depreciative of constitutional democracy and parliamentary institutions, preferring the romance of armed struggle to the mundaneness of political debate, but their leaders were prepared to stoop to conventional politics when it suited. Thus, after 1889, under the impetus of Vázquez de Mella and Cerralbo, members of the upper echelons of Carlism reentered the electoral fray, fighting for seats in the Cortes. However, the fruits of their bid for conventional power were few. Although Carlist deputies had wielded a disproportionate degree of influence in the Cortes in the years before the outbreak of the Second Carlist War, in the period between 1890 and 1923 the Carlists in the chamber rarely constituted anything more than a small and ineffective minority, albeit a vociferous one. The only time more than thirteen of its candidates were elected was in 1907, when local Carlists joined a short-lived alliance of Catalan parties. While participation in parliament yielded few political returns for Carlism, merely exposing its electoral weakness in most parts of the country, the adoption of this new pragmatic approach had not changed the ultimate aim of the movement: the creation of a new state. Members of its elite were entering the parliamentary system only for tactical reasons. If, at that time, they could not overthrow the liberal state from without, they would attempt to destroy it from within.

Throughout this period, Carlism continued to be perceived as a movement with its own powerful military organization, capable of mustering from the villages a large number of soldiers whenever the need might arise. This was largely a myth, perpetuated both by Carlists, who were keen to maintain their bellicose traditions and the sense of armed threat behind their political statements, and by the liberals, ready to exploit the specter of Carlist rebellion to prevent their own factions from deviating too far. The political unreality of this talk of supposed military organization was most dramatically revealed at the end of the century when the restoration monarchy suffered its first major crisis. In 1898 Antonio Cánovas del Castillo, the architect of the regime, was assassinated, and the next year, after a short but disastrous war, Spain lost three of its major colonies to the United States. Thinking their time had come again, Carlists plotted another uprising. But all that occurred were a number of uncoordinated, and easily suppressed, outbreaks by armed bands in Cataluña, Gijón, and Jaén.[17]

Despite the efforts of Vázquez de Mella and Cerralbo to bring their movement up to date, Carlism continued to look to the past for inspiration. The trouble was that the gradual development and modernization of the country began to make many Carlist ideals seem increasingly irrelevant, if not anachronistic, to some former stalwarts of the movement. On top of that, in certain areas, the Carlist defense of the *fueros* came to be overshadowed by the rise of nationalist parties with their own program for boosting regional autonomy. In Cataluña, onetime members drifted away from the movement as the rise of industries began to improve the living conditions of the previously rebellious poor, and as provincial politicians started to take up the regionalist issue.[18] In the Basque provinces of Bizkaia and Gipuzkoa, some former Carlists went over to the side of Sabino Arana, pioneer ideologue of the Partido Nacionalista Vasco (PNV, Basque Nationalist Party). His racialist version of ethnic difference attracted those indigenes caught up in the social upheavals caused by the extremely rapid industrial expansion experienced in certain confined areas of the Basque Country. In the southerly provinces of Álava and Navarre, few factories were constructed, agriculture remained the dominant economic mode, and the Carlists continued to prevail. After the loss of so much support in other parts of the country, Navarre became, almost by default, the heartland of the movement, the "Spanish Vendée." And it was trumpeted as such in common Carlist sayings, such as "Sparks will cease to fly in forges before there are no more Carlists in Navarre."[19]

In the first decades of the new century, Carlism, already debilitated by the integrist exodus, was weakened yet more by defection and further schism. In 1905, some Carlists, correctly perceiving that the chances of their pretender reaching the throne were extremely slim, chose to support the cause of religion by joining the neo-Catholic party of Alejandro Pidal, a politician who thought backing the ruling monarchy offered the greatest guarantee of safeguarding conservative Catholic values and privileges. In 1919 Vázquez de Mella argued with Don Jaime, Carlos VII's son and the contemporary pretender. Although Vázquez de Mella's dispute with his leader was based more on differences of personality than on political approach, he still left to set up his own separate conservative faction. While this split, together with the integrist schism and the defections to Pidal's party, enfeebled the movement, they did not politically incapacitate it, since integrists and *jaimistas* were occasionally prepared to ally for electoral purposes, and since only minorities followed Pidal or Vázquez de Mella.[20] During this period one could speak not of "Carlism" as such, but of several Carlisms: integrists, *mellistas,* and *jaimistas.*

Many leading Carlists welcomed the dictatorship established by General Miguel Primo de Rivera in 1923, given his inclination toward certain aspects of traditionalism and his promise to revitalize and to strengthen regional administrations. But their support for the new regime changed to rejection as they began to realize its strong centralizing policies and liberal tendencies.[21] However, Carlism was unable to take political advantage of its opposition, since the movement, like all other political parties, had been declared illegal; thus much of its organization continued to languish during this period. What was to bring Carlism so remarkably back to life was not the end of the dictatorship in 1930, by which time it had become politically nonviable, but the flight of the discredited king, who had condoned the regime, and the establishment of the Second Republic a year later.[22]

Although Alfonso XIII's departure revived hopes of installing a traditionalist monarchy, and though the proposed land reforms of the Republic directly threatened the interests of the Carlist landowning elite, it was the sternly anticlerical proposals of the new government that above all stimulated Carlists into action. For no conservative upholder of the faith could agree with the latest attacks against the Church: the removal of crucifixes from classrooms, the limiting of religious education, the secularization of cemeteries, and the introduction of civil marriage and divorce. Such measures menaced ecclesiastical authority and Christian conceptions of morality. The separate Carlist factions, commonly opposed to these antireligious measures and to the desecration of religious sites by uncontrolled mobs, came together in January 1932 and re-formed as a single organization, the Comunión Tradicionalista, headed by Tomás Domínguez Arévalo, Conde de Rodezno, a Navarrese aristocrat and political pragmatist.

Conservative Catholics incensed by the Republican reforms swelled the Carlist ranks, and the Comunión rapidly grew in numbers. Much of this increase was due to the efforts of Manuel Fal Conde, a remarkable organizer from Andalucía who was appointed secretary-general of the Comunión in 1934. In Navarre alone, forty-six new Carlist "Circles"—centers for social and political activity—were registered during the six years of the Republic. In many Circles, however, the customary lectures on traditionalism were soon replaced by training in the use of arms, as Carlists, living up to their warlike reputation, prepared to impose their political opinions by force. For the rise of Fal Conde represented the ascent within Carlism of former integrists who, unlike Rodezno and his followers, upheld an uncompromising strategy of winning power by armed rebellion. Thus the new secretary-general oversaw the revival of Carlism's own paramilitary organization, the Requeté, first formed in Pamplona in 1908. Soon, uniformed Carlists could be seen on most weekends participating in mass exercises in the hilly areas around Pamplona. Not afraid to show its strength, the Junta Regional de Navarre of the Comunión even staged a military parade, 3,000 *requetés* strong, in March 1935 through the streets of Estella in homage to the great general of the First Carlist War, Tomás de Zumalacárregui. Meanwhile their leaders put their intentions into effect by conspiring with the generals to overthrow the government, end the republican experiment, and halt the continuing and seemingly ever-rising crisis of public disorder, caused by both right- and left-wing violence. The exact terms of their collusion were left vague, but by the time it was hurriedly agreed on, in mid-July 1936, the momentum for the uprising seemed unstoppable. Whether or not the agreement was precisely what senior Carlists hoped for, not since the 1870s had a nationwide crisis offered them such a good chance of installing a traditionalist system of government.[23]

The insurgents rose up on 17 July 1936, and Navarre, thanks to the Carlists, was the first province that came out in their support. On 19 July, a Sunday, the main plaza in Pamplona filled with thousands of excited, zealous *requetés*. As one participant remembered, people, seemingly delirious, were shouting, "Long live Religion! Long live the King! Long live brave Navarre!"

Shouts of joy, happy faces. The population was sweeping in off the land. Lorries, tractors, farm carts bringing red berets from every side into the square. Most of the people in their Sunday best. A man in shirtsleeves leaped from a lorry crying: "Here we've come, confessed and communed, for whatever God demands."[24]

Chapter Two

Representing the *Requetés*

In November 1937, Generalísimo Franco, in a rare gesture, granted the province of Navarre as a whole Spain's highest military honor, the Cross of Saint Ferdinand with oak leaves. He gave the military decoration, which was to be added to the provincial coat of arms, in recognition of the *requetés'* contribution in the first, crucial months of the war. At the official ceremony of conferment in Pamplona, he stated:

> In the resurgence of Spain, Navarre was conspicuous for its heroism and sacrifice. Navarre was the province on which the eyes of Spaniards were fixed in the sad days of the collapse of the Patria; it was the credit of its virtues that transformed it into a solid military base of our uprising, and it was its youth in arms who in the first moments formed the backbone of the army of the north. During the entire campaign, the Navarrese, with their legendary bravery, formed up in the *Tercios* (regiments) of *requetés*, *Banderas* (regiments) of the Falange, and in battalions, rivaled in valor the most distinguished forces of the army.
>
> All Spain renders homage and sympathy to the virtues and high spirit of a people in whom it is not known what to admire most, the valor of those who bravely died on the fronts, or the generosity and patriotism of those who, happily, gave up to the Patria the most beloved of their hearths.[1]

Franco called Navarre "the birthplace of the Movimiento." The province was presented as a bastion of the Right, unanimously insurgent and distinctively Carlist. Its men had gone to war, emptying their villages of adult males; its women had worked as nurses, made clothes for the troops, and toiled in the fields usually tilled by their menfolk. Navarre exemplified the principles of the crusade, and its exemplar was the *requeté*. No matter that many Navarrese had supported the Republic or that the Navarrese contribution to the war was proportionally no greater than that of any other province. The important points were that Navarre had been the first province to declare for Franco and that two-thirds of the Navarrese who had joined the insurgents had done so *voluntarily*.[2]

Requeté Literature

Like most modern wars, the Spanish Civil War generated its own particular subgenre of literature. On the Carlist side, demobilized officers, chaplains, journalists, and writers produced memoirs, novels, and accounts of wartime episodes. These texts, like Franco's speech in Pamplona, contain a certain representation of the *requeté*. They reveal, in a narrative fashion, the idealized image, as then held by members of the movement's elite, of the *requetés:* the homes from which they were said to come, the life they were supposed to lead, the death they were meant to enact. This literary image was not a spontaneous creation, rather a modern elaboration of one already held to varying degrees by Carlist leaders and villagers. Authors drew on what already existed and then refashioned it to fit the contemporary setting.

These written accounts are constituted by a particular discourse within which the life of the *requeté* was expressed. Analysis of the terms and themes of this discourse is one way to comprehend how the culture of the movement was publicly expressed by the Carlist elite in the immediate postwar decades. Comparing this literary image with the recollections of veteran *requetés* today, as detailed in chapter 3, suggests how far the elite's version tallied with that of Navarrese villagers. These analytical approaches—one literary, the other local—may also serve as an introduction toward understanding how ceremonies such as Montejurra were represented and understood by both the officer class of the movement and by its rank and file.

One means of specifying this literary genre is by comparing it with others. Unlike realist accounts with their drive toward personal and social exploration, documentary form, and commitment to truth in inner and outward experience, these Carlist texts are written in a romantic mode as ethical, improving tales. Around the turn of the century, Miguel de Unamuno, Ramón del Valle-Inclán, and Pío Baroja had portrayed the Carlist Wars as, respectively, degrading, disenchanting, and nefarious. The Carlist writers of the Civil War would have none of this. To them, armed combat for a cause that was true was exemplary, ennobling, and unquestioned. In contrast to the British poets of the First World War, these authors speak, not of homoeroticism in the midst of ugliness, but of comradeship in the face of adversity. They do not talk of sorrow at the sight of fallen youth, but of manly companionship on the battlefield or behind the lines. In contrast to the French novelists of that conflict, they do not portray man as epic victim but as epic hero. Their tone is not ironic but declamatory. They do not disparage heroism or courage, nor is there any "collision between events and the language available to describe them."[3] In sum, to Carlist writers the Civil War does not seem unspeakable, untranslatable. No author appears to be grasping for words to contain the horror he has witnessed. Instead, quite simply, these writers use an inspirational prose infused by a belligerent spirit. In print at least, they displayed no qualms about what they had done or why they had done it.

In their books the thousands of *requetés* were homogenized into a collective "they," a pronominal plurality most often presented as a stereotypic "he" evincing the appropriate forms of Carlist behavior. This almost superhuman image is so consistently maintained that literary anecdotes of action on the battlefield often fail to lend the men any individuality. According to their scribes, the *requetés* were humorless characters without any sense of play: it was not until 1982 that a veteran admitted in print to the jokes and pranks he and his fellows got up to.[4] Otherwise, in the books written about them, these armed apostles of the faith are made to seem unreflective actors impelled by their traditions. Deviations from this ideal, the natural variety within human groups, and the vagaries of individuals' experience were ignored or only grudgingly admitted to in side comments when the image was too fantastical even for its intended audience. The aim was not to portray diversity, but to detail and color the standardized image.

This literary image of the *requeté* was part of the public face Carlism presented, both for its own members and for outsiders. The memoirs served to justify and glorify the military deeds of their authors and stood as memorials to their dead friends, whose endeavors they preserved in print. Some of these books are themselves examples of Carlist dedication to their cause. For example, S. Nonell Brú's *Así eran nuestros muertos del Laureado Tercio de Requetés de Ntra. Sra. de Montserrat* is a compilation of vignettes of *every* single *requeté* that died in the author's regiment. These memoirs were not meant to be mere recollections of past events, but uplifting tales of the past for the present. Instead of detailing the tedium of time in the trenches, they chronicle stimulating examples of Carlist values in action, of Carlists doing what came "naturally" to them, and doing it well: taking up arms to defend and propagate their ideals. As both testimony to the feats of the dead and stirring moral tales for the living, these martyrographies were seen as storehouses of "magnificent lessons" from which generations to come could learn.[5]

The books produced during wartime were meant to boost flagging morale and to reassure those in the rear guard concerned about their kin and neighbors fighting at the front. Those published later sought to counter any liberal backsliding and to reaffirm the Carlist spirit. Francisco López-Sanz, editor of the Carlist newspaper *El Pensamiento Navarro*, wrote his novel *¡Llevaban su sangre!* in reaction to the proposals then being made by some of the dialogue between the opposed groups and to calls of the need to forget the war.[6] His earlier account of heroic deeds committed during the war, *¿Un millón de muertos? . . . pero con ¡Heroes y Martires!*, was explicitly intended as a rebuttal of José

María Gironella's long novel *Un millon de muertos,* a best-seller that advanced the then-daring thesis that the Republicans and the insurgents should be considered as morally equal, and that portrayed the *requetés* as a monstrous mixture of faith and ignorance, as a fanatical, superstitious rabble. In Navarre, the effect of this partisan literature was supplemented by textbooks "educating" primary schoolchildren in the Carlist tradition of the province. As one Navarrese later complained about his schooling in the postwar years, "With the bellicose passion of a crusade, they inculcated us with the feeling that we were the best in everything, the only ones, the bravest."[7]

Bowing to the dictates of the regime's censors, the authors of this improving literature tended to ignore the issues of their day. They made no comments about disputes within the unitary party established by Franco nor about contemporary Carlist attitudes to the dictator and his government. Unlike the antiregime authors of the *novela social,* they did not even indirectly criticize the present social problems of the country, such as widespread rural poverty, mass migration, and urban deprivation.[8] Instead they perpetuated an arcadian image of Carlist homes, as though they existed outside of historical time. These traditionalist tomes were not, however, politically empty; for by lauding the original ideals of the uprising, they helped to bolster the unreformed rhetoric of the regime. Like other forms of Franquist historiography,[9] though in a Carlist mode, these accounts contain a unified, single vision of events, where polyphony is absent and what is presented is the unquestionable truth.

By default, these stylized memoirs and accounts of life at the front also contributed to the popular belief of Carlists as warriors unfit to govern. A movement of such single-minded soldiers was seen as too narrow in its interests to be capable of running the country. According to this outsiders' view, the Carlists knew how to fight but not how to rule.

Sacrifice, Saints, and the Good Death

Within the camp of the insurgents, the *requetés* were not the only militia to espouse Catholic ideals. The founder of the Falange, José Antonio Primo de Rivera, for instance, told his proselytes to be "half monks, half soldiers." But it was the *requetés* who were perceived as by far the most committed group of Christians among the rebel militias. The image of the *requetés,* moreover, unlike that of the Falangists, owed nothing to Nietzschean ideas of supermen or superior races. They were inspired by their version of God, not by nineteenth-century racist ideas transposed to an Iberian setting.[10]

As portrayed in Carlist accounts, the *requetés'* deeply held faith in Catholicism strengthened their bellicose resolve, shielded them from death, and made them seem unworldly almost to the point of questioning their masculinity. This exaggerated religiosity makes them appear two-dimensional characters, since they harbor no doubts, do not waver in their aim, are unable to exact revenge, do not indulge in looting, and flatly refuse to join a firing squad. For a *requeté,* executing someone officially was said to be "worse than attacking an enemy parapet." As one officer explained, "They are incapable of killing anyone because their Christian feelings prevent them." Polycarpo Cia Navascués, a *requeté* chaplain, said though many may call the Carlist soldiers *mogigatos* (innocents, believers), this was not a source of shame, rather of honor and worth: it was *because* of their religious conviction that they made the best infantrymen. Unstained by sin and sexually chaste, they went to war in a state of grace. And conversely, a *requeté* who had sinned could be neither brave nor heroic. As some *requetés* put it, "The cleaner our soul, all the braver and more enthusiastic we enter battle." They liked to quote the socialist Indalecio Prieto's statement to the men on his side, "Beware the worst enemy you could meet on the battlefield—a recently confessed *requeté* is a terrible creature!"[11]

Such stalwart, religious soldiers are not frightened of death, for it is but the road to celestial happiness. Death is merely the point of transition from one section of the Carlist community to another, from those living on earth to those living on high. A woman asks one soldier, "And if they kill you?" "I'll go to heaven," he answers immediately and without hesitating. A *requeté* asks a companion-in-arms on his deathbed if it grieves him to have been a Carlist soldier.

"No, I'll always be one."
"Are you scared?"
"Today I took Communion!"

Another writes in a letter to his family that they should not worry about him, "for, in the worst possible case, death will never catch us better prepared."[12] López-Sanz gives examples of *requetés greeting* death because they will be united in heaven with family and friends. At one excited moment in his bloody chronicle, the author feels compelled to exclaim, "What happiness in the face of death!" He continues, "One of the things that was most admired and produced most emotion was to die without a protest, without any resentment, but with an enviable joyfulness."[13]

The death of these men is a "sacrifice" for the cause of God and the Virgin, to whom they offer up their lives. And they are meant to see it as such. Their imitation of the crucified Christ is a further demonstration of their beliefs and, because the dying will go to heaven, a means of glorifying their cause. *Requetés'* readiness to die for the sake of traditionalist ideals is represented as a form of sacramental communion with God. Surrendering one's life for the sake of religion—a definitive way to ensure meeting one's Maker—is experienced with the literalness of a sacrament. The field of battle is called "a worthy temple" where the sacred ritual is performed, and the soldiers' preparation for union with the Lord is a "novitiate." In one account, a *requeté*'s fiancée places a medal of Saint Michael Excelsis on him with hope in its protective power. Although accepting the gift, he says, "I'll put it on myself with much pleasure, but don't delude yourself that it is to free me from death, because this morning I said goodbye to the Virgin of Pilar (the patron saint of his hometown) and I have offered her my life." Another, "as a good *requeté*, acted like a missionary helping [his wounded captain] to die well, praying in front of his chief and reciting prayers and ejaculations that he had learned in childhood."[14]

It was not just that these men were prepared to die *for* the cause, but that they knew *how* to die for the cause. "The good death" is a common motif in Carlist writings. Some men, in their last moments, attempted to utter a final prayer before meeting with their deity. Others made more dramatic gestures. One nurse, the head of the Pamplona branch of the Carlist women's wing, is quoted as saying that she had never seen anyone with the faith and resignation of the *requetés:* "One day as I was passing by the bed of a gravely wounded man . . . he called and, groaning with pain, asked me to stretch out his arms in the shape of a cross. I did so, thinking that it relieved his pain. 'No, sister, it's not for that,' he replied, 'It's because I want to die like Christ on the Cross.'" We read of one "hero" who died "like the saints and like the martyrs: with many pains and without a complaint. In this way the suffering has to be more meritorious." To their Carlist hagiographers, *requetés* who died in combat fulfilled the definition of martyrs, because they loved God and their killers hated Christ. The most exemplary of these holy warriors were to be regarded as saints and their trappings as relics, such as the blood-stained catechism (its owner received a bullet through the heart) kept by the Dominican missionaries of Pamplona. As one *requeté* is supposed to have said, "We firmly believed that if we died at the front we would be martyrs to God and country—and that we would be assured eternal happiness." Although no *requetés* have yet been canonized, one is in process of beatification.[15]

God is all-powerful, all-seeing, as emphasized by the Carlist saying, "Before God you are never an anonymous hero." According to this *requeté* motto, invented by Fal Conde as a counter to the "atheist" symbol of the Unknown Soldier, no *requeté* death was pointless, for the Omnipotent perceived all. As one *requeté* whose leg had been amputated told his nurse, "If it hadn't been for God, we wouldn't have gone."[16]

The *requetés* kept themselves so morally clean by constant performance of Catholic ritual while at the front line. They said the Rosary every evening—

even in the trenches if need be—and Mass was celebrated whenever they could congregate. Participating in these habitual ceremonies helped to make the war seem less extraordinary, more comparable to life in the villages, for *requetés* knew their kin back home were saying the Rosary at the same time as them. Families were religiously reunited by their spatially separate but simultaneous performance of the same familiar rituals. On the field of battle, moreover, the soldiers' felt need for these ritual performances was all the greater. One *requeté,* speaking of Holy Communion in times of recreation, said, "Although we do it continually, we like to take advantage of the days of rest in order to fill ourselves with fervor." Preparing for an attack "and thinking of God and of Spain, with the force of our ideals, we made general Communion, offering the (local) population a spectacle of moving religiosity, in order to fight more bravely and without fear of anybody." On a different occasion, *requetés* who had advanced to within a few meters of the Reds' trenches readied themselves by saying the Rosary and receiving penance from their chaplain.[17]

One Carlist priest thought the daily Rosary was "like the muster or rations" for the *requetés.* "I obtained a rosary for each one [of his men] and they all guard it like the best of gifts." Chaplains were very close to their men, speaking of "my" *requetés* in a somewhat possessive way, similar to that of an anthropologist talking of "his" or "her" tribe. After taking Bilbao, Cia Navascués's men used their day of rest to celebrate the Feast Day of Saint Ignatius Loyola with a Mass, a parade, and a feast. At times in his narrative, Cia Navascués exploits the emotive contrast of moments when these trained killers display their gentleness in a religious manner. Returning to the battlefield one night, he wrote:

> Already near the front line, I let myself be lured by the soft murmur like a quiet sea on a sandy beach, of the Hail Marys . . . which fell from their Rosary, like leaves of divinatory pearls, the *requetés* of Montejurra.
>
> I reach them when they end praying the Rosary. Not interrupting them with profane words, my lips murmur: "The Angel of the Lord declared unto Mary"; and all the *requetés* answer, "And she conceived of the Holy Spirit." God save you Mary. . . . [18]

In Navarre alone, eighty-two Navarrese clergymen joined up as chaplains. Some were not pacific pastors attending to the spiritual needs of their flocks but energetic recruiting agents and active combatants. Once in battle, some made up for the lack of officers by taking command and directing the troops themselves. Peter Kemp, the only Englishman to fight as a *requeté* officer, saw one chaplain urging soldiers to shoot at fleeing Reds and helping them in their aim. The same priest, mounted on a white horse, even led the assault on the heights overlooking Bilbao. As Julio Caro Baroja, the distinguished Basque anthropologist of Spain, later complained, "We have seen too many priests and monks with the red beret and the two stars of a lieutenant marching with the jaunty swagger of the victor."[19]

Requetés did not leave their religious symbols in the rear guard but took them into battle. Conjoining the two main sources of power, religion and the military, each regiment carried both a crucifix on a pole bearing the motto "With This Sign We Will Overcome" and the national banner on a staff. These were seen as "two sacred symbols": the cross filled volunteers with faith, while the flag "speaks of the one and variegated Spain we dream of with hardy patriotism." *Requetés* bivouacked around the cross, "shield of our regiments," and fortunate ones died under its "sweet company." After the taking of the hill of Urcullu in the battle for Bilbao, Cia Navascués wrote: "Next to the red and gold flag, painted red by its creases and caressed by its undulations, the Cross of Montejurra. There I stuck in its shaft and left it upright, so that on the highest point of Urcullu it would crown the triumphant, living and dead, would aid those toiling close by in the work of fortification, and would give solace and refreshment to the tired hearts and bodies."[20]

In this bloody setting of religious banners, prayers, Christian fervor, and supererogatory valor in the almost constant face of death, seemingly unusual events could be interpreted as the result of the hand of God at play, as the direct intervention of divinity in earthly matters. Equivocal signs are read in supernatural terms. In one battle, the *requetés* gain ground and come upon the charred bodies of their fellows, all burned by the Reds, except for the arm and prayer book of one. As a priest later proclaimed on the radio, "Do we not see here the canonization of that *requeté's* prayer-book?"[21]

Requeté Demonology

To Carlist writers, the Civil War was a contest to the death. It was a stark, supposedly final contest of Spanish spirituality versus the specter of Russian materialism. The traditionalist notion of Spain these authors adhered to was so rigidly constructed that any suggested alteration by nontraditionalists implied disorder. Medicalizing political discourse, they spoke of disorder as though it were a disease where foreign ideas "infected" the pure Spanish body politic. Thus the apparent collapse of public order in the last years of the Republic could be used by them to legitimate the *requetés* taking up arms against the government of the day. These righteous soldiers were not to be seen as rebels, but as crusaders in a modern-day crusade that was to be "ennobled by the renunciation and the blood of those energetic and brave paladins of the Cause of Religion and Country." Publicly compared to the supposedly

Moor-hating Spaniards of the first centuries of the second millennium, the *re-quetés*—"grandchildren of el Cid"—were bent on a "Reconquest" of their country.[22] They were the men who would purify the land of anti-Christian forces.

If the Catholicism of those days exaggerated Manichaean division, loading moral right exclusively on the side of the Carlists, then the Christian rectitude of the *requetés* gained by unbridgeable contrast with the "infernal" enemy, Red "devils of hell." The *requetés* were defined in dichotomous opposition to their diabolical opponents, and Carlist writers delighted in vituperatively cataloging the unattractive attributes of their enemies. Possessors of "an African hate," these "hapless illiterates," "poisoned" by traveling marxist speakers, were "selfish," "envious," "vengeful," "vindictive," and "rancorous." "Satanic subversives," they could not love because they had no love of God; they had no God. Like the Devil himself, they were cowards who fled at the sound of a Carlist shot in the air. In Carlist discourse, these two warring factions were *not* equal because the atheists systematically shot nuns and priests. *Requetés* buried the enemy dead, but the Reds did not return the obligation. Lacking the idea of divinity, they could not be differentiated from beasts and so acted like barbarians or animals. In one incident, when the Reds had been repulsed after breaking through Carlist lines for half an hour, the chaplain held Mass at the front in order "to purify with the Blood of the Lamb and the collective sacrifice of the *requetés*, the land trodden by the horde." The Spanish soil, polluted by the diabolic and the immoral, had to be cleansed of their sign. In sum, in a list, the leftists were cataloged as "the enemies of our beliefs, our good customs, our traditions, our hearth, Religion, and the Country." To their opponents, they were not compatriots but foreigners, if not beings of a lower order or even extraterrestrials.[23]

This set of polarized oppositions did not accommodate ambiguity. Within its scheme, all Spaniards were categorized as either ally or enemy. In the effort to score the divide between Carlists and their foe, the devout Christianity of the Basque nationalists in the ranks of the Republicans was ignored. Although some nationalists in Navarre came out on the side of the insurgents in the first days of the uprising, most wished to stay out of the conflict. Some *requetés* refused to fight on the Basque front. Basque representatives met secretly with Carlist leaders but could not reach agreement. They finally decided to join the other side only because the government promised to grant them autonomy. But in the official Carlist war frame, those who did not actively support the insurgents were against them. That the nationalists initially had doubts over which side to choose, if either, was forgotten. So the nationalists became the enemy, and their religious kinship with the traditionalists was disregarded as Carlist writers incorporated the Basques into the opposed side of their antagonistic taxonomy.

Associations from past political oppositions intensified this sense of armed enmity. The Republicans were seen as the modern-day version of the nine-teenth-century liberals against whom the Carlists had fought in several wars. The elderly patriarch in López-Sanz's novel ¡*Llevaban su sangre!* educates his grandson by constantly comparing the liberals and the Republicans, iterat-ing how both committed atrocities against the Church. José María Resa, au-thor of *Memorias de un requeté*, says his grandfather, "a veteran of the wars of the past century, felt a natural aversion to both the adjectives 'liberal' and 'republican.'"

Requeté Military Traditions

Like most wars, the Civil War demanded comparison with past, not with imagined future armed conflict. It militated identification with previous Car-list wars; it encouraged a form of looking backward that helped to underline the moral steadfastness of Carlist tradition over the previous hundred years; and it allowed *requetés* to dwell both on the splendid feats performed in pre-ceding wars and on the idyllic periods enjoyed by Carlist homes in the times of peace. The *Ordinance of the Requeté* called its soldiers "inheritors of your glori-ous ancestors" and explicitly told them to "remember old glories." One bard of the cause portrayed the war as endowing the dead with almost Lazarus-like powers:

> Carlos the Fifth, like el Cid,
> Returns, dead, to battle.
> Tomás de Zumalacárregui,
> The loyal, good soldier,
> From his wound in Begoña,
> Has managed to recover.
> At the side of their grandchildren,
> Grandfathers and fathers, go
> The great-grandfathers of Estella,
> The shadows of Saint Martial.
> All enter the ranks,
> Oh, my God, what a source! . . .
> General Emilio Mola,
> You carry a century behind:
> Which is like carrying ahead,
> Captive, Eternity![24]

In one song of the period, the "return" of Carlos VII was used to underline the duty of Carlists to join up, for "this time, we will win the war!"[25] To some of those who went to fight in 1936, the military uprising was not "the Spanish Civil War" but "the Fourth Carlist War"; one writer called the insurgents' encirclement of Bilbao the "third Carlist siege of the city"; the term "*requeté*" was itself redolent of past Carlist conflicts.[26] Federico García Sanchiz mentions *requetés'* "ingenuous pride in the ancestry of their arms, a genealogy that innumerable lads even carried to the extreme of wearing sideburns in the style of Zumalacárregui." Like their forebears, many *requetés* also wore *detentes* (Christian amulets) and had the Cross of Saint Andrew sewn onto their shirts. When the *requetés* filled the main plaza in Pamplona in the first days of the uprising, they were joined by a veteran of the 1872–1876 war, dressed in his old cavalry uniform and dragging his rusty sword along the ground. According to one officer who witnessed the scene, though the man was too infirm to get on a horse, let alone charge, he was generally regarded with admiration and sympathy.[27]

The skills of warfare are described in these books in almost chivalric terms. By loyally keeping to their faith and by honoring their moral code, *requetés*, though often from humble rural backgrounds, are seen as "noble," and, at times, as "gentlemen." They are meant, after all, to be fighting for elevated ideals, not for some grubby material advantage.[28] In his *La historia triste de Fernando y Belisa*, Jesús Evaristo Casariego writes of a valiant, though poor, *requeté* who is in love with both the war and his girlfriend. But her narrow-minded father withholds his letters from her, and he dies on the battlefield. She is then forced into a marriage of convenience with the son of a successful merchant, a man with a "great future" in business. The *requeté* ascends to heaven; she is condemned to a living hell.[29] The moral is all too plain: only noble sentiments, not mundane interests, lead to eternal happiness.

Because the *requetés* were idealistic troops fighting for a worthy cause, their level of training was held to be less important than their attitude. They were meant to be courageous amateurs, rather than calculating professionals. As one Carlist novelist claimed in 1937, "The majority of those volunteers of Spain are ignorant of the rudiments of military instruction, and yet it does not occur to any of them to be concerned about this lack. They all know what they want and what they have to do to achieve it, and they think that, with a good cause and a bold spirit, victory is unquestionable."[30] At times, whether the *requetés* will win or lose seems to concern their scribes less than the idea of the struggle itself. The men are meant to throw themselves into battle, no matter the consequences. And if the chances of victory are small, then all the more glorious their effort. According to one of these writers, "In the Carlist army, those undertakings that did not agree with the rules of tactics, and in which there was a 99 percent chance of losing and only one of triumph, were known as *carlistadas* [Carlistries]."[31]

These Carlist authors, reveling in an unrepentant romanticism, depict war in deeply anachronistic terms. They seem to take pride in portraying *requetés* as quixotic characters who prefer to tilt at windmills rather than question the mode of mill production. Instead of acknowledging the nature of modern mechanized warfare, these writers delight in detailing any military event that involved the use of that antiquated vehicle of aristocratic association, the horse. Rather than discuss anonymous, grand battle plans, they choose to focus on the exploits and actions of individual *requetés,* especially when engaged in hand-to-hand combat. The British poet Laurie Lee might have confessed that he and other green members of the International Brigades had at first felt themselves so righteous that they had yet to learn "sheer idealism never stopped a tank"; but at least one Carlist writer evidently thought otherwise, for he describes an attack in which a clutch of *requetés* supposedly beat back enemy tanks with picks and sticks, and even managed to take one of them.[32] This stress on individual effort, rather than on modern modes of coordinated military strategy, was a way to deny historical change. For these Carlist authors presented history as not so much progressive and irreversible but as static and repetitive. To them, it was not open ended and alive to the possibility of radical change, but closed and dedicated to the trumpeting of continuity. According to their accounts, the *requetés* of the 1930s were the same as their forefathers of the century before; in battle, they had to face the same sort of challenges.

While the Carlists were being presented as, once again, pugnacious counterrevolutionaries who preferred overthrowing the state to following the dictates of an unfriendly government, their socialist opponents thought their present methods and level of organization owed more to the Italian fascists who had trained some of the *requetés'* key officers than to any century-old tradition of warriorhood and guerrilla bands.[33] The First and Second Carlist Wars had been, at their start, primarily rural uprisings later coordinated into nationwide struggles. In each case, the Carlists had chosen first to rebel, and only then to train their troops. It was only with the accession of Don Jaime in 1909 to the Carlist throne that leaders of the movement broached the question of setting up a permanent military organization. The new pretender, who lived in Paris and was influenced by the ideas of the French radical Right, was interested in establishing a special section whose trained members would combat the leftist street gangs that were beginning to threaten law and order. Unlike the rural irregulars of the last century who had acted independently of their generals, this new kind of militia would constitute an integral part of the Carlist structure. Although such Carlist paramilitary groups were never set up outside of Madrid or Barcelona, and though the groups that did exist languished during the dictatorship of Primo de Rivera, their example laid the foundations for the establishment of the Requeté in the first years of the Republic.[34]

Partisan writers may have wished to stress the similarities between the *requetés* of the Civil War and nineteenth-century Carlist soldiers, and even to claim their identity, but the centrally organized, at first urban-based militias were above all a modern creation, meant to fit the political demands of their time. Although, on the outbreak of hostilities, a few Navarrese and Aragonese Carlists did form their own bands of rural irregulars, the overwhelming majority of *requetés* entered the ranks of a predominantly twentieth-century organization: the Requeté.[35] One may thus see Don Jaime's paramilitaries as less the inheritors of the customary Carlist military style than as the precursors of fascist squads and bullyboys. To this extent, the Carlist writers' representation of the *requetés* was as much a recruitment of tradition, to veil recently created elements, as it was a modern portrayal of a supposedly habitual bellicosity. They were not exactly inventing tradition but exploiting traditional elements of Carlism for modern political ends. Carlism might hail from the nineteenth century, but the *requetés* were very much part of the twentieth.

Family, Blood, Beret

Whether describing domestic or military life, traditionalist authors portray the Carlist world as overwhelmingly masculine in orientation. Strength, bravery, and heroism are stressed at the expense of values marked as feminine. The austere, the muscular, and the inflexible consistently overshadow the tender, the sensitive, and the compassionate. This pugnacious predisposition had already been starkly stated in the orders given to the *requeté* street squads that saw action in Barcelona in the 1910s: "To an insult, reply with a fistful, to a fistful with a stick, and to a stick with a shot."[36] The same bloodthirsty aggressiveness is underscored in the following popular Carlist song:

> Put my espadrilles on me, give me my beret, give me my rifle,
> For I'm off to kill more Reds than the month of April has flowers.[37]

While some Republicans had wanted to change the traditional status of Spanish women, Carlists (and other factions of the Franquist forces) wished only to reinforce it. To them, the fact that women on the Republican side took up arms and fought alongside their menfolk only demonstrated the depths of moral misery to which the enemy had sunk. Women who so dramatically transgressed the sexual divide could have no shame or dignity. In the traditionalists' accounts, female voices are rarely heard and those women who do appear in their narratives are consigned to predominantly passive roles. They are not meant to educate themselves in political matters. As one of these chauvinistic writers put it, "Without political science, which was absolutely unnecessary for them, [the women of the village] intuited the greatness of the problem raised and the sublimity of the great exploit embarked upon. They knew that the war was for Christ or against Christ, and they did not need to know anything more."[38]

Women are portrayed in these texts only as supportive kin: as mothers, sisters, or fiancées who keep the home fires burning and who, in their own way, uphold Carlist ideals as staunchly as their menfolk. García Sanchiz refers to the legends about mothers refusing to feed sons who had not yet joined up, and about the grieving but resolute grandmother who offered her remaining grandson (the others already dead) in the *requeté* recruiting office. But other than employing these restricted modes of action, women were not supposed to agitate, only to feel and to grieve. One author states that Carlism does not just live in the houses, objects, and acts of the faithful: "But, above all, Carlism lives in the figure of a mourning, pallid, and sweet mother, that is, the holy mother of the martyr *requeté*. . . . It lives in her silent resignation. I have seen her serene, tranquil, quiet. With that august and mystical immobility of the *Dolorosas* on the altar."[39] Mortifying herself for the sake of her son and the beliefs he held, this stricken mother is identified with a particular avatar of the Virgin. The two women are united by a common pain for their departed child.

In their typically masculinized mode, none of the *requeté* memoirs refers to the work of the Margaritas, the Carlist women's organization named after Doña Margarita, the wife of Carlos VII, who worked as a nurse in the Second Carlist War. Founded in 1919, ostensibly for the provision of aid to impoverished traditionalist families, during the Republic it was used by the Comunión for propagandistic purposes: senior Margaritas proselytized in homes, put on musical evenings, and arranged religious acts, all for the sake of the cause. During the war, these white-bereted women organized and worked in hospitals at the front, and visited *requetés* on active duty, bringing them food and clothing. At home they knitted and darned garments for their menfolk and performed the agricultural tasks their absent fathers, husbands, or brothers usually did. According to their ordinance, a Margarita was "an example of Spanish woman, intrepid defender of the Christian family, vigilant guardian of the traditions of the patria." They were meant to constitute a moral rear guard, stimulating the *requetés* to ever greater feats and shaming those who had not yet gone to fight.[40]

While Carlist authors denied women much space in their texts, they made the family the institutional bedrock of their faith. According to José María Co-

dón, who summarized traditionalist thought on the matter, families constituted the fundament of society. If they ceased to exist, the structure of society
would collapse and social life would inevitably degenerate into anarchy. This
was not an arbitrary social fact, for the family was a divine creation, instituted
by God when He made Adam and Eve. It was part of His plan for us, and we
could not go against His will: family life was sacred. Besides these pseudosociological and theological assertions, Codón also argued—perhaps unsurprisingly for a traditionalist—that the traditional Spanish family had the weight
of history to back it up. Using the Bible, Aristotle, and Numa-Denis Fustel de
Coulanges as trustworthy sources, he claimed that patriarchy had been characteristic of families from the beginning of time. The fact that the patriarchal
family had survived, and thrived, as an institution since that time was a clear
measure of its perfection. Although liberals in the last hundred years had tried
to weaken and destroy the family, their attempts to alter such "an indefectible,
perpetual, and insecularizable institution" had failed completely. The family
remained in its ordained place, in the very center of Spanish life.[41]

The authors of more popular works on the *requetés* took a slightly different
approach in their attempts to justify the primacy of the family. When trying to
explain the strength, nobility, and moral fortitude of the *requetés*, they claimed
"the secret of everything" was the "hardy virtues" of the "inviolable" hearths
in which Carlist children were brought up. These were virtues "inherited from
their parents as the best and richest legacy." The familial home was seen as a
rural refuge of "the peaceful Christian virtues," a bulwark against "the social
and political anarchy vomited by the cities and the industrial centers." And
the symbolic center of these homes was the kitchen, or more specifically its
fireplace: "the flame of the faith, the embers of tradition, and the forge where
the souls of crusaders were wrought." In steadfast Christian homes, this fireplace was "the distilled drop from the still of traditionalism" that such homes
were. It was the favored domestic site where familial members gathered; at the
hour of the patriarchal circle, people repaired here "to the entreaty of the
flame." It was here that fledgling Carlists learned traditionalist values. When
José María Resa and his fellows went to fight, "very proud . . . to defend our
sacrosanct ideals," he thought all this "the fruit of the good example of our
ancestors and of the spirit of sacrifice inculcated by our parents."[42]

Priests of the day drew a close analogy between the structure of the family
and that of the Holy Family. Both the Almighty and the paterfamilias were
represented as distant, powerful figures who could dictate to their people or
children but could not be dictated to. Women, as the example above implied,
were told to model themselves on the Virgin. Children were meant to ask their
mother to intercede on their behalf, while Christians had to seek the aid of
Mary when they required the assistance of God. Both types of family were

also meant to be bound by the same mutual ties of affection. Carlists extended this familial analogy to themselves: their organization was not a "party," but a "communion," a term meant to signify coexistence, communication of ideas and of feelings, and participation in the common good. Their king was portrayed as a "father" to his people, one as remote, authoritative, and benevolent as any male head of a household or supreme being. Carlist villagers were not to approach him directly but to make their feelings known to their local representatives—some of whom were so highly regarded that they were known as *santones* (men so influential they were almost revered)—who would pass the word on to their leader. Although inaccessible in life, the king could be met after death: in the notebook of a dead *requeté* was found the following poem:

> I want to go up to heaven,
> giant step by giant step,
> to give an embrace
> to Don Jaime de Borbón.[43]

The Carlist analogy could influence the others reciprocally: the family was called a socially sovereign unit, a miniature monarchy, with the mother as "queen of the hearth," while God was "the supreme King of Carlism" and "King of the Martyrs." Some village Carlists blurred their notions of god and king; for in an evocative passage on the image of Carlos VII, Pablo Antoñana—a Navarrese writer who has taken an especial interest in the Carlism of his area—states:

A majestic king when on his horse, a great lord when on foot, with the halo of a saint in a hagiography. And a saint he was for his needy subjects, whose children in 1933 still (true and checked) worshipped that unique portrait of him in a blue greatcoat, buttoned up, his goat's-udder beard, the dalmatian at his feet. The image hung on meat hooks, to which were lit pure beeswax candles on days of thunder and lightning, which was invoked when the woman of the house was in labor or one of her children set out on a voyage for Asia or the Antilles. That almost deified man, God on earth, was deeply impressive, in contrast with the feeble, wan body of that Alfonso XII, which made a die-hard Carlist woman say, on seeing him enter Estella as conqueror, "But *this* is a king?"[44]

The reciprocal modeling between the three types of family meant that each type could be imbued with the associations of the other two. The analogy with the Holy Family lent an air of sanctity, that with the royal family provided a note of regal distinction, and that with the family supplied connotations of love and propinquity. The overall effect of these resonating analogies was to underline the centrality of the family in otherwise distinct spheres of Carlist activity: what happened at home, in church, or at Carlist meetings was not to be understood separately but as similarly structured parts of a greater whole.

Many writers on war present time spent on the battlefield as a rite of passage from callow youth to aware manhood. Not so the Carlist authors, for they wished to stress how popular and compelling the cause was. They wanted to underline the fact that not just headstrong youths but men of all ages had joined up. In a well-known piece of verse, one *requeté* is asked who should be informed if he is killed. The soldier mentions his son, who is in the same regiment. "And if your son is dead?" "Then inform my father who is also among us." This much-publicized Hernandorena trio of grandfather, father, and son, who went out to fight *en famille* in July 1936 is perhaps the most striking example of the commitment across generations to the same movement. Memoirists liked to stress this continued adherence by sons and grandsons to the creed of their forefathers, for it highlighted the enduring, familial nature of Carlist tradition. As one author stated, "It goes without saying that my father, my brothers, and myself, we all have been just like [our Carlist grandfathers] were." Men were said to feel that their families had to be represented on the battlefield: one Carlist, the father of thirteen children, went to the front in order to stand in for one of his sons whose wife was about to give birth. One widower was so keen to participate that he took his young son with him to the front, where he helped in the kitchens and soon became the mascot of his father's *tercio*. Some grandfathers were said to have joined up. Romero mentions an eighty-three-year-old *requeté*. More infirm veterans simply urged, if not censured, the youth of their villages to "go fight" (*echarse al monte*, "to throw oneself up the mountain").[45]

Good Carlists, ever constant, did not just maintain their faith until death but kept it up even beyond the grave. For Resa, the greatest of victories will be to join in heaven his fellow *requetés*, men who fell in the field, and for them to sing "all together in union and eternally,

> For God, the Patria and the King
> our fathers fought;
> And for God, the Patria and the King
> we will also fight."[46]

Resa's grandfather, on his deathbed, said that should King Carlos return to the Court of Madrid, he wished his ashes to be disinterred so he could contemplate this Carlist victory.[47]

This consanguineal continuity, this ideological steadfastness within the same families over generations, is expressed metaphorically as "blood." López-Sanz entitled his novel, which was primarily concerned with this theme, *¡Llevaban su sangre! (They Carried Their Blood!)*. In the final scene, the bereaved mother shows once again the relics of her dead father and son, both *requetés,* to her daughters and exclaims, "Let us always be like them! Let us carry their blood!" The author goes on to speak of "feelings that were indestructible because they were born in the blood." Resa, reflecting on the violence in his hometown during the Republic, says the Carlist blood of his grandfather runs in his veins, and that it is now "even more energetic and convinced due to everything I had witnessed earlier."[48]

The trope of blood is both genealogical figure and vital constituent of personality. Events are meant to inflame the blood, which, once kindled, "pushes" its owner into action. Veterans of the Second Carlist War, censuring youths not yet in uniform, rubbished them by saying, "It is that you are not like us! It is that you do not bear our blood!" Shedding this blood "ennobles" the crusade. One *requeté* dying in battle, unable to shout "Long live Christ-King!" is said to have written it instead in his own blood on a stone. After one victorious battle, the *requetés* literally merged Church and Carlist blood by soaking for forty-eight hours the gory blankets used to shroud a dead companion and by mixing the resulting solution with cement for the restoration of a church burned by the Reds. "In this way, we *requetés* will say that the church of Villanueva de Argecilla has been restored with our sweat and with our blood." Traditionalist writers did sometimes use other physiological metaphors to communicate the nature of their beliefs, speaking of people who were "Carlist to the guts," whose ideals were "stuck in as far deep as the marrow [*el tuétano*]," defined as "the most profound physical or moral part of man." But "blood," with its connotations of vital essence and vivacity, remained the most popular way of naturalizing the cultural, of explaining beliefs in physiological terms.[49]

These themes and metaphors of tradition—its continuity, the familial frame, armed violence, and blood—all come together in the red beret, the epitome of Carlist symbolism. The beret first became a distinctive part of the uniform during the First Carlist War, as a way of distinguishing Carlists from liberal soldiers with their morions (a type of helmet without beaver or visor). By the 1860s, the beret had become a badge of Carlism generally, not just of the Carlist military. Some wore blue berets, others white. Not until the Second Carlist War did wearing a red beret become general. As metonym, the red beret came to signify Carlism and all it implied. When López-Sanz wishes to express the grief of a bereaved mother in his novel, he says that she had no other son on whom to place the red beret. One *requeté*, about to be shot by a Republican firing squad who have removed his beret, shouts, "Please leave me the beret! I want to die with it on as the best safe conduct to present myself before the Tribunal of God, for whom I die." Another, on his deathbed, tells a nun to stop trying to remove his bloody shirt because "I want to present myself before God as His defender with my *requeté* shirt and my Carlist beret." A third, also on his deathbed, insistently asks his parents for the beret he had worn in battle. Using it to wipe away "the cold sweat of his agony," he says, "This is the beret that you gave me: with it I have lived, with it I have defended the Holy Crusade, and with it I want to die and enter into the Kingdom of Heaven."[50]

Using headgear as a symbol for the movement itself was so pervasive that staunch Carlists were said to wear the beret "on the outside and on the inside." The offering made to Saint James by a Carlist pilgrimage to Santiago de Compostella in 1965 was a red beret, "discolored, but much loved by us all"—that of Antonio Molle Lazo, the *requeté* currently in process of beatification.[51] According to the accounts of Carlist writers, the homage paid to this piece of headgear could at times seem fabulous. When the *requetés* took the Basque town of Durango, they searched the streets for a place where they could celebrate Mass; they were allowed into a convent once the nuns and Catholic refugees hiding inside realized they were not Republicans; the nuns led the *requeté* chaplain into their church and sat him in front of the organ; as he started to play, they removed his red beret and passed it among themselves. They kissed it respectfully, "imprinting on its crumpled wool the kiss of lips hot from the fever of their emotion and the ardor of their perilous wait. With resplendence in their misty eyes, they examined it from a distance, placed on a table, without wrinkles, without sinuosities, and they contemplated it with a veneration almost religious, for a long time."[52]

While Carlist authors of the Civil War laud the role and actions of the *requetés,* they quietly pass over the progressive development of the Nationalist army and the absorption of the *requetés* into its ranks. But as the war progressed, the army grew ever larger and the proportional contribution of the *requetés* that much smaller. The Carlist soldiers may have played a crucial part in the beginning of the conflict, but by its end they had simply become another section of the forces under Franco's command. As Peter Kemp observed in August 1937, "For all their courage and endurance, their patriotism and self-sacrificing idealism, they lacked the strict discipline that are so necessary in modern warfare. This war had altered radically since the early days, and the old qualities of willingness and valour were no longer enough."[53] In military terms, the *requetés* had become out of date. Kemp transferred to the Legion.

Chapter Three

Village Carlism

The literary representation of the *requeté* was a standardized image aimed at several audiences. It historicized *requetés* by masking modern realities; it generalized at the sake of local specificities; it dehumanized at the expense of personal individuality. A *requeté* from northern Navarre might secretly lament, "For me the saddest thing about this war is that not only Spaniard is fighting Spaniard, but Basque is fighting Basque," but such opinions were not fit to print.[1]

Chapter 2 discussed the idealization and depersonalization of the *requetés*. In contrast, this chapter particularizes the *requetés* by viewing them in a specific situation: the Navarrese village of Cirauqui. Village Carlists were aware of how the educated elite of their movement portrayed the cause, because they read the traditionalist press, attended talks given by visiting representatives of the Comunión in Cirauqui and in nearby towns, and had to listen to the harangues while in the ranks. But they knew Carlism in primarily local terms: the contexts in which it was expressed, and the forces against which it was defined. In this setting, the movement has its own history, genealogically set and topographically placed rather than bounded by a political context of national scope. While continually affected by events beyond the municipal boundaries, and while influenced by the picture presented by the literary Carlist elite, traditionalist villagers have much their own way of speaking about the movement. Those who experienced the war know how the publicized stories of the *requetés* could simplify, if not misrepresent, what they had gone through. If the previous chapter examined the statements of an educated officer class, then this one tries to give voice to "other ranks."

To put their words into context, though, we need first to review the histories of Carlism in Cirauqui: socioeconomic, politicomilitary, and sociopolitical.

Cirauqui, Socioeconomic History

To the traveler, Cirauqui appears a series of closely built stone houses climbing up a small hill. Its gradients, in places quite steep, provide a natural defense for its inhabitants. The remaining sections of a high wall, which once encircled the whole settlement, supply further protection. The two impressive churches of the village, one topping the hill, the other on its northwest slope, both date from the thirteenth century, and both were renovated and expanded about three hundred years later. While records of the village exist from medieval times, most of the houses that can be seen today were raised in the seventeenth or eighteenth century.[2] The mound on which they sit, bordered at its base by slightly more modern buildings, is set above a long valley that runs from east to west. Views to the north are blocked by a range of high hills, and to the south by a slightly more distant, lower range. Land down the valley, along whose bottom a river flows, and up the less inclined slopes is cultivated with various crops. Livestock graze in the steeper areas.

The strategic position of the village, plus the existence of a Roman road along its southern edge leading to an equally ancient bridge, suggests the antiquity of the settlement. The Roman bridge and road, sections of which can still be walked, lay on the pilgrim route to Santiago.[3] Near the bridge was found a votive altar to a Roman divinity. Further evidence about the human prehistory of the site has been provided by the recent discovery of Neolithic dolmens half a kilometer to the northwest of the village. The earliest records referring to Cirauqui detail its successive transferals from one overlord to another. In 1045 the incumbent king of Navarre donated the estate to a local monastery. Two hundred years later, the monarchy received it back from a noble in exchange for other lands. Finally, in 1425, the then-reigning king gave it to his bastard daughter and her husband, the Conde de Lerín, in whose family control the village remained for the next three centuries.[4]

Until very recently, agriculture was the primary means of production, the villagers cultivating grapes, a mixture of cereals (in order of importance: wheat, barley, oats, rye, maize), and olives, and rearing stock. The extensive commons of the village provided pasture for livestock to graze, and its forested parts firewood. From the beginning of the seventeenth century, villagers started to shift from an economy of self-sufficiency to one that exploited the market values of their crops. Thus, since a good wine could be produced in the immediate area of Cirauqui, and since the government introduced a range of measures favoring the export of Navarrese wines, villagers began planting more vines. In other villages of the region, where the soils were more suitable for other crops, locals began to specialize in the production of either cereals or olive oil. This relative specialization led to increasing commerce and contact between different villages of the region, and boosted the importance of its market town, Estella.[5]

Unlike many other areas in Navarre, the population of Cirauqui increased steadily from the fifteenth century on (figure 1). This rise in numbers was sustained primarily because, over the centuries, locals progressively cultivated more of the village land and because land that could produce cereal crops only

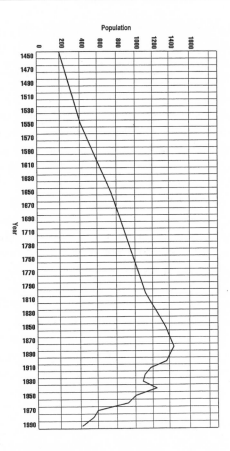

Fig. 1. The Development of Cirauqui's Population, 1450-1990

every other year could yield, when turned into vineyards, annual harvests. In 1607 about 25 percent of the land within the boundaries of Cirauqui was cultivated; by 1888 about 40 percent of it was being exploited. This gradual expansion at the expense of the commons did not go unopposed. The *Libros de Acuerdos* (*Books of Agreements*) of the Cirauqui town hall detail a series of conflicts during the eighteenth century between livestockmen and those bent on tilling the commons. These disputes were finally resolved in 1792 to the relative detriment of the livestockmen.[6]

Accounts in the town hall records of disputes give us some idea of the interest groups within Cirauqui. But in order to discern, in a detailed manner, its socioeconomic structure, it is necessary to analyze the one cadastral survey of Cirauqui, carried out in 1897. This survey details the holdings of everyone, whether a villager of Cirauqui or an outsider, owning taxable goods in the village. A computer analysis of the survey (summarized in appendix 1) suggests that there were very marked inequalities of wealth in the village. Sixty percent of the taxpaying villagers provided less than 11 percent of the villagers' total tax bill, while the richest 20 percent paid more than 71 percent of it. The majority of villagers owned plots of land covered with poor soil; most of the wealthier minority owned large tracts, some of top quality. People with the means to choose did not specialize economically but invested their wealth diversely. They made money by cultivating grapes and cereals, running businesses, letting houses, and, to a much lesser extent, by harvesting olives. The production of wine, however, was the major source of income for most villagers: the better-off all paid 75 percent of their tax bill on vineyards.

The existence of marked rural inequality is also strongly suggested by data from the census of Cirauqui, carried out eighteen years previously. According to the census, the village was then inhabited by 693 males and 725 females, living in 370 "hearths." Of the active male population over the age of twenty-one, 184 were classed as farmers working their own holdings *(labradores)*, 60 as landowners *(propietarios)*, 5 as *labrador propietarios*, 4 as landowners who exercised another profession at the same time, 45 as day laborers *(jornaleros)*, and 1 as a *labrador jornalero*. There were also 55 men primarily engaged in other occupations, such as shepherds, merchants, cobblers, bricklayers, clergymen, carpenters, millers, municipal constables, schoolteachers, and tailors.[7] These data indicate that at least 19.5 percent (69 men) of the active males in Cirauqui employed others to work their land, and that at least 12.9 percent were primarily dependent on being offered employment by others. The proportion of men who were economically dependent, at least seasonally, on the landowners was most likely much higher, since many of the smallholders would have rented land, sharecropped, or worked occasionally for the larger landowners, some of whom were outsiders and hence not included in the census. Thus, if the analysis of the survey results and the data drawn from the census enable us to draw a single picture of Cirauqui at that period, it is of an agricultural village where, above all, the sale of wine generated wealth and where the few could economically dominate the many, getting them to work their fields, pick their crops, and clean their houses.[8]

This domination did not always go unopposed. Let me give two examples, taken from either end of the nineteenth century. Because of the continued economic crisis experienced between 1800 and 1820, many of the village's poor escaped destitution by joining the national forces fighting Napoleon's armies. But with the end of the war, demobilization offered these men little. In May 1815 some of these impoverished youths expressed their discontent by helping to stage a riot during the fiestas of a nearby village. Frightened locals huddled in the church while cavalrymen quelled the disturbances, which ended in a mass arrest. According to one of the lawyers in the subsequent case, the rioters were "ungovernable churls" who dedicated themselves to stealing food from fields and terrorizing local populations and municipal authorities. The Cirauqui leader of the riot, Vicente Guembe, was "a subject of relaxed conduct and capable of every evil." In other words, he was a former soldier who had turned to banditry in order to survive. He received a sentence of six years.[9] At the turn of the century, discontent was expressed in a similarly violent manner when someone blew up the small dam in the valley bottom used to power the village generator. The culprit was never officially found, but it is thought the explosion was the work of a poor villager, disgruntled that only the local rich could take advantage of the electricity the generator produced.

Many Spaniards had themselves long recognized that structural inequality was a pervasive feature of rural society. From the 1800s on, liberal reformers had tried to correct this injustice by progressively selling off the land entailed on the Church. However, the main buyers had not been, as originally hoped, those with insufficient land, but those with sufficient resources. Thus the well-intentioned reforms tended to aggravate rather than to reduce the difference between the relatively rich and the less well-off. In Navarre, the worst effects of this increased economic disparity were mitigated by the carefully regulated exploitation of the commons. Compared to most other provinces, the majority of Navarrese municipalities still controlled a particularly high proportion of common land. *Vecinos* (natives and established residents) of each municipality had the right to cultivate designated plots of land *(parcelas)* and to cut down trees for firewood. Also, town halls could enrich their coffers by auctioning off the leasehold of certain uphill stretches of their commons to the owners of herds.

The costs of the Carlist Wars, however, left many town halls close to bankruptcy, and they were forced to sell off part of their commons. The municipality of Cirauqui had been affected worse than most. Between 1862 and 1898, in a series of attempts to pay off its debts as well as to meet the legal obligations of the disentailment reforms, it had to auction over 2,000 hectares: only two other town halls in the whole of Navarre sold off a higher proportion of their territory.[10] According to the cadastral survey, by 1897, 19 percent of all village land, excluding the commons, was owned by outsiders. The *parcelas* available to the villagers became smaller, and fewer in number. The size of smallholdings, moreover, diminished as familial plots were progressively subdivided. As the cadastral survey showed, by that time, the majority of villagers had only small tracts covered with poor soil.

In the first decade of the twentieth century, villagers began to change their mix of crops, because the phylloxera pest had by then destroyed many of the vines, the French market for Navarrese wine had shrunk, and the government had started to implement a policy of promoting the production of cereals. People began to sow seed in their former vineyards. By 1935, the land area devoted to vines had halved, compared to forty years before, and the area devoted to cereals had doubled. However, this shift in emphasis from one kind of crop to another did not sufficiently improve the position of the poorest villagers. At this time, in some parts of the province, the increasing pressure on the land caused by the rise in population led people to plow up areas previously left fallow. But those inhabitants of Cirauqui who had adopted this strategy in the eighteenth century had managed to maintain the land they had begun to cultivate only by winning the approval of the town hall and overcoming opposition from herd owners. If, in the first decades of the twentieth century, the latest generation of impoverished smallholders and landless villagers wished to start digging up part of what was now left of the commons, they still needed the formal permission of the town hall, and that was not readily forthcoming.

Some tried to escape the threat of indigence by emigrating; the population of the village went from 1,354 in 1900 to 1,121 in 1930, a drop of over 17 percent. The coming of the world depression in the 1930s only worsened the plight of those who stayed. According to a survey carried out in 1932 by a provincial workers' association, about fifty men in the village—a significant proportion of the adult male population—were unemployed.[11] By January 1933, those worst off had become so desperate that they were prepared to act illegally, by plowing up the commons without municipal agreement. The resulting violent confrontation with the police, plus the many arrests that followed, made the town hall so unpopular that its representatives backed down, allowing the villagers to plow some of the commons. Once again, the needs of those who worked the land had eventually prevailed over others with interests in the commons.

Cirauqui, Politicomilitary History

Like many Navarrese villages that lie along important routes, since the beginning of the nineteenth century, Cirauqui has often suffered the passage of armies of various kinds. Perhaps because of its strategic placement on a steep hill overlooking the highway, its inhabitants have also had to bear several times with the protracted residence of bands of soldiers. However, though it is one of the villages along the Carlist belt of central Navarre, Cirauqui is not famed for its allegiance to the Carlist cause. Rather, it is known locally as a village of divided interests: of Carlists versus liberals in the nineteenth century; of Carlists and conservatives against leftists and Basque nationalists in the twentieth century. This opposition has not always remained within conventional bounds. In the nineteenth century it led to a notorious massacre within the village, in the twentieth century to a number of politically inspired murders.

Documentation about the political life of Cirauqui in the early nineteenth century is sparse. Accounts of military activity in the village, however, are more plentiful. A summary of these accounts and of the years of the Republic and the Civil War will serve several purposes: (1) to illuminate key periods in the recent past of the village; (2) to underline the fact that the dramatic events of the Carlist Wars were not simply external occurrences about which resident villagers only heard; and (3) to provide a historical context within which the remarks of veteran *requetés* about the nature of Carlism can be critically appreciated.

During much of the First Carlist War, Carlist forces occupied and controlled the village. In 1834 a French legitimist who presented himself to their commanding general, Tomás Zumalacárregui, then based in Cirauqui, described the village as being "full of soldiers and *confidentes* [trustworthy men], the squares crammed with horses and baggage, and the barrels full of wine."[12] By this time, the inhabitants of Cirauqui were used to the reality of armed conflict, for in late October 1811, during the War of Independence, the Spanish general Francisco Espoz y Mina had stationed two battalions of irregulars there. These men were meant to detain the advance of a French column 4,000 strong, which they did, for a short period. In the early 1820s a significant number of male villagers volunteered for the Royal Division of Navarre, which won over much of the province to the absolutist cause. In 1823, toward the end of the war, 234 royalist troops, stationed in Estella, mutinied against poor conditions. The majority of them, from Cirauqui and a neighboring village, walked home. Zumalacárregui, then a royalist captain, smartly dispatched companies to the two villages. There they rounded up the discontents and returned them to barracks, though their demands were to be quickly met.[13] During the Carlist war, the resident villagers witnessed action in their hometown only toward the end of the conflict, in July 1839, when liberal forces attacked. The Carlist troops based there put up fierce resistance, and the liberals, in revenge for their defeat, destroyed everything in their path as they beat a retreat.[14]

THE SECOND CARLIST WAR

The Carlist banner was raised again in Navarre in May 1872, when Carlos VII entered the province from France in a premature attempt to foment uprising. Although his ill-prepared expedition was roundly defeated a few days later at the Battle of Oroquieta, and he was forced to return across the border, a sizable contingent of his troops continued the fight for several more weeks. The military governor in Pamplona declared the province to be in a state of war. In Cirauqui, as in other Navarrese villages, a group of committed anti-Carlists formed their own armed band, Los Voluntarios de la Libertad (Volunteers of

Liberty). They took control of the village and dismissed the mayor, his two assistants, and six aldermen. The new administration was immediately ordered to provide the military commander in Estella with sixty fully equipped large horses, as well as supplies of wheat and barley. In August, the military governor told the mayor and his men to remain on their guard, as he had heard that the Carlists were aiming to raise bands of irregulars throughout Navarre; their job would be to distract the attention of the troops stationed at the border so that their brethren in France could smuggle arms into the country that much more easily. The governor urged all local authorities to be extremely vigilant and to prevent any attempt at insurrection.[15]

His directive had little effect, for by the end of the year the Carlists were openly regrouping. This time the pretender's lieutenants were better prepared: they ensured there were sufficient rifles, uniforms, and supplies to arm, dress, and maintain a full-fledged army. Many hundreds throughout the greater Basque area promptly left their homesteads to enlist. Within months the Carlist forces had swelled into a well-organized army of over 7,000 men, most of them Navarrese, under the command of General Antonio Dorregaray. Between April and July they won several important battles and began to occupy much of northwestern Navarre.

Bands of Carlist guerrillas attacked Cirauqui twice but were beaten back on both occasions by the Voluntarios. This liberal squad did not confine itself to the village but several times sallied forth to skirmish with enemy groups based in the surrounding hills. It could not, however, dislodge the Carlist company that had gained control of the fort of San Isidro, perched on the crest of the southern range of hills overlooking Cirauqui, and that fired cannonballs on the village from time to time. As the mayor put it, the Carlist cannon fire had "regrettable" effects on the inhabitants. On hearing that a small detachment of government forces was going to "disturb" the troops entrenched in the fort, he beseeched the military governor to cancel the raid. Otherwise, the cannon fire would start up again, causing more "regrettable" effects.[16] On the afternoon of 12 July the liberals of Cirauqui had to contend with more than a few cannonballs, as the large Carlist column that had just taken the nearby town of Puente la Reina was now marching up the valley to attack them.

The Voluntarios and their enemies fought hand to hand in the village streets. But there were fewer than eighty on the liberal side, and despite their valor (which even a Carlist eyewitness, called Gorriti, attested to), they were forced to retreat and barricade themselves in the village's second church. In the early months of the uprising the liberals had turned this building into a fort. Unlike the church on the summit of the hill, this one, halfway down the northern slope, commanded a view of the highway that ran from Pamplona to the important market town of Estella. If the Carlists wished to move their troops freely in the area, they had to take it.

In February, General Dorregaray had sent the leader of the Cirauqui Voluntarios a message recommending that they lay down their arms. On that occasion the leader had refused and said that, given the rightness of the liberal cause, it would be more appropriate for the Carlists, not for the liberals, to hand over their weapons. This time Dorregaray sent him a letter urging him and his men to surrender. Once again the liberal leader refused, saying that he and those under his command would rather die than give up. The next morning the Carlists moved a cannon onto a small promontory overlooking the church and began firing at its tower. They also started to throw petrol bombs and to mine the foundations. The besieged managed to resist for a while. But by midday, with the church already alight and with no chance of countermining the Carlist excavations, they decided to put their future to the vote. Of the sixty-two Voluntarios inside the church, thirty-two thought they should give up; the rest voted to continue fighting, though the only imponderable was whether they would all be killed by fire, gunpowder, or bullets. At two o'clock in the afternoon, they raised the white flag.

The liberals agreed to surrender to Dorregaray on the same conditions as had their fellows in Puente la Reina: in return for their handing over all their arms and munitions, the Carlists would escort them to neutral territory, respect their property, and not harass their families. When some of the villagers heard the terms of the agreement, they rioted and shouted for the heads of all the prisoners. They were joined by some of the Carlist soldiers, especially those in the band of one Idoy, all of whose men came from Cirauqui, Puente, and a village in between the two. According to Gorriti and also to the liberal historian Antonio Pirala, during the fourteen months the liberals had controlled Cirauqui, they had treated some of the other villagers, particularly some of the women, very badly. When they had fortified the church, they had ordered women to carry water up from the river. They had sometimes humiliated them even further by emptying their buckets on the ground, so forcing them to make a second arduous trip to carry more water up the hill. The traditionalist historian Melchor Ferrer states they also "abused" the women in other ways, while Gorriti refers more generally to the "horrors and ill-treatment" of which the liberals were guilty. He claims that they repeatedly profaned the church, damaging images, committing "a thousand obscene acts" in time to the music of the organ, and removing a crucified Jesus from its cross and telling Him to leave now that He was free.

According to Gorriti, Dorregaray tried to contain the tumult by keeping the liberals inside the church. At five o'clock he decided to take the main body of his force into Estella, and to leave the prisoners under the custody of Idoy. In a heated response to this order, Idoy told his general that since the angry villagers and his own mutinous men were now at the door of the church, he could not answer for the lives of the imprisoned. Dorregaray ignored this reply and went off with his troops. Idoy, not knowing what to do, held up a battalion that was about to leave and spoke to its colonel. The senior officer, determined to take resolute action, told his men to fix their bayonets. However, neither the warnings of the colonel nor the threat of his soldiers could move the crowd at the door. Meanwhile, the liberals, who were able to observe all that was going on from the windows of the church, armed themselves with rifles that they had earlier hidden in fear that the surrender might not proceed as originally agreed.

At six o'clock the mob at the door finally forced it open and charged inside. The liberals fired, wounding three men, one of them mortally. The crowd, now more enraged than ever, set upon their assailants, bayoneting and knifing as many as they could find. Before the regular troops could reestablish order, the rioters had massacred forty-two of the Voluntarios and mortally wounded three others; another four were wounded, but later recovered, while the remaining thirteen saved their lives by hiding in a large vat. Two days later the seventeen survivors of the carnage were escorted to Puente, where they were set on the road to Pamplona. The widows and wives of the Voluntarios were expelled and their houses ransacked.

One survivor was Tirso Lacalle Yabar, nicknamed "El Cojo" (The Lame) after an agricultural accident damaged one of his legs. He later gained notoriety as the leader of a bloodthirsty band of liberal guerrillas. Lacalle Yabar tried to sum up the feelings of his fellows in his report of the event to the civil governor of Navarre:

> My brave Volunteers do not ask for vengeance; they ask for justice, Illustrious Sir, they ask for reprisals, those reprisals authorized by the laws of war; they do not ask for vengeance because they do not feel it in their breasts; they do have strong feelings, Illustrious Sir, but they are republicans and they only want Justice! Justice!! Justice!!! They want eye for eye, tooth for tooth and man for man, house for house, furniture for furniture, money equal to that which has been taken from them. They want, as I have said, justice, but a quick and efficacious justice.

The news spread quickly throughout the country. Within days of the massacre, the town hall of Pamplona voted to commemorate the dead by changing the name of one street from "Saint Anthony" to "Martyrs of Cirauqui." Liberals regarded the event as a tragically good example of Carlist murderousness. Pirala, while understanding the reasons for the mob's rage, blamed the Carlist officers for failing to subdue the mob; Ferrer thought the liberals had

committed equally barbarous deeds and so should not be overhasty in damning the Carlists; Gorriti judged the slaughter a retributive act of "the Divine
Justice that never errs."[17]

The new masters of the village dismissed its two schoolteachers and installed a Carlist administration in the town hall. The change of municipal officeholders was done out of necessity as much as self-interest: the mayor that
had been installed by the liberals and at least three of his aldermen had all
been killed in the massacre. One of the mills was commandeered as a barracks;
according to the subsequent testimony of the miller, the soldiers billeted on
him insulted him so much that he felt forced to leave for Pamplona.

To help ease the burden of maintaining a resident army in the area, the military authorities now began to impose a series of demands on the town hall.
On 24 August, for example, the municipality had to supply a squadron of
cavalry with a hundred rations of beef, bread, and wine. Three days later it
was told to send the troops in Estella a thousand rations of beef, eight hundred
of bread, and one hundred of barley. At other times it had to provide horses
and mules for the army, espadrilles for the foot soldiers, bedclothes for the
wounded, beds for the military hospital near Estella, carpenters and laborers
to fix a war-damaged bridge, and cartloads of dried vine shoots for the production of coal. Sometimes the Carlist authorities gave less than a day's notice
for the completion of their demands. Sometimes the town hall did not respond
with sufficient speed or in the appropriate manner. Company commanders
protested about the quality of the bread they were given and threatened pu-
nitive sanctions. The military hospital also complained it was not receiving
the rations of food and wine ordered, and it warned the mayor that it would
"energetically castigate" any disobedience.[18]

The municipal authorities were not the only people in the village dragging
their feet. In 1874, the Carlists started to conscript all able-bodied bachelors
and childless widowers between the ages of eighteen and thirty-five in the
areas they controlled, unless these men could give good reason otherwise.
Six men from the village bought their way out, four won exemption on the
grounds of physical or mental deficiency, and three others were excused from
service for being the only sons of widows; the secretary of the town hall succeeded in staying out of uniform by arguing that he was the only child of his
sexagenarian father. The commanding general of Navarre threatened to fine
or imprison the fathers, or grandfathers, of those who, while eligible for conscription, had fled or not yet joined up. One man who persuaded his son to
flee had his house ransacked by troops, who stole two casks of wine and all
the fruit they could find. In the following weeks, they took to stoning the
house and threatening to bayonet him to death. As he later complained to the

liberal Deputation in Pamplona, "the wickedness of those savages became such that, at the beginning of this July, they inhumanely threw me, my wife, and my daughter out of my house."[19]

The more well-to-do of the village were also pressed into lending money to the army. In February 1874, ten local landowners were told to hand over quantities of money ranging from 400 to 5,800 *reales de vellón* (copper coins) "within the inextensible limit of eight days and without any excuse or protest." Although they were promised 5 percent interest on their "loans," the money would never be paid back.[20]

The villagers had had to suffer the liberals in the first months of the war, and they had to suffer them again in the last ones. In February 1875, the advancing liberal troops took a series of hilltop forts, including that of San Isidro, in the Middle Zone of Navarre. Their progress northward was halted only by their defeat at the Battle of Lácar, a village seven kilometers to the west of Cirauqui. For the first time in the course of the conflict, the liberals did not retreat but proceeded to dig themselves in. The detachment occupying San Isidro bombarded the village day and night, pausing in their firing only if the mayor met their exorbitant demands for rations. An attack on the fort in April failed. The liberals, threatening to pound Cirauqui until it was destroyed, continued to extort supplies from the locals. They were not released from this burden until February of the following year, when the massed liberal armies in Navarre and the Basque Country forced the Carlists to retreat and Don Carlos to return to France.[21]

THE REPUBLIC

By the time—fifty-four years later—the dictatorship of Primo de Rivera collapsed and the king fled into exile, the coordinates of local political debate had shifted from a contest between Carlism and liberalism to a clash between conservative and left-wing forces. And, within the spectrum of right-wing groups, Carlism was the single most powerful party in Navarre. Although its fortunes had languished in the decade before Primo de Rivera's coup, the perceived threat of the reforms proposed by left-wing Republicans to the established position of religion was sufficient to revive support for the Carlist cause and for right-wing villagers to close ranks.

In March 1933, the Carlists of Cirauqui formed their own Circle in a private house. The membership grew rapidly, and within six months the club had eighty-seven dues-paying members on its books. Nine more joined before the end of the year. There were no more new members until 1936. In March that year nine men were admitted to the club, and they were followed in the first nine months of the war by another twenty-three. The Circle, decorated with pictures of the Immaculate Conception and San José and portraits of the pretender, Alfonso Carlos, and his wife, ran a bar and invited leaders from Pamplona to come and speak on the tenets of Carlism. Villagers would also journey to Estella and other towns to hear Carlist speakers there. Every year on 3 May, members celebrated the Day of the Holy Cross, designated by the pretender as the date of the annual fiesta of the Comunión Tradicionalista. After attending Mass, members set off fireworks in the main plaza, and the club served alcohol and biscuits free to its members.[22]

As opposition to the Circle, a local member of Unión General de Trabajadores (UGT, Workers' General Union), the socialist union, set up a Casa del Pueblo on the edge of the village. But it was never registered with the authorities and does not appear to have been very active. Only a small minority of villagers, a clutch of independently minded leftists, regarded themselves as its members.

During the six years of the Republic, political tension in the village was expressed more in personal terms, as clashes between individuals, than as a contest between opposed institutions, such as the Circle and the Casa del Pueblo. The long list of local cases dealt with by the village and the regional courts between 1931 and 1936 suggests that the antagonism between villagers of different political persuasion was steadily maintained throughout this period. In the politically charged atmosphere of those days, a shout, an insult, or a song was enough to provoke a violent reaction. In August 1932, two villagers were brought up before the court of Cirauqui accused of causing a public scandal. The village constable had tried to imprison one of them for shouting, "¡Viva la Republica!" Aided by a friend, he had resisted arrest. In the trial, the friend claimed that justice was not being done, for others had shouted "subversive cries" like "¡Viva Cristo-Rey!" The constable claimed not to have heard the latter cries, and the two were found guilty. Three months later a known loudmouthed drunk insulted a woman of the village for being the wife of the local president of the UGT. When she replied that her husband, unlike her detractor, did not blaspheme, he tried to stab her with a large knife. He was imprisoned for three days and was fined five pesetas. When, on the night of New Year's Eve that year, some conservatives began singing political songs in one of the village bars, some left-wingers who were also drinking there made their disapproval plain. A heated discussion ensued at the doorway between a member of each faction. A friend of the Carlist involved in the dispute arrived and tried to take him home. But the Republican then pulled out a knife and stabbed his disputatious opponent three times. His injuries kept him off work for thirteen days; his assailant was locked up in the village jail for fifteen days and fined 102 pesetas.[23]

The bloodiest event of this troubled period, though, was yet to occur. On

20 August 1933, the mayor and a relative of his (his mother's brother's daughter) met, by chance, at the village washhouse where both had gone to draw water. The mayor made plain his wish to have sex with the woman, a married mother of three children.[24] In reaction, she called him a thief, for a past transaction in which he had supposedly cheated her. As the mayor was leaving, her son, who had arrived on the scene, threw a stone at the man and then grabbed him. His mother jumped on the mayor, but, catching her by the hair, he managed to pull her off. Her son then warned him that he would not live another twenty-four hours. That night the mayor ordered his assailant to appear at the town hall. When he did turn up, the two men argued and the young man shot the mayor dead with a bullet to his neck. The murderer was sentenced to over twelve years' imprisonment, fined 15,000 pesetas, and made to pay costs.

When villagers today relate the story of this killing, they emphasize that it was primarily a dispute between kinsfolk, and that the two families had long been at odds. But they also recognize the political dimension of the murder, as the murderer was of the Left and his opponent was Cirauqui's leading representative of the Right. Furthermore, moments before being shot, the mayor had threatened his assailant that he would starve to death all the Republicans of Cirauqui. In an extraordinary session of the town hall held the day after the event, the acting president underlined the municipal dimension of the killing when he said that proof of the late mayor's dedication to his job was the fact that he had died as a martyr to it. For an hour before the funeral, his corpse was laid out in state in the main chamber.[25]

Instead of insulting or otherwise challenging opponents to their face, some politically inclined villagers chose a slightly less direct method of injuring their enemies: destroying their property, usually on a Sunday. On the night of 2 April 1933, someone set fire to the barn of a leading Carlist, causing damage to a total value of 2,380 pesetas. Two weeks later, over one and one-half acres of flourishing vines belonging to the local chief of the Requeté were cut down. The damage was estimated at over 900 pesetas. One night in late May, a further 475 of his vines were destroyed. In November that year, one or more arsonists vented their anger by starting fires in the communal woodlands on the slopes of San Isidro, destroying trees and stacks of firewood worth over 6,000 pesetas. In the last months of 1934, another barn was burned down and, in the first days of the following year, yet another—this one belonging to a Basque Nationalist—was put to the torch. On the night of 8 September 1935, the barns of three right-wingers were set alight. One of the sheds was so close to the small Civil Guard station in the village that the policemen had to evacuate the building until the fire was put out. This last case of arson was unusual, for a villager, an eighteen-year-old member of the Left, confessed to the crime. He was sentenced to four months imprisonment.[26]

The villagers may have been divided, sometimes violently, by politics, but the more impoverished among them could be united by a common concern for improving their wretched lot. In November of this same year, one of the village Republicans presented himself to the town hall as a representative of the unemployed of Cirauqui and formally asked for work. When he did not receive a reply, seven workers began to work on the municipal paths on their own account. The town hall ignored them. The following January, a group of land-hungry villagers petitioned the town hall for permission to plow up some of the commons on San Isidro. Once again, the town hall did not reply and, once again, the locals took matters into their own hands. They ascended the hill, chopped down a large number of trees, and started to dig up the land. The Civil Guard arrived, stopped the illegal works, and, after some angry confrontations, arrested six of the trespassers. A month later a much larger band of villagers, 190 strong, climbed the hill and took up where their fellows had left off. But when a squad of over twenty Civil Guards appeared, they did not offer any resistance and pacifically agreed to suspend their labors. Once back in Cirauqui, however, the mood of the men, who were now milling around the main plaza, changed. When the Civil Guards tried to disperse the crowd by wielding their batons, the angry villagers turned on them. The policemen were forced to flee into the town hall, where they attempted to hold off the crowd by raising their rifles. But the rioters were not to be put off by this threat: a number pushed their way into the building, grabbed one of the policemen, and tried to throw him off the balcony. The guardsmen, however, managed to expel the intruders and immediately rang their headquarters in Estella for reinforcements. With the forces of law and order now effectively besieged in the town hall, the rioters had temporary control of the village. They lit bonfires in the plaza and cut the telephone wires. One man who lived in the plaza supplied them with wine, and, according to participants, an almost fiestalike atmosphere ensued. When the reinforcements eventually arrived, they fired several shots, relieved the besieged, and arrested nineteen of the rioters.[27]

All but five of them were freed within a few days. The mayor and his councillors, realizing the unpopularity of their previous measures, agreed unanimously not to take part in the subsequent court case and not to forward any claim of compensation for damage done by the rioters. Trying to cover up their previous mistakes, they argued that the villagers had not thought they were damaging the commons, but rather exercising their rights. And the mayor and councillors explained that the only reason the villagers' request to plow the land had not been quickly acceded to was the long administrative procedure such petitions had to undergo. In a further effort to regain some standing among their neighbors, the municipal officeholders also drew up a list of those unemployed in Cirauqui and agreed to hire four of them to repair the village paths. The mayor and his men, however, did not forget whom they represented. When they accepted the petition by the Sociedad de Trabajadores sin Tierra (STT, Society of Landless Workers) for the construction of a new bridge, the town hall did not contract any of the village leftists, though they had been the very ones to promote the project.[28]

Veteran *requetés* emphasized to me that these various incidents have to be seen in context. They stress that village life used to be much less sedate than it is today, that fights and riotous behavior were then almost commonplace. One claimed that a young man who woke up on a Sunday morning in the village jail with a hangover would not have been surprised nor particularly ashamed to find himself there; some middle-aged women remembered having seen on several occasions women openly fighting in the main plaza, pulling each other's hair and shouting insults. The words of these villagers are borne out by the catalog of cases dealt with by the Cirauqui court in the first half of the 1930s: besides politically motivated incidents, they include disrespect to the village authorities, mutual insults, drunken brawls, violent quarrels, threats with knives, stabbings, and one homicide.[29]

If the use of violence for politically based reasons was not out of key with the general tenor of those times in Cirauqui, nor were the fights, knifings, and murder committed during the Republic the first occasions, outside of periods of war, when factional difference was expressed physically. In Navarre as a whole, the political campaigns of the 1910s were marked by the increasingly virulent language of candidates toward their opponents. In August of 1914, when a large group of Carlists returned home to Cirauqui from attending a rural pilgrimage, a serious fight developed between them and village liberals, and a number of the combatants were later tried in the provincial court for rioting.[30]

Similarly, during the years of the Republic, not just Cirauqui but many Navarrese villages were the scene of persistent social conflict. While the province as a whole did not experience the revolutionary upheavals that characterized parts of Asturias, Cataluña, and Andalucía, there was a long series of politically provoked outbreaks in the Ribera and the Middle Zone of the province. Since trade-union activity was not well organized in Navarre, compared to other regions of Spain, social tension was expressed less by strikes than by arson, destruction, and occupation of the commons. In these terms of political violence, the village of Cirauqui is exceptional solely for the number of fires started there: only three other Navarrese municipalities reported more cases of arson.[31]

After the burning of the three barns in November 1935, the sergeant at the Civil Guard station in the village asked the Carlists to follow the movements of the socialists. Five young *requetés* formed a patrol to keep watch over their opponents. Five months later, a visiting speaker told Carlists that the uprising was near and that they would soon be given pistols. When it started, they were to arrest all the leftists in the village. He also told them to put up posters for the coming elections and not to insult any of the local Republicans. If their political opponents started to abuse them, however, they were to draw their pistols. When the two groups did meet in the narrow streets of the village, both sides quietly stuck up their posters on different parts of the same wall and nothing was said. In the elections (the last ones staged by the Republic), 399 villagers voted for the right-wing coalition and 41 for the Frente Popular de Navarra (Navarrese Popular Front). The Basque Nationalists did not participate, and 28.6 percent of the electorate did not vote. As in the rest of Navarre, the high level of abstention affected the Left more than it did the Right.[32]

THE CIVIL WAR

On the morning of 20 July, when the *requeté* patrol learned of the uprising, they immediately asked the police sergeant if they could raise the national flag, which has one gold band flanked by two red stripes. He seemed doubtful, then admitted he did not have one. So the armed youths went up to the town hall, tore the purple band off the Republican flag, burned it, then hoisted the remaining bit of bunting, with its one gold and one red stripe, as a substitute for their faction's banner. Within a short time, the two Nationalist councillors, the schoolteacher, and the postman of the village were all dismissed. The president of the Casa del Pueblo, the president of the Sociedad de Trabajadores (Workers' Society), and the vice-secretary of the STT were arrested along with eleven other known leftists. Most were imprisoned for eight months. A few nationalists and socialists, fearing for their lives, quickly joined the Falangist militia. The postman fled the village, and in his absence all the goods in his shop were looted. He was later spotted in Pamplona and killed. In all, five villagers, including a gypsy woman, were shot. It is thought that there would have been more killings had not the police sergeant made clear his distaste for any "butchery."[33]

Of the 164 villagers who fought on the side of Franco, 93 volunteered as *requetés*, 37 joined the Falange, and the remainder were later conscripted. No one signed up for the regular army. While almost 75 percent of the men who entered these militias were under the age of thirty, several of those Carlists who joined up were in their forties and one volunteer was sixty. The ambience of war was so strong and its attractions so tempting that some adolescents ran off to the front and had to be brought home by their fathers. In total, seventeen *requetés* from Cirauqui died in the war. The body of each was laid in state in the town hall overnight, and a band of *pelayos* (Carlist minors) played at the funeral the next day.

Carlist authors like to give the impression that all the *requetés* were willing volunteers. But as one veteran pointed out to me, though he and his friends had volunteered, they knew that if they had not, they would have been eventually conscripted anyway. Moreover, while sixty villagers joined the *requetés* within the first two weeks of the uprising, those who did not sign up quickly were frequently shamed into uniform by women shouting "¡Falso! ¡Falso!" beneath their windows.[34] Such men were "volunteers" only in name.

Cirauqui, Sociopolitical Composition

Perhaps the most pertinent question for us to ask at this point—"Who exactly were the Carlists of Cirauqui?"—is also one of the most troublesome to answer. Any attempt to tackle this topic is hindered by a lack of detailed documentation, by the biases of the documentary information that is available, and by the nature of political allegiance in the area at the time. While it is probable, bearing in mind the geographical position of Cirauqui within the heartland of Navarrese Carlism as well as its structural similarity with neighboring villages, that a good number of its inhabitants sympathized with the cause, it is extremely difficult to calculate with any precision how many liberals or Carlists there were in Cirauqui, and what proportion of the main occupational groups sided with either of the factions.

One might think initially that a study of the political complexion of the village during the two Carlist wars could provide an approximation to an answer to these questions. In fact, documents covering the events in Cirauqui during this period are among the least revealing for our purposes. The local leader of the Carlists and the organizer of the initial rebellion was a major landholder, Don N. Urra, who was assisted by at least two other notables of the municipality. During the occupation of Cirauqui by the troops of Carlos V, it would seem that the majority of the inhabitants were Carlist, since a report to the Navarrese section of the pretender's administration says the villagers were "fully committed" to the cause, there being only one "doubtful subject." However, it is probable that most of the liberals in Cirauqui, however many or few there were, had already fled to Pamplona. The fact that no one from Cirauqui is included in the list (compiled by the provincial authorities after the end of hostilities) of liberals whose property or goods had been confiscated by the Carlists might seem to suggest that most villagers adhered to the cause of Carlos V. But at the same time, it is quite possible that kinsfolk had managed the properties, and protected the possessions, of their absent liberal relatives.[35]

The information I have obtained about the villagers during the Second Carlist War is almost as inconclusive. One hundred and thirty-eight of them entered the ranks of the Carlist army, but we do not know how many of these actually supported the cause of the pretender; at least seventeen of these conscripts were sufficiently disgruntled to cross the line and join the liberal forces. Of the villagers who fled to Pamplona, seven joined the Compañia de Emigrados, a section of the liberal army, and several entered the Foral Guard, a provincial militia.[36] However, these numerical data, like those for the proportion of villagers within the Carlist ranks, do not necessarily inform us about people's political allegiance. The Compañia was not trusted by liberal officers, as they suspected that some of its members were not true liberals but shirkers evading the rigors of the Carlist army. In the same way, membership in the Guards did not necessarily denote commitment to liberalism: since the Foral Guards spent most of the war within the city walls, only occasionally venturing out as escorts or reinforcements, joining this militia was seen as a relatively safe way for rural refugees to support their displaced families. The claims of indemnity brought after the war by supposedly liberal villagers against the degradations committed by the Carlist occupiers are similarly unrevealing, and for much the same self-interested reasons. As administrators in the provincial Deputation were well aware, many Carlist villagers were quite prepared, once the hostilities were over, to deny their former allegiance in order to claim monies to help cover the cost of any damage done during the war. None of the petitions made by the inhabitants of Cirauqui was accepted.[37]

Checking names from the rolls of the Compañia, of the Guards, of the liberal and Carlist administrations of the war-struck village, and of the Carlist recruits who did not desert against those that appear in the cadastral survey of twenty years later, it is possible to construct lists of apparent Carlists (22 men) and liberals (26) and of which tax decile they belonged to. Figure 2 shows that the ranks of Carlists were drawn from all deciles of the village, while the liberals came from all but two. Comparative examination, within each decile, of the holdings of members of the two sides suggests that there was no important difference between them. Both sides have similar proportions of traders and merchants, and of large, medium, and small landowners. Comparing the two sides across groups of deciles, there does appear to be a tendency for the liberals to come from the higher taxpaying groups (69 percent of the liberals and 50 percent of the Carlists are from deciles 7 to 10), and for a relatively greater proportion of the Carlists to come from the lower to middle deciles (15 percent of the liberals and 32 percent of the Carlists are from deciles 3 to 6). But the numbers within each decile are too low for us to be able to make any finer, statistically significant generalizations about the social composition of taxpaying Carlists and liberals.

Given the potentially misleading nature of some of the wartime and the

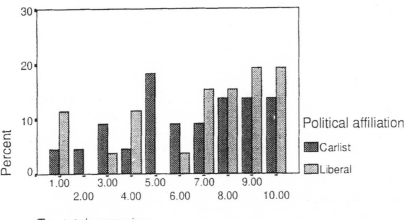

Tax totals grouping

Fig. 2. Political Parties by Tax Group

survey data, it might be thought that the results of the hustings in Cirauqui would be more informative. In fact, the particular forms of social structure that existed in both the village and the province from the end of the Second Carlist War to the dictatorship of Primo de Rivera in the 1920s mean that the voting patterns discernible during this period reveal more about the patron/client relationship then current in Cirauqui than about villagers' political sympathies.

Some of the more powerful men in Cirauqui exploited their position to advance themselves and their cause. Aging men in the village today state that politics was "much harder" then, for those who did not vote the same way as their patrons might be sacked or ejected from their tied houses. Electoral politics throughout Navarre was organized in the same corrupt manner, with bribery and systematic violence against sectors of the electorate as the order of the day. One journalist of the period complained that "Workers and subordinates have necessarily to give up their own ideas and to identify with the thought of the owner of their workshop or business."[38] The local liberal newspaper, *El Eco*, put it more ironically: "In elections, all means are good for achieving the end and, if a request is not sufficient, offers and threats are used, which have always given good results; and to all those who have been promised appointments as judges, magistrates, or canons, it is above all because they deserve to be appointed; and, as regards threats, we will use them only on those who owe us a favor, such as tenant farmers or debtors." [39] Votes were often sold on an open market. In 1897, *El Pensamiento Navarro* claimed the current rate was one duro (five pesetas) for one vote. Eight years later it reported that some electors had bought food on credit against the proceeds of the hustings. But the electoral struggle had not transpired, and they were left in debt.[40] Besides buying votes, provincial politicians, the immense majority of whom were landowners or lawyers, also gerrymandered district constituencies, coerced members of the foral administration, and had ballot boxes broken into. In these circumstances of bribery and bullyboys, electoral results tend to be more a reflection of how well organized political groups were than of voters' sympathies.

In Cirauqui, the results of elections to the Foral Deputation suggest that, after the failure of the Second Carlist War, the village anti-Carlist faction led by the family of "El Cojo" were able to prevent local Carlists from reorganizing themselves successfully until the 1890s. In the 1882 elections for a provincial deputy, the vote was split almost evenly between a pioneer Basque Nationalist and a Republican. Four years later, the same Republican candidate won 94 percent of the vote and his Carlist contender 6 percent. In 1898 the Carlist share of the vote went up to 58 percent, while the conservative who stood gained 42 percent. In 1903, the village vote was divided between the Carlists (47 percent), a conservative liberal (34 percent), and a conservative (19 percent). In 1907, the Carlist candidate won 69 percent, the conservative 20 percent, and the conservative liberal 11 percent.

The results for elections to the Cortes suggest a similar pattern. In the 1891 elections to the chamber, the Carlists won 37 percent of the vote and the conservative liberals over 60 percent. Less than 40 percent of the enfranchised turned out for the following elections, held two years later, and the Carlists' share of the vote went up to 75 percent and the conservatives' went down to 19 percent. In 1896, the Carlists maintained their leading position in the village, with 60 percent of the vote compared to the liberals' 34 percent. Two years later, the Carlists' share of the village vote had declined to 43 percent, while that of the conservative liberals had risen to 44 percent. In 1901, the Carlists won 63 percent and the conservative liberals 37 percent. Four years later the vote was divided between five candidates: the Carlist gaining 39 percent, the Integrist 31 percent, the Conservative 22 percent, the Republican 5 percent, and the Democrat 4 percent. In 1907, the Carlists and the Integrists together won 71 percent, the conservative liberals 27 percent, and the Republicans 3 percent. In 1914, the Carlist and Integrist candidates gained 61 percent between them, and the conservative liberals 28 percent.[41]

Taken all together, the results of these elections to the provincial and national chambers suggest that, from the 1890s on, the Carlists were always able to organize themselves as a major force in Cirauqui, winning the votes of never less than a third of its enfranchised. But neither these electoral data nor the documentary evidence dealing with the Carlist Wars allow us to make any definitive statement about the number of villagers during this period who regarded themselves as Carlists or which social classes they belonged to.

Since electoral politics was far less corrupt by the time of the Second Republic, the results at the hustings during this period provide a more accurate idea than any of the above data of contemporary villagers' political attitudes. In the first municipal elections after the dictator's departure, held in April 1931, the people of Cirauqui voted into office five Carlists, two right-wing Republicans, and two Basque Nationalists. In the national elections for deputies to the Constituent Cortes, staged in June 1931, in which 89 percent of the village electorate participated, candidates of the right-wing coalition of Carlists, Basque Nationalists, and other conservatives received 240 votes apiece and the left-wing alliance 23.[42] On the basis of these results, it would appear that, as happened elsewhere in Navarre, Carlism was gaining popularity and reemerging as a significant political force.

When I asked aging villagers about the social and political composition of Cirauqui at that time, they stressed that there were Carlists and "liberals" in all social strata of the village, and that the relatively few leftists tended to come from the poorer families and the few Falangists from the more well-to-do ones. They also emphasized that they could not be more precise in their statements because a number of people kept very quiet about their political affiliation. At least during the years of the Second Republic, it appears that the Carlists of Cirauqui were not restricted to any one social category, but counted within their membership people from almost all walks of life in the village. Thus both the locally popular view and the results of our documentary surveys corroborate the common representation of Carlism as a cross-class movement.

Perhaps the most important point that emerges from the examination of all these different types of data is that the popular conception of the Middle Zone of Navarre as being traditionally almost solidly Carlist is much less well grounded than Carlist writers would have us believe. While there is little doubt, given the oral testimony of aging villagers today, that a number of families in Cirauqui did maintain, and value highly, their continued allegiance to the Carlist cause over generations, it also seems to be the case that other villagers supported Carlism only when it suited them. It would thus appear that the Carlist writers' portrayal of Navarre in 1936 as a province so naturally, and so densely, Carlist that "even the cherry trees bore *requetés*" is an exaggeration, for political ends, of the extent of traditional support for the movement. Although the proportion of people in the Middle Zone of Navarre who supported Carlism appears to have been significantly higher than in most other parts of the country, that does not mean that the majority of people in that zone saw themselves as traditionally Carlist, or even as Carlist.

Requeté Culture

Although everyone in Cirauqui depended, directly or indirectly, on the working of the land, lived within the municipal boundaries, and had their needs administered by its town hall, they appear to have had relatively little else in common that might have contributed to a sense of village unity. As we have seen, people were divided by their access to wealth into the rich, the peasants, and the landless; by political faction into Carlists and liberals in the nineteenth century, and into Carlists, Republicans, and Nationalists in the twentieth; and at times by livelihood into livestockmen and those keen to till the commons. Furthermore, the wealth of the municipal area was not exclusive to locals but was divided between villagers and nonvillagers; according to the cadastral survey, a few *foráneos* (outsiders) owned some olive groves and houses within Cirauqui. Also, it is very likely that the wealth of the locals was not restricted to the boundaries of Cirauqui; a number of residents probably owned land, inherited or purchased, in other villages.

The only other cultural elements that held the potential of uniting these villagers—living in an area not wholly owned or worked by them and whose limits did not define the extent of their own wealth—were adherence to a communal religious code, a sense of local history, the domestic mode of production, and notions of political steadfastness. At various times in the past, the prospect of a common threat might have united villagers to an unusual extent. But the sole event I found in my historical analysis of Cirauqui that even begins to approach this was the popular reaction to the religious reforms of the Second Republic, mentioned below.

Although the common cultural elements of religion, history, familial economy, and notions about political allegiance might draw people together, when variously interpreted, they could be more sources for separation than motives for community. Thus local Carlists' religiosity was a heightened, extreme version of village Catholicism; their sense of history was a contested reading of the past; their appreciation of the importance of the family as an institution was a politically framed one; and they applied the local idea of political steadfastness in a highly partisan manner. In the following subsections, I discuss aspects of this "*requeté* culture" within the contexts of village culture.

REQUETÉ RELIGION

Veteran *requetés* with whom I talked said that the stories of the highly fervent *requetés* are "a little exaggerated" but added that there were indeed men like that. They said that some *requetés* did take Holy Communion at every available opportunity, but that others attended Mass only on Sundays, as they did at home. In contrast to the humorless image produced by Carlist authors, one old man happily admitted that after a successful attack, he and his mates would go "mad" enjoying themselves. To be wounded four times was considered the greatest of good luck, for it meant one would be off on leave for long periods. It is important, however, to remember that these veterans are survivors. Conspicuously brave, or foolhardy, soldiers who perform supererogatory deeds are often the very ones killed in battle. Religiously inspired heroes *are* heroes because of the risks they take. And, in a war that lasted three years, they did not always survive those risks.

Many of the veterans stated that it was above all the issue of religion that had motivated them to fight, for "the Reds were burning churches." They were Carlist, they said, *because* it was rooted in religion. One woman recalled that her father used to say that if another party defended the Church as well as the Carlists were doing, and that if the Carlists were not defending the Church, then he would be for that other party. One priest and former *requeté* leader from a nearby village declared, "Carlism represented the mode of Christian-humanist being. When I was seven years old, my father told me that Carlism is authentically Christian and that if it is necessary to die for it, one must do so." It was better to die than suffer the religious persecution of the Second Republic. "The *requetés*," he added, "were ready to die." As one Navarrese, speaking on the radio, put it, such devout men regarded "war as marker in the memory of the passage of man through the earth, and in the end martyrdom, anteroom of the face of God."[43]

When *requeté* veterans speak of their support for religion, they do not discuss Christianity in a restricted ecclesiastical or theological manner; rather, they are promoting a traditionalist conception of local identity expressed in a religious idiom. In this sense, Catholicism becomes a symbol of their notion of community, of how people should live together in peace, harmony, and mutual respect. Although the villagers could be divided by politics, they were meant to be united by religion. Those few who stayed away from church on the Sabbath were notorious to the whole village. When, in 1897, the parish priest had to report to his bishop on the moral state of his flock, he said there were only four parishioners who did not observe their Easter obligations, and only two of those were "public and scandalous sinners." One refused to marry the woman he had once lived with, though the priest had "used all the means within my reach" and had gotten figures of authority and influential persons to try to persuade the man. The other was an avaricious moneylender who had been in America and had "antireligious ideas." The priest's efforts to reform the man failed, and he classed the sinner as "an obstinate ignoramus."[44]

Christianity could be a symbol of the local Carlists' notion of community because so much of their way of life was given substance and shape by their religion. Catholic rites and structures organized and framed people's life cycles, the agricultural calendar, and the ordinary work routines of both individuals and families. The rites of baptism, First Holy Communion, confirmation, marriage, and funeral structured people's trajectory through life. Families said grace before meals and the Rosary every evening before supper. Many attended Mass daily. Sunday Mass was a major social occasion for which people (especially women) dressed up and after which they passed the time chatting with fellow villagers in the main square. It was imperative that all the faithful observed the Sabbath as fully as possible: shepherds and the municipal gamekeepers had to return specially to the village in order to hear Mass; in the autumn, farmworkers had to seek permission from the bishop if they wished to gather in the harvest on the Sabbath, and he would not allow them to carry out any other task on that day.

The annual religious rites were many and various, dividing up the village year in ceremonial terms and providing locals with a regular series of occasions by which they could mark the passage of the year and date the occurrence of events. In January, on the feast day of Saint Anthony, all the livestock in Cirauqui were made to circle the church three times and were blessed each time by the priest. On the seven Sundays preceding the feast day of Saint Joseph on 19 March, villagers sang novenas as they processed around the village. Villagers were meant to observe the Lenten penances rigorously; they had, specifically, to abstain from meat and, more generally, to eat only the most frugal of meals. From Palm Sunday to Good Friday, the church bells were silenced, children were not allowed to play games in the streets or the plazas, and people attended services every afternoon. On the night of Maundy Thursday, heavy floats portraying scenes from the Passion of Christ were carried around the village in procession. The morning of Easter Saturday marked the end of all restrictions. On 1 May, villagers made their annual pilgrimage to the hermitage of San Cristóbal, where they celebrated Mass and then spent the rest of the day drinking, eating, and dancing. On 9 May, the feast day of Saint Gregory Ostiense, patron saint of the countryside, the priests celebrated Mass and then distributed holy water for the blessing of the fields. The water came from Sorlada, a village in the west of the province, where it had been passed through the head of the saint whose remains were kept in the basilica there; no villager worked on this day. On the feast day to celebrate Corpus Christi, villagers dressed in their best clothes, the parochial treasures were displayed, and a procession was held through the village. On 13 September, the Day of the Holy Cross and feast day of the Saint Román, patron saint of Cirauqui, a similar procession was staged. This event was the religious high point of the annual village fiestas, which were held around this date. Every day in October, at dawn and twilight, people performed novenas and processed around the village as they sang the Rosary for the sake of the Virgin of the Rosary.

Adult villagers could also manifest, and intensify, their faith by joining some of its church-based associations. Most men in Cirauqui belonged to one of its two confraternities. Members of the Confraternidad de la Cruz Verdadera (Confraternity of the True Cross), which included most of the adult male population of the village, organized the Good Friday procession and, masked in long black cloaks, carried the floats. They also paid for the celebration of a sung Mass on the first Friday of every month and for the performance of sung Masses on the two days before and after the Day of the Holy Cross. Members of the Confraternidad del Rosario Sagrado (Confraternity of the Sacred Rosary) paid for a Mass for the living and dead members of the association, to be held at dawn on the first Saturday of every month. Before each Mass, the Salve was intoned, and would be followed by a member singing the Rosary. The confraternity also paid for special Masses on the day after Christmas, and on the days celebrating the Purification, the Annunciation, and the Ascension of the Virgin. In both confraternities, when the viaticum was performed for a gravely ill member or when the funeral of a member was held, other members attended the event bearing the crosses, flags, and other insignia of their association.[45] In 1909, a male Asociación de Adoración Nocturna (Association of Nocturnal Adoration) was established in the village. Once a month, the Eucharist was exposed on the altar of one of the village churches, and members of the association took turns keeping a vigil over the Host throughout the night. Vigils were also kept by members on Christmas, during Holy Week, and on the eve of other important liturgical occasions. Women joined the Asociación de las Hijas de María (Association of Daughters of Mary). Once a month, members had to attend church on Sunday evenings; the priest would give a sermon and discuss religious practices with them, for up to two hours. Children were formally educated in the tenets of their faith in weekly classes of catechism. In 1924, the parish priest of Cirauqui stated in a letter to his bishop that every one of the 110 boys and girls who were obliged to attend did so. As the priest admitted, one of the reasons attendance was so high was his exhortations to parents that they ensure their children turned up.[46]

Almost every important event was celebrated in a religious manner. Prayers were said before meetings of the town hall and other village organizations, and any major new project either was blessed with holy water or had a Mass celebrated for it. Also, unpredictability and the threat of misfortune were countered in a Catholic manner: people lit candles and prayed to Saint Barbara and Saint Tirso when their crops were at risk from thunderstorms; if Cirauqui suffered a bad drought, the parish petitioned the bishop in Pamplona for permission to carry the image of Saint Christopher in procession down to the river where the congregation would pray to God for rain. Given the pervasively Catholic ambience of village life in those days, where every significant event and many seemingly insignificant ones were marked in religious terms, where people turned to Christianity in an effort to control both their destinies and the forces of nature, and where much of people's nonworking time was taken up fulfilling the duties of their faith and performing its practices, it is not surprising that those *requetés* who during the war were stationed in the provinces of Castile were shocked to find how unkempt the churches were and how worldly the parish priests.[47]

Carlist leaders often liked to boast that it was necessary to "Navarrize" Spain and to "Hispanicize" the world. According to several indices, Navarre was the most religious region in the whole country. From the 1870s to the 1940s, the number of priests per capita in the province was the highest in the Catholic world. Even in 1967, Navarre had the highest proportion in the country of seminarians (26 for every 10,000 inhabitants) and of priests (1 for every 371 inhabitants), while a contemporaneous survey showed that 90 percent of Navarrese attended Sunday Mass, a figure higher than that for any other diocese in Spain. In Cirauqui, where, up until the 1940s, villagers' pastoral needs were tended to by one parish priest and three benefice priests, the ratio of clergy to inhabitants was about 1 to 400. To villagers, joining a clerical order was a recognized way to get an education, gain a living, and reflect prestige back on one's family. Parents were pleased and proud if their offspring became priests or nuns, and a very high proportion of people from Cirauqui joined an order of the church. As one parent put it to me, "It was both a good thing and one less mouth to feed." Even today, most middle-aged villagers have several relatives who have taken Holy Orders.[48]

A parish priest had status and power; a good one was regarded as a *santón*. Besides organizing and controlling much of the locals' lives (as the parish priest of Cirauqui said in his 1897 report to the bishop, he and his assistants "were assiduous in the confessional box"), parish priests acted as privileged intermediaries between villagers and the official world beyond the municipal boundaries. Some exploited their position for political ends. In 1839, the sacristan of Cirauqui was expelled for his Carlist beliefs. Sixteen years later, an acting benefice priest in the village was imprisoned in the nearest episcopal seminary for preaching about the sins committed by the liberal troops in the First Carlist War. At the end of the Second Carlist War the parish priest, who had been the incumbent during the Carlist occupation of Cirauqui, was transferred for similar reasons to the closest seminary, while another priest of the village was amnestied.[49]

Since Christianity ordered and gave meaning to so many different aspects of local culture, any threat to the established Church, in turn, imperiled the village way of life. Many people in Cirauqui regarded the planned reforms of the fledgling Republic as menacing. On 7 June 1931 the town hall, "interpreting the unanimous desire of the inhabitants," unanimously agreed to protest against the *profanaciones* and *sacrilegios* recently committed against churches and religious communities in other parts of Spain. They also objected to the proposed expulsion of Jesuits from the country and formally stated their common disapproval of the decrees enabling freedom of worship and of religious education in schools. When the government passed a bill for the removal of crucifixes from places of education, the mayor, councillors, and the parish priest headed a large procession that formally carried the crosses from the village school to the church on the summit. Since the government had banned the singing of *auroras* (religious songs sung at dawn), those Catholics who did sing them around the village streets at break of day were accompanied by others for their protection. These escorts regarded themselves as guards for the choir, to shield them in case of attack by supporters of the government. In the first month of the uprising, the parish priest had the parochial treasures secretly buried to save them from theft in the (extremely) unlikely event of the Republicans taking Cirauqui.[50] The enemy might occupy the village and desecrate its churches, but they were not going to be given the opportunity to desecrate and sell off the most valued material symbol of the Catholic-based conception of the community.

Local Carlists were not the only village defenders of religion, nor was the Comunión the only political organization that protested strongly against the Republican reforms. What differentiated the Carlists from most other villagers in this respect was that Carlism had *always* made the defense of Catholicism a central part of its platform. Non-Carlist conservatives had often compromised with liberals; liberal (and later, Republican) reforms had frequently threatened the Church; and socialists were usually stereotyped as atheists. It is this centrality of Catholicism to the Carlist creed and the historical length of that centrality that helped make Carlism locally so distinctive and that enabled the *requetés* to see themselves, like their forebears, as the self-proclaimed "guardians of the Church." Unlike village Falangists or other militant members of the Right, the *requetés* could pride themselves that only their organization had so signally defended, over so long, the cause of Mother Church whenever she had been threatened.

REQUETÉ HISTORY

When I asked the *requeté* veterans, not why they had gone to fight, but why they had become Carlists, some looked taken aback, as though finding it difficult to explain what was never explained, what was obvious—to them. "Carlism is very old," said one. "It comes from way back." Its history has been linked with that of the village for over one hundred and fifty years; it is an unquestionable and, to staunch Carlists, proud part of the village traditions. Once again, it is this historical depth that distinguishes Carlism from all other political groups within the village. In contrast, liberalism, its old adversary, had become a spent force by the time of the Republic and disappeared altogether under Franco.

The introduction of Carlism to the village predates people's familial memories. No one can remember named ancestors who did not live in a Carlist milieu. As far as the present-day Carlists of Cirauqui know, members of their families have always been in the movement. Their fathers and grandfathers brought them up on stories of Carlist feats. Some veterans, with manifest pride, spontaneously recounted to me the exploits of their grandfathers (and even, in one case, of a great-grandfather) in the Second Carlist War. But it is interesting that no one in the village could remember being told anything about their family's involvement in the First Carlist War. It is as though the remembered events of the second war have buried those of the earlier conflict.[51]

To staunch former *requetés*, the Second Carlist War is not remembered as a military defeat but as a stirring tale in which Carlist soldiers, villagers, showed what they were made of. Convinced of the rightness of their cause, they did not regard losing a battle as any reflection on the merits of their cause. Their understanding of this nineteenth-century war is made up of various incidents and gory battles fought in the neighborhood. They are not concerned with grand strategy or the pendulum swings of advance or retreat. Their memories are of dramatic events and familial involvement, and they can read the surrounding countryside like a military map, pinpointing the sites of Carlist victories. They rarely mentioned places where the liberal armies had won the day.

When the village town hall was renovated in the early 1980s, a nineteenth-century military standard with the embroidered message CIRAUQUI TODO POR LOS FUEROS was discovered in the attic. Although this sign from the past is now safely encased behind glass in the municipal meeting room, no one ever mentioned it to me, and when I asked veterans about it, no one had any idea when it was made or what exactly it had been used for. They might be proud of this bit of bunting as a further example of village participation in events beyond its boundaries, but it did not fit into their localized and personalized conception of the Carlist past.

While *requetés* in Cirauqui mention battles fought in the locality as examples of the Carlist spirit, villagers in general regard these events as part of their home's history. People constantly, and spontaneously, mentioned to me the massacre of the liberals and the cannon fire from San Isidro. One local stated how, to this day, farmers from the nearby village of Lácar continue to discover lumps of lead when plowing their fields. To villagers, the memory of the massacre and other events during the two wars are not the exclusive property of the Carlists but part of all the villagers' common heritage. The events are further evidence that Cirauqui has its own distinctive history, which is passed on to children irrespective of their parents' political leanings. The most notorious of these events is the massacre of the liberals. Although villagers are aware of most of the details I discovered in historians' accounts of the event, the non-Carlists among them tend to end their version of the tale in a way that emphasizes common humane concerns over partisan division. They say that the bloodletting was only halted when a Carlist general on a white horse arrived on the scene. While riding by the village, he was approached by a liberal who had escaped the carnage and was now trying to flee. The liberal recognized the general, for they both came from the Estella area, and told him what was going on, whereupon the general intervened to halt the bloodletting. A final detail of the account, in both Carlist and non-Carlist versions, suggests the divine attitude toward the slaughter. As the cart carrying the corpses began to descend toward the cemetery, one of the oxen pulling the load dropped dead and the cart overturned, spilling the corpses onto the cobbles. Blood, some say, can still be seen in the stones of the walls where the liberals were bayoneted. Veteran *requetés* recognize the immorality of these killings, but are quick to mention other atrocities, committed by the liberals in nearby villages, at least one of which was carried out in retaliation for the massacre in Cirauqui. To these *requetés,* the Carlist soldiers were not alone in sinning.

Just as the non-Carlists of Cirauqui interpret the story of the massacre in their own way, so they contest the historically grounded image that *requetés* have of themselves and their predecessors. These non-Carlists say their opponents were violent, hot-blooded, infested with lice, and usually excessive in their behavior. Caricaturing Carlists as untamed creatures or cave dwellers, they lampoon them as animalistic hillbillies who preferred the untrammeled ways of life in the wild to the civilized domesticity of the village.[52] Among the traditional sayings of these anti-Carlists are the following:

Two Carlists together are all right, but three and there'll be a quarrel.
Always friends of *la pólvora* [gunpowder, liveliness, irritability].
The Carlists run about the mountains like rabbits, and they don't dare come down because they are full of lice.

The Carlist is a red-crested animal
Who grazes in the mountains of Navarre.
When he takes communion he attacks men.
And on the cry of "Long live Christ-King!"
Attacks everybody.[53]

These opponents interpret Carlist zeal as blind fanaticism, as a highly dangerous form of self-righteousness. As examples of this bellicose zealotry, they
mention the massacre of the liberals in 1873 and the rear-guard killings in
1936. Left-wing villagers stress that the *requetés* were *ignorantes* (uneducated,
unaware, uncivilized) who were used in the Civil War by the rich to do their
dirty work. One old man said that at the beginning of the uprising, *requetés*
would come into Pamplona from their villages, go straight to Mass, and,
drunk with excitement, start shouting, "Long live religion! I shit on God!" ("I
shit on X!" [most often God] is a common exclamation in the area.) When the
Navarrese novelist Felix Urabayen wished to express in one of his books how
shocking a group of people found a particular incident, he wryly wrote "that
even the Carlist stopped blaspheming."[54]

REQUETÉ FAMILY

The veteran *requetés* say they went to war because of the threat to religion, but
that they became Carlist because of their families. They supported the cause
because their parents had done so.

In Cirauqui, until very recently, the family was both the primary vehicle of
identity and primary mode of production. For many, the ideal was a three-
generation family—grandparents, adult child and spouse, unmarried adult
children, grandchildren—living and working together under the same roof,
often with their animals. To achieve or to maintain this state, only one child
could inherit the house and the land. The parents chose which of their children
was to inherit and when he or she was to take control of the land.[55]

Fathers were able to exert a great degree of authority and to demand much
respect, largely because of their continued control of the main economic resources of the family. Even adult sons, those chosen to inherit and granted
usufruct over their aged parents' holdings, still had to bow to the dictates of
their elders. The only way for a young man to escape this familial gerontocracy
was to establish himself independently, setting up house and gaining economic liberty by, for instance, successfully practicing a trade. But this alternative was not available to the majority, whose livelihood depended on working their family's land.

Veteran *requetés* and villagers of their generation state that when they were
children, families used to be more united and that offspring were meant to pay

great respect to their parents, especially to their father. A good husband and father was hardworking, responsible, generous, and capable of making decisions, while a good wife and mother took care of the household in all its different facets, including domestic finances. Within families, men were able to exercise power, and learned to be distant, haughty, and proud; in times of misfortune, they could express irritation or annoyance. A father had his own seat at mealtimes, and in certain households no one could begin eating until the father had sat at the table. Women, in contrast, were supposed to be more humble; they learned to suffer and feel more. Children were taught to be quiet in the presence of their elders, and were not even to tell jokes to one another when in the company of their parents. When speaking to their parents, children had to use the respectful mode of address, "Usted" (originally from "Vuestra Merced," meaning "Your Grace"), instead of the more informal mode, "tú." The commands and requests of the father or mother were to be obeyed without hesitation or question. Indeed, a child who was disrespectful to any adult villager might later be punished by his father. Some middle-aged villagers today complain that when they were young there were "dominant fathers" who seemed to spend their time dictating to others; in one extreme case, the male head of the household was locally notorious for deciding "even when his wife and daughters bought their underwear."

The authority of one generation over another stretched beyond the immediate circle of the family. Any man in the village could ask a child to perform a simple task for him—for example, to get him some tobacco from one of the local shops. A child who refused to comply would be reported to his father, who would very likely beat him for his insubordination. As an example of parental power over offspring, some villagers today like to give the example of the young man who, in the 1940s, was taken to Estella *a vistas* (to look). This matchmaking custom consisted of parents from different villages with children of marriageable age meeting in Estella on market day. If the two sets of parents could agree, the potential fiancé/fianceé were introduced to one another on the following market day. In this particular case, on their journey home to Cirauqui, the parents asked their son what he thought of the young woman he had just met. "Well!" he replied, "whatever *Ustedes* tell me."

Some villagers, now in middle age, wished to make it clear to me that though children's relations with their parents were highly rule bound, these rules should be seen as just customs or habits. They stressed that these rules were mere behavioral formalities, guidelines of conduct, which did not necessarily imply that children were scared of their fathers. Some fathers, they emphasized, abused these rules. Others did not.

During the cold months of winter, members of a family spent much of the day together in the kitchen. This was the season for the hearth and its traditions. Houses in the village had thick walls and small windows to keep the cold out, and the kitchen was often the only room heated, its temperature slightly raised if cows were corralled underneath on the ground floor. Around the hearth (itself a site of folkloric faiths and spirits),[56] the family gathered to eat, play cards, say the Rosary, and, above all, talk. It was around the fireside that elders recounted tales about the village's past. Aged Carlists told stories about the great Carlist events they had heard of or participated in; it was here children learned the values of Carlism, by listening to their grandfathers yarn about their warrior past.

Offspring were meant to respect their father during his life, and beyond. For the funerals of their parents, bereaved adult children paid—if they could afford to—for the village choir to sing, for the organist to play, for giant candles to illuminate the church, and for the priest to perform the ceremony with the parochial treasures. Before the coffin was carried out of the church, and later in the cemetery before it was lowered into the earth, the priest and choir performed on each occasion a *responso* (a sung responsory followed by a liturgical prayer for the dead). The bereaved might also hire the priest to perform Masses daily for the soul of the dead for the first nine, or thirty, days after the funeral. They could also pay for a Mass to be celebrated on the first anniversary of the death; and some went further, having the priest perform a Mass on the second anniversary as well. On the days preceding All Souls' Day, people cleaned the tombs of their dead; on the day itself, so many people attended church that three consecutive Masses were celebrated in the morning, with another in the cemetery in the afternoon, and a final one back in the church at twilight.[57] It was also customary for people to visit the tombs of their late kin on Maundy Thursday and Ascension Day.

Widows wore weeds for the rest of their lives. Those villagers who had lost one of their parents dressed in mourning for at least one year, and some did not put on brighter clothes for two years or more. Some also wore black when their grandmothers died. Not to do this, villagers said, would have been seen as showing contempt for one's late parents. The great importance of having kin mourn one's death is highlighted by the example of the villager from the nearby valley of the Amescoas, who dressed in black for six months because his late aunt had no closer relatives to commemorate her decease. Some villagers stated that, where possible, it was important to live in the house of one's father or father's father, and to keep it clean, both as a form of memory of, and sign of respect for, one's dead.[58] Villagers mentioned that the memory of the dead was also kept alive by saying an Our Father for them during the daily reciting of the Rosary and by invoking their name in exhortations, at times of danger or affliction. Also, wayward offspring might be admonished with phrases such as "If your father could see you now!" The paterfamilias might be long dead, but the memory of him, of the respect he was still owed, and of the ethical code he wished upheld, could still be used to exert moral pressure.

Pierre Lhande Heguy, writing in the first decade of the twentieth century about Basques in Lower Navarre, just over the national border, said that the proposals made by the paterfamilias of a homestead about, say, the chores to be carried out that morning had the character of directives that experience had consecrated. The implicit reasoning was, "If I think in this way, it is because the ancestors have taught me it." According to this logic, ancestral tradition was an argument to which people were meant to submit without discussion.[59] If—as their military support for Catholicism suggests—what Carlist villagers revered was their fathers, the community they and their families collectively embodied, and the apparently unchanging nature of that community, then one's forefathers were to be respected, for they had maintained the traditional way of life as a legacy for their children to inherit and, in turn, transmit. Thus, this conservative rural worldview had its own integral logic of reproduction, thanks to the high value attributed to the attitudes and actions of one's familial predecessors.

This motivating sense of respect toward one's father and forefathers is given by many Carlist villagers as a fundamental reason for their adherence to the cause. One man said he had joined up "for the feelings of my father, who couldn't bear to see liberals," because they had deported *his* father to Cuba, where he had died. The man's father had even worked his passage to the Caribbean in order to visit his father's grave. One woman said she was Carlist because of her father, "whom I hold very high." If her father, who had died when she was young and who, people told her, was such a good person, was a Carlist, then she would be one too.[60] When I spoke with another Carlist, he repeatedly referred to the framed snapshots of dead *requetés* that were mounted on the wall in the Carlist Circle of his village, as though the continued existence of this delicately decorated collective portrait exemplified present reverence for the memory of the forefathers' fatal upholding of their ideals. On this interpretation, their deeds were not forgotten.

Some *requetés* expressed their pride in the military past of their fathers by wearing *their* berets, the more washed out, beaten, crumpled, and moth-eaten the better. In rural areas of the Basque Country and in the north and center of Navarre, it is still customary for many middle-aged and elderly men to wear black berets all the time. One woman said her grandfather had been buried with his beret on because "it had become part of his personality." A beret could become integral to a person's character, and a red one was memorably associated with its owner's days of war, fighting for the Carlist cause he proudly believed in. So the occasion of it being given to a grandson was all the more charged. One middle-aged Carlist said that his grandfather on his deathbed had given him (when he was fourteen) his Carlist trappings to look after. The youth, in turn, promised the old man that he would continue the Carlist tradition of his family. The red berets were often stored in *kutxas*, large antique chests, where (as one man put it) the "most sacred" objects were stored: wedding dresses, First Communion outfits, and other clothing worn on only the most memorable of occasions. Removing the beret and placing it on the head of the young male was seen as a deeply significant occasion. Those who chose to hold on to their red berets went to the grave with them, perhaps carried on a separate cushion behind the coffin as the cortege entered the church.[61]

Whereas a father was to be respected, it was the mother whom a child was meant to love. Mothers were the transmitters of values, especially religious ones, informally teaching their children Catholic beliefs and practices, and making sure they fulfilled their religious obligations. They, rather than their husbands, were the mediators between God and the living or the dead.[62] Women attended church more than men; it was also they who put candles by the window and began to say the Rosary if, during July or August, they feared an impending storm that might destroy the harvest. For the weeks preceding and following the feast day of the Sacred Heart of Jesus, women (and not men) wore scapulars strung about the neck with an image of the Sacred Heart. For these reasons of gender-defined sentiment, it was the *requetés'* mothers and fiancées who gave protective religious objects to their beloved. To shield "her" *requeté* against danger, a woman hung a scapular around his neck, embroidered the Cross of Saint Andrew on his left breast pocket, and placed inside the pocket, over his heart, a *detente*—a small piece of cloth bearing the image of the Sacred Heart and the words "*Detente bala* [Stop bullet!]; the Sacred Heart is with me."[63] It was a woman's prerogative to present her beloved with these Catholic tokens of her concern. A father would never have given his son such items. His badge was the tired beret his boy wore.

To *requetés*, the objects they carried in their shirt pockets were constant personal reminders of those human *and* supernatural women closest to their heart. Elision of the two was easy, for women were meant to regard Mary as their model: obedient, receptive, docile, pure, denying herself pleasure for the sake of others. And the particular avatars of the Virgin whose medals the *requetés* bore were very often either the patron saint of their hometown or especially associated with it in some way. Carlist soldiers from the Navarrese village of Mendigorría always carried in their breast pocket a small piece from the cloak of the Virgin of Andion, the Roman settlement within the municipal boundaries. "I carried it as a thing of faith," one *mendigorriano* said, "the Virgin protecting me." The *requetés* of Artajona, the first village southeast of Mendigorría, invoked their "beloved" Virgin of Jerusalem, a small image in the parish church said to have been brought back from the Holy Land by an Artajonan captain who was given it as payment for his worthy services during the Crusades.[64]

Although the expression of Carlist emotion was oriented in this female mode, and though sentimental association with a particular avatar of the Virgin further linked a *requeté* to his home ground, this feminine connection to the heart of Carlist soldiers was not exclusive. Some *requetés* carried medals of the Sacred Heart of Jesus, a male, albeit One who loves us all, because if one went to Mass the first Friday of every month (a day dedicated to the Sacred Heart) for nine months, one would be saved. Bearing these medals, moreover, carried national Catholic overtones, since in 1919 Alfonso XIII had officially dedicated Spain to the Sacred Heart. The connection with place was also expressed by the formation of the regiments themselves, which were often made up of men from one particular area: the name of the Tercio (Regiment) de Artajona is a continuing tribute to the extraordinary number of *requetés* who set out from one particular medium-sized village in the Middle Zone of Navarre.

Men were associated with reason, authority; a man placed the beret—symbol of forefathers' exploits—on his son's head. Women were associated with passion, sympathy; a woman placed religious (often "female") objects—symbols of religious continuity linked to place—over her beloved's heart. Men occupied public, political space; the beret was visible to all. Women occupied private, domestic space; the objects they gave their beloved were hidden from view in breast pockets or under shirts. Together, these gender-defined sets of oppositions—female, private, hidden versus male, public, open—organized military dress. This symbolic duality of male and female, which was rooted to place, religiously expressed, and literally mapped onto the body of the *requeté* son, *could* be seen as a corporeal manifestation of another family—the most exemplary of all. Since the soldiers fighting in the Second Carlist War of the 1870s had also worn *detentes* and had had the Cross of Saint Andrew sewn onto their shirts, the decorated uniforms of the Civil War *requetés* could be taken to symbolize the persistence of Carlist militancy over time and thus, in this sense, to deny the passage of time. On this reading, a fully dressed *requeté* became a walking advertisement of his hometown values. In one poem about a *requeté* leaving for the front, the young soldier asks his grandfather to bless his departure, his grandmother to give up her rosary, his mother to buy him a beret, a little girl (*niña*) to sew three lilies on it, and his sisters to embroider his breast pocket with the Carlist Cross of Saint Andrew.[65] Suitably decorated by his family, he can now go off to war.

Once again, at the village level, the Carlist concentration on the importance of the family is not unique, for other parties of the Right lauded the family as the bedrock of society. What makes the Carlist concentration distinctive is the particular way it was made an integral part of the Carlist self-image and, over the decades, developed a genealogical depth that no other political organization or ideology could match. Come the Civil War in 1936, there were no members of other parties who could say, "I am X because my father and grandfather were X."

REQUETÉ STEADFASTNESS

Those born and brought up in a Carlist family were meant to remain Carlist for the rest of their days. One veteran, placing his right palm over his heart, said he still supported the cause: "You don't give up. You carry on with your own." A common reply to the question, "Are you Carlist?" is "Until my death!" The idea of unchanging commitment was not exclusive to Carlism. In Unamuno's famous novel about the Basque phase of the Second Carlist War, *Paz en la guerra*, the Bilbao-born author has one character underline the central importance of people keeping to their family's political traditions, whether they be Carlist or liberal: "It's suckled with mother's milk, and what is suckled with mother's milk is lost only in the shroud. So it was in my time and so it will continue to be. . . . Anything else would mean chaos . . . ; you couldn't trust anyone if a person can be one thing or the other at the same time."[66] One day, on being driven into Pamplona, I persisted in asking a local why he thought it so important that people should stick to a certain set of political beliefs throughout their lives. In reply, he said several times, "Well, because no, because no." Then he pointed to the white button of his black car radio. "That is white. You know it is white. It is not black. If it changed color, you wouldn't know what it is. You wouldn't know what was going on." What these two examples suggest is that, according to local attitudes, one can trust in people only if one knows where they stand. Without this knowledge, without this certainty about others' allegiance, one cannot categorize them. And if one cannot classify others in an unambiguous manner, disorder ensues. Thus the idea of political steadfastness is a basic organizing principle of local society, a pole around which village life turns.

If sustained commitment is so highly valued, then a *chaqueta vuelta*, or *chaquetero* (turncoat), is to be particularly despised.[67] The phrase is itself revealing, highlighting local attitudes that those who treat political allegiance not as an integral part of their social identity, imbibed at the breast, but as something as lightly worn—and as easily cast aside—as a jacket, are worthy only of their opponents' criticism. Branding someone a *chaquetero* is still considered by many today such a strong criticism that it is not done to the culprit's face. This insult, moreover, is applied only in a partisan manner. Villagers of one political persuasion might deride someone who deserted their own side, but they do not rubbish a person from the other camp who switches allegiance to them.

What one side sees as betrayal, the other regards as enlightenment. Carlists took evident pleasure in informing me that one of El Cojo's sons became a minister of state in one of Franco's governments. One octogenarian of the village told me that her grandfather had been a die-hard Carlist. His son had made friends with liberals in the village and their ideas had won him round. The political differences between father and son had then become so great that they had to separate. In recounting this to me, she in no way suggested that her father's political conversion was untoward. *Chaquetero* is an insult aimed at men. A woman was usually supposed to adopt the political line of the man she married; if a woman wed someone of the other side, she was to switch to the political affiliation of her husband.

For some of the older villagers in Cirauqui, steadfast adherence to one's side was above all a social statement, which might say little about the detailed content of one's political opinions. As the octogenarian said to me, "I'm liberal and I hope to die liberal. I listened to my father and I liked what he said. There isn't anything prettier in the world: each person to his side and there you stay. You don't get on the wrong side of anybody. You follow your own road without annoying anybody. Your side is already enough for you. You know me, I like everybody, but I'm liberal and I'll stay that way." On a later occasion, I asked her what exactly she meant when she said, "I'm liberal." In answer, she immediately began to list the families and people in the village that were liberal when she was young, saying that they were liberal and the others were Carlist. Placing her right hand over her left breast, she said, "I'm liberal and that's what I feel in my heart." When I pressed further and asked what liberal ideas she still believed in, she replied, now clearly peeved, "How do I know what are the political ideas of the liberals!"

Naturalizing the cultural, converting social statement into a quasibiological one, veterans say Carlism was an *herencia,* "something of the blood, something inherited." The legacy bequeathed by one's parents was not restricted to material items, such as land and buildings; it included immaterial ones as well, such as political affiliation. Being Carlist was seen as a familial trait, on a genetic par with other supposedly inheritable aspects of one's personality such as temper, taste, and certain idiosyncracies. To rural supporters of the cause, this conception of Carlism-in-the-blood helped to explain both the persistence of Carlist tradition and its future maintenance by the as yet unborn. As one aging former *requeté* chaplain from a nearby village said to me, "Children came out of their mothers already with the ideas of Carlism. They had to follow the same road."

When an educated young woman from Cirauqui wanted to express to me the pervasiveness of Carlism in the Middle Zone of Navarre, she employed a different, but still naturalistic, metaphor. "In those days," she said, choosing

her words carefully, "Carlism was *breathed* in these villages." One Carlist, formerly a deputy in the national parliament, said becoming Carlist was "as rational as learning a language." Like a language, one learned it unconsciously
from one's parents. Just as one later learned the grammar of the language
consciously, so one later became a convinced Carlist by learning its ideology
and program from pamphlets, bulletins, and newspapers (especially *El Pensamiento Navarro*), as well as from sermons, talks, and speeches given by visiting
spokesmen. But most veteran Carlists, unlike the former deputy, had not received years of education. To them, Carlism was not primarily a developed
political philosophy to be carefully examined and discussed, but a "way of being"; in the religious terms of one Carlist, it was "consubstantial with the mode
of being." For these people, being Carlist was not a rational process on a par
with formal linguistic instruction, but an "irrational" (i.e., socially grounded)
process whose integral position in the time-honored local way of life was justified in terms of naturalistic metaphors like "blood" and "breath."[68]

DIOS, PATRIA, REY, FUEROS?

Some historians of Carlism study the political ideas of the movement in the
terms of its famous quadripartite slogan: DIOS, PATRIA, REY, FUEROS. They
analyze the evolving role of each of these four constituents within the Carlist
political program, to what extent and in what way, at any one time, its leaders
promoted particular forms of Catholicism, patriotism, monarchism, and foralism. While this intellectualist focus may tell us something about the opinions of the traditionalist elite, the material documented in this chapter suggests that the content of the slogan was largely irrelevant to the rural Carlists
of Cirauqui.

None of the veterans to whom I spoke mentioned foralism or sang the
praises of the Spanish state, unless I asked them specifically about them. I
never overheard the word *"fueros"* in villagers' conversations. In our discussions, none of the veterans spontaneously referred to the Carlist pretenders of
their time. When I asked one veteran whether, in the 1950s, he had supported
the claim of Don Javier or of Carlos VIII, he appeared surprised, as though
unsure of how to answer, and then said that Carlists in the villages had not
concerned themselves with such matters. To the former *requetés* of Cirauqui,
their king was a distant figurehead, someone to shout for at massed gatherings
of the faithful, and not much more.

Although these stalwarts of the cause, who made up the backbone of the
movement, were apparently indifferent to *patria, rey,* and *fueros,* they did care,
and passionately so, about *dios*. Catholicism was an intimate, intricate part of
their way of life. They did not want it altered. However, while they had gone
to war to safeguard their religion, they were Carlist in the first place because

of their upbringing by their parents. In a world where respect for one's father was a primary organizing principle, offspring were meant to follow their paternal example. And if Carlism was part of the tradition a father bequeathed to his dutiful children, then the Carlism of villages such as Cirauqui should be seen not so much as a political statement but as a filial one. Being Carlist was a traditional way of maintaining paternal tradition. This was a major structural reason for its successful continuance over the decades—and when radical change finally came to rural Navarre in the 1960s and 1970s, a major reason for its decline.

Chapter Four

Postwar Carlism

Veteran *requetés* like to stress that they won the war but lost the peace. As one leading Navarrese Carlist put it, "Each military victory was for us a political defeat because they needed us less."[1]

During the war Franco had already established himself as the absolute ruler of the ever-increasing areas his forces controlled. By its end he had become the dictator of the whole country with no limits to his power other than those he might impose on himself. His main political means of remaining in position over the next three and a half decades was to manipulate the political families into which his supporters grouped themselves. Each family was given a share of power. Whenever necessary, he would juggle these shares to maintain a balance of forces. Those outside this interfamilial network were castigated as "the vanquished" and excluded from any sphere of influence. Any opposition to the regime was suppressed, as was much opposition from within it. There was little serious extrafamilial opposition anyway, for most of the regime's adversaries had been shot, imprisoned, or gone into exile, while the general war-weary populace was more concerned about surviving within the battered economy than about fighting on.

As cities were "liberated" by the Nationalist troops, their Carlist Circles were not allowed to reopen, and those who objected forcefully were put into jail. Any traditionalist hope of maintaining an autonomous, nationwide body was dashed in April 1937 when the Decree of Unification was proclaimed. This edict prescribed the creation of a single, national organization, the Falange Española Tradicionalista y de las Juntas de Ofensiva Nacional-Sindicalista (hereafter FET). This awkwardly named body, also known as the Movimiento, incorporated all the forces that had supported the uprising. Besides the Carlists, it included the Falange, small reactionary groups, and those supporting the liberal monarchy of King Alfonso XIII, who had fled the country in 1930. Although some Carlists were prepared to work together with members of these groups, relations between them were often strained, and sometimes violent.[2] The organization of the Comunión was assimilated into that of the Movimiento, almost all of its Circles were shut, its trade unions were dissolved, its newspapers and radio stations were closed down, its juntas were suppressed, some of its members were imprisoned, and any independent political activities were banned. Come the end of the war, the *requetés* were demobilized, despite some protest. From now on, with rare exception, the Comunión could operate only unofficially, in areas where it was regarded tolerantly by senior soldiers who had fought alongside the *requetés*. Elsewhere it survived on a semiclandestine basis.

The Carlist response to the dictatorship was complicated and plural. Those, probably the great majority, who believed in the ideals of the insurgents' "crusade" were pleased that the new military order had smashed the hated forces of the Left and had removed any threat to the continued existence of the Catholic Church in Spain. They could take pride in the fact that they had participated, sometimes crucially, in the campaigns that had led to the downfall of the Republic. At the same time, those Carlists who had hoped to see the political program of the Comunión implemented were dismayed that Franco showed no signs of establishing a traditionalist monarchy nor of devolving power to the regions, and many of them were outraged by the statewide repression of their organization. As a consequence of this difference of opinion between dictator and the dictated to, the question as to what sort of relation the Carlist community should maintain with the new government was never satisfactorily resolved. During the war and the years afterward, different groups within the Comunión moved in disparate, sometimes surprising ways along the political spectrum of open collaboration, a discriminating cooperation, assertion of a separate identity, mild dissension, and obdurate antagonism. Indeed some leading Carlists changed tack so often that the traditionalist historian Manuel de Santa Cruz has tried to justify his fellows' behavior by claiming that "Everything [concerning the Comunión] related to Franco was complex, confusing, difficult, contradictory, and paradoxical."[3]

What was not complex, but painfully evident, were the limitations of the Comunión, which was constantly hamstrung by a shortage of money and a pervasive lack of professionalism. Its leaders were not keen on those members who constantly called for "War!" and would later ask their superiors to pay their subsequent fines. Only a handful worked seriously for the Carlist cause, and they had to divide their time between their jobs and matters of the Comunión. According to Santa Cruz, meetings tended to become chat shops where good conversation was seen as an entertaining end in itself. Many senior Carlists did not carry out the assignments given to them, and most were notoriously slow correspondents.[4] A lot was said but little was done—an almost general attitude among the opposition to Franco at this time. Those Carlists active in the universities and regions distributed fliers and published Cyclostyled bulletins. But production of these newsletters was spasmodic, and most ran to only a few issues.

During this period, Carlist leaders did not spend much time on rallying the faithful and ensuring their maintained support, other than staging occasional mass gatherings presented as religious events. It appears they regarded local Carlists as forever ready to rise up in defense of Carlist ideals and not in need of persistent animation. Instead they expended much effort on trying to find a suitable regal figure ready to lead them. This search, which lasted from the Civil War to the mid-1950s, left Carlism enfeebled, divided, and headed by a prince disinclined to accept the mantle of power. If this period of Carlism can be characterized easily, it was one of too many pretenders and too little political activity.

The Camps of Postwar Carlism

During the Republic the exciting prospect of violently overthrowing the secular state had united Carlists of different persuasions into a single body. Now that that task had been accomplished and the fledgling regime had fulfilled only some of Carlism's hopes, old internal divisions resurfaced and new ones emerged. While the different groups within the Carlist elite did not harden into rigid factions, it is still possible to profile the main camps within the Comunión and their protagonists.

The undisputed leader of one group was the Conde de Rodezno, the "boss" of Navarrese Carlism. He and his followers (who also were often titled) were usually more concerned with the propagation of traditionalist ideas than with the promotion of the Comunión as a political body. To them, it was worth compromising themselves with the new regime to see at least some of their ideas made an integral part of official policy. At the same time, the count and his supporters could take pride in the fact that, by working with the new rulers of the country, they could strive to ensure that the political complexion of the fledgling dictatorship did not take on too fascist a tone.[5]

Of course, collaboration with the dictator also had its more tangible benefits, in the form of jobs for the "boys." Tactically apportioning cabinet posts among the different political "families" of his government (traditionalists, Falangists, Franquists, etc.), Franco appointed Rodezno minister of justice and made Luis Arellano, a friend of Rodezno, his subsecretary. This ministry and the presidency of the Cortes were to become virtual fiefdoms of Comunión collaborators for the next thirty years.[6] The Generalísimo also granted the Carlist leaders of Navarre control of their province and, in an exceptional move, officially recognized its *fueros* as well as those of Álava. With time, many of those who accepted, and held on to, public office during the regime came to be regarded not so much as Carlists, but as *carlofranquistas*, men whose primary allegiance lay with their paymaster.[7]

Manuel Fal Conde, chief delegate of the Comunión, headed the camp of

Carlist intransigents. He and his associates did not wish to see the well-structured organization they had helped to create neglected for the sake of winning a few political gains. While they were at times prepared to negotiate, they were far more wary than Rodezno and his circle of cooperating with other groups within the coalition of insurgent forces. This stubborn resistance to the compromising of Carlist identity came to be known as *falcondismo;* though Fal Conde himself, in an effort to suppress an undesired cult around his own personality, denied its existence and chided those who believed in it.[8] But the regime established by the dictator left little room for party leaders who insisted on affirming their band's independence, and between late 1936 and 1940 Fal Conde was exiled to Portugal for seeking to boost the political autonomy of the Comunión. During his absence, Rodezno became the de facto leader of the Carlist movement in Spain.

Men Who Would Be King

The key Carlist questions that Rodezno, Fal Conde, and other prominent members needed to resolve concerned the succession of the movement: Who was to be their royal leader? Was he to be a regent or a king? Resolution of these questions became all the more pressing as Franco began to contemplate the restoration of monarchy and the possible return of the Alfonsine line, represented by the exiled son of Alfonso XIII, Don Juan, and by his young son, Juan Carlos.

In 1936, Alfonso Carlos, the last direct male descendant of the Carlist dynasty, had appointed his wife's nephew, Prince François Xavier de Bourbon-Parma, as regent of the Comunión. The aging pretender, who died childless a few months later, had not wished to designate Don Javier (as he was henceforth known) directly as his successor because so few Carlists knew anything about him. As the legitimacy of Don Javier's claim in terms of blood was debatable, Alfonso Carlos thought that letting him act as regent for a while would be a way to demonstrate his legitimacy of conduct and so improve his chances against other candidates for the title of pretender.[9]

Like so many of his kingly Carlist predecessors, Don Javier was not an ideal aspirant to the Spanish throne. For besides playing the part of regent, he had other roles of comparable importance to perform on the European political stage: he was a pretender to the French crown; and as a diplomatic prince who spoke eight languages, he was frequently called on by governments and the Holy See to act as an intermediary to assist negotiations between various chancelleries.[10] Moreover, at times his different commitments pulled him in opposed directions. In his book *Les Accords secrets Franco-Anglais de décembre de 1940*,[11] he attempted to restore the reputation of his old friend Marshal Philippe Pétain by trying to justify the statesman's actions during the German invasion. Throughout the book he spoke, like a natural Frenchman, of "our troops," "our prisoners," and "our interests." Although in its pages he mentions his contacts and negotiations with Madrid several times, he had in fact never made use of his well-placed Carlist friends, as though it had not been necessary, or even convenient. Publication of the book irritated many of his supporters and only aggravated their doubts about his dedication to the Carlist cause.[12]

More important, perhaps, than the worries about Don Javier's competing commitments was the question of whether his personality suited him for political leadership. The regent, as some of his supporters admit, was a relatively weak man who could be influenced, and at times dominated, by those immediately around him. An indecisive character, he persistently vacillated and contradicted himself, much to the frustration of his supporters. He might, for instance, expel dissidents from the Comunión, but continue to treat them as fellow Carlists, as though nothing had happened.

While prepared to head the Carlist movement, he regarded the regency as, above all, a duty he had been obliged to take on at a time of both internal and national crisis. He was reluctant to assume responsibilities any greater than those of a party chief, and he frequently appeared unwilling to seek the highest office in the land. As he was later to confess privately to a traditionalist sympathizer, he thought that Carlist legitimism had ended with the death of Alfonso Carlos, and had always considered himself simply as a leader charged with maintaining the traditional essence of the movement.[13] To him, the most appropriate way to resolve the problem of succession, for both Comunión and country, was the establishment not of a Carlist regency but of a national one, based on traditionalist principles and headed by the most suitable candidate, presumably not himself. Personally, he preferred to remain a prince without a principality than ascend to the rank of king without a kingdom.

Senior Carlists believed that the mass of their ancient, royal movement was deeply dissatisfied that it was represented by a regent, not a sovereign. They wanted to shout their support for a particular person, not for the impersonal institution of kingship itself. "Long live the Monarch!" did not have the same evocative force as "Long live King Javier!" The discontent of their leaders was heightened by the absence of Don Javier himself. Banished by Franco in 1937, he was imprisoned by the Germans for most of the war for aiding the French Resistance. Since Alfonso Carlos had stipulated that the future pretender was to be recognized by a "truly constituted Cortes," the prolonged existence of the regency plus the enforced exile of the regent encouraged different Carlist factions to search for other solutions and to seek out their own heirs presumptive.[14]

With his leader incommunicado in a foreign land, Fal Conde sought a rapprochement with Franco by proposing a national traditionalist regency assisted by a council of three members, one of whom would be the dictator. Fal Conde thought Franco could use this idea as a counterweight to pressure from those pushing the Alfonsine claim, but the dictator would not even countenance sharing his absolute power.[15] Undaunted, Fal Conde then advanced the cause of the Duke of Seville, great-grandson of the younger brother of Ferdinand VII and Carlos V. He thought advocacy for the duke might combat the attraction that some Carlists had for the new liberal pretender, Don Juan, who, on the death of his father in 1941, had promptly started to cultivate other political factions, including groups within the Comunión. But many leading Carlists, committed traditionalists, regarded the duke as too liberal, and his claim was quietly forgotten.[16]

In 1946, Fal Conde's fears were realized when Rodezno and other Carlist pragmatists sided openly with Don Juan. Received by Don Juan at his residence in Estoril, Portugal, they agreed to recognize his claim if he would declare his support for traditionalist dogma.[17] Unlike Fal Conde, Rodezno and his associates were prepared to divide the higher ranks of the Comunión for the possibility of having their political program implemented by a more likely candidate to the throne than Don Javier, even though Don Juan's political opportunism was already notorious. Rodezno's move led to a complete break with Fal Conde, and was followed by a period of mutual accusation and insults between the partisans of both sides. However, since the Carlist hierarchies of Navarre and the Basque Country, as well as important sections of the Catalan and Madrid leadership, backed Rodezno's switch of regal allegiance, his supposed betrayal of the Comunión had little effect on his great influence or authority within it.[18]

The internal division of the Carlists, however, had been further aggravated by the arrival on the scene of yet another pretender, the Archduke Karl Pius of Habsburg, son of Doña Blanca, the daughter of Carlos VII and thus the niece of Alfonso Carlos. His claim had been first put forward during the Second Republic by a small group of fervent traditionalists who had wished to prevent any rapprochement with the Alfonsists. At first this self-styled Núcleo de Lealtad (Nucleus of Loyalty) had comprised a compact elite without a mass following. Their chance for greatness came in 1943 when Karl Pius, fleeing the Allied advance in Italy, was invited to live in Barcelona. Several influential traditionalists came out in his support, but more significantly perhaps, "Carlos VIII," as he titled himself, was also aided by non-Carlist sectors from within the regime. Prominent Falangists have since claimed that they "invented" the new claimant, and that their intention was less to divide the Carlists than to promote an authentically traditionalist candidate who could compete with Don Juan, who seemed far too liberal for them. Carlos VIII's "Catholic-Monarchist Comunión" was promptly provided with money, mayorships of villages, and posts within the Movimiento. In turn, this latest aspirant to the crown, who said he stood for a traditionalist monarchy, but one very much within the frame of the present state, praised the dictator lavishly, impugned the regency, and denigrated Don Javier.[19]

In some significant ways, Carlos VIII clearly outshone his rivals: unlike them he lived in the land of his subjects and was backed by the head of state; he wrote in perfect Castilian, in marked contrast to Don Javier's defective Spanish; and he was said to speak traditionalism like a mother tongue, whereas Don Juan made it sound like something he had learned as an adult. "Blond, strong, and with blue eyes, like a prince in a film,"[20] he even acted in an appropriately regal fashion, creating nobles and awarding decorations and honors to those who served him well. Accompanied by police, Carlos VIII toured parts of the country to meet his supporters, while his supporters busied themselves publishing journals in Santiago (*Lealtad Gallega*), Lugo (*Alerta*), Oviedo (*La Verdad*), Barcelona (*Boletín Oficial de los Requetés de Cataluña*), and Madrid (*Boletín Carlista*). In Pamplona, a group of more than forty Carlists set up a students' wing, and juntas were formed elsewhere.[21] *Carlosoctavismo* was rapidly gaining political weight.

From what we know of this period, it appears that within a relatively short time Carlos VIII came to be the indisputable candidate for an important section of the Comunión's elite.[22] He seemed to attract, above all, those Carlists (many of them wartime recruits to the movement) who, uncomfortable with the apparent intransigence of Fal Conde, were prepared to compromise their traditionalism, yet were suspicious of Don Juan's true leanings. Apparently favored by Franco, Carlos VIII seemed at the time the most likely Carlist who could be king.

Unsurprisingly, *falcondistas* attacked Carlos VIII for his patent Franquism. For instance, during the strikes and civil unrest in Barcelona and the Basque Country in early 1951, he came out in support of the regime, while the Comunión remained neutral, quietly watching both sides. Derided as collaborators, the *carlosoctavistas,* in turn, criticized the regency as but the despicable result of an interested family intrigue led by Doña Maria de las Nieves, the wife of Alfonso Carlos, for the sake of her favorite nephew, Don Javier. This mutual hostility between the opposed factions could at times become physical. At a grand ceremony in Pamplona in 1945 on the feast day of Don Javier's patron saint, a supporter of Carlos VIII shot one of the crowd and was then stabbed. *Requetés* pulled out their firearms and began shooting. Three Carlists and nine armed policemen were wounded in the resulting fray. For this action, the most important Carlist Circle of the Comunión, that of Pamplona, was closed. Six years later to the day, *falcondistas* assaulted a small group of the enemy band and, once again, pistols were drawn.[23]

Don Javier: From Regent to Pretender

Those activist Carlists loyal to Don Javier felt cramped by the inertia of the Comunión. They wanted traditionalism revitalized, able to address the questions of the day and to provide guidance for the rank and file. But, they argued, the rejuvenated movement had to be led by a committed pretender prepared to dedicate himself to the task at hand.

In February 1947 they took advantage of a limited relaxation in the level of official repression to stage a meeting of the Junta of Regional and Provincial Chiefs, which, with forty-two members present, was the largest gathering of the Carlist elite in ten years. Its members agreed to restore the structure and various sections of the Comunión: the National Council, the local juntas, the Asociación Estudiantil Tradicionalista (AET, the Carlist student association), the *requeté* organizations, and the Margaritas. They also planned to boost the circulation of their newssheet, *Boletín de Orientación Tradicionalista*, and to have it printed more frequently. To reverse the image of Carlists as incapable of governing and as useless for anything but waging war, they decided the National Council should meet regularly to discuss current political, economic, social, and religious issues, and to publish pamphlets on selected aspects of policy.[24]

The councillors' intentions were good, but few of their aims were realized, for most members of the movement's upper echelons remained as disorganized and sluggish as ever. One region where Carlists had overcome the otherwise pervasive lassitude was Cataluña. Under the able leadership of their regional chief, Mauricio de Sivatte, the Catalans had become the most dynamic and well-organized Carlist group in the country. Their journal, *Tiempos Criticos*, was the oldest and best-produced publication put out by Carlists since the war. The annual gathering at Montserrat, which they put on, was at this time the most important ceremony in the traditionalist calendar, attended by speakers of national rank and by Carlists who had come from as far away as Granada. Sivatte and his men had challenged, badgered, and cajoled the military and civil authorities so insistently that a new status quo had been established in the region: the Catalan Carlists were allowed to celebrate with a regularity unknown in other parts of the nation the feast days of Corpus Christi, the Holy Virgin, the Carlist kings, and the Mártires de la Tradición. In turn, this local liveliness made Catalan Carlists more anxious about the quiescence of the Comunión as a whole.

In December 1946, Sivatte openly aired his criticisms in a letter to Fal Conde and the National Junta. A spirited man of action, he accused his chief delegate of being impractical, unrealistic, and too theoretical, while the Comunión, in the eyes of the public, appeared divided and was kingless. The only remedy was rapid reorganization and the greater involvement of Don Javier, who should assume effective command.[25] Such blunt language was comparatively rare within the Carlist hierarchy, and a division opened up between "hard" and "soft" wings, led by Sivatte and Fal Conde respectively. Both sides wished Don Javier to become king of the Carlists, but they differed on how best to persuade him. Sivatte and his supporters wanted brazenly to ask Don Javier to dedicate himself more to the cause; Fal Conde was against any move that the regent might take as censure. From this time on, the topic was raised for discussion at every meeting of the National Junta. Sivatte wrote several stiffly worded letters, quasiultimatums, to Don Javier, urging him to take the helm of the Comunión as soon as possible. He also called for the holding of a grand Carlist assembly, which, acting like the "truly constituted Cortes" specified by Alfonso Carlos, could decide in favor of Don Javier as pretender. The regent, unused to such forthright demands, was not prepared to brook what he regarded as repeated insubordination from one of his subjects, and in March 1949, he sacked his regional chief. In sympathy with their ousted leader, the members of both the Catalan regional and the Barcelona juntas left the Comunión; contributors to *Tiempos Críticos* joined in this counteroffensive by writing vitriolic articles against Fal Conde.[26]

As the split between the unrepentant Catalans and the national leadership deepened, discontent with the inactivity of the Comunión and the prolongation of the regency was next voiced in Navarre, where 280 priests signed a letter to Don Javier respectfully urging him to end the regal interregnum. National councillors, appreciating the great authority of Navarrese priests over their flocks, took this letter to be representative of Carlist opinion in the province. They were also concerned to learn that a group of Carlists rebellious to Fal Conde had started to form in Navarre.[27] To contain the effects of these growing protests and to forestall any further erosion of his authority, Fal Conde applied all his efforts to getting Don Javier to commit himself to Spanish matters. Backed by the National Junta, he began to persuade his superior, in the politest possible terms, that he and his family were the best solution to the dynastic dispute.[28]

Don Javier finally responded to the continuing worries and repeated demands of his subjects, though not exactly in the manner they wished. From

1949 on, he began to play a progressively more active role in the affairs of the Comunión. He also recruited his children to the cause. They started to learn Castilian and to pay visits to the country, where they were introduced at gatherings of the party faithful. In 1950, Don Javier attended a plenary session of the National Junta, and visited Navarre, where he met with local leaders and representatives of the priests who had written to him. Acting like an archetypal Carlist king, he also swore respect of the Basque *fueros* under the ancient tree at Guernica, Bizkaia. The following year, accompanied by his eldest daughter, he toured Carlist strongholds throughout the land, ending in the monastery of Montserrat where he swore respect of the Catalan *fueros*. Wherever he went, he was enthusiastically received by forewarned Carlist crowds, while Comunión leaders exploited these occasions to remind him personally of the general wish that he assume the throne.

In 1952, at a meeting of the National Junta in Barcelona attended by their regent, the assembled councillors solemnly declared that the legitimate succession to the crown of Spain belonged to Don Javier. This time he succumbed to their petition, but immediately and unexpectedly stated that his acceptance was not to be promulgated until the opportune moment, and that, until then, he would only pretend to be king of the Carlists and not of the whole country. By thus taking on the Carlist crown, yet eluding the proclamation of his rights to the Spanish throne, Don Javier left his followers disillusioned and confused. He had felt cornered by their stubborn insistence and had given in to their requests, against his own will, only out of feebleness. Although this Act of Barcelona temporarily advanced the *javieristas* against other Carlist factions, Don Javier soon afterward denied its importance and silenced any allusion to the awaited proclamation. Franco was even more displeased than the Carlists about the act, and he had the regent promptly expelled.[29]

Monarchy without a Monarch

With the end of the Second World War, the Western democracies became increasingly hostile to the Spanish dictatorship, which they represented as the last fascist regime in Europe. The General Assembly of the United Nations voted against diplomatic recognition of Spain, most countries recalled their ambassadors, and France closed the frontier. In response to this foreign pressure, the Generalísimo tried to improve the image of his government by distancing Franquism from fascism. Among a host of other measures, he accentuated the Catholicism of his regime, began to play down the importance of the Falange, and suppressed the fascist salute. He also amnestied those imprisoned for Civil War crimes, announced the preparation of a Fuero de los

Españoles (a sort of bill of human rights), and signed the Ley de Referéndum, which envisaged that the government could submit issues of transcendent national concern to plebiscite.[30]

In his speeches at the time, Franco seemed to be moving toward traditionalism, though one very much of his own concoction. While much of this apparent change was merely cosmetic, the Comunión publicly declared its approval and stated that it would happy to associate with the Movimiento if Franco continued to veer toward traditionalism. Since so many Spaniards, arguing "Either Franco or the Communists!" rallied to their leader during these years of international ostracism, the Carlists felt obliged to fall into step; it would have been impolitic to disparage him. In line with this pacific policy, the Comunión urged its members to avoid fights with Falangists after Carlist ceremonies. The *requetés,* ever patriotic to a right-wing notion of Spain that transcended factional division, offered their services to the army in case of a widespread "Red" uprising.[31]

In partial reaction to this change in Carlist policy, Franco began to ease his repression of the movement. This mild letting up of the pressure on the *requetés* suited his purposes, for a strengthened Comunión could be a useful counterweight, above all to the supporters of Don Juan but also to the overbearing and sometimes arrogant Falangists. Fal Conde was permitted to journey about the country, and in 1946 was allowed to speak at the annual Carlist ceremony in the Catalan monastery of Montserrat. The anticommunist rhetoric of one speaker at the following year's gathering pleased Franco so much that he offered the man the San Sebastián bullring to hold a meeting. The Caudillo's aid, however, remained highly specific. The Carlist Circle at Zaragoza, one of the very few still open, was closed in 1945, and a great *requeté* celebration to be held on the site of one of their recent battles was banned. In 1948, the ceremony at Montserrat was suspended; the journal *Misión* was closed down; and police joined Falangists in attacking a Carlist crowd leaving a commemorative service, and arrested forty-two.[32] Despite the limited relaxation of repression, the Comunión clearly remained on the very margins of official approval.

Franco persevered in remodeling his government, which was now called an "organic democracy." He sought to legitimate his powers further (and perhaps also to make his regime more respectable internationally) by turning his form of state into a monarchy. The first article of the Ley de Sucesión, passed in 1947, stated, "Spain, as a political unit, is a Catholic, social, and representative state that, in keeping with her tradition, declares itself constituted into a kingdom." The law also proclaimed that Franco would rule until his death and that he had the right to nominate his regal successor. Spain was now a monarchy without a monarch, and Franco had his job for life.

The great loser, of course, was Don Juan, since the law treated all candidates as equal and denied the right of hereditary succession. Since this legalistic leveling of different pretenders' claims cut the ground from under his feet, he refused to acknowledge its validity. Although the law theoretically benefited Carlist candidates, Don Javier opposed it, and the Comunión told its people to vote no in the referendum on the issue.[33] The only claimant who did speak in its favor was Carlos VIII. Mindful of his patrons, he called the law "another, and a very important, step in the return toward tradition."[34]

The following year, Franco, in a gesture of appeasement, passed a law recognizing the titles up till then conferred by both Alfonsine and Carlist branches.[35] But at the same time, he made a move that suggested his true leanings on the question of the succession. In a meeting with Don Juan aboard the state yacht *Azor,* Franco agreed to a suggestion by his guest that Juan Carlos, Don Juan's eldest son and heir, should be educated in Spain.[36] If the sonless dictator thought Don Juan an unattractive character and too liberal for his liking, he could at least try to raise the man's son according to his own beliefs. For, according to the Law of Succession, only a person espousing the principles of the regime could sit on the throne. Carlists might dream of their own candidates winning the day, but it seemed that Franco was already preparing the way for his own chosen successor.[37]

The meeting on the *Azor* had a further, immediate consequence: the meteoric fall of Carlos VIII, initiated by Franco's withdrawal of support and funding. Some *carlosoctavista* acts were banned, and in Navarre, amid a general persecution by the civil governor, mayors sympathetic to the cause were sacked. After losing his patron, the pretender then lost his wife, who in 1949 commenced proceedings for the annulment of their marriage, and went to live in Italy. This was a critical setback for a man whose family was meant to personify traditionalist domestic values. He died childless in 1953, and the movement he had orphaned was left desperately seeking a new candidate. His brothers were considered first, then their children. But none was particularly suitable, nor very interested. Although no new pretender could be found within the *carlosoctavista* line, many of his supporters did not immediately desert his cause. A commemorative mass held two years after his death was still able to draw a crowd of three thousand.[38]

Don Javier Takes the Helm

Those *carlosoctavistas* who wished to continue upholding a viable Carlist candidate to the throne had little choice but to join Don Javier's fold. Others stayed at their posts in the state bureaucracy, preferring to collaborate rather than emphasize their Carlist identity. If the cause of the regent had been indirectly advanced by the demise of his competitor, it had also been assisted by the death of Rodezno the previous year. On the *conde's* decease, many of his supporters moved over to the side of Don Javier. Although the cause of the *javieristas* was, in this manner, gaining strength from within the greater Carlist community, their main worry—the attitude of their leader—persisted. For at the very time that previously opposed sectors began to unite behind one man, that man continued to fail them.[39]

Javieristas were particularly concerned about the strong rumors that Don Javier had gone so far as to enter into secret negotiations with Don Juan. They feared he was preparing to renounce his rights in favor of the liberal pretender. When Don Javier met with his regional leaders in April 1954, they called for the dissolution of the National Junta, which in their eyes had become as suspiciously *juanista* as its leader. Don Javier compromised by admitting the fervently *antijuanista* regional chiefs of Cataluña, Navarre, and the three Basque provinces onto the council.[40] Although this move somewhat appeased the worries of the die-hard traditionalists, the next meeting of Franco with Don Juan to discuss the education of Juan Carlos only rekindled their concern about the general advance of the *juanista* claim. They were also unsettled by a remark made to some of them by Hugues, Don Javier's eldest son, to the effect that Carlists should be on good terms with Don Juan because he could become king. One Navarrese leader asked Fal Conde to explain the lad's words; when he did not receive a good answer, he resigned. The *antijuanista* regional chiefs remained distrustful of the National Junta, which they thought might move to exclude them from its composition. At an unofficial meeting in Zaragoza, they wrote a letter to Don Javier urging him to dissolve the National Junta and, once and for all, to proclaim himself king of Spain.

The regent's immediate response to this independent activity within his higher echelons was to send his older children to Seville for Easter, while Fal Conde counterattacked personally in a meeting of the National Junta, where he made the rebellious regional chiefs of Aragón, Cataluña, and Valencia back down. The regional chief of Gipuzkoa was forced to resign, so the council of his province followed suit. Fal Conde then tried to reinforce his authority over the Comunión by executing the very act the regional chiefs had feared: excluding them all from a reformed National Junta.

Opposition to the chief delegate now began to mount, and came from many sides. The traditionalist minister of justice, Antonio Iturmendi, and Rafael Olazábal, an old friend of Don Javier, wanted to bring the Comunión closer to Franco and were prepared to act as intermediaries between the two leaders. To them, the independently minded Fal Conde could only be a hindrance. At the other end of the Carlist spectrum, the forces opposed to Fal Conde's continued incumbency included prominent Gipuzkoans who wanted to take an even firmer line against collaboration than he did; members of the Baleztena family, leading Navarrese who had previously sheltered under Rodezno's umbrella, and who were now informally allied with Sivatte's group; regional leaders, and others, who thought Fal Conde too dictatorial; and various groups of Carlist youth who saw him as senile and old-fashioned. On top of that, and perhaps crucially, Fal Conde had lost the support of Don Javier, who personally blamed his chief delegate for pushing him into the Act of Barcelona. A personal assistant of Franco who had visited Don Javier in Paris in April 1955 had said it was necessary to reorganize the Comunión rapidly if it wished to play a decisive role in the future of Spain. But first, Fal Conde would have to go; the head of state had not forgotten his intransigent attitude at the beginning of the war. In August 1955, the regent, unable or unprepared to resist pressure from so many different quarters, dismissed his chief delegate in what is reported to have been a rather cowardly, backhand manner.[41]

Having dropped his pilot, Don Javier set about renegotiating the relations of the Comunión with the dictatorship. Since the war, leaders of the Comunión had tried to keep up their friendships with generals and other power holders who, it was thought, might succeed Franco. But by the mid-1950s, it had become clear that the dictator was not going to disappear from the political scene soon. Don Javier, thinking that Franco had to evolve, considered it best that the Comunión participate in any evolution of his system of government. At first, this move toward the regime was simply presented as "an understanding with Iturmendi." Gipuzkoan, Navarrese, and Catalan Carlist chiefs, however, remained set against any maneuvering with the minister of justice, which they saw as part of an increasingly *philojuanista* tendency within the national leadership.[42] These stalwart traditionalists wanted no truck with the regime, nor with an unprincipled pretender like Don Juan.

Many senior Carlists were pleased that Don Javier had taken on the duties of the chief delegacy himself, since they thought that would bind him closer to the movement; they were disappointed that he remained averse to playing the role of pretender and seemed content to retreat back into the part of regent. But Don Javier, as reluctant as ever to assume what his supporters regarded as his rightful title, continued to search for a solution that would free him of his responsibilities. At one point he even considered his sister's son, Otto of Habsburg and Bourbon-Parma, as did some Carlists in Madrid, Navarre, and San Sebastián. When he realized his nephew's candidacy would not prosper, he revived the idea of a national regency, this time composed of himself, Don Juan, and one other. Don Juan, however, was not prepared to compromise what he regarded as his legitimate right to the throne, and he refused to recognize the authority of any regency.

With Fal Conde now out of office, the Comunión needed skillful, committed leadership if it was to survive as a unitary organization with any political pretensions. But Don Javier, rather than dutifully steer the movement he had been given by his uncle, continued to seek a release from the increasing burdens of his inheritance. He might have been a successful diplomat, but he did not wish to take on a political post that would end only with his death. He had been willing to act as an international negotiator when the occasion required but, now in his midsixties, he was disinclined to spend the remainder of his days coping with the pressures from competing Carlist factions. To put it simply, this prince had tired of noblesse oblige and wanted to have done with the whole business. To his friend Olazábal, he secretly pleaded, "Rafael, free me of this weight."

Chapter Five

The Rise of the Progressives

If Don Javier did not covet the position of pretender nor of Comunión leader, then, from the mid-1950s to the early 1960s, he could at least fulfill the duties entailed until his elder son, Hugues, was ready to take the reins. The aging prince would stay at his post while Hugues, aided by his sisters, readied himself for his Carlist inheritance and cultivated his candidacy for the Spanish throne. It was this younger, more energetic generation of Borbón-Parmas who could both stimulate and help direct the revitalization of their disorganized movement. Unlike Don Javier, who had been expelled from Spain twice, they could enter the country, get to know the Carlist people, and guide those young activists who had already started to campaign for reform. In the meantime, Don Javier would pilot the Comunión from afar, usually trying to steer a middle course between the options of single-minded collaboration and outright particularism—a task that would be complicated, if not occasionally impeded, by the increasingly vociferous demands of the youthful militants.

The need for reform had become ever more pressing, because by the mid-1950s Spanish society had started to undergo a profound social and economic transformation, thanks primarily to American aid and loans that had stimulated industrialization and a tourist boom. The rate of change was so rapid that between 1950 and 1975 Spain experienced the greatest proportionate growth of any country in the world except Japan. This restructuring of the economy led in turn to massive rural emigration, a rise in the standard of living, and the first signs of a consumer culture. Centers such as Madrid and Barcelona mushroomed as people from impoverished regions came to find work. Economic change was also reflected in political change. Meritocratic members of the secret Catholic society Opus Dei won positions in the cabinet. Once inside the center of power, they managed to persuade Franco to end his now floundering policy of autarchic nationalism for the sake of economic liberalism. The old policy of self-sufficiency was to be succeeded by one based on international commerce and foreign intervention. Falangists and Christian Democrats were replaced by technocrats, an outmoded spiritualism by an aggressive materialism.

Even Catholicism would begin to change, stimulated by Pope John XXIII's convocation of the Second Vatican Council in 1959. It is worth stressing that it is very difficult to exaggerate the liberalizing effects of the council on Spanish life in general. With its emphasis on human rights, justice, ecumenism, and dialogue, and its assumption of pluralistic societies as the norm, conciliar Catholicism justified the separation of the Church from determined political positions and legitimated discontent on regional issues, political repression, and other social questions.[1] Churchgoers would no longer have to side automatically with the Right. Instead of being influenced by a formal religiosity, they could begin to apply Christian values to a political context.

In these different ways—economic, social, and religious—the very foundations underpinning the civil society constructed by the regime were slowly being demolished: strikes were more and more common, political unrest was becoming an established fact of university life, and a new generation of socially aware, outspoken priests was emerging. In this context of flux, a static, backward-looking traditionalism would gain few new recruits and stood to lose many. As peasants deserted the land to find relatively well paid work in factories, a movement that extolled the virtues of the countryside against the evils of urban life began to make less and less political sense. And since factories, as many realized with hindsight, provided workers with a stark lesson in the depersonalizing nature of capitalist exploitation, a political movement that stressed interclass harmony started to appear out of date and ill informed about the contemporary reality of Spanish life. The Comunión would have to change if it was to revive as a force to be reckoned with.

Within a decade of Don Javier's assumption of power, the combined, though frequently conflictive, activities of the conservative and the progressive factions within the movement, together with the monarchic aspirations of Hugues, were to prepare the way for a remarkable transformation of Carlist identity. The symbolic and political centrality of the royal family was to be reasserted, while some of the cherished concepts of the *requeté* old guard were to be pushed aside for the sake of advocating social change. In their own muddled, disputatious way, the Carlists began to turn their ancient cause once again into a significant force within Spanish politics—perhaps for the last time.

The Appearance of Hugues

In May 1957, those attending the annual Carlist ritual of Montejurra were surprised by the sudden appearance of Hugues on the mountaintop. With the exception of 1939, when Princess Isabel, Don Javier's sister, had graced the inaugural ceremony with her presence, this was the first time that any of the Borbón-Parmas had turned up for the occasion. Three of Don Javier's daughters, Francisca, María-Teresa, and Cecilia, had walked up the mountainside with the party faithful, but Hugues had ascended by a different route and joined his sisters only at the summit. Styling himself "Prince of Asturias," a title reserved for the heir to the throne, he spoke to the assembled multitude of "my father the King" and "my forebear Carlos VII." He went on: "Called by the laws of succession to be the inheritor of the Spanish monarchy, I have taken on all the weight and responsibilities that that inheritance demands from me as Prince of all Spaniards."

To Hugues's listeners, it seemed that Don Javier and his son had finally accepted their familial duties. Their regent had at last become a pretender; there was to be no more suggestion of a "truly constituted Cortes" deciding who was to be appointed to the post.

For leading *javieristas,* the sight of Hugues forcefully speaking to "his" people was explicitly intended as a way to demonstrate publicly that the pretender had a heir, and a vigorous, youthful one at that. Because Don Javier's almost constant shuffling back and forth had discredited him in the eyes of many, the physical presence of his daughters at the ceremony and, above all, of his son on the mountaintop was deliberately designed to reaffirm the Borbón-Parmas's leadership of the Comunión. At the same time, it was an overdue attempt to reanimate the political fortunes of the movement they headed.

Although Don Javier did not officially and conclusively take on the title of pretender until 1965, by the Montejurra of 1957 it had become clear to most that he had given up prevaricating and had effectively assumed the role.[2] This belated change of heart may have pleased his exasperated supporters, but it ran the risk, as he had presumably calculated, of alienating those Carlists who had put up with the interregnum precisely because it left various options open. *Sivattistas,* aghast at the talk of "King Javier," turned their split with the Comunión into a definitive rupture by creating the Regency of Estella, a separate Carlist body with its own organization and its own ritual calendar.[3]

Juanistas, who had hoped that Don Juan would be designated the legitimate traditionalist successor, wrote a joint letter to Don Javier, strongly criticizing his son's words at Montejurra, and then formally broke with the leadership of the Comunión. After a series of meetings in the provinces to sound out local opinion, sixty-three representatives assembled in Madrid before many of them, including a large number of peers, traveled to Estoril, where Don Juan accepted their allegiance in return for his espousal of traditionalist principles. Those among them who had not met Don Juan before were on the whole very impressed with the man they encountered: "He is Carlos VII all over again," one of them exclaimed enthusiastically, "but without the beard."[4] Although some Carlists regarded this collective defection as a reversal for the Comunión, and an especially grave one coming at a time when the movement was trying to relaunch itself as an effective political force, committed *javieristas* saw it as a self-inflicted purge of the unwanted. If these *carlojuanistas* were so opposed to Don Javier as pretender, it was best that they went their own way.

Reorganizing the Comunión

If Don Javier was to preside over the Comunión until such time as Hugues could take command, then one of his most pressing tasks was to reorganize its direction, and to do so rapidly. In 1956 regional leaders, disappointed that he had not fulfilled his recent promise of returning the movement to a more representative and decentralized structure, had spontaneously constituted a Junta of the Regions. In a bid to control this unofficial body and to forestall any further regional unrest, Don Javier set up a five-man secretariat. Its two key members, both of whom had served on Fal Conde's National War Council, were José Maria Valiente, whose task was to establish liaison with Franco and senior generals, and José Luis Zamanillo, who was to head the initiative within the Movimiento and the Cortes. Their main aims were to pursue the "neocollaborationist" policy initiated by Don Javier and to promote the candidacy of his son.[5] They wished to take advantage of the increasing tolerance of the regime by making the Comunión an evident force within the government while avoiding any "stain" by this contact. In the contemporary circumstances, they considered a finely judged degree of collaboration to be not an abandoning of principles (as some stalwarts claimed) but a valid tactic to be maintained for the time being.

The turnabout in the strategy of the Comunión was criticized from both ends of the Carlist spectrum. *Carlofranquistas* begrudged the *javieristas'* rush to cooperate, and tried to embarrass these newcomers to the dictator's camp by reminding them of their opposition to unification in 1937.[6] More pertinently perhaps, die-hard opponents of the dictatorship contended that any form of collaboration, however discriminating, was still collaboration and that, in politics, fine distinctions could rarely be drawn, and even more rarely perceived by others. Prominent Basque Carlists strongly disagreed with the Comunión's new line. "Intransigents," as they were dubbed, in Cataluña and Navarre distributed leaflets and circulated open letters arguing against any dealings with the regime; very few veteran *requetés* marched in the huge Victory Parade celebrating the twenty-fifth anniversary of the outbreak of war, despite the call to attend made by the leadership. Although the Comunión was now informally allied with the Falange in common opposition to Don Juan and in their support of the "original spirit of 18 of July," Zamanillo had to be very careful what he said at Carlist gatherings. If he mentioned the fascist organization by name, some of his audience would heckle, and others would leave.[7] Feelings against the sudden switch in policy ran so high that one young Navarrese, disguised as a priest, assaulted Valiente in a Pamplona street.

But Valiente, a former professor of law and widely acknowledged to be a brilliant orator, did manage to win over the Carlist priests of Navarre. At the same time, Don Javier tried to persuade skeptical members of the National Junta by arguing that the *requetés* had collaborated with the army in the war and, now that Franco seemed ready to restore a traditional monarchy, the Comunión could not let the memory of its war dead down. The efforts of the Carlist leaders paid off; if it could not be said that unity had been restored, then at least opposition to the change in policy had been quieted.

The new lineup of political forces was refracted ritually, and is most dramatically thrown into relief by comparing the same event on different dates. In 1955 Iturmendi and the secretary-general of the FET, amid a small congregation, had attended the official ceremony for the souls of the Carlist martyrs, while the unofficial traditionalist service at a nearby church had attracted a large crowd, including pugnacious Falangists waiting outside for the end of Mass. On the same anniversary five years later there was only one sizable service, and that was attended by Iturmendi, accompanied by two Falangist ministers. After the Mass, a *juanista* gang scuffled and fought outside the church with those congregants who shouted "Long live Don Javier!" and "Death to Don Juan!"[8]

Though Don Javier and his secretariat were prepared to assist the regime and to laud its founding principles publicly, their repeated efforts to win either Valiente or Zamanillo a ministry failed.[9] Franco was satisfied with the two traditionalists he already had: Iturmendi and Esteban Bilbao, president of the Cortes, both of them longtime collaborators who had not let their Carlism get in the way of their careers. The dictator was not going to oust these loyal servants for the sake of *javieristas* who had only recently moved toward his side. However, he was so pleased with the new attitude of the Comunión leadership that in a meeting with Valiente in April 1961, he granted them several favors.[10] But these concessions could not mask the fact that the Carlists were a minor force within Franco's ambit. Valiente was granted an audience with the Caudillo only once a year; the supporters of Don Juan met him weekly.

Hugues and His *Huguistas*

For leading *huguistas* (as they came to be known), the decade beginning with the first appearance of Hugues in Montejurra corresponds to an "awakening" of their movement, the beginning of its political evolution after years of lethargy. These young men had been children at the time of the Civil War and had grown up during some of the worst years of the regime. They had not experienced the disorder and violent anticlericalism that had galvanized their elders into action. Instead, they had been forced to live through *los años de hambre* (the years of hunger), when the state had been unable to ensure an adequate diet for millions of its citizens. They had had to witness the true, repressive nature of the dictatorship, and to observe firsthand the disillusionment of former *requetés*, who felt betrayed by the government they had helped usher in. More open to the new currents emerging within Spanish society, they were not disposed to accept the contemporary situation passively; yet neither were they prepared to seek change along the lines of what seemed to them to be an anachronistic and perverted interpretation of the Carlist message perpetrated by self-interested integrist leaders. Members of the AET worked for a renovated, politically engaged but independent Carlism, concerned with social reform, and they publicly repudiated any strategy of collaboration.[11] By the mid-1950s members of the AET, working alongside other groups of the recently emerged student opposition (which ranged from revolutionary communists to orthodox Christian Democrats), had helped to break the monopoly of the state-run Sindicato Estudiantil Universitario (SEU) and had started to win posts as student representatives within the academic hierarchy. To these AET members, the universities were one of the few arenas where they could act effectively, winning new adherents to the cause and campaigning for causes such as a free press and democratic syndicates. Over the next decade their organization was to prove the major school in practical politics from which most of the next generation of Carlist leaders graduated.[12]

These activist youths were opposed to the traditionalist conception of religion as the fundament of national unity. They wanted a prudent and progressive secularization of the almost mystically religious content of Carlism as promoted up to then. To these progressives (as they became known), the "angelism" (exploitation of Catholic imagery and values for reactionary ends) of the old-guard leaders controlling the Comunión prevented people from feeling responsible for their own destiny. Instead of helping to perpetuate an internal power structure that was uneasily akin to that of the hated regime, they wished to democratize Carlism and to return it to what they saw as its original raison d'être: to act as an organized vehicle of popular protest against the dominating forces of the state. In the process of propounding these reforms, they were to replace the old-style chiefs with leaders supposedly in the new mold—in other words, themselves.

It was a Bilbao-based group of these activists, led by Raymond Massó, national secretary of the AET, who realized that their renovative ideals could best be promoted by a youthful prince of the line. In 1956 four of them visited

Hugues, then studying in Oxford, and, after some difficulty, overcame his initially strong resistance to take up their banner. They then arranged for him to spend the seven months prior to Montejurra living incognito with an old Carlist syndicalist in Bilbao. He passed the days improving his Spanish and the evenings in long political discussions with Massó and his like-minded friends. The activists did not just want a Castilian-speaking prince who worked for the cause; they wanted one who spoke the right political language.

Hugues returned to Montejurra in 1958 and 1959. On each occasion he spoke of the need to reform Spanish society, yet was careful not to criticize the regime directly. In 1959 Valiente and the secretariat, as good neocollaborationists, did not want him to attend the ceremony because orders had been issued to bar his entry into the country. But since national newspapers had publicized Juan Carlos's participation in the Madrid Victory Parade a few days before, it was felt that the Carlist prince, who was already in Spain, should make his presence similarly evident. Shortly after the ceremony, he was arrested and driven to the French border. Neither the government nor the Comunión publicized the expulsion; neither wished to increase its distance from the other.

But if Hugues was to help reanimate the greater Carlist community, reorganize the structure and program of the Comunión, and establish definitively the central position of the Borbón-Parmas within the movement, and if—to him, perhaps most important of all—he was going to present himself to all Spaniards as a worthy competitor to Juan Carlos for the throne, then he needed to reside permanently in the country. Carlists in Madrid used all their government contacts to try to get the prohibition against Hugues's entry lifted. It was not until 1961 that Franco relented. In return for the dictator's tolerance, Hugues, who based himself in Madrid, did not reappear at Montejurra, and refrained from making any public speeches.

One of Hugues's first moves was to reform the Comunión executive. Meetings of the National Junta could be held only with difficulty, since its membership included all regional chiefs. So, with the agreement of Valiente, Hugues substituted the overlarge junta with a much smaller Permanent Committee, composed of Valiente, Zamanillo, and other neocollaborationists, as well as a few intransigents and progressives. The prince appointed such a heterogeneous crew to this new body as an initial attempt to integrate some of the diverse groups within the movement. Leaving the practical business of running the Comunión in the hands of his appointees, he and his team of youthful secretaries, headed by Massó, got on with the business of trying to advance their reformist political line within the Carlist ranks. They were to find that if ideological inflexibility had helped maintain an independent Carlism during the barren years of the first postwar decades, then that same stubbornness would prove an obstacle to any group bent on change.

Carlos Hugo's Bid for the Throne

Shortly after establishing himself in Madrid, Carlos Hugo (as he now styled himself) embarked in a resolute manner (which contrasted strongly with the cautiousness of his father) on an almost frenetic program of activity, much of it chosen for its value as publicity.[13] He met with politicians and influential businessmen, visited ministers, was received by Franco, and crisscrossed the country visiting Carlists, often being received triumphantly. Navarrese who had barricaded the entrances to their villages to prevent Juan Carlos from visiting them turned out en masse when Carlos Hugo passed through the area.

His sisters aided his efforts by publicly performing good works and going out to meet the Carlist people.[14] In 1962 all four sisters attended Montejurra. From that year on, at least one of them would turn up for the annual event, with Cecilia, the youngest and perhaps least politically inclined, filling in whenever her more committed sisters were unable to make the date. In these different ways, the younger generation of the Borbón-Parmas could be seen to be playing exemplary roles as socially concerned participants in Spanish life and as committed members of the Carlist royal family.

Many people, and not just Carlists, began to regard this industrious prince as a promising contender for the crown, one more fit for the task than Juan Carlos. Journalists for the Navarrese Carlist magazine *Montejurra* underlined the point by writing articles comparing the various qualities of the two young men; other *huguistas* made their point by demonstrating against Juan Carlos, and against *El Diario de Barcelona,* which supported his claim.[15] Franco, however, thought the Borbón-Parmas "foreign princes" making illegitimate claims in Spanish territory. Don Javier and Carlos Hugo repeatedly requested Spanish nationality, to which, according to certain legal experts, they were entitled.[16] But Iturmendi, as minister of justice and a traditionalist loyal to his true master, opined that their petition should be rejected. Franco agreed. He regarded the meetings of Don Javier's court as "operetta" and complained privately that the pretender, as a foreigner, should not be conceding noble titles, crosses, and medals. As he told his cousin, Francisco Franco Salgado-Aranjo, "The traditionalist branch cannot be the solution, since the monarchic succession lies legitimately in Don Juan or his son Juan Carlos. The traditionalists, with Don Javier, want to destroy what God has made legitimate." Although he personally liked Carlos Hugo, he would not help him to the throne: "I am fond of him, he is very courteous and likeable, but he does not seem to me to be the right prince to be King of Spain."

To his cousin, a close confidant, Franco seemed obsessed with the issue of the monarchy at this time. Hardly a day went by without him speaking of it.

He was uncertain about Don Juan, but he was definite that if Spain was to be a kingdom, it would be ruled by a member of the Alfonsine, not the Carlist, lineage. Nonetheless, as the Opus Dei minister Laureano López Rodó recognized, it was convenient to work with the *javieristas* in order to keep them quiet. So long as the Comunión worked in league with the regime, Franco was prepared to allow Carlos Hugo's residence in Spain, and he played along with Carlist hopes by telling Valiente he had decided nothing about the succession. Franco's apparent approval of the prince was also a way of keeping Juan Carlos in check by reminding him that he was neither his automatic nor sole choice for the crown. When, immediately after their marriage, Juan Carlos and Sofia made a special trip to Madrid to pay him their respects, Franco made a special point of also granting a long audience to Valiente.[17]

To some, Carlos Hugo's wedding to Princess Irene of the Netherlands in 1964 marked the high point of his chances. To others, it merely crystallized the attitudes of different groups toward the Borbón-Parmas. After the romantic interest of the King of the Belgians, Baudouin I, in María-Teresa had ended abruptly when sectors within the Belgian parliament made clear their opposition to the princess, the courtship of Carlos Hugo and Irene throughout 1963 was conducted in the strictest secrecy.[18] Well liked in her native Holland, though recognized as something of an enfant terrible, the princess spoke fluent Castilian and had long had a deep interest in Spanish culture. Shortly before the announcement of their engagement, she entered the Roman Catholic Church. Her parents had been opposed to the union of their wayward daughter with a Catholic adventurer who had no obvious throne. But the publicity already given to the affair, partially engineered by Carlos Hugo's secretaries, forced the Dutch monarch to accept the forthcoming marriage as a fait accompli.[19]

The anti-Carlist campaign mounted by the national *juanista* press during this period was so virulent that Valiente urged all regional and local chiefs to protest in writing to Manuel Fraga Iribarne, then minister of information. Carlos Hugo had also wanted Fraga to stop the Spanish press from reporting that the Dutch royal family had not allowed the marriage to be held in The Hague. But the minister, whom Carlos Hugo had until then counted as a friend, refused to intervene.[20] Franco was irritated by the anti-Spanish reports in the Dutch press, which in his opinion had ridiculed national organizations and important persons, especially himself. Shortly after the wedding, he warned his cabinet, "This man is going nowhere. . . . I would beseech you to take note, and that each one of you in your own specific area do everything possible to clarify that."[21] Although Carlos Hugo and Luis Carrero Blanco, Subsecretario al Presidente, lived in the same Madrid apartment building,

Franco's trusted minister would not even speak to the prince when by chance they met in the elevator.[22] No open support for Carlos Hugo was to come from official quarters.[23]

Carlist Reactions to *Progresismo*

While many Carlists were at least ready to listen to the renovative ideas of Carlos Hugo, steadfast intransigents were not prepared to brook any tinkering with the traditionalist program, whether or not propounded by a prince of the blood. Progressives might have seen the late 1950s and early to mid-1960s as a time of "awakening," but to the men they branded as conservatives it was a period of increasingly bitter internal disputes, as a new form of Carlism started to emerge and members of the old guard were slowly ousted from their positions. Contributors to the journals of both the conservative and the progressive wings began to spend their time sniping at one another, and meetings chaired by Carlos Hugo could easily become very heated.[24] Some traditionalists, not bothering to resist the rise of the young leader and his team of advisers, went straight over to the *juanistas*. In March 1961 250 Carlists, unattracted by Carlos Hugo's approach, made the journey to Estoril bearing a message of loyalty to Don Juan signed by 700 *requeté* officers.[25] Most *sivattistas* were unimpressed by the prince. Opposed to both Don Juan and Carlos Hugo, they joined with the remaining *carlosoctavistas* to form a nationwide organization, the Juntas de Defensa del Carlismo.[26]

Perhaps the most visible manifestation of this frequently generational conflict was the dispute between Zamanillo and his prince.[27] As the war leader of the *requetés*, Zamanillo commanded greater prestige than Valiente, who had converted to the cause only during the Republic, and he came to represent the most conservative wing of the *javieristas*. A brusque man with an unshakable sense of his own authority, he had differences with Carlos Hugo from the very beginning of the prince's residence in Madrid. He and his supporters complained of the cost of maintaining the prince in Spain, disapproved of the almost frenzied activity of Carlos Hugo and his secretaries, and were jealous of the power these newcomers had effectively usurped. In the eyes of these conservatives, the secretaries acted as though they were chiefs, directly contacting provincial leaders and bypassing the established hierarchy. On top of that, the secretaries spoke openly of "victory" and of "the struggle for power," but kept the plans of their prince secret. Zamanillo and his predominantly *requeté* cohort looked up to Don Javier and regarded his son as unstable, overhasty, materialist, inexperienced, and ignorant of Carlist history. To them, he was a domineering absolutist who tried to put pressure on well-entrenched chiefs.

They were also not impressed when he refused to intervene on behalf of leading Navarrese who were worried about proposed legislation to abolish the
fueros of their province; they were not persuaded by his argument that, until
he had won the throne, it was best not to jeopardize his chances in any way.

In early 1963 Zamanillo toured the country giving public speeches about the
need to reaffirm the 1937 Decree of Unification. Next, he and like-minded colleagues revived the idea of a national regency, whose controllers would first
declare their full commitment to the "original spirit of 18 of July," and only
then decide who was most suitable to be king of the Carlists. Both of these
maneuvers failed ignominiously. Although some *antihuguistas* and some *juanistas* close to the regime supported the proposals, the majority of active Carlists did not because the proposals amounted to the Comunión giving up those
shreds of its former autonomy that it had only recently regained and because
they questioned the eminence of the Borbón-Parmas.

Zamanillo's bid failed, and he resigned from his official positions within the
movement. But the leadership of the Comunión then accused him of overzeal-
ous collaboration, of open criticism of Carlos Hugo, Valiente, and Fal Conde,
and of discourtesy to Don Javier's daughters. He quickly became so discredited that within a few months he had lost all influence within the Comunión
hierarchy. He had been purged, and the position of Carlos Hugo's secretaries
strengthened. In the meantime, Don Javier reminded regional chiefs that Carlos Hugo was his representative in Spain, and that he had full confidence in
him, while Fal Conde sent an open letter to the National Junta in which he
praised the prince and his work. The message was clear: fidelity to the dynasty
was to take precedence in contemporary Carlism. From now on "King" was
to come before "God" or "Patria" in the movement's slogan.[28]

While conservative *javieristas* were unhappy about the infiltration of Carlos
Hugo's men into the hierarchy of the Comunión, they could always comfort
themselves that their movement was still headed by an exemplary traditionalist: the rush to change desired by the headstrong son would be tempered by
the steadying influence of his father. All the more reason for their shock, then,
when in January 1965 Don Javier made a speech in which, using the phrases
of his son's secretaries, he spoke of "democracy" and acknowledged the importance of nonmonarchic forces in the "guts" of the country. Leading conservatives, scandalized by the statement, published an *Ideario Tradicionalista*.
At the same time, the Delegación Nacional de Requetés produced a pamphlet propounding that all veteran insurgents reassert collectively the values
for which they had gone to war.[29] Both documents failed to sway those already inclined toward Carlos Hugo—the traditionalist antipathy to change
expressed in both pamphlets serving only to clarify publicly the sort of blink-
ered opposition that reformists faced.[30]

Later that year the progressives consolidated their position within the Comunión when its executive was restructured, with a Governing Junta replacing the Permanent Committee. Although the junta was composed mainly of conservatives, most of them lived in the provinces, so it could meet only occasionally. Thus, power effectively passed to its technical secretary, the energetic José María de Zavala, an intimate of Carlos Hugo. At the same time, young activists were put in charge of the press office, the AET, the finances of the Comunión, and the development of a workers' wing, Movimiento Obrero Tradicionalista (MOT), created that year.[31] Members of the old guard were retained in senior, if at times almost nominal, posts, while their youthful antagonists were taking over more and more of the direction of the Comunión.

Despite these gains, Carlos Hugo's secretaries were becoming disheartened. Impatient for success, they were dissatisfied with the political advances already made and felt that Carlos Hugo, now comfortably settled into marriage, was not pushing his candidacy hard enough. Massó, deeply discouraged by the thought that his prince would not be crowned, resigned.[32] The remaining secretaries estimated that their best policy was to forget their regal hopes for Carlos Hugo and to try to carry the Carlist majority with them by accelerating the pace of ideological change. To that end, they started publishing new periodicals, such as *La Mina* in Asturias and *Campos de España* in rural Castile, both of which adopted a much more radical tone in their political commentaries. In January 1966 they staged a National Carlist Congress, attended by national and regional leaders as well as by a disproportionate number of students and young professionals, some workers, and, for the first time in a major meeting, some women. In its final declaration, the congress defined Carlism as "a constructive and inevitable group of the opposition" whose principal mission was "to propose solutions for authentic political and syndical representation for all Spaniards." According to this statement, the official stance of the Comunión was not to be a discriminating quasifranquism, but a determined antifranquism.

The secretaries had miscalculated badly. Carlist neocollaborationism, far from being moribund, was about to take on new life. Veteran leaders complained to Don Javier about the declaration, and most refused to fill in a lengthy questionnaire handed out at the congress, which they had regarded as a form of "brainwashing."[33] In the Montejurra of that year the speakers ignored the scripts given them by the secretaries and chose not to criticize the government in their speeches. The final reversal for the secretaries came when their protector, who since his marriage had become far less dependent on them, followed his father's wish and withdrew his support. At that point, all of them but Zavala resigned.[34] Don Javier proceeded to calm conservative disgruntlement and to halt any further desertions to Estoril by temporarily abandoning any strategy of opposition.[35]

The conservatives might have won a brief victory with the departure of the secretaries, but the reformists continued to gain further positions within the movement. In 1966, they won the editorship of *El Pensamiento Navarro*, the Carlists' only daily newspaper, and in 1968 attained control of *Montejurra*. The year before, four Carlist deputies in Navarre and Gipuzkoa had been elected in the elections for the "family" representatives to the Cortes, where they quickly gained a reputation as lively members of the antifranquist opposition within the chamber.[36] And when, in January 1968, Valiente resigned over differences with Carlos Hugo on strategy, Don Javier did not replace him but left the direction of the Comunión to his son, assisted by Zavala as secretary-general.[37]

In many ways, this brief period from the mid to the late 1960s is a confusing one for an analyst of Carlism, as perhaps it also was for much of the rank and file. Articles in the very same issue of *Montejurra* might be couched in the style of an adamant traditionalism or a committed *progresismo*. A column entitled "Why I Am Not a Democrat" might be placed alongside one on the lessons of Maoism. A piece by a conservative remembering Carlos Hugo's earlier words in support of "the spirit of 18 July" might be followed by one on the errors of integrism. As both counterrevolutionaries and their opponents continued to wrestle for control of the movement and for the hearts of their readers, it could be difficult to ascertain who exactly was in the ascendant, when, and for what reasons. For instance, the specific causes of Don Javier's dramatic about-face in policy remain unclear.[38] Whatever the precise reasons for it, this sudden switch back to neocollaborationism was relatively short-lived.

Amid this seeming political confusion and pervasive air of ideological contest, Carlos Hugo and his immediate circle appear to have had, at least by 1968, a clear vision of their own position, and of their future. With a gradually increasing number of the leading conservatives now marginalized, they believed they were close to winning effective control of the Comunión. Unfettered by prestigious former *requetés*, they could proceed to reshape the movement according to their own designs. Carlos Hugo, moreover, had recently been freed from the restraint entailed by the role of polite pretender. Since Franco, now in his midseventies and well aware of his failing powers, seemed finally on the point of officially proclaiming Juan Carlos as his successor, Carlos Hugo no longer needed to curry favor with the dictator. The prince and his progressives could afford to proclaim a more radical program, no matter the consequences.[39]

Chapter Six

Kings and Common Phrases

To my knowledge, Carlism is the only example in the modern history of Europe of a political organization that has moved, with a certain degree of success, from the extreme right to the center-left. This dramatic shift from one end of the ideological spectrum to almost that of the other, made in less than fifteen years, was not achieved without much dissension, internal disputes, and desertions. But while progressives were keen to replace those officeholders who were stubbornly resisting the emergence of the new party line, they did not at the same time wish to alienate the Carlist base but to carry it with them as they groped their way toward new solutions. In order to minimize the divisive effects of reformation, they therefore chose to emphasize the supposed underlying continuity in the midst of so much change. They did this in two key ways: (1) they maintained fundamental terms within the movement's discourse while simultaneously reinterpreting them; and (2) they reaffirmed the focal role of the royal family within their community. As far as they were concerned, the third term in the traditional slogan of DIOS, PATRIA, REY, FUEROS had been neglected for too long.

The Exemplary Images of Don Javier and Carlos Hugo

Javierista journalists presented their prince, his wife, and their children as a living embodiment of the dynastic continuity of Carlism. In their articles, the Borbón-Parmas were portrayed as a regal family who lent an air of majesty to the notion of ideological steadfastness over the generations. Their close connection by blood to the lineage of Carlos V, VI, and VII was repeatedly depicted in cleverly devised genealogical trees, their right to Spanish nationality was stoutly defended in a string of vehemently couched commentaries, and their exemplary conduct was persistently praised. Line drawings of their many castles and châteaus frequently illustrated Carlist periodicals, and their princely possessions were lovingly lingered over. Of course, partisan journalists, as dutiful professionals dedicated to advancing the cause, kept mum about any details that might detract from this image of royalty and commitment.

Don Javier himself was taken to personify unswerving regal fidelity to the movement over the course of several decades, for his biography linked Carlism from the time of the Civil War to the reformist days of the 1960s. However, when his elder son had first appeared at Montejurra, Don Javier had been still little known by most of his subjects. Very few had ever seen him, let alone spoken to him. Although he had been commander in chief of the *requetés* and had visited some of them at their battle sites, he had been expelled from Spain before the war was even a year old. He did not return for a decade, and when he did start to revisit the country, he never stayed long and rarely met any Carlists other than national or provincial leaders. But once he accepted the role of pretender and his elder son firmly committed himself to the cause, *javierista* journalists worked swiftly to rewrite his past, singling out different parts of his life according to which audience they were addressing. For conservatives, they iterated that his legitimacy lay partially, but importantly, in the fact that he had signed the order for the *requetés* to rise up with the insurgents. They would also mention that his father, Prince Roberto, had campaigned with his wife's brother-in-law, Carlos VII, in the Second Carlist War; that he had fought in, and been decorated by, the Belgian army in the First World War; and that his brother, Don Cayetano, had enlisted incognito as a red beret in the Civil War and seen action many times. On this evidence, Don Javier was a brave man from a family of brave men. For reformists, the journalists emphasized achievements that displayed attitudes and values that progressives held dear: his secret attempt to bring peace to Europe in 1916, his clandestine endeavor in 1936 to end the Civil War in the Basque Country, his supposedly intractable opposition to Franco from the first months of the uprising, and his aid to the French Resistance, for which he was interned in the concentration camp of Dachau. In terms of public image, Don Javier was thus usefully Janus-like, with a face for either audience.

While it appears to be true that Don Javier was a morally upright character who evinced the values of bravery and dedication, the portraits of him painted by Carlist journalists omitted many aspects of his multifaceted life. For Don Javier was a man with several loyalties. As well as having over thirty noble titles and being pretender to both the Spanish and the French crowns, he also had blood ties with the Portuguese monarchy and affinal links with the Austro-Hungarian empire, both of which he had been prepared to support, militarily or diplomatically, when their incumbents lost their thrones, or their lives. Moreover, the allegiance of Don Javier and his siblings, as polyglot princes who moved within a European ambit, was not automatically tied to any specific country or bound by international border. As he often told his children, "There are no Pyrenees for a Borbón." When war broke out in 1914, Don Javier and his brother Sixtus entered the Belgian army, while two of their younger brothers joined the Austrian forces. Don Javier's Carlist hagiographers may have wished to assert the Spanishness of him and his family, but when his sister Zita, as a child, had asked their father Roberto, Duke of Parma, what exactly the Borbón-Parmas *were*, he had replied, "We are French princes who reigned in Italy."[1]

Both traditionalists and progressives might be grateful to Don Javier for having remained at the head of Carlism since 1936, but Carlos Hugo was the kind of leader the reformers wanted. While Don Javier, in his own dithering way and sometimes in spite of his own desires, had helped to keep the Carlist flag flying, it was not he but his son who was capable of taking up the standard of change. In the words of one militant, "Don Javier was very pious, a gentleman, someone from another epoch." Born in 1889, he was now reaching an age where he was becoming more venerable than effective. Even the physique of this tall, almost skeletal septuagenarian seemed to embody the ascetic values of a rapidly disappearing time. Reared to be a discreet diplomat rather than a public politician, he was recognized by leaders of the Comunión to be a relatively uncharismatic figure and an undistinguished speaker. His son, in contrast, embodied youthful energy, gave speeches in a most competent manner, and appeared highly adroit at playing the political game. If Carlism needed a skillful leader to steer its progress within the modern Spain that was already emerging, then Carlos Hugo was the man for the task.

Any serious candidate to the Carlist kingship was meant to "personify the values of the monarchy." As Carlos Hugo himself proclaimed, "A prince is worthy to the extent that he goes in the lead [*va el primero*]. However, if princes do not have to be superendowed and cannot, therefore, be the first in everything, they ought to be the first in fulfilling their duties. Hence a prince who impoverishes his mission in life to the extent of reducing it to the simple bearing of a title does not deserve to call himself a prince."[2] An aspirant to the throne had to prove himself qualified for the position by his conduct as much as by his parentage. In order to demonstrate that Carlos Hugo could amply fulfill this regal requirement, partisan periodicals stressed the years and variety of his scholastic education: he had finished his baccalaureate in Quebec, and had studied law at the Sorbonne, economics at Oxford, and sociology at Cologne University. They boasted of his linguistic gifts: he was said to speak French, English, German, and Spanish fluently, and to have a conversational command of Italian and Portuguese. They emphasized his wide range of experience: the month he had spent down an Asturian mine; his attachment to the Deutschbank, where he had worked with the former chancellor of the country, Ludwig Erhard; and the two years he spent studying the economic and social problems of various European countries that he visited with his father. At times, his journeying from one place to another could occur at a vertiginous rate. On one occasion, *Montejurra* claimed, he lunched in Santander, had tea in Madrid, took an aperitif in Milan, dined in Vienna, slept in Frankfurt, and breakfasted in Paris.

Carlos Hugo's loyal scribes also gave much space to events where he displayed his vitality and masculinity. In Carlos Hugo's own words, "What in an ordinary citizen is heroism, in a prince ought to come naturally."[3] He liked physically strenuous, sometimes dangerous sports, such as skiing and parachuting, and once he even ran with the bulls in the Pamplonan fiesta of Sanfermines. He neither smoked nor drank much, though photographs of him at home often included a bottle of *pacharán* (sloe anis), a distinctively "Navarrese" drink, prominently placed in the background. These diligent journalists heavily publicized any occasion where he showed his commitment to the cause and his concern to deepen his knowledge of the country. There are articles on his visits to Carlist Circles, factories, chemical plants, trade fairs, the opera, and even an art gallery, as well as on his meetings with Franco, cabinet ministers, city mayors, and other important persons. At times the journalists credited Carlos Hugo with singular, only hinted-at capacities. In one press photo, the prince, on a factory visit, watches a man operating a machine. The caption reads, "The look goes beyond pure observation."[4]

The publicity given by Carlist journals did not of course reveal Carlos Hugo's "real" character, but rather the abstract ideas of personality valued by his loyal subjects. However, he was not just playing a role when he appeared in public. For, unlike an actor who can relax after a performance and return to his usual life, a prince such as Carlos Hugo was expected to manifest regal values at every moment, whether at open events or behind closed doors. There was not supposed to be any distinction between his public and private lives. Indeed, given the unrelenting publicity trumpeting his almost every act, Carlos Hugo could not have had much of a "private" life, even if he had so wished. Partisan journalists could, however, choose not to mention certain details: they did not admit that Carlos Hugo never rid his Castilian of a light French accent, while those close to him say he was clever and very hardworking but could also be cold and calculating.[5]

Like the present queen of England,[6] Carlos Hugo benefited from a mystique far more powerful than that enjoyed by any film star or successful politician. He had "glamour," in its original sense of "a magical or fictitious beauty attaching to a person." For he was simultaneously an ordinary man with pursuits and interests any Carlist could identify with, and an extraordinary one given the irrevocable nature of his royalty. After all, the Borbón-Parmas were the only family in the movement whose claim to status relied partly but necessarily on the criterion of birth. However, though he stood at the top of the social tree, he was identified not with the aristocracy but with the common people. He was both royal *and* human, different from yet the same as any man.

Carlist journalists liked to publicize his continuing friendship with the Asturian miners with whom he once worked for a brief period. Villagers who met with Carlos Hugo in informal meetings emphasize his apparent simplicity, his lack of pretension, and how easy he was to talk with. This princely openness to common folk only increased the sense of mystique. As Nairn points out about the British royal family, "The inner meaning of the belief that 'They're just like us' ('ordinary beings,' 'got their own problems,' etc.) is the certainty that they are not, and cannot be conceivably be just like us. . . . The actual sense is more like: 'They're just like us *in some ways* (and what *this* implies is how absolutely extraordinary—unlike us—the rest must be).' Thus—since what's marvellous about them being like us is that it shows they aren't just like us— each new glimpse or revelation can only reinforce the glamour rather than dissipating it."[7] The glamour of royalty enhanced the otherwise banal details of the Borbón-Parmas's daily lives, transforming their performance of quotidian tasks into objects of general interest. That some of Carlos Hugo's sisters were physically attractive only added to this glamour. An early adviser to the prince fell in love with one of them and had to be quickly transferred.[8]

The story of Carlos Hugo's engagement to Princess Irene of the Netherlands smoothly fits into the context set by the created image of him as an exemplary prince. Educated Carlists today agree that the story has all the ingredients of a good romance. A young prince still awaits his first serious girlfriend. The independent daughter of a Protestant queen comes to Spain. The prince starts to woo her, in secret. Rumors circulate: the Dutch princess is in love with a foreign prince; she is going out with a Spanish grandee. Her parents oppose the match: the man is a prince, but where is his future crown? Irene struggles against the opinions of both her family and parliament. Carlos Hugo refuses to lay his commitment to Spain aside. For the sake of her love, she converts and gives up her claim to the throne. But the marriage cannot be held in Holland. On hearing of the engagement Carlists throughout the country, greatly stirred by this tale of romance and female self-sacrifice, of a princess who has forsaken her crown for the sake of her heart, hold solemn Te Deums to bless the union. Three thousand travel by train, car, or chartered plane to Rome to attend the ceremony. A crowd of 20,000 gather outside the church, and the service is transmitted live by Eurovision. To Carlists, their prince was acting in a manner befitting his position, and in marrying the regal daughter of the world's second-richest woman, he had gained a great prize.[9]

If I give so much space in my account to the work of Carlos Hugo, that is because Carlist values multiply the action of the youthful pretender, giving him a disproportionate political effect. Centrally placed thanks to an accident of birth, his royal status granted him an apical authority to legitimate ideological evolution—a potentially very advantageous privilege denied to any Carlist commoner, no matter how prominent. Carlos Hugo was well aware of his position from the first; writing to a Spanish friend in 1957, he stated, "I am convinced that Carlism has to undergo a revolution and to change its form. As it is now, it is incompatible with the needs of today. This revolution is one only I can bring about."[10] For Carlists, the legitimacies of blood and of conduct, embodied together in one person, constituted a potent combination without equal. One senior traditionalist said to me that until Carlos Hugo's leanings toward socialism became patent, "What the prince said was the gospel truth." Die-hard reactionaries might argue with their regal leader in private meetings, but in acknowledgement of his position and out of their great respect for Don Javier, they did not dare to voice their comments in public. Rather than criticize him in print, they wrote generally worded articles reaffirming the principles of traditionalism. The only occasion on which a subject came near to open censure of his prince was an article by Raimundo de Miguel, a close associate of Don Javier, in which he merely suggested that there were certain topics on which a responsible prince should not opine.[11] At the same time, those who criticized Carlos Hugo even in closed meetings were sometimes forcibly reminded by assertive senior *huguistas* of the duties of loyal subjects. As one wrote to the increasingly restive traditionalist General Luis Ruiz Hernández in 1968, "[Don Javier and Carlos Hugo] are the only ones with the authority to correct deviations or to judge loyalties. Only they, and the persons in whom they have deposited their confidence, are the definers of, and responsible for, the official performance of the Comunión. Whosoever fails to recognize this principle, however much merit they may have previously gained, has ceased to be Carlist."[12] Leaders of the Comunión were on occasion prepared to demonstrate in a highly dramatic manner the special status of Carlos Hugo. On his second appearance on the summit of Montejurra, some of them advertised their fealty to this youthful prince by theatrically falling to their knees in front of him. Some of the crowd followed suit.

The power of Carlos Hugo's example was enough in itself to coax some prematurely retired Carlists to return to the movement and to persuade some uncertain conservatives to follow the new party line, though they might find the sudden change traumatic. Manuel Rego Nieto, a prominent Galician Carlist, admits that he and his fellows painfully "reconverted" from traditionalism to *progresismo* because of a personal meeting with Carlos Hugo.[13] The prince even managed to win over some of his father's most outspoken opponents: at a meeting in Barcelona with some of the *sivattistas*, he succeeded in seducing them away from the Regency of Estella.[14] Others were apparently not so hard to woo: one distinguished former *requeté* is quoted by María-

Teresa de Borbón-Parma as saying that he had at first followed the ideological shift of Carlism purely *because* it had been preached by Carlos Hugo; only later had he come to understand and to appreciate it.[15]

Leaders acknowledged that the enthusiasm of the rank and file depended partially, but still significantly, on the image of a royal personage at the helm. They recognized that the majority preferred the rights and values of Carlism to be personified in a fitting pretender. As one of the Carlist deputies to the Cortes claimed, the Carlist people had always had an intensely emotional bond with their standard-bearers.[16] The level of some followers' enthusiasm could at times reach almost delirious heights. One villager of Cirauqui complained to me about the excitement any news of Carlos Hugo could cause among her Carlist neighbors. When the woman next door told her she wanted to send the prince a gift on the birth of his first child, the villager could not contain her irritation. "Shut up! You filthy creature!" she cried, "You never gave me anything at the baptisms of my children!"

As partisan journalists pointed out, without "the extraordinary example of our singular prince," who evinced "the traditional virtues par excellence," Carlism would appear to be like so many other, merely political doctrines: it would lose much of its distinctiveness. However, this regally based difference was not neutral, for it brought with it a sense of superiority: having a royal family at its head meant that Carlism was not merely dissimilar to most other parties, but better as well. As Carlos Hugo stated in a speech in 1967, "We are the best because we have a king and not a president."[17] This somewhat narcissistic approach led some Carlists to see others as envious. On the evening after one Montejurra, a female Carlist of Cirauqui, still dressed in a white beret and clothes, went to buy fresh milk from a neighbor. The milk seller, who was a Basque nationalist, tried to make polite conversation by referring to the presence of the royal princesses at the ceremony. "What class you Carlists have!" she exclaimed. The Margarita smartly replied, "You! You're one of the bad ones! I'd grab you by the neck and throw you into the street! You lot don't have anything so beautiful of which you can be proud!" She clutched her purchase, turned on her heel, and walked out.

Although the prince enjoyed the legitimacy of birth, he underscored his connections with former Carlist kings, all but two of whom had been called "Carlos," by occasionally referring to Carlos VII as "my ancestor" and by officially changing his name in the Paris registry from "Hugues" to "Carlos Hugo." The change is noteworthy, for in Unamuno's *Paz en la guerra*, one character says, "that name carried all the hopes and memories of some, and the rancor of others. Carlos! Name full of history, evoker of years of youthfulness, of nature, and of the land [*verdura*]!"[18] Combining respect for his father with the remembrance of his predecessors, Carlos Hugo named his first-born son

"Carlos Javier." His presentation of his infant to a Carlist crowd at a French village near one of the family castles and Irene's subsequent bringing of the child to Madrid was meant to signify "the fulfillment of the pact between the Carlist people and its dynasty." The Navarrese Carlist journal *Montejurra* published several photographs of the princess with her child wearing a red beret.[19] The birth of an heir showed that Carlos Hugo was not neglecting his duties toward the future. Carlism could continue into the next century, with a new generation of the Borbón-Parmas at its head.

Familial Values and Extended Kinship

In the early 1960s conservative Carlists still spoke of their king as a "father" to his people, and of God as "the supreme King of Carlism."[20] But the notions of paternalism and almost absolute authority underlying the reciprocally modeled metaphors of the divine, domestic, and Carlist families were gradually becoming more and more out of place. Within the Comunión, the nature of authority was being openly called into question by progressives, who were trying to replace the unreformed traditionalist emphasis on hierarchy with more democratic conceptions. According to these youthful activists' notions of political organization, there was little room for conservative *santones* within the movement, while the king came to be seen less as an independent autarch and more as a helmsman responsive to his people's needs.

Within the Church, the key cause of change was the liberalizing decisions passed by the Second Vatican Council. Up to then, the Virgin had played a crucial intermediary role between the Omnipotent and the people. But now the cult of Marianism began to decline, and the divinity ceased to be represented as a transcendent monarch ruling over his realm and was instead understood to be immanent in the world.[21] He was incarnate in humanity and participated in the suffering of people who were bound together in "the Brotherhood of Christ." God was no longer above us; he was among us.

As the people of Cirauqui will state today, relations within families, between fathers and their children, started to become far more relaxed from about this time. Major reasons for the change in this structure of authority were the increased educational opportunities for the young and the rise of new sources of employment as the Deputation of Navarre stimulated a belated program of industrialization. Many offspring, no longer forced to follow in their parents' footsteps, sought jobs in factories and offices in Pamplona and in the nearby towns. Many of them, thanks to their years of schooling, were also more knowledgeable than their parents about what was happening in the world beyond the village boundaries. The old paternal style of authoritarianism came increasingly to be seen as inappropriate; sons and daughters became more independent, and fathers became closer to their children. As one man put it to me in 1990, "the father has come down from his pedestal."[22]

Within the royal family itself, Don Javier and Carlos Hugo were not portrayed as a strict figure of authority commanding a meekly obedient son, but as a fatherly guide watching over an energetic but mature young man. At the same time, the homology between heavenly and earthly realms did not disappear; it was just suggested in another manner. The familial division of tasks represented in the image of Don Javier supervising from afar while Carlos Hugo was active spreading the word to his people bore strong Biblical overtones of God the Father looking down on his son's progress in Israel. Born in 1930, Carlos Hugo was even similar in age to Jesus during His last three active years.

The existence of the royal family might make Carlism different from, and better than, other political movements, but the Borbón-Parmas were not represented as superior to other Carlist families. Rather, they were "an exemplary and united family." Theirs was the first among Spanish hearths: it was simply primary, not above others. Their royalty did not impede their humanity. Just as Don Javier and Carlos Hugo were represented as personifying the male virtues of decision and activity, so Don Javier's wife Doña Magdalena and her daughters were seen to evince the female virtues of empathy and care for others. The children of Don Javier had been brought up by "our much loved Doña Magdalena" in such a mindful manner that "they know how to feel love for the people, understanding their needs."[23] All the charitable work done by her daughters in Spanish organizations and publicized in Carlist publications fits into this feminine mold. In the performance of their duties and the fulfillment of their obligations, the different members of the royal family were meant to set a standard by which male and female Carlists could measure themselves morally.

The Borbón-Parmas, together with their supporters, were said to make up the "the great Carlist family," a loose social unit bound by common history, genealogical persistence, and an effusive emotional bond. Like the relationships within a close-knit kin group, those within the Comunión were presented as mutual rather than instrumental: people did not become Carlists for the sake of self-interested gain. The metaphor of "the great Carlist family" was a means to emphasize the strong links between the people and the Borbón-Parmas. At the same time, it was both an emblem of historical homogeneity differentiating Carlists from outsiders and a template for social relations within the movement. It was a particularly resonant metaphor in the Basque Country, where the image of the intergenerational family working as one economic unit and living together under the same roof had long been extolled in

Basquist writings. According to Raimundo de Miguel, there was a real sense of affection and intimacy between the Carlist king and his people, *because* the monarchy was based on a familial institution. In contrast, a cold and impersonal state aroused feelings of suspicion and animosity. Just as members of a family remained loyal to one another, in good times or bad, so, supposedly, had the royal and greater Carlist families remained faithful to one another over the last 130 years, despite the sacrifices they had all made. Indeed, according to another traditionalist writer, the "truly astonishing" loyalty of Carlists was ultimately based on and fed from the "warmhearted" loyalty of the Carlist royals to their historic mission and the Carlist people.[24] As one eulogizer of Montejurra put it, "Carlism has something that makes all we Carlists *hermanos* [siblings, brothers, sisters], and which allows us to say to our prince, without it being a metaphor but a palpable reality, that all we Carlists form part of the royal family, to which we feel so linked that, without losing respect, we commit the greatest breaches of protocol, simply out of affection."[25] On the mountaintop one year, Zavala said that just as families have their big fiestas, so the Carlists gathered annually *en famille* at Montejurra.[26] The annual ceremony, with its image of unity, fellowship, and communal conviviality, was meant to objectify the metaphor, to reveal the discourse of family as an evident reality.

The concept of "family," however, is open to several readings. Besides signifying social reproduction or kin-based harmony, it can also refer to a collection of individuals joined by blood but separated by opposed attitudes. It can connote both dutiful children *and* rebellious offspring. The metaphor of "the great Carlist family" was designed to promote unity and to mask the differences between *javieristas,* and even between Don Javier's various children. Articles by Carlists on their royal family often failed to mention his younger son, Don Sixto, and his eldest daughter, Doña Francisca, both of whom maintained right-wing views and did not assist Carlos Hugo in his project of reform. Enemies of democracy could exploit this potentially subversive element to shatter the symbolism of familial harmony and divide the movement. Shortly after the death of Franco, that is what they did.

Clarifying Carlist Discourse

Progressives tried to mask change, or at least to smooth its effects, both by reaffirming the central role of the royal family within their community and by claiming that they were maintaining fundamental Carlist concepts. Although their political vision was couched within the terms of a renovated Carlist vocabulary, they argued that they were not breaking with the past and creating a new Carlist discourse; they were just, in their own terms, "clarifying" the lexicon of their movement's ideology. So when traditionalists complained that their vocabulary was influenced by political philosophies alien to Carlism, progressives could reply that it was their opponents, not themselves, who were misrepresenting the "true" traditions of their movement: "There are those who say that the terms that the Carlists use are terms imposed or taken from Marxism. Since when have the concepts of liberty, of participation, and of democracy been foreign to Carlism?"[27] According to progressives, what their critics failed to appreciate was that it was not Carlism that was changing, but rather the parameters within which political life was conducted: "Let them call us what they wish, but we are what we are [*somos lo que somos y estamos*] and we will remain in the same position in which we find ourselves."[28] Thus progressives argued that they were changing neither their philosophy nor their vocabulary, merely elucidating them. As far as they were concerned, the key words employed by Carlists were not, despite appearances, being modified; it was only that their meanings were, at long last, being illuminated.

"The Carlist *pueblo*," for instance, was to remain a central term in the speeches and writings of Carlist leaders, for its inherent vagueness could be exploited to provide lexical continuity between old and new visions of the movement. In everyday discourse, "*pueblo*" means both a place and the people who belong to that place. Thus to conservatives, *el pueblo Carlista* signified *a* people, a geographically definable community of politically like-minded persons (including its local upper class) who automatically passed their allegiance on to their children. Some Carlist spokespersons liked to assert the distinctiveness of their movement by pointing out that Carlism, unlike conventional political parties, had both its own program and its own *pueblo*. In reaction to this traditionalist usage, progressives preferred to draw out the more socialist meaning of the term: *pueblo* in the sense of plebs, a social class exploited by others. Although nineteenth-century Carlists sometimes used this vulgar sense of the term "*pueblo*," leaders in those days tended to regard the mass as a group of souls who were meant to play only a strictly limited role in the business of the nation. Twentieth-century progressives, in contrast, wanted to replace this conservative notion of interclass harmony with one of a single class ready to agitate for its just deserts. To them, the Carlist *pueblo* was not meant to be passive, but active and participatory.[29]

The notion of "martyr" was similarly updated. According to progressives, to be a martyr for contemporary Carlism did not mean dying on the field of battle, or heroically suffering hideous tortures at the hands of the enemy. Instead of throwing away one's life in a grand, fatal gesture, modern-day martyrs had to labor steadily for the movement. Some veterans might still be speaking of "the eloquent plebiscite of blood, the most authentic vote of national will,"[30] but most progressives saw things rather differently. As one proclaimed at the annual commemoration of the Mártires de la Tradición:

> To be a martyr is simply to make a sacrifice for a cause, in our case for the cause of a regime of justice and liberty. That is to say, we can and we should all be Mártires de la Tradición. We are living in difficult times, times of persecution and of imprisonment, times of negation of the three basic liberties—political, regional, and syndical—on which a democratic and just state should be based. For that reason, he who today is not a martyr, that is to say, is not committed to the communal sacrifice, is not Carlist. As an example of this commitment and of this sacrifice, we have all the royal family and all those Carlists who are suffering repression in all its forms: from jail to exile. . . . Of course these cases of imprisonment and physical persecution are of the few; they correspond to the activist vanguard to which we do not all belong, nor are called to belong; the many should embody this struggle and this sacrifice in a more prosaic, but equally necessary, form. . . .
>
> I believe that on this day of the Mártires de la Tradición, it is right that we should remember the martyrs of yesteryear, but above all we should commit ourselves to imitate the martyrs of today, each of us doing it within our own sphere of action and according to our possibilities.[31]

In this broadly inclusive interpretation of the term, not just those who dressed for war and for likely death, but any Carlist, whether male or female, could be a martyr, each in his or her own way.

Perhaps the central term that progressives were in the late 1960s concerned to retain was the one constituting the very name of their movement's established political philosophy: "tradition." They liked to iterate that traditionalism did not equal "immobilism," for tradition and progress were mutually dependent; there could be no tradition without progress and, vice versa, no progress without tradition. Tradition should thus be viewed not as a state but as a process, which represented "the action of people in history." Its content, progressives argued, was not timeless, but subject to agency and historical circumstance. One did not break with tradition; one built from it.[32] As was pointed out, the highly respected traditionalist ideologue, Vázquez de Mella, had said much the same thing over eighty years before: "Tradition is the continuity of life and does not signify, not even etymologically, stasis, but movement. . . . Progress invents, discovers an unknown truth and the derivations of that unknown, and that truth is conserved, through the work of generations, which transmit them to their successors, and an intermediate, rebellious generation has no right to suspend the work of previous generations."[33] Carlos Hugo was emphatic on this issue: "Tradition is not the repetition of the past.

It is that part of the past that survives in order to make itself the future"; "When new problems arise, it is necessary to invent new traditions."[34] This claimed openness of traditionalism to the possibilities of the present meant that there could be more than one version of the philosophy: "Traditionalism is not, and never has been, a rigid unity of positions, but rather a historical vision of Spain, . . . which allows the richest variety of postures within itself."[35] Thus the traditionalism of the Comunión could not be defined in a dogmatic, constrictive manner by conservatives. Rather, it was to be understood as sufficiently ample to accommodate both conservative and progressive interpretations.

Progressives also emphasized the continuity of Catholic standards within the Carlist code. God had always been the ultimate referent for the movement's ethics. According to Carlos Hugo and his supporters, He would remain so, but now in a manner more appropriate to present-day concerns. Progressives claimed that conservatives chose to follow not the edicts of the recently concluded Second Vatican Council, but of the medieval Council of Trent, and that they characterized God as a distant, transcendental deity who evinced timeless values, ones that legitimated a static conception of society (with themselves at the top, or near it). Instead of lauding this self-promoting conception of the Absolute, progressives preferred to concentrate on the figure of Jesus as a man in the world, as one who wished to improve the lot of the common people. He did not believe in stasis, but in steady evolution, achieved through continual struggle. Thus *Dios* would remain an integral part of the Carlist motto, though His meaning for the world was open to interpretation by earthlings.[36]

While progressives liked to profess continuity between the past and their present, at root here lie opposed conceptions of the Carlist world. Traditionalists classified according to their starkly Manichaean scheme of irreconcilable opposites where the good, Catholic, traditional Spain was stacked against the bad, Protestant, socialist/communist/anarchist anti-Spain. Those who thought in the terms of this crude conceptual scheme had no need for debate or reflection. Little wonder that their prose, empty of self-criticism, is triumphalist and, when not punctuated by a series of militaristic exclamations (such as "¡Firmes! ¡Carlistas!"), is weighted by a seemingly unending series of laudatory tributes. It is the literary style of dictatorship, deaf to dissenting voices. Perhaps its finest Navarrese exponent was López-Sanz, writer of a rolling, dramatic prose that, if not stentorian, has its own rhythms, a charged vocabulary, and an almost convincing tone of passionate authority. The versifiers who eulogized Montejurra were not of the same standard.

Progressive propagandists, reacting against the grandiloquent, almost baroque clichés so beloved by conservative speakers, used a pedestrian prose

that seemed to be inspired, though at several removes, by Marx and his inter-
preters. In pointed contrast to the directorial and declamatory style of their
immediate political forefathers, progressives liked to boast that *their* unifying
feature was an open-ended critical stance, both of self and others. Thinking
that they had dismantled the dichotomous schemes of their conservative opponents, these activist youths portrayed themselves as people who engaged
with the problems of the contemporary world, as people who sought for new
political solutions through a process of questioning and discussion. According
to them, their vision was dynamic, not static, and as they learned to publicly
deprecate individualism, they came to laud the values of dialogue, mutual
respect, and collective decision.

In sum, while leading progressives were prepared to stress continuity between previous versions of Carlism and theirs, the continuity they perceived
and promoted was of a very particular kind. As some conservatives were later
to declare, progressives were thus in effect guilty of the very same prescriptiveness that they charged others with.

Chapter Seven

Past Masters

Carlism is not a purely dynastic and regressive movement, as the lying, well-paid liberal historians insist on saying. It is a free and popular movement in defense of traditions much more liberal and regionalist than the official, possessive liberalism, infested as it is with simpletons who copy the French Revolution. The Carlists defended the best legal Spanish traditions, those of the fueros and the legitimate Cortes, which were trampled on by the monarchist absolutism and the centralist absolutism of the liberal state. They represented the great fatherland as the sum of the local fatherlands, with their own peculiarities and traditions. There is no country in Europe that does not contain residues of ancient populations and popular forms that have been knocked down by the advance of History. . . . In France it was the Bretons and in Spain, in a much more voluminous and national manner, the defenders of Don Carlos. Carlist traditionalism had some authentically popular and national bases, of peasants, petty notables, and clergy, while liberalism was embodied in militarism, capitalism (the new classes of merchants and speculators), the latifundist aristocracy, and secularized interests that in the majority of cases thought with a French head or translated, in a confused way, from German.

An ancient movement undergoing radical reorganization needs a new past to match the future it is fashioning for itself. The novel goals being set by its renovators require legitimation by "rediscovered" historical precedents. An uninterrupted unity of purpose is thus made to stretch from a movement's genesis through the present up to the advent of their version of the millennium, which, its proponents hope, is not too far off. To that end, a collection of progressive historians reanalyzed the Carlist past, for the sake of the future, on *huguista* lines. Ever keen to rewrite Carlist chronology, they delighted in quoting any favorable comments made in the last century by highly respected intellectuals. Perhaps their favorite was the one above, penned by Karl Marx.[1]

It is a truism that all histories are constructed, that all have their focal points and their blind spots. No single account can encompass all details, and selection, by definition, entails interpretation. However, though the *huguista* telling of the traditionalist tale is a highly partisan reading of the past, it is still important to recount and to assess this historiography, if only because of the way it became a significant part of the lived reality of party members. Progressive historiography gave them an identifiably modern way of understanding the past, in a Marxist-inspired language similar to that used by would-be allies on the Left. A new vision of old times, it helped to secure them against potential criticism from possible bedfellows. Metaphorically, it was a means to cover one's back while continuing to look forward.[2]

The History of Carlism, According to the Progressives

The leading light of these progressive revisionists was Josep Carles Clemente, a Catalan journalist and editor with a degree in contemporary history. Born into a non-Carlist family, he had joined the AET in the mid-1950s because it had then seemed the only student organization to be mounting any opposition to the regime. Besides contributing to a variety of progressive journals, Clemente became a member of Carlos Hugo's inner circle, with the special responsibility of managing Carlist relations with the press. Other progressives, such as José Maria Zavala, Evaristo Olcina, Carlos Hugo, and his sister María-Teresa, who also lent their aid to the task of rewriting Carlist history, were neither as well read nor as prolific as him. Rather than provide their own original accounts, they helped to disseminate the historical message that Clemente was putting together.

These academic manqués wanted to rephrase the history of Carlism and to clear it of the cobwebs spun by their misguided predecessors. In contrast to the quasiromantic approach of traditionalist narrators, these modern-day revisionists did not wish to compile a chronicle of dashing pretenders, theocratic crusaders, and unreflective reactionaries. Instead of putting together a gory catalog of individual glories won on the battlefield, they wanted to present an analytical, social history of popular demands. They wished to help steer the movement away from a bloodthirsty exaltation of violence and military achievement toward a more pacific celebration of the Carlist people's sustained political commitment. The point of their efforts was to laud the life of Carlism, not to rebury, once again, its many dead.

Traditionalist historians had merely romanticized the Carlist past. Official historians had done far worse; they had portrayed it unjustly. According to Clemente, the work of these historians—"liberals of the time, adherents to the Alfonsine monarchy, political absolutists, and partisans to the centralism of the *Ancien Régime*"—had given their readers a false image of the nature of Carlism. Failing to understand the "true" nature of the movement, they had confused the authentic version with those bastardized forms perpetrated by intrusive outsiders, and thus they had misrepresented it as essentially clerical, legitimist, and right wing.

As Clemente put it, one unfortunate consequence of what he called Carlism's "democratic" structure and its respect for freedom of opinion had been its frequent infiltration by interlopers. On several occasions, self-interested conservatives had succeeded in commandeering the movement and diverting it from its true ideological course. These nefarious intruders could be classed into two main groups, integrists and traditionalists. The integrists who had inserted themselves into Carlism in its first years, and who had "infected" its ideology, were senior ecclesiastics and their sympathizers. As fiercely reactionary Catholics, they had called for the reinstitution of the Inquisition, advocated a "pure absolutism," and had opposed even the moderate reforms of Fernando VII. The early traditionalists were a slightly more heterogeneous band. They included several sectors of the nobility, important landowners, and members of the well-off who eyed the economic innovations of the liberals with great suspicion. It was, above all, thanks to these moderate absolutists and royalists that the dynastic claim of Don Carlos, and later his descendants, had become so central to the movement. Unlike the integrists, many of these traditionalists were pragmatists who were occasionally prepared to bend their principles for the sake of practical gains. The epitome of this group was General Maroto, who had ended the First Carlist War in the Basque area in such a shameful manner, negotiating with the enemy and shooting fellow officers opposed to appeasement.

According to Clemente's imaginative reinterpretation of nineteenth-century Spain, "genuine" Carlism was a movement of "the people" (i.e., of the poor, the impoverished, and the less well-off), untainted by the errors of either pure or moderate absolutism. To him, these humble countrymen, who constituted the core of the movement, were the only true Carlists. They were, in Carlos Hugo's phrase, "espadrille socialists": unable to afford leather soles, they had to go about in hemp-soled shoes.[3] The only authentic Carlists, they had never been greatly concerned with the dynastic question and had supported pretenders only because, given the nature of leadership in those days, they had had need of a royal champion. They were not, at root, monarchists. Nor could they be judged rightists, since they had not tried to preserve privileges. Far from wishing to maintain the exclusive rights of certain advantaged groups, they had wanted to create a just society based on their *fueros*. Unlike the integrists, whom Clemente considered capitalist, conservative, Manichaean, and deeply bigoted, true Carlists were socialist, democratic, and far more tolerant of others. These lovers of freedom wished to retain the *fueros* because they safeguarded a degree of both political and economic autonomy at the local and provincial levels. To them, the standardizing plans the liberals wished to impose would diminish their liberties, threaten their livelihoods, and subject them to a centralizing oligarchy.

Clemente and like-minded progressives extended their highly original re-interpretation of Spanish history even further by asserting that the supporters of Isabel, Fernando VII's daughter, had fought against change; it was they, not the Carlists, who had desired to keep the hierarchical structure imposed by her father. Thus the wars of the last century were not to be understood as armed conflicts led by competing contenders for the throne, but as radical confrontations pitting the supporters of a federal and populist Spain against those liberals who defended the idea of a bureaucratic state divided by class. These armed conflicts were to be seen as clashes between a Carlist concern for change and a conservative vision anchored to the past. They were not to be compared with contemporary legitimist disputes in other European countries, but with the "revolutionary" wars of our own time, in which a people rises up against its oppressors.

Clemente viewed the internal history of Carlism as one of sustained struggle between the three sections he had identified—true believers, integrists, and traditionalists—with members of each group constantly battling to occupy the moral and political high ground. Sometimes one faction would win hegemony, sometimes another. During the First Carlist War, integrists and traditionalists had control. Afterward, they gradually integrated themselves within the liberal regime. On the fall of the monarchy in the late 1860s, members of these two groups returned to the fold and participated in the Second Carlist War. After the liberal victory in that conflict, the contemporary leader of the integrists quarreled with Carlos VII over the need to modernize the political program of the movement. He left Carlism and took most of his supporters with him. The next schism came in 1919, when the leading traditionalist ideologue, Vázquez de Mella, and his *mellistas* deserted the cause to set up their own political group.

The three sections of the movement came together again only when, in the 1930s, they were faced with a common, powerful enemy: anti-Church Republicans set on change. Once again, integrists and traditionalists wrested control of the movement. While spokesmen of these two groups thundered against the policies of the left-wing government, the Carlist people did not at first participate in the conspiracy to overthrow the Republic. They eventually sided with the insurgents because the increasingly violent antireligious offensive of the Left pushed them toward the Right. "If it had not been for this simple detail," Clemente claimed, "the Carlists would have fought on the other side."[4]

After the war, the integrists and traditionalists remained at the reins and collaborated with the Franquist regime that was so hated by the rank and file. But once Don Javier had finally recovered from his wartime incarceration, he returned to Spain, where he realized that true Carlists had little say in the movement he headed. Opposed to Franco and the Falange, he expelled from the movement all those who accepted posts within the regime. He also decided to send his son to Spain, with the task of reorganizing Carlism and initiating "the return to ideological authenticity." Subsequently, in the course of a long series of internal battles, most integrists and traditionalists were forced out of the movement, whose popular, foral nature could thus be finally and definitively reestablished. Out of the remnants of the Comunión Tradicionalista arose the Partido Carlista, a modern political party that advocated socialism, global self-government, and the autonomy of the various nationalities that constituted the Spanish state. The infiltrators had been banished, and the true ideology of Carlism had at last been "clarified."[5]

To bolster their reinterpretation of the movement's past, progressive historians liked to emphasize the occasions when Carlism had shown itself to be something other than an ultraorthodox, extreme right-wing movement. In 1860, for instance, Carlos VI had issued a manifesto that stated, "The liberal system has not assisted the people in any way and it is no more than a new feudalism of the middle classes represented by lawyers and orators. . . . The most honorable undertaking for a prince is to free the productive classes and the disinherited from the tyranny of those oppressors who govern the nation in the name of liberty."[6] Shortly before the outbreak of the Second Carlist War, leading Catalan Carlists had agreed to meet with José Alsina, deputy to the Cortes, senior representative of the Sociedad de Trabajadores (Society of Workers), and founder of the International in Spain. He pledged the workers' support for the Carlist cause in return for a quantity of money. Carlos VII regarded the proposal sympathetically. But when the Freemasons, to whom the Sociedad was indebted, heard of these maneuvers, they immediately and successfully sought to undermine them.[7] In the 1910s Jaime III founded the Sindicato Libre (Free Syndicate), whose goal, according to progressives, was the abolition of capitalism. He welcomed the establishment of the Second Republic with joy and suggested to his followers that they join the recently constituted Federación de Naciones Ibericas (Federation of Iberian Nations).[8]

Progressive historians, in an effort to show that it was not just they who regarded the Carlists of the last century as socialist in style, liked to quote the commentaries made on the movement by Karl Marx in the 1850s and by Unamuno at the turn of the century. Like Marx, Unamuno saw Carlism as a quasisocialist movement of the people opposed to the centralizing liberals. Unamuno also differentiated between this popular form of Carlism, which he regarded as one of the "intimate expressions of the Spanish people," and "historic Carlism," which was best characterized by integrism, "that scholastic tumor, that misery of babbling graduates, canons, priests, and fawning sophists and rationalizers."[9] To back up the progressive case a little more, María-Teresa de Borbón-Parma cited in her brief history of Carlism part of the anti-Carlist document published by some local Catalan liberals at the close of the War of the Early Risers: "Nor is it constitutional monarchy, such as we have, or as Don Carlos pretends to have. No, fellow mountain-dwellers: it is deadly communism in all its extension and horrors; it is this world-disorganizing system; it is, in the end, *the terrible conflict between the haves and the have-nots.*" [10]

In order to solve a problem of their own making, progressive historians had at times to employ extrahistorical notions. The nub of their difficulty was the following: they wished to claim that true Carlists had always adhered to the same basic ideas (such as socialism and democracy), though the early Carlists had never employed such terms and had, in fact, gone to war under the banner of DIOS, PATRIA, REY, FUEROS. Thus the progressives, in order to demonstrate that the Carlist people of the 1830s were fighting for the same fundamental political reasons as their *huguista* descendants, felt the need to claim that the true Carlists of the last century had unconsciously "intuited" that liberalism was capitalist and therefore to be opposed. Zavala argued that the early Carlists had supported Carlos V only because they knew "instinctively" that he was opposed to the absolutist oligarchy then effectively controlling the country.[11] Clemente used the same kind of claim in his attempt to explain why the *requetés* had battled against the Left in the Civil War. In his words, members of the Carlist youth wing had, in the early 1930s, "intuited" that the real reason behind the antagonism of their integrist leaders toward the Republic was economic more than religious, that they were organizing the Comunión as a military force in order to defend private property and capitalism. On the outbreak of war, they dutifully obeyed their superiors' order for them to participate in the insurgency, but "in their innermost being they intuited that their political chiefs were making a mistake; they did not understand how they, who had neither capital nor properties to defend, could sally forth to defend capitalism." [12] By using this kind of argument, progressive historians did not have to put words into the mouths of dead Carlists: instead they put capacities of political perception into their brains, capacities of which even their possessors had been unaware.

Assessing Progressives' History

Clemente and his peers were keen to criticize the ideologically self-serving work of their scholastic forebears. But in fact, their own particular compilation of the Carlist past suffers from the same general fault of politically guided group self-interest. This is unsurprising, given that they were paid politicos, not professional historians, and that their ultimate aim was to contribute to the promotion of *progresismo* rather than to produce a disinterested history devoid of passion or political purpose. Nevertheless, since they wished their writings to be taken seriously and not to be written off quickly as mere propaganda, they may still be judged according to commonly accepted standards of historical scholarship. And as such, their work may be found guilty of the sins of omission, gross simplification, prescriptiveness, misleading quotation, and misrepresentation.

Perhaps the most distinctive feature of progressive historiography is its patently prescriptive and exclusive definition of Carlism. Only the Carlism of the people, *as interpreted by the progressives,* was "genuine." Any other form was politically suspect and to be regarded as inauthentic. Of course it was just as easy, and as dictatorial, for traditionalists to counterargue, as some of them did, that *theirs* was the only true version of Carlism. They could claim, with some justification, that for most of the movement's history many Carlists had supported a traditionalist conception of the world and had fought against changes that threatened their customary way of life. To them, the progressives' prescription was a politically biased definition employed by *huguistas* in their bid for hegemony, and was to be derided as such.

Nineteenth-century Carlism was a complex phenomenon, resistant to any simple generalization. Clemente and his colleagues wished to portray the movement as one of a deprived "rural proletariat." While it is true that Carlism was used in some areas by the economically aggrieved as a way to express their discontent, many rural notables and minor aristocrats also participated in the movement, and many disadvantaged peasants did not. The social complexion of Carlism cannot be confined to the members of one particular subclass without grave distortion. The progressive historians also tried to characterize the Carlist Wars as ones of popular insurrection, yet support for the cause outside the greater Basque area was very patchy. Even in Navarre, the famed heartland of the movement, there were whole areas whose inhabitants did not heed Don Carlos's call. If progressive historians thought this socially and geographically uneven support for Carlism equaled "a people in arms," then it is a very reduced notion of "people" they have in mind.

For the sake of advancing their argument that the Carlist populace were motivated primarily by social and economic demands, progressive historians also asserted that the people espoused the cause of religion only because of their priests' self-interested harangues against the ecclesiastical reforms proposed by the liberals. From the evidence available,[13] however, one cannot easily disentangle defense of the *fueros* from support for the Church. If, as I tried to demonstrate in chapter 3, Navarrese villagers saw Carlism as a means to maintain their local traditions, then Catholicism was an integral part of that way of life. Defending the Church was of a piece with defending their own community. They did not want either tampered with.

The most daring aspect of the progressives' thesis was their notion of the Carlists as socialist revolutionaries, for the weight of historical evidence very strongly suggests that the Carlists were not attempting to overthrow the established order. On the contrary, they were, on the whole, trying to shore it up. They were not budding revolutionaries but classic counterrevolutionaries. It was not they but their enemies, the liberals, who were resolute for change and for modernization of the Spanish state. For instance, during the First Carlist War in the Basque area, much of which was controlled by Carlists, the occupying authorities made no attempt whatsoever to reform the pattern of land ownership. Although they did confiscate land from local liberals, the consequent financial gains did not go into the pockets of the rank and file but into the coffers of the Carlist administration. The point of these confiscatory measures was political and fiscal, not social. The policies of Don Carlos's government did not include the redistribution of land to the peasants who supported him. Apparently they agreed, or at least did not violently disagree, with this omission, for contrary to what happened in France on the outbreak of the revolution there, Basque peasants who joined the Carlist cause did not start occupying the land, burning notarial records, or destroying manorial archives. They did not want to overturn the present order; they wanted to maintain it.[14]

It is true that in certain highly specific areas, groups of peasants bearing the banner of Don Carlos did advocate communalist or even collectivist reforms. It is also the case that the overriding desires of some Carlist leaders to bring down the liberal system did at times bring them politically closer to certain republican groups. But these isolated examples do not justify labeling the whole movement as "socialist." Just because a popular reactionary movement wishes to improve the daily lot of the mass of its supporters, or at least to safeguard it against the threatened reforms of others, does not make that movement left wing.[15] As so many examples from the modern history of the European Right demonstrate, a party can be populist without being in any way socialist. A right-wing movement may choose to represent the social demands of the underprivileged without at the same time calling for an end to economic difference between classes. Don Carlos and his regal successors might have championed the cause of the Carlist people, but that did not mean they had to become bedfellows to politicos committed to a fundamental and equitable reorganization of Spanish society. Carlists wished to preserve the traditional hierarchy, not to eradicate it. They simply wished to ameliorate some of its worst aspects, not demolish the whole structure.

Leading Carlists knew who their "people" were, and that conception of community, though broadly based, did not include socialists. In the 1870s Carlists were more than ready to launch diatribes against the socially destructive effects of the industrialization that had begun to affect parts of the country, but they did not side with those workers whose way of life had been transformed by it. To them, the once happy and honest peasants who had left their rural hearths for jobs in urban factories had been irremediably corrupted by their new environment into ambitious, atheistic, and potentially very violent thieves. The Carlist ranks were largely filled by those impoverished smallholders, sharecroppers, and artisans who still clung to precapitalistic modes of production; the urban proletariat were not their brothers-in-arms but their most dangerous opponents. According to Carlist writers of the day, the hated socialists wanted to "devour" society and to do away with any individual rights to property. The liberals, whose ideas had engendered those of the socialists, were too timid to deal with their revolutionary threat. But the Carlists, as they liked to emphasize, were not so pusillanimous. They claimed to be the only national force strong enough to defend the social order and to squash the subversives by meeting the threat of violence with the reality of it.[16]

Progressive historians might have wished to argue that this antisocialist rhetoric reveals the contemporary attitudes and fears of the hegemonic elite rather than of the Carlist people. However, the history of Carlist activism in the turbulent Barcelona of the 1910s and 1920s suggests otherwise. During that period *jaimista* workers, who had kept the faith of their fathers when they had moved into the city, formed their own political bodies to advance the lot of the local proletariat. But they did not ally with the socialist groups then active in the area. In fact, they regarded them as among their worst political enemies. Employing a rhetoric that was almost as anticapitalist as it was antisocialist, these young Carlists looked forward to a vaguely formulated corporative future. They cannot be classed as revolutionaries because they defended the social (though not the economic) order: under the regime they wished to establish, property, family, and religion would all be safe from threat. Even the most radical among them never developed a full-fledged theory of class struggle nor resolutely advocated the triumph of labor over capital. As good Catholics, they bewailed the spiritual decadence of industrialized society, but at the same time they treated the clerical establishment with contempt, regarding it as the servant of the liberal status quo. Perpetuating the Carlist cult of violence and martyrdom, the trade unions they founded—the Sindicatos Libres—practiced a murderous form of pragmatic activism, which, besides strikes and boycotts, included the extermination of their anarcho-syndicalist opponents. Fighting their way to political prominence, these subversive pistol-bearing traditionalists came to be greatly feared by the Left, and by the Right, who viewed them as attempting to dominate through terror.[17] No one would have dared calling these gunmen socialists.

Clemente and other historically minded members of Carlos Hugo's crew are not just guilty of trying to impose a socialist predilection on earlier generations of Carlists, who in all probability would have rejected the imposition even if the full meaning of the term had been explained to them. They are also culpable of misrepresenting the authoritative non-Carlist commentators whose words they so loved to cite. As the quotation heading this chapter suggests, Marx clearly perceived the popular nature of early-nineteenth-century Carlism, but on no occasion did he call it socialist. While deriding the "imbecile legitimists" who supported the cause of that "Quixote of the auto-da-fe," Don Carlos, Marx was also aware of the dubious motives of some of those sheltering in the Carlist army: "It was the Carlists who gave origin to the *ladrones faceiosos* [insurgent thieves], that combination of robbery and pretended allegiance to an oppressed party in the State. The Spanish guerrillero of all times has had something of the robber since the time of Viriathus; but it is a novelty of Carlist invention that a pure robber should invest himself with the name of guerrillero."[18] Similarly, Unamuno's vision of the movement was quite distinct from the version of it that progressives relayed to their readers: perhaps that is why they deleted so many phrases from the passages they quoted. To Unamuno, Catholicism and monarchism were superficial components of Carlism. Its defining essence, however, was not a primitive form of socialism, but traditionalism; the movement, he thought, should be renamed accordingly. For him popular Carlism, as a protest by people who wished to maintain their age-old way of life, opposed any introduced novelty, whether it came in the form of centralization, intellectualism, or Jacobinism.[19] In this account, radical democracy was as foreign to the Carlist populace as a *fueros*-free form of government. According to Unamuno, the majority of those in the movement were, more than anything else, inarticulate lovers of their own traditions. They did not think out their ideals; they felt them, deeply. "Popular Carlism is ineffable, that is to say, inexpressible in speeches and programs; it is not material for oratory."[20] This was a conception of the movement that offered no space to voluble progressives with ideas of debate, tolerance, and thoroughgoing democracy. Only when gravely distorted could it lend them support.

The residual, idiosyncratic aspects of progressive historiography may all be seen as supplementary means to the political end of portraying the Carlist past in a way that no modern left-winger could criticize. Thus the *fueros* are not presented as antique privileges ensuring the advantage of some over others, but as the basis of a "just society." The Carlists of the nineteenth century are not viewed as conservatives who supported the traditional hierarchy, but as democrats keen for change. Jaime III's call for Carlists to assist the fledgling Republic in maintaining public order is not regarded as a calculating political move that would soon be superseded by an aggressively anti-Republican strategy,[21] but as a sign of his democratic convictions. The collaborative tendencies of the Comunión in the postwar period is not blamed on Don Javier's constant equivocation and apparent lack of interest in the movement, but on the almost decade-long period of convalescence he is supposed to have needed after spending the last year of the world war in German camps.

If we are to believe Clemente and his colleagues, the Carlist people and most of their pretenders were, and are, incapable of almost any wrong, while the generations of leading integrists and traditionalists have been persistently unable to do anything morally right. It seems that Clemente, though damning the Manichaeanism of the integrists, revived it in another form. In this sense, the old Carlist vice of intolerance toward their opponents had not disappeared, but had been dutifully inherited by the progressives.

It is perhaps ironic that the very progressives, such as Clemente, who were so convinced of the need to distinguish "true" members of the faith from self-interested infiltrators should themselves, when they left the movement in the late 1970s, come to be regarded by the rank and file as inauthentic Carlists who had entered the organization for a while and used it for their own ends. To those Navarrese villagers who, in the 1980s and 1990s, were still prepared to put on their red berets, the former leadership of the progressives had not been the saviors of Carlism, but the latest in a long line of its abusers.

Chapter Eight

Montejurra

On the morning of 3 May 1939, several thousand Carlists, mostly Navarrese, met in the village of Ayegui to celebrate the memory of their war dead. People came in coaches, trucks, cars, and carts; some rode into the village; others walked. To mark the ceremony and underline its significance, Rodezno, Arellano, the civil governor of Navarre, the president of the Navarrese Deputation, the mayor of Pamplona, the provincial chief of the Movimiento, and Don Javier's sister, Princess Isabel de Borbón-Parma, all turned up for the occasion. Villagers had specially decorated the windows and balconies of their homes. At the beginning of the path up to Montejurra, the neighboring small mountain, they had erected a commemorative arch.

Priests said Mass in the parish church and private houses. After breakfast had been served, the church bells tolled, firework rockets were let off, and the procession started, most people walking, but some on horseback. Carlist soldiers and horses carried heavy crosses, each dedicated to the memory of certain Requeté regiments. As the procession climbed the mountain, the *requetés* secured the crucifixes in a series of prepared holes. Priests said a station of the cross in front of each one as they journeyed up the mountainside. Pilgrims, fingering their rosaries, recited Hail Marys between stations. Once they had all reached the summit three priests, accompanied by two choirs, celebrated Mass in front of the assembled multitude. After the service, prominent Carlists made speeches glorifying the cause. Then people went off in groups to lunch in the countryside, while the Ayegui town hall staged an official banquet for important guests. The day closed with everyone singing the repertoire of songs from the Carlist Wars before starting for home.[1]

The idea of staging this ceremony had first come from Asunción Arraiza, the "godmother" of the First Company of the Tercio (Regiment) de Montejurra. Don Joaquin Vitriain, the parish priest of Ayegui, the mayor of Ayegui, and some fervent Carlists of the area had taken up her idea and organized the event. The president of the Navarrese Deputation had lent his enthusiastic support. The crosses had been made in workshops belonging to Carlists, as the organizers thought partisan craftsmen would do a better job at a cheaper price.[2]

The pilgrimage was so successful that it was decided to stage it annually. After its first performance, however, the numbers attending soon began to decline; in 1940 the pilgrimage was postponed for two days because it rained heavily on the chosen day.[3] The event soon became known as "the pilgrimage of the Navarrese mothers," since the only people who participated in it regularly were a reduced group of the ever-faithful, mainly widows, bereaved mothers, sisters, and girlfriends ("eternal fiancées" as they were known), all dressed in mourning. And, on the whole, it was the women who carried most of the crosses.[4] *El Pensamiento Navarro* stopped giving much space in its columns to reports of the ceremony, and *El Diario de Navarra* did not even mention it at all between 1945 and 1953. In that latter year, *El Pensamiento* admitted that Montejurra was "no longer the clamorous reunion of the times close to the end of the war, when we all felt in our souls the necessity to give thanks to God for the victory that he gave us and the life that we held on to."[5] If it had not been for the grieving women who could not forget their losses, it is very likely that the annual pilgrimage would not have survived these lean years of the immediate postwar period.

Despite these inauspicious beginnings, the ritual of Montejurra went on to become the central event in the Carlist ritual calendar. For almost fifteen years, from the mid-1950s to the end of the 1960s, it was also to be the most important mass gathering in the country not staged by the Church or the state. Outside these ecclesiastical and dictatorial realms, no regularly performed ceremony gained anything approaching the level of public significance of the pilgrimage to Montejurra. The purpose of this chapter is to detail the contents and changing contexts of this annual event: to track the course of its development, lay bare its structure, and analyze the discourses by which it was understood. Thus the following sections of this chapter deal, successively, with the revitalization of the ceremony; its ritual context in historical and contemporary terms; the reasons why, out of all the different Carlist ceremonies, Montejurra became the most important; the way traditionalist journalists reinterpreted it; how die-hard Carlist villagers regarded it; the more nakedly political aspects of the event; and the particular ways it was used to generate solidarity among believers.

The Traditionalist Development of Montejurra

The initial impetus for reanimating the pilgrimage came from prominent Navarrese Carlists, who, since the late 1940s, had been trying to rebuild their movement within the province. Their desires dovetailed with those of their national leaders, who themselves sought a platform where they could publicly, but safely, express the contemporary views of the Comunión. For the members of both these groups, the ceremony of Montejurra was a privileged opportunity to rally the faithful and regalvanize their enthusiasm for the cause.

The first move of these prominent Navarrese, made in 1954, was to have the now badly deteriorating wooden crosses replaced by stone ones, which were to be affixed at strategic points along the length of the mountain path. The Navarrese Deputation, then still controlled by the Comunión, approved their proposal and paid for the crosses to be specially made with stone from a local quarry. Their second move was to have the ceremony publicized much more than usual, and to present that year's staging of the event as especially important: now that the fourteen stone crosses were in place, the Vía Crucis (Stations of the Cross) de Montejurra could be publicly blessed and inaugurated. On the morning of the event, thousands of pilgrims turned up, including Carlist representatives from all over Spain, three foral deputies, and mayors and councillors from several Navarrese municipalities. After Mass and speeches on the summit, the veterans, united by a common memory of war but separated by geographical distance and the intervening years, greeted one another effusively. People lunched in the shade, then sang and danced before descending. In the nearby market town of Estella, they sang and made music in the streets until it was time to leave for home.[6]

From that year on, in the week preceding the pilgrimage, *El Pensamiento Navarro* would devote one or two whole pages every day to articles about the history of Montejurra, and to *romances montejurreños*, verse compositions commenting on the history, meaning, and emotional content of the ceremony. One year the paper included an unprecedented twenty-page supplement on Montejurra in its edition on the day of the ritual. Thanks to this publicity, and to the spirited speeches given by Carlist leaders at the ceremony, the fame and size of the pilgrimage continued to grow and grow. So that more people could attend, the date of the ceremony was changed from the feast day of the Holy Cross (May 2) to the first Sunday of the month. In 1959 the day of the celebration was moved yet again, to the second weekend of May, in order not to coincide with the annual Victory Parade put on by the regime. By the mid-1960s there was a regular attendance at the ceremony of at least 40,000. The number of journalists covering the event rose similarly; in 1964, 300 of them came to report on the ceremony.[7] By this time, there were so many people turning up for the event that Masses had to be held every half-hour in the monastery of Irache before the procession started. It was even becoming difficult to find space on the summit during the Mass there. Photographs of the time show people perching on rocky outcrops to avoid the crush of the crowd. Those who wished to lay claim to a good spot had to climb the mountain at dawn.

The municipality of Estella, which, like the Deputation, was then dominated by Carlists, rose to the occasion by providing the same sorts of entertainment as it did for its own fiestas. The beginning of the pilgrimage was announced by setting off rockets from the balcony of the town hall at noon the previous day. At nighttime, bands played in its main plaza and a firework bull was let loose. Bars stayed open until they finally emptied of people at three or four o'clock in the morning. There were so many visitors that cinemas did not close; some pilgrims slumbered in the stalls while others serenaded in the streets.[8] Many of those traveling from afar were billeted in Carlist homes of nearby villages. Some houses were so full that many of the guests had to sleep in the corridors. As visitors and hosts got to know one another over the years, the same group of people would always go to stay with the same householder. Those Carlists who had brought their musical instruments formed into bands, which would trumpet the cause and drum up enthusiasm for the big event by doing a round of the village they were staying in. The small village of Mañeru, famous for its Carlism, was so packed with pilgrims that on the night before the ceremony four bands filled its narrow streets with their noise.

The revitalization of the ceremony was accompanied by a militarization of the event. On the morning of the day itself, after Mass in the monastery of Irache, bemedaled veterans and youths in military uniform, a few of them on horseback, formally paraded en masse in front of members of their royal family or Carlist generals. In the Montejurra of 1963, for instance, two thousand *requetés,* holding their flags and standards up high, and led by military bands, stiffly marched past Doña Magadalena and María-Teresa, wife and daughter of Don Javier.[9] The pilgrimage proper started in Irache with bugle and trumpet calls. Mass on the mountaintop also began with a bugle call; at the moment of consecration, the regimental flags were lowered, a band played the royal march, and a series of rockets and exploding fireworks were set off.[10]

At Holy Communion, any member of the royal family attending the ritual joined Don Joaquin Vitriain in taking the host. When Mass ended, he gave a traditionalist speech about the religious and Carlist meanings of Montejurra. He ended his oration by leading the congregation in cheering Carlism and "King Javier." Next came the political speeches given by Comunión leaders and, if present, by one of Don Javier's children. On several occasions in the 1960s, at this point in the ceremony a light aircraft, sometimes rumored to be piloted by Carlos Hugo, flew over the multitude, performing acrobatics or dropping carnations as gifts "from heaven" on the visiting Carlist princesses.[11] Once the speeches and these aerial stunts were over, pilgrims had a leisurely snack before descending. Usually people went to Montejurra in groups, each from a particular village or area. At the foot of the mountain they regrouped and went off to cook their lunch in the fields nearby. Their meal finished, people wandered from fire to fire visiting friends.

The increasing popularity of the event also stimulated a certain commercialization of it. Along the mountain path, energetic petty entrepreneurs set up kiosks for the sale of refreshments to wearying pilgrims. Between the cries of "Viva!" to Navarre, Christ the King, Spain, and the *requetés*, could be heard shouts of "Beer, lemonade, Coca-Cola, tobacco, sandwiches!" The closer one got to the summit, the higher the prices.[12] In the years before the mountaintop became too congested, one man even used to set up a small bar there.

By the early 1960s the summit had become so crowded during the ritual that the time and place of the political act was changed to the midafternoon in the Plaza de los Fueros in Estella. Orators, speaking from the balcony of a well-known restaurant, praised the undying virtues of Carlism and gave the current line of the Comunión, while the crowd shouted their agreement. Messages of support from notables were read out and cheered.[13] From the mid-1960s on, the movement tried to demonstrate its support of regionalism by staging performances of Basque dance and music before the political act started. Some orators even began by uttering their first few lines in Euskera (the Basque language), cheered on by the crowd shouting "Viva Euskal-erria!" ("Long live the Basque Country!").[14] The speeches over, inebriated pilgrims, led by a brass band, danced around the kiosk in the center of the plaza, singing the "Oriamendi" and other beloved Carlist tunes. Most pilgrims then spent their time touring the bars of the town in the company of friends. Others sought out the armed representatives of the state; in the late 1960s, violent clashes between demonstrators and the police became almost a norm. The official events of the day usually ended with a solemn Salve in homage to murdered Carlist generals of the Second Carlist War, held in the Estellan Basilica to the Virgin of Puy.

The Ritual Contexts of Montejurra

This preliminary sketch of the revitalized, expanded version of Montejurra may make the annual ritual seem an extraordinary event, unique in its time. But the exceptional features of the pilgrimage should not blind us to the fact that its basic ceremonial structure is common to, and derives from, the popular, vigorous tradition found throughout Spain of *romerías*. These predominantly local events are pilgrimages held by the people of a village, set of villages, or town. To an anthropologist, they seem classic "rituals of integration," concerned with promoting moral and solidary corporateness, and centered around the figure of the group's patron saint, its special intermediary with God.[15] Usually only members of the particular community staging the ritual attend, outsiders are not invited, and those locals who left to find work elsewhere often return home in order to take part. These pilgrimages, most of which are performed in the spring, normally start with a religious procession headed by a priest. At his side are men bearing a cross and an image of the patron saint. The pilgrims process from their village, praying as they go, and walk through the countryside, stopping at sacred sites along the way, until they reach the shrine of the patron saint, usually located on the municipal boundary. Etymology underlines this sense of excursion out of town, for *romería* comes from *romero*, which may signify either a person who has made a pilgrimage to Rome, or the plant rosemary, which is not cultivated in villages but grows wild in the countryside.[16] After the celebration of Mass at the shrine, the pilgrims enjoy themselves by eating, drinking, singing, and dancing together. This skeletal description may suggest some of the similarities between a run-of-the-mill *romería* and the elaborated version of Montejurra: the conjunction of a community, religiosity, and fiesta; the season of performance; the passage from the urban to the rural, with a peripheral spot as the destination; and the pauses of the procession at significant sites along the path. But there is an important difference as well.

Unlike the destination of conventional pilgrimages, the summit of Montejurra is neither the shrine of a patron saint nor a marked "site where some manifestation of divine or supernatural power had occurred."[17] Rather than being the home of a historic theophany, the mountain is a historically marked site, where military events of political import occurred, and which post–Civil War *requetés* chose to hallow in the name of their dead brethren. Three battles have taken place on the mountain. In September 1835, during the First Carlist War, the liberals briefly occupied Estella, but had to leave hurriedly when a Carlist army appeared. The Carlists attacked the retreating enemies and the two sides then fought for possession of the strategically important summit of Montejurra, alternately winning and losing it. The liberals finally managed to break out of the threatened Carlist encirclement and headed southward, pursued by their opponents.[18] Since both sides claimed this encounter as a victory, twentieth-century Carlist eulogizers tended to pass over the event quietly. They also tended not to mention the third of these battles, fought on Montejurra on 18 February 1876. In this, the last great armed engagement of the second war, Carlist troops tried to defend the mountain against a much larger government army. But they lost, Estella was occupied by the enemy, and the war ended a few weeks later.[19]

Instead of wishing to remind their readers of these two events, Carlist panegyrists preferred to publicize the second battle of Montejurra, in which an army of 17,000 liberals spent three days in early November 1873 failing to dislodge a much smaller Carlist force entrenched on the mountaintop. To commemorate this great victory, which definitively established Carlist superiority in the Basque theater of war, a Te Deum was solemnly sung in Estella, and the troops were reviewed by Carlos VII, who commanded that a medal be struck. The king himself had been present on the battlefield, where a grenade had exploded at his horse's feet. The next year the foothills of the mountain were the scene of the Gran Parada de Montejurra, a celebration of the Carlist victory over the liberals in the nearby village of Abarzuza.[20] Because of the battle honors they had won on the slopes of Montejurra, and because of the great review they staged at its base, Carlists marked out the mountain as one of their most revered battle sites. Thus it was fitting when, in 1939, local veterans of the Civil War who wished to hallow the name of their dead brethren did so by instituting an annual pilgrimage to what their leaders called the "Monte Sagrado de la Tradición" (Sacred Mountain of Tradition).

Within Navarre, the partisan tone of the pilgrimage to Montejurra was not particularly unusual for its time, since from the beginning of the century many local *romerías* had taken on a markedly politicoreligious character.[21] Nor was the Carlist creation of a new pilgrimage a particularly innovative act in the province; during the same period, other annual religious excursions with comparable political connotations and similarly triumphalist rhetoric were also established. In 1937 Don Marcelino Olaechea, bishop of Pamplona, set up the Javierada, a fifty-kilometer pilgrimage from the city to the east Navarrese town of Javier, birthplace of the provincial patron saint, Saint Francis Xavier. He had instituted this mass ceremony, which was attended by thousands of people and many dignitaries, in order to maintain "the spirit of the crusade."[22] Two years later, another annual, but much smaller pilgrimage to the summit of Montejurra, performed in the second week of September, was established by the Hermandad de los Caballeros Voluntarios de la Cruz (Brotherhood of the Gentlemen Volunteers of the Cross), a fraternity of former *requeté* officers. An eyewitness account of the event describes it in the same emotive language as used by Carlist journalists reporting on its springtime counterpart.[23]

Within the general Basque area, the idea of incorporating a performance of the stations of the cross within the ritual was neither unusual nor out of tone with other public ceremonies of the time. During the war, throughout areas of the Basque Country controlled by the insurgents, patriotic interpretations of the stations of the cross were celebrated weekly "for Spain." The politico-ecclesiastical discourse within which these events were couched spoke of the need for penitence as a means to expiate the sins committed during and by the Republic, and of the dead both as a form of purification and as a punishment for the faults of the nation.[24]

Montejurra also needs to be placed in its contemporary national context. During the Civil War, the rise of a strident national Catholicism had led to the nationwide performance of a series of ostentatious acts of faith: grand processions, enthronements of the Sacred Heart, spectacular funerals for the fallen, and mass confirmations and First Holy Communions. Ecclesiastics sympathetic to the regime were clear about the point of these mass ceremonies. As the apostolic administrator for the Basque city of Vitoria stated in 1939 on the feast day of Christ the King: "The annual festivities of the sacred mysteries are more effective than the solemn documents of ecclesiastic teaching in order to mold people in matters of the faith, addressing not only the intelligence but also the heart and the senses by the suggestive force of the sacred rites and ceremonies."[25] The regime, just as aware as the Church of the manipulative power of ritual, used to stage its own grand ceremonies: for example, to celebrate the liberation of the Alcázar, the work of the Caudillo, the anniversary of the uprising, and victory in the Civil War.

While the ceremony of Montejurra may be seen in these various contexts, it is important to note its difference from the broader of these ritual frames. Unlike the mass performances staged by the national Catholic hierarchy (most of which had ended by the early 1950s), Montejurra was, until 1954, a locally organized event attended by a faithful few. Only for its inauguration in 1939 did the event attract non-Carlist dignitaries and large numbers. Unlike the nationally common and markedly formal rituals of the regime, where the massed ranks of the armed forces would set the dominant tone, Montejurra was a relatively informal event. For its first two decades there was no military parade, nor any of the pomp associated with the ceremonies of the dictator. Even when, from 1959 on, uniformed *requetés* did begin to line up on the morning of Montejurra, the ceremony still remained much more relaxed than the strictly regulated events staged by the government. Today, former progressives claim that these parades were far less disciplined and more shambolic than proud veteran *requetés* might like to admit. Montejurra, in short, was based fundamentally on local practices. It had more in common with provincial events than with state-organized ones.

Montejurra and Other Carlist Rituals

The reasons why Montejurra became the largest among modern Carlist ceremonies are a compound of mathematics, history, and contemporary politics.[26] In the mid-1950s the Navarrese Junta, by then one of the most organized regional bodies within the Comunión, wished to revitalize the movement and to reassert the place of their province within it by transforming the local ceremony into one of national importance. They well knew that the number of Carlists living in or near the region of Estella was proportionally greater than in any other part of the country. This simple arithmetical factor plus the fame of Navarre as the traditional heartland of the movement gave the pilgrimage a potential sense of significance that other regular Carlist rituals lacked. Andalucian and Catalan Carlists might journey to Montejurra, but their Navarrese and Basque brethren did not return the visit, to attend the annual events at Quintillo and Montserrat, respectively. Andalucian Carlism was a relatively recent phenomenon compared to its northern counterparts, and there were insufficient Carlists in the zone to pack Quintillo with the sort of numbers that Montejurra could command. In 1963, for instance, a truckload of Sevillan *requetés* made the cross-country trip to attend Montejurra. The provincial chief of the *requetés* in Seville hoped that, in return, the leadership of the Comunión in Madrid would dispatch an equal number to Quintillo. He was to be disappointed, and he expressed his feelings in a letter to his superiors in the capital:

> It is a shame that in the highest ranks of the Comunión, there is so little aid for Quintillo (and please note that that is not censure). But it pains we Andalucians, and especially we Sevillans, to see that everything is for Navarre, where every stone yields a Carlist, and that here everything demands so much work and sacrifice, since we are not the cradle of Carlism, nor have ancestors to imitate. It is for these reasons that, according to my own meager understanding, You Sirs should try to stimulate yourselves a little more and to spare less effort when dealing with us. This year we did not have any representative from the highest ranks of the Comunión. Just as well we had the great satisfaction of having present our Don Manuel Fal Conde.[27]

Catalan Carlism, in contrast, had a much greater historical depth, and the Aplec to the renowned local monastery of Montserrat was the oldest annual pilgrimage in the ritual calendar of the Comunión. Inaugurated shortly after the Second Carlist War as a pilgrimage of thanks to the Virgin of Montserrat for having saved a contingent of Carlist troops from what seemed to be inevitable annihilation, the Aplec became an especially important traditionalist ceremony during the turbulent years of the Second Republic.[28] It was revived after the war by the well-organized Catalan Carlists, who had a crypt built near the monastery as a memorial to the *requetés* of the Regiment of Montserrat. By the late 1940s, it had become the most prominent regional ceremony in the Carlist year, with leaders of national rank coming to speak and former *requetés* journeying from as far away as Granada to attend. But the split between the *javieristas* and the *sivattistas* led to both groups performing their own versions of the Aplec on different days, with some people attending both events. Since each group questioned the legitimacy of the other's ceremony, this contested ritual could not serve the *javieristas'* interests of celebrating Carlist unity in a ceremonial manner. In the same way, this majority wing of the Comunión could not exploit the September pilgrimage to Montejurra because the fraternity that controlled its performance was composed of die-hard traditionalists opposed to the machinations of their national leaders. Thus, if the *javieristas* wished to make a particular Carlist ceremony the ritual focus of their efforts to refortify the Comunión, then the May pilgrimage to Montejurra was their best bet.[29]

For Carlist politicos concerned about the revival of their movement, the repeated performance of these rituals was centrally important, because the dictatorship had banned almost all forms of conventional political activity. Demonstrations were outlawed, free elections were never held, and any open-ended, public debate about politics was suppressed. Since propagandists of the regime liked to underline the association of their system of government with the Church by staging large Catholic ceremonies, the only way Carlist leaders could hold mass gatherings that would be tolerated was to frame their events as religious ceremonies, most commonly as pilgrimages. This is not to suggest that the organizers of, and participants in, these events were not religiously motivated, but that these acts were usually an almost inseparable mixture of both religion and politics.

As political parties officially did not exist, the pilgrimage to Montejurra was not organized by the Comunión, but by the Hermandad Penitencial Canónica (Canonical Penitential Brotherhood) de la Vía Crucis de Montejurra. This ecclesiastically recognized body was the legal authority responsible for the annual ritual. It was created by Navarrese Carlists in 1957 because organization of the day's events had become too much for the Carlists of Ayegui. In effect, the Hermandad was used as a convenient legal cover, for it looked after only the religious aspects of the ceremony; the more political parts of the day's events were taken care of by the Navarrese Junta. If the authorities did decide to prohibit the political act in the plaza, speakers would give their speeches on the summit immediately after Mass. Banning the religious service simply on the suspicion that the Carlists were going to stage a political act as soon as Mass ended would have been seen as a lack of respect both for the Church and for the memory of the valiant *requetés*. Instead, speakers who criticized the dictatorship too strongly at particularly sensitive moments were fined heavily. From the very first performance of the pilgrimage in 1939, a few Civil Guards would always attend the ceremony on the summit. But their presence was purely testimonial: they could have done little against a large crowd of fervent, excited Carlists. Over the years, as the ceremony became more political in tone, policemen would often set up roadblocks on the main approaches to Estella. But the Carlist convoys usually knew ways to bypass these obstacles.[30]

Montejurra in Traditionalist Discourse

The numerous and extensive articles that *El Pensamiento Navarro,* and later *Montejurra,* printed about the annual ceremony in the days leading up to it provided readers with particular ways of understanding the possible meanings of the annual event. Analysis of the discourse employed in these articles provides modern-day outsiders, such as foreign anthropologists, with a means of attempting to comprehend the intended significance of the rite. Looking at the language of these articles gives us an idea of how their influential authors wanted the rank and file of their movement to interpret the multifaceted event of Montejurra.

These journalistic pieces are already skillful précis of Carlist symbolism. They were written to guide and to enrich participants' experience of the ceremony. There is little need for an anthropologist to *impute* symbolism here: it is already given. Much of the journalists' symbolic interpretations, moreover, were not freshly created for the occasion but drew on, if not merely rewrote, already extant Carlist metaphors and images. Unlike most indigenous commentaries on rituals or other aspects of their social lives, these writings are not native exegeses purposefully elicited by an intrusive ethnographer. They are not "folk explanations" given in an interview by a particularly articulate and perceptive "informant," to be accommodated within an ahistoric ethnography. Rather, they constitute a loose set of metaphorical directives explicitly manipulated by fluent professionals at a certain time for political ends. All I try to do in the following pages is present the key notions within this discourse in a systematic manner.

HISTORICAL GEOGRAPHY

In the first years of the ceremony, there were still elderly *requetés* who could point out the positions that they had defended against liberal attacks in November 1873; after Mass on the summit, pilgrims relaxed by picnicking in the trenches, still evident eighty years later.[31] These physical reminders of past military achievement were considered insufficient by some. By 1956 the editor of *El Pensamiento Navarro* thought that many Carlists did not know enough about their history of the area and that some had even forgotten it. So he started an annual series of articles on the Carlist past of Montejurra, Irache, Estella, and neighboring villages. These articles thickened pilgrims' understanding of their performance and directed their gaze. From the top of the mountain they could learn, or relearn, how to read the landscape in Carlist terms, remembering different villages for their historical associations: one was the birthplace of a renowned Carlist commander; in another, a glorious battle had been fought; in a third, a famous general had fallen wounded; and so on.

One journalist, professing to tire of cataloging the Carlist memories that could be evoked by the view from the summit, confessed grandly, "Why list more, if every corner of this land is the place of the holocaust of a Mártir de la Tradición?"[32] Carlist history is made so rich on Navarrese soil that its signs can be interpreted everywhere, and from the top of a small mountain dominating a plain the possibilities are limited only by the horizon.

Closer to base, readers were reminded, stood the monastery of Irache, where pilgrims gathered before ascending the mountain. It had been a hospital in the Carlist Wars; Doña Margarita of Parma, wife of Carlos VII and aunt of Don Javier, had worked there as an *ángel de caridad* (angel of charity); General Mola, one of the insurgent triumvirate, had met the Carlist leader Fal Conde there in June 1936 to negotiate the preparations for the uprising. At the start of each pilgrimage Irache, "dressed again with red berets," was said to "relive" history.[33] Further down the road lay Estella. This market town already had a special place in Carlist traditions, as Carlos VII had established his court there during the second war. Since his provisional government of the Basque Country had made the town its administrative center, Estella came to represent the closest Carlists had ever been to having their own capital.[34] Carlos VII had passed many mornings in its Plaza de los Fueros, the same square where, in the 1960s and 1970s, Carlist orators spoke to the assembled multitude. One reason why Montejurra had come to occupy such a central site in Carlist geography was its strategic proximity to Estella. Unamuno called it and the adjacent small mountain of Monjardin "sentries of the city"; to the former *requeté* officer and Carlist historian Jaime del Burgo, it was "the key to the city."[35] In other words, the army that controlled Montejurra controlled Estella: if the city symbolized the urban hopes of Carlism, then Montejurra was its military gate.

Montejurra "was not just any mountain, but one without peer." Given that it rises only 600 meters above the plateau on which it stands, Carlist journalists searching for striking metaphors preferred to dwell on the physical qualities of Montejurra rather than on its altitude. They described it as being as hard and as firm as Carlist ideals. This "austere mountain" was meant to remind pilgrims of "the message of tradition": its solidity and supposedly gigantic dimension were said to be capable of revitalizing and renovating their faith.[36] Geogeny, as well as geology, was brought into play, for the mountain's volcanic origin, "which stirred up the bowels of this zone of Navarre, which still displays the hard mortar of fire and stone," was made to symbolize "the idealist volcano" of the *requetés* in the Tercio de Montejurra. And when cloud covered the mountain, locals said it had put on its beret.[37] According to this almost fantastical set of metaphors, Montejurra was Carlism petrified, its ideals made rock hard.

Journalists seeking for ways to magnify the significance of Montejurra could also exploit the Christian connotations of mountains, which carried with them Biblical echoes of divine revelation. In the Old Testament, epiphanies frequently occur on mountaintops, as do many important events in the life of Jesus.[38] In each case, the summit acts as a place where Heaven conjoins Earth, as the apical meeting point of mundane profanity with a higher spirituality. The idea of a mountaintop as a place on which a person can feel whole and from which one can put the world in perspective lies also at the core of Unamuno's *Paz en la guerra*. In this novel about the Second Carlist War, he replicates traditionalist dichotomies by contrasting the corruption, depravity, political disputes, and "indecent things" found in towns with the balmy calm of the countryside—best exemplified as a mountain. At the end of his tale, an old Carlist whose son has died in battle goes up a small mountain and, on reaching the summit, experiences a tranquilizing vision of the unity of all things. While contemplating the view, he fuses the "eternal sadness of the depths of his soul with the temporal happiness of life." It is the mountain that has provided "spiritual freshness" and allows him to feel whole.[39] Thus for both Biblical scribes and the Bilbao-born philosopher, a summit is the preferred site of personal revelation and self-integration. The journalists' interpretation of Montejurra merely relied on and bolstered this already extant cultural conception of a mountaintop as a special site of conjuncture. By utilizing this sort of religious cosmography, they could turn Montejurra into a key reference point for Carlists and so reorient their readers' conception of the world. They could portray ascent of the mountain as a way for pilgrims to realize the lofty ideals of the Christian movement they embodied, as a way for them to come closer to God and their dead fellows in heaven. By climbing to the summit Carlists were supposed to be reaching the boundary where the terrestrial could encounter the divine.

Besides linking the mountain's topography with traditionalist cosmology, Carlist journalists also exploited the associations of its toponym, by asserting that the battle record of the Tercio de Montejurra was as brilliant as the memory of its name. "When the bugle of war was blown in June 1936, the *requetés*, who had the same spirit as those who, sixty years before, had clambered up the cliffs of Montejurra, wanted to render homage to their forefathers, imitating them in the struggle and choosing a name for their unit of combat, a name that was so familiar to them and that they had so many times heard talk of: Montejurra! The battle of Montejurra, the fort of Montejurra, the parade of Montejurra. . . ."[40] The Tercio de Montejurra had the second-highest proportion of dead and wounded of all Carlist regiments in the Civil War, because "its *requetés* honored the name they carried. Montejurra! It didn't deserve less."[41] To Melchor Ferrer, "Montejurra" was a heroic slogan, a password calling future generations to repeat the feats of the regiment. Thanks to the efforts of its *requetés*, "Montejurra" as a name "echoes deeply in the hearts of admirers of Carlism."[42] Even the phonetics of the toponym were put to use, as the spoken sound of the word was said to be, like the mountain and the movement it symbolized, "rugged and intractable."[43]

REENACTMENT AND SACRIFICE

Each stone cross of the Vía Crucis de Montejurra was inscribed with the names of certain Carlist regiments. They were generally placed where the wooden crosses had been stuck into the ground, though the position of a few was changed. All the crosses were deliberately sited in "the most strategic places, the highest crags, so that they appeared more striking, more propitious." The explicit aim was to impress pilgrims, to remind them of the fallen, and to make them "pray like Catholics pray."[44] Some writers further stressed the symbolism of war by noting that the procession was usually headed by men bearing the national flag and a tall crucifix, and that beneath them were others carrying their regimental banners and crosses. As one panegyrist noted, these crosses had served in the Civil War as pointers and foci of spirit in the advances, and as images in military Masses; they had blessed the companies preparing for attack, and they traced out in the air the sign of pardon over those who fell dead. Thus, the ceremonial conjunction in Montejurra of these pairs of "sacred symbols," of the regimental flags and crucifixes, was said to make the procession appear "a warlike column."[45] Following this line of argument, the uniformed *requeté* pilgrims, by acting like troops going into battle, were metaphorically reenacting the war itself.

For its first fifteen years, Montejurra was characterized as exclusively a "pilgrimage of the Navarrese mothers." In the mid-1950s, journalists wishing to extend the significance of the ceremony started to call it both one of mourning and one of happiness, because those attending demonstrated "the vitality of spirit of a race of idealists."[46] These correspondents' accounts of the event emphasize its religious nature, the sacrifice made by participants, the emotion they displayed, and the spirit they evinced. Ascending the mountain was seen as a sacrifice; the track was difficult, muddy, and painful, and the gradient in places steep. Until the Ayegui town hall improved the path in 1956, many used to trip or fall. Newspaper articles mention "trembling knees," "heaving chests," "foreheads bathed in sweat," and pebbles sliding under one's feet. Their readers were reminded that, in the first years of Montejurra, several warwounded *requetés* had managed to struggle up the mountain path: these onelegged men on crutches, together with a blind soldier leaning on the arm of his wife, had animated others by their example. One senior Navarrese Carlist stressed to me that, in the first years of the ceremony, those who had carried crosses up the mountainside were genuinely shouldering a weighty burden, since the life-sized crucifixes were made of heavy oak; he said they really did look like Christ ascending Calvary. Journalists of the time reported that grieving parents had asked to carry the crosses dedicated to the memory of the regiments in which their sons had fought; they felt they had to make some sacrifice, just as their *requeté* children had sacrificed their lives.[47] Some pilgrims performed a sacrifice by *walking* to the mountain from their Navarrese village, by journeying from distant provinces of the peninsula, or by fasting from the night before so they could take Holy Communion on the summit.[48]

Some oblation, whether of comfort, convenience, or food, was said to be necessary to prepare oneself spiritually and emotionally for the Mass on the summit. Climbing Montejurra was meant to be a form of mortification, to be offered for the eternal rest of the dead *requetés*. It was satisfying, writers claimed, to tire oneself out voluntarily, for one did it with the same spirit and hope as those Carlist soldiers who voluntarily fought in the battle of Montejurra. On a more self-interested note, Don Joaquin Vitriain reminded readers that salvation lay in sacrifice.[49] Sinners, by imitating the last steps of Christ and the efforts made by their *requeté* forebears, could redeem themselves from damnation. Inflicting a little pain on their bodies was good for their souls. At the same time, the "legions of martyrs" who had died for the cause in Carlist Wars since the 1820s showed their gratitude for the sacrifice of their successors by blessing those who ascended Montejurra.[50] Those who joined the Hermandad de la Vía Crucis were also granted a 200 days' indulgence, plus a similar amount every time they climbed the mountain.[51]

EMOTION, SPIRIT, BLOOD

One writer described the feelings he claimed to experience on achieving the summit: "Uplifted, elevated above earthly things and closer to heaven, in an ambience more propitious to contemplation, meditation, and pleasurable evocation of inerasable events, one feels stronger, more integral, more Carlist, more bound to the spirit and memory of the heroes who gave glory, fame, and meaning to Montejurra. . . . We have climbed Montejurra. . . . We feel ourselves more in love with, and more fraternal toward, those who so deeply professed ideals for which one dies."[52] To adopt these writers' sanguinary metaphor for a moment, we might characterize the ceremony as a cathartic opportunity to pick the scab of memory, to make the blood run afresh, and to relive the pain of loss. For Montejurra was *meant* to be emotive; the tears were *meant* to run. Partisan reporters extolled the ceremony as a series of acts "full of emotion in which the entire soul of our people was present," where "the enthusiasm, the shaking of the people made itself felt." It was said that participants, especially in the first years, wept openly during the pilgrimage, above all during the stations of the cross, at the moment of Communion on the summit, and at the playing of the Royal March. After Mass, during the responsory to the Mártires de la Tradición, some were overcome by great pain, "a pain that redeemed and ennobled the Christian sacrifice of our brave crusaders"; in 1954, Holy Marian Year, people "shook" with emotion during the Salve to the Holy Mother held after the Mass; even in 1966, thirty years after the war, journalists reported that people cried while listening to the national hymn in Estella.[53] To Don Joaquin Vitriain, Montejurra was so evocative to Carlists as a symbol of resistance and of persisting faith in the cause, and had become *"so effective, so intimate, so familial, so Carlist,* that we cannot speak of it without getting emotional."[54] In the reported words of one *requeté,* the meeting on Montejurra of a people full of faith in the true ideals of Spain excited him and touched his heart: "Montejurra," he confessed, "forms part of myself." One Carlist correspondent used a similarly emotive (and revealingly male-oriented) language: "It is necessary to be with the men of Montejurra, in the essential, and there the essential is Spain, and there what does not deceive is called heart, and it is only the heart that speaks."[55]

Besides provoking strong emotions in participants, the performance of the pilgrimage was meant to generate "spirit," the same "spirit" as shown by those who went to fight in 1936. Montejurra was to be an annual renovation of the meaning of 18 July, a way to maintain "the spiritual elevation" of those first months of the uprising. Everyone was to go up the mountain "with the same spirit and the same immortal ideal." Singing the old Carlist songs in unison was said to excite that spirit while the potent ideals of the Comunión were meant to "push" pilgrims up the gradients of Montejurra.[56] Even Carlos Hugo's secretaries recognized the ability of Montejurra to shake "people's drowsy spirits"; as they put it, with everyone shouting together, "the sensation of force, of power was felt."[57] Those "symbolic pilgrims" who stayed at home yet thought of the pilgrimage during the day of its performance were to be considered "present in spirit."[58] Thus an extended notion of "spirit" was made to unite the dead, those assembled on the summit, and those unable to come that day. It was a metaphoric means of connecting the Carlist people, both living and dead, both present and absent. It was also an implicit reminder of the wartime opposition between the "spirituality" of Carlist Spain and the "materialism" derived from bolshevist Russia. Thus stalwart traditionalists who maintained the spirit prevented base material considerations from polluting their doctrinal purity.

"Spirit" was the most common metaphor in accounts of the ceremony. "Blood" was used less frequently, as sanguinary trope for the dead as well as physiological figure of speech for ideological steadfastness: the blood of the martyrs was said to have taken spiritual form in the crosses; their sacrifice was meant to have revitalized the stations of the cross. The first prayer of the ceremony ran, "Lord, let the perennial essence of that martyrial blood purify our prayer, comfort our desire to serve You, and vitalize all our national being with their ideals of being the Christian vanguard." [59] One correspondent, watching hundreds of red-bereted men move up the mountain, was reminded of the blood shed in the Carlist Wars. To another the sight of thousands of mobile red berets along the path was "like an artery of fresh blood maintaining the life of the quiet mountain. The names change and the generations succeed one another and the blood continues flowing and reflowing from the foot of the mountain to its summit, from the Carlist heart of Navarre." [60] Individuals might die, but the Carlist people continued.

FAMILY

Montejurra was presented as unity amid variety. Journalists liked to stress that pilgrims came from different classes and different regions of Spain: there were farmhands, professionals, war wounded, priests, officers, and students; there were Basques, Galicians, Castilians, Catalans, and members of other peninsular groups; and all of them participating together in the same great ritual enterprise. [61] The night before in Estella was called one of "deep brotherhood," as Carlists from different parts of the country chatted at the same tables. Literal companions, they shared the same bread and slept under the same roof. "All are one," *El Pensamiento Navarro* stated, in "the great Carlist family." [62]

And some Carlists did ascend *en famille*. Newspaper photos published in 1954 and 1955 show an elderly Carlist going up the mountain escorted by his son and grandson. In 1957, a seven-year-old went up the path with his great-grandfather. [63] Speeches made during the day of the ceremony emphasized this genealogical continuity. The crowd applauded one orator who said that speaking to the Carlist people there signified the greatest distinction, the greatest evidence to his wife and sons standing next to him, of his heritage of faithfulness, like that of his parents, to the ideals of the cause. The next speaker on the platform said that Montejurra was a ceremony for veterans, for youth, and also for those as yet unborn because they were predetermined to be Carlists if their parents already were. His words were greeted with great applause and shouts of "Very good!" According to journalists' reports, when speakers invoked Carlist youth, excited fathers would pluck their infants out of their prams and raise them in the air, as though offering them for the cause. [64] It was this sustained hereditary component of Carlism that had made it so distinctive and so strong, "because there is not in the universe an equivalent example, where five or six generations have stubbornly maintained the heroic defense of certain principles and of a cause that neither promised nor offered anything, but demanded constant renouncements and the sacrifice of life and wealth." [65]

This sense of successive generations maintaining the same traditions is bluntly portrayed in the story, "Those Men of Iron . . . !" published in *Monte-jurra* in 1967. A young Carlist shames his aging father by saying that he will not be going to Montejurra that year. Although ailing, the old man insists on going himself. "It is the first year that someone from this house would be lacking there. And because you don't want to go, I will go there myself. In one of those crosses is the regiment where your brother died. . . . Since you are so cold toward everything that is ours, I must continue, while I live." Coming down from the mountain, he slips and has to be carried to his couch by his anguished son. At the bedside, the son confesses that he has spent all day thinking; he voluntarily promises that, beginning the following year, it will be he attending Montejurra, and wearing the beret of his father, who clearly has not long to live. His son's voice sounds "a little hoarse, as though it came from deep down." But neither cries, for "those Carlist men are made of iron." [66]

Requetés were told that they *ought* to go to Montejurra, and that they were to take their family and friends along too. Making the pilgrimage was a duty, like Muslims journeying to Mecca: it had to be done, at least once. Journalists tried to coax those deaf to these directives by pointing out that the ceremony was an excellent opportunity to meet old wartime comrades and to revive fading memories. Parents were also admonished to take their children so that they could learn how to pray and to do good works. "Everyone to Monte-jurra," read the headline one year; "there's no excuse for absence." [67]

Perhaps the most dramatic demonstration of transgenerational commitment and of the ceremony as a site to rekindle old bonds occurred on the mountain-top in 1957. To telling political effect, a leading Navarrese Carlist introduced the prince to the multitude: "He is the son of our king, who has come to put himself on our side. Do you know why he is here? Why he is ours? His grand-father, Prince Roberto of Borbón, and my grandfather fought together here in Montejurra. Today is a day of reunion." [68]

The act of Montejurra was meant to provoke emotion, demand sacrifice, generate spirit, display unity in variety, underscore genealogical continuity, and demonstrate the dutiful nature of committed Carlists. It was a rounded performance that was supposed to manifest in a concentrated manner the ideals for which the *requetés* had fought, of their conception of Spain. Monte-jurra can thus be considered a celebration of both a political and a moral com-munity, whose members were meant to judge themselves and others along the lines of their unbending standard—a standard raised every year on a small mountaintop in the west of Navarre. In this sense, journalists could call the ceremony of Montejurra "the very heart" of the country. One writer, mind-ful of the hegemonic and nation-building aims of his movement's ideology, claimed that the summit contained "an altar sculpted into the earth, a priest, a people, a dynasty"; at this ceremonial moment, "All Spain was dominated."[69] Following this logic, if the Comunión was to reemerge as a significant force within national life, if it was to attempt to impose its views on the rest of the country, then the meeting on the mountain was one annual appointment all able-bodied Carlists had to keep.

Veterans' Views

Senior Navarrese and Basque Carlists stated to me that pilgrims used to read the articles in *El Pensamiento Navarro* and *Montejurra* as assiduously as radical Basque Nationalists today pore over the editorials and commentaries in *Egin*, the highly successful daily newspaper of the political party associated with the terrorists. Because for many years of the dictatorship there were few means of publicly printing and widely disseminating the contemporary attitudes of the Comunión leadership, both *El Pensamiento Navarro* and *Montejurra* were regarded as invaluable, because they were almost the sole sources of information and opinions for local Carlists. Literate Carlists of Cirauqui acknowledge the importance this pair of periodicals had in their day. Some had subscriptions, and those who did not could read the latest issues in the village Circle. The discourse of the Carlist journalists might have been more elaborately developed than that of local former *requetés*, but the articles they wrote were phrased in a traditionalist terminology that could be readily understood by any minimally knowledgeable supporter of the cause.

In my conversations with these veterans, some were diffident about the exactitude of their historical knowledge of Montejurra when talking to a person whom they took to be a scholar. But while they were prepared to profess relative ignorance in this field, they at the same time took great pride in the fact that fluent professionals had written about the history of Montejurra in books and in *El Pensamiento Navarro*. Even if villagers could not remember all the dates and events exactly, prestigious others could, and had written them down.

Like the journalists, who employed an affective, stirring style, former *requetés*, in our discussions on the matter, spoke in a highly enthusiastic, passionate, and at times almost oratorical manner about Montejurra. They portrayed the well-attended performances of the 1960s as grand, emotive occasions where experienced speakers roused the excited crowd into clamorous support of their movement. To these villagers, the events of the great day were something Carlists could be openly proud of. As one put it, the small airplane that flew low over the crowded summit in two successive Montejurras was an admirable "madness." To them, the tempting possibility of seeing and hearing at least one member of their royal family at the event was a further, glorious reason for going to the ceremony. In 1964 newspapers suggested that so many attended the Montejurra of that year because they had hoped to see Carlos Hugo and his bride. For participants, the day of Montejurra was one to remember with pride and, for some, with a hangover.

In our talks, former *requetés* liked to emphasize the conviviality of the event and the sheer sense of occasion—boosted by the rise in numbers. The offspring of *requetés* said how much they, as children, had looked forward to the festive night before Montejurra, when the village was filled with people, noise, and music.[70] One Carlist now in his seventies laughed as he remembered the violent clashes with the police: everyone singing antifranquist songs or shouting "Franco is a traitor" and similar slogans right in front of Civil Guards. To him, such daring, such crazy things *(burradas)*, showed how "blindly the Carlists held to their faith." Most villagers stressed to me the "spirit" of those attending, especially in the first years when the memory of the war was most vivid. Some of them admitted that they had seen, or heard of, particularly aged men or war-wounded *requetés* trudging up the mountainside, and talk of such exemplars often led them to mention excitedly the glorious history, the staunch idealism, the tremendous nature, and the staying power of Carlists. When these villagers recounted past Montejurras, the emotions and the values were expressed simultaneously, mutually reinforced in the stories they were giving me. Like the journalists' discourse, the villagers' vocabulary compounded sentiment and ideals, fortifying one another and together glorifying the name of the movement to which they all belonged.

Montejurra as Political Stage

According to the journalists' interpretation of Montejurra, the Masses, in the monastery for the multitude and on the summit for the elect, associated Carlist ideals with otherworldly powers and so sanctified the proceedings of the day. This religious facet of the ceremony, together with the evocative power of ceremonially remembering one's dead and celebrating one's community at a historically hallowed site, framed and heightened the political speeches that followed. They provided a stirring context within which orators reaffirmed Carlism and criticized others. Preceded by a military parade, Christian services, and an alcoholic lunch break, the speakers were listened to by an already well-charged audience. The sense of occasion and the uniqueness of the event in Franquist Spain only served to lend the speeches even further significance, giving them a power and weight unknown to other, lesser gatherings of the time.

The journalists' interpretations of Montejurra in all its multifarious aspects contained implicit pretensions toward timelessness, as though they thought the movement had lived, and would live, forever in the same traditionalist mold. Despite the historiographical nature of their articles, they did not tell their tales of Carlist history as if the movement were located irretrievably in the past but as if it were metaphysically present.[71] In marked contrast to this essentially atemporal vision, which disregarded important differences between *requetés* of different centuries, and which paid little heed to the current political state of the country, some of the speeches made at each staging of the ritual always discussed the present political scene and the official Carlist attitude to it. These addresses to the assembled were meant to provide them with a succinct statement of the political opinions of the Comunión leadership at that particular time. For the speakers on the platform, it was the most public opportunity they would have in the year to inform their followers of the current stance of the movement's elite and of any shifts in policy.

In the early years of Montejurra, almost all the speeches concerned the glorious history of Carlism and the *requetés'* contribution to the war. As dissatisfaction with the regime increased, orators had begun to make their speeches more and more political in content. But since the numbers attending the ritual were then small, their rhetoric had little political effect. When the Navarrese Junta relaunched the ceremony in the mid-1950s, speakers of greater rank started regularly attending the event, their words were listened to by greater numbers of people, and some Carlist periodicals published their speeches. The political act at Montejurra quickly became such an important platform that members of different Carlist factions would compete behind the scenes to control the sorts of speeches given. They wanted to have their say.

Carlos Hugo used the political act of Montejurra as a way to present both himself and some of the progressives' ideas to the general Carlist public. At his first appearance, in 1957, he advocated the creation of independent syndicates, that municipalities and regions should be allowed to regain their foral personality, and that economics, rather than religion, should be the theoretical base of Carlist policy. In his speech the following year, which had been drafted many times by members of the AET, he spoke of the need for dialogue between all levels of society, of pluralism, of the injustices in a society where wealth equaled power, and of syndicates working together with the government and business in running the economy. He was against both popular capitalism, because it turned workers into members of the bourgeoisie, and socialism, because it curtailed too many freedoms. In order to appease Carlist conservatives, Carlos Hugo would also make reference in his speeches to "our glorious crusade" and other concepts beloved by the intransigents. Although in 1958 he rejected the speech that leading reactionaries had sent him, he still felt the need to incorporate a few of its more "poetic" traditionalist phrases into his address.[72]

As Carlist conservatives and progressives began to tussle for power, the various speeches made at any one performance of Montejurra could differ markedly in style from one another. In 1961 Carlos Hugo's message, though generally neocollaborationist in tone, criticized those who continued to justify their actions by reference to the crusade, and those who wanted a paternalistic monarchy that would treat "the people" as children. He called for a social monarchy, in tune with the needs of the people, and for the establishment of democracy, then still regarded as a subversive concept by some Carlists. On the same platform, Valiente gave a solidly traditionalist speech; Pedro Lombardia, a progressive professor of law, launched a virulent attack on capitalism; while Zamanillo reasserted "the spirit of Montejurra"—in other words, religious unity consubstantial with national unity.[73] Two years later it was decided that most of the speakers, who included Carlos Hugo's sister María-Teresa, would try to establish once and for all the position of the Borbón-Parmas within Carlism by stressing the central importance of the royal family within the movement. In contrast to these speeches, Blas Piñar, an invited speaker who was to become a leader of the extreme Right during the transition, couched his oration in a reactionary discourse that dwelt on the aims of the Civil War and their continuing validity. In a bid to compensate for the absence of the recently dismissed Zamanillo, Fal Conde attended the event that year. Don Javier, in a message read out to the multitude, underlined both his regality and his appreciation of his former chief delegate and his successor, Valiente, by making them "Oficiales de la Orden de la Legitimidad" (Officers of the Order of Legitimacy); Zamanillo was a mere "Caballero" (Gentleman) of the august body.[74]

The speeches made at the Montejurra of 1964 were similarly varied in style. Blas Piñar and two leading regional Carlists all spoke in defense of the idea of a traditional monarchy, while Massó gave one of the most vehemently critical speeches pronounced up to then in a public event in Spain. Reacting to the press campaign against Carlos Hugo during the period of his engagement, he attacked the *juanistas* and disparaged the government, but carefully refrained from passing any comment on Franco himself.[75] At the next Montejurra, the speakers jointly presented a much more coherent political message, marking the gradual shift of the Comunión leadership toward the camp of the opposition. Carlos Hugo's message referred to the need for an economic, social, and administrative renovation of the country; a professor of civil law argued for the legitimacy and Spanish nationality of the Borbón-Parmas, whose petition for passports had been rejected by Franco; the contemporary head of the Requeté, though employing a triumphalist style, accentuated the distance between the regime with all it signified and "authentic" (i.e., *javierista*) Carlism; a delegate of the MOT spoke on the virtues of a fully participatory democracy and derided the excesses of capitalism; and Valiente closed the proceedings with a highly measured speech that avoided both immobilist and progressive extremes.[76]

The rhetorical tone at Montejurra in 1966 was very different and starkly expressed the waning influence of Carlos Hugo's secretaries. Although the event that year was presented as the "Montejurra of freedom," and though Don Javier's message suggested for the first time that, alongside regional and syndical representation, a means should be found for representing the diversity of political opinions, his words were virtually the only ones that contained any hint of *progresismo*. All the speakers on the platform disregarded the scripts written for them by the secretaries, and rather than laud political progress toward a thoroughgoing democracy, they chose instead to praise a static traditionalism. Raimundo de Miguel, for instance, who was later to become a strong opponent of Carlist progressives, argued that "the people" could not be sovereign if there was to be representation and that Carlism was not like political parties whose programs were contingent, changing according to circumstances. In contrast to this undesirable flux, he claimed, the Carlist motto of DIOS, PATRIA, REY, FUEROS was the true expression of the Spanish political constitution and thus, implicitly, did not change.[77] At Montejurra the following year, the revived neocollaborationist policy was firmly in evidence. In his message, Don Javier told Carlists to integrate themselves fully within public life without, at the same time, breaking the law. Lauding the work of the *requetés*, he asked God to enlighten Franco and to protect and to bless "our patria." Valiente, in his speech, confirmed this sudden about-face of the Comunión leadership by inviting the dictator to attend Montejurra the next year, and by crying, "Lord, save us from modernism."[78]

While different speakers might put forward varying visions of Carlism and of the future, they did not directly criticize one another, nor were differences of opinion openly discussed. The highly public platform of Montejurra was not a place for those who wished to debate. There was no space here for extended discussions about different attitudes held by various factions. Rather, for most speakers, Montejurra was an opportunity to restate powerfully the movement's ideals and aims as they understood them. The only time any dispute was seen to occur on the platform happened in 1974, by which time the progressives had long won control of the movement and shifted it toward the Left. On that occasion, José Maria Codón Fernández, a Catalan traditionalist, had started to say that it was necessary for Carlism to come to an understanding with the army. Zavala was so horrified by this unexpected and unorthodox opinion that he immediately snatched the microphone from Codón. But this event is remembered only because of its exceptional nature.[79] Otherwise, the speakers on the platform in any one year presented a very loosely united front. The idea was to rally the faithful and point them in the right direction, not to divide and confuse them.

The Construction of Solidarity

The religious and political acts of Montejurra, together with all other associated aspects of the ritual, were meant collectively to reinforce a sense of solidarity among participants. The ritual both presupposed and was intended to generate solidarity. As the articles in the partisan press pointed out, people were to assemble on the day in order to revitalize their faith in the movement, to remember the deeds of their dead, and then to enjoy the festive ambience of Carlists together in a Carlist setting. Those attending met not as villagers, professionals, or priests, but as Carlists—an identity not bounded by hometown or job but by allegiance to a nationally framed movement of the people, one with universalizing pretensions. Participants could shed their quotidian roles for the day, hold in abeyance much of the usual social structure they were defined by, and affirm a somewhat different way of organizing the world. As brothers and sisters of the great Carlist family, they could also temporarily lay aside particularistic relationships for the sake of a politically generic kinship. The very journey from one's village to Montejurra both effected and symbolized this short-lived distancing from the onus and constraint of their ordinary lives,[80] while the temporary occupation of the otherwise uninhabited mountain underlined the extraordinary nature of the day's events. This is not, as Victor Turner would have it,[81] the creation of a liminoid antistructure, but the temporary fabrication of a distinct social structure, the Carlist one.

This striving for a regulated union of equals at Montejurra was tempered by a mild statement of regimental identity, which often subsumed a regional sense of belonging: veterans proudly carried the fading banners and the crucifixes of their regiments, and placed flowers and wreaths at the foot of the cross dedicated to their fallen; demobilized officers wore the insignia of their rank, a fleur-de-lis, on their berets; and the bereaved rendered homage to the *requetés* in general by participating in the pilgrimage, and to their deceased kin in particular by praying devoutly in front of the cross dedicated to the memory of his unit. But fellow pilgrims could excuse these claims to military distinctiveness as an acceptable, personal focus on specific individuals or groups who had collectively made the recent Carlist past so memorable.

Any strong sense of hierarchy was muted in the religious act and was only gently reasserted in the later political act when representatives rose to speak before the represented. Even though orators might extol the virtues of unity in their speeches, by the authority of their position and by their place on the platform they expressed difference from the crowd in political and spatial frames. However, speakers could express solidarity by common physical gesture. At the morning Mass in the ceremony of 1954, the Carlist deputies in the Navarrese government made manifest the widespread disapproval of the incumbent civil governor, a highly unpopular figure, by refusing to sit with him and moving across the aisle to another bench.[82]

The search for solidarity was pursued generally by downplaying difference. More specifically, it was partly achieved by effectively ignoring, and thus devaluing, women as a distinct group. In the first years of Montejurra, when women made up the majority of pilgrims and the religious sense of the ceremony was very strong, the ritual—first thought up by a woman—was not much publicized in the local periodicals, and the Navarrese Junta did little to stimulate its growth. In the late 1950s, as attendance began to rise and the event's political aspect grew in importance, the glories of the *requetés* were lengthily and elaborately extolled in the pages of *El Pensamiento Navarro*, while the wartime role of the Margaritas was all but forgotten. The newspaper columnists made general calls for Carlists to go to Montejurra but, on examination, almost all the examples they gave of "people" at the ceremony were men. Although women were present on the day, and often in great numbers, they were usually absent from journalists' accounts of the ceremony. Carlist women, as though accepting the male devaluation of their distinctiveness, stopped wearing white berets and switched to red ones, sometimes lightly decorated with a few daisies *(margaritas)*. Thus women, excluded from the columns of *El Pensamiento Navarro*, retained their associations with the hidden, the private, and the religious. Montejurra had become a newsworthy, public event, dominated by men. Only a woman with the status of a Carlist princess was allowed to stand out.

The very organization of this ceremony of solidarity concealed a longstanding division between the Carlists of Madrid and those of Navarre. As Montejurra became larger and more important, the Carlist leadership in Madrid became increasingly keen to take over its management, but the proud provincials of the Navarrese Junta refused to hand over responsibility. Influential local Carlists cherished the historical, and continuing, distinctiveness of their province within Carlism as a whole. Navarre, after all, had been one of the few areas where Carlists had revitalized their organization in the postwar period without the aid of the national leadership. Furthermore, the Navarrese Junta was the only one to appoint all its own members: while the regional chiefs of other areas were simply appointed by the pretender according to his own judgement, a candidate for the chieftaincy of the Navarrese Junta was suggested to the king by the junta itself, and he always followed their wish. To leading Navarrese members, the Carlism of their province was a more popular brand than that of Madrid Carlists. According to these Navarrese, the men of their area would just put on their red berets and go to Montejurra no matter how they were dressed, even if they had to go straight from working in the fields. In contrast, the Madrid leaders were seen to attend the ceremony in a more lordly style: they dressed up for the occasion, were better organized, and paid more attention to the *santones* of the movement.

The organizers of Montejurra were not aiming to achieve anything so difficult as consensus, but rather trying to prevent the lack of consensus from reaching a point where oppositional attitudes would be translated into political, or pugilistic, action. "Bloody incidents, like that in 1942 in Begoña, were always expected. . . . When the events of the day finished without any, leaders would sigh deeply."[83] To forestall potential conflict, the organizers attempted (but usually failed) to prohibit the distribution of any unofficial pamphlets, and they allowed only approved vendors to sell Carlist periodicals.[84]

Despite the efforts of organizers to generate solidarity among participants, the conflict between certain Carlist groups could not always be contained pacifically. When Massó spoke of "King Javier" in 1956, infuriated *juanistas* shouted their vehement disagreement and were forced to leave. The next year, committed *carlosoctavistas* were so angered by the appearance of Carlos Hugo and by his arrogation of the title "Prince of Asturias" that they booed him loudly and quickly became involved in heated arguments with a crowd of *javieristas*. Like the *juanistas* in 1956, they too had to quit the scene. The year after that, a coachload of *estorilinos* had to flee after being met by a hail of stones from their Carlist opponents, who were outraged that these renegades had dared to show their faces at Montejurra. In 1963, during the reading out of the prince's annual message, a group of *sivattistas* started to cry "Carlos Hugo is no good!"; they were immediately set upon and ousted. Three years later, progressives hooted at Blas Piñar during his speech. Since Montejurra was not meant to provide cause for internal division but to promote public unity, he was not invited again. In 1968 two taxiloads of bellicose traditionalists, most of them in their late sixties and styling themselves the "*Batidores* [Scouts] of Don Javier on the orders of Franco," were shuffled off the scene by Civil Guards when one of them replied to insults from *javieristas* by drawing his pistol.[85] In 1970 isolated groups of assertive progressives and traditionalists insulted one another, which in some cases led to fights. None of the veteran pilgrims with whom I spoke acknowledged any of these incidents to be particularly significant. They said they did not disturb the general atmosphere of Carlist celebration. From 1959 on, Montejurra was after all a predominantly *javierista* event. Most of those who gave their allegiance to other factions of the movement attended, not to shout out their opposition, but to pass time with fellow Carlists.[86]

In sum, the Carlists at Montejurra might appear united to curious outsiders regarding the event from afar, but the participants achieved a ritual-long solidarity only by the temporary denial of dissimilarity—whether military, hierarchical, sexual, or factional. The public face that the Carlist elite wished to present in their annual ceremony and in their articles about the occasion was not of internal discord aggravated by ambivalence, but of fraternal unanimity charged with ideological purpose.

The solidarity shown by the majority of the crowd at Montejurra was not, however, solely Carlist. In 1959, the event was attended by low-ranking officers and other disgruntled members of the regime who still believed in the political possibility of a national alliance of all "the men of 18 July." Groups of Falangist veterans, some of them dressed in their blue shirts, also started turning up for the ritual. In 1962, a few weeks before the marriage of Don Juan's son Juan Carlos, Comunión leaders, in an effort to show the range of forces opposed to the Alfonsine claim to the throne, invited famous Falangists to the event and read out messages sent by Pilar and Miguel Primo de Rivera, sister and brother of the martyred founder of the blue shirts. The organizers of the ceremony, anxious both to attract even more non-Carlists and to avoid giving the police an excuse for interfering, warned activist youths not to shout slogans against Franco or Opus Dei. Their conservative policy, aimed at improving relations with the regime, bore some fruit. In the Montejurra of 1963, for instance, telegrams of support were read out from the vice-president of the government, General Agustín Muñoz Grandes; the president of the Cortes, the *carlofranquista* Esteban Bilbao; and the captain-general of Madrid, Rafael García Valiño. In return, the Hermandad de la Vía Crucis de Montejurra sent a similar telegram of support to the Generalísimo. Given the Carlist leaders' concern for appeasement with the authorities, it is noteworthy that at the same Montejurra, a group of Asturian miners who had once worked with Carlos Hugo down in the pit bore placards calling for social and political change, while reformists in the crowd spent the time shouting mildly progressive slogans.[87]

The heterogenous appeal of Montejurra was even more marked in 1966, when the Falangists on the sidelines were joined by observers from Catalan and Basque Nationalist groups, together with representatives from the union of democratic students in Madrid. A little color was added in the mid-1960s by the repeated attendance of a Scots legitimist who used to turn up dressed in his kilt and sporran. He told a journalist he was "very impressed by the ceremony, the enthusiasm, the friendly atmosphere."[88] The event was also attended in these years by people who, quite simply, just enjoyed this rare opportunity for political expression. As some said to me, they liked the atmosphere. The sight of thousands of red-bereted Carlists clambering up the mountain path was, they said, "very pretty." To these political tourists, Montejurra was a very rare ritual of opposition—however mildly the dissent might be expressed—and they attended it as such. Although these onlookers may have appreciated the scene, some of them were unmoved by the oratory. When I asked one veteran Basque tripper to Montejurra his main impression of the event, he replied, "A strong feeling of the absurd."

Montejurra as Active Process

Montejurra, with its massed crowds, gave literal substance to the idea of a Carlist community. The ceremony reified Carlism, objectifying what was otherwise invisible. If the *requetés,* for instance, could not rearm, then they could at least re-form and parade in front of their monarch. The number of people attending the ceremony, their degree of animation, and their reaction to the speeches were an integral part of the proceedings. Carlists gathered at Montejurra in order to be with their fellows, to commemorate collectively their dead, and to glorify the movement of which they were a part. This was less an "imagined community," as Benedict Anderson[89] would have it, than a real one given momentary substance by and within the ceremony. On the mountainside, the massed Carlists were meant to stand closer to God and to join with the spiritual company of their predecessors. Here, both the living and the dead met under the eye of God. As a group celebration of Carlism's existence, Montejurra thus comes close to the Durkheimian conception of ritual as a means for society to worship itself. But unlike the Australian Aboriginal rites he described, the Carlists crowded on the mountaintop were celebrating community without the aid of a mediating referent, whether totem or deity.[90] To them, Montejurra was a pilgrimage, not to some god but to themselves. In these terms, we could characterize the ritual as less Carlism reified than Carlism self-deified.

Except for non-Carlist bystanders, Montejurra was no mere spectacle. It was not a grand sight to be contemplated from a distance; it was a participatory experience in which the audience, and its number, was intrinsic to its performance. Participants as well as outside commentators partially judged the effectiveness of the event in terms of the crowd's size and its degree of animation. A Montejurra with political intent but attended by very few was regarded as a disappointment, while the years when the summit, or the plaza, overflowed with people shouting "*¡Vivas!*" to their leaders are vividly remembered occasions. The success of the ceremony was thus, to a certain degree, self-generating: the larger it grew, the more of an event it became, and hence all the more worth attending.

In this sense, Montejurra is unlike, say, a rite of passage, a transformative ritual centered around a group of initiators and initiates where the number of onlookers is often largely irrelevant. In the performance of Montejurra in the 1960s and early 1990s, the officiating priests, the speechmakers, the uniformed *requetés*, the bereaved pilgrims, the journalists, the political tourists, and the rest of the crowd together created and performed the ceremony, all of them helping to make the annual ritual either a memorable occasion or a relatively run-of-the-mill event. To this extent, the police standing by on the sidelines were themselves part of the events of the day. Whether quietly watching the different phases of the ceremony unfold, or actively intervening by setting up roadblocks or charging riotous demonstrators, they indirectly legitimated Carlists' sense of their own political importance and, thus, of the ceremony itself: if the Carlists had had nothing to say or had not been perceived as a force to be reckoned with, then the police would not have turned up.

The form of participation required of the Carlists at the ritual was not meant to be passive, but energetic and energizing. They were not supposed to come simply to remember their dead, but also to *reenact*, physically and mentally, some of their deeds. The Masses celebrated at Irache returned the monastery to a place of succor for Carlists; the effort involved climbing the mountain was said to simulate the sacrifice of the *requetés;* the procession itself imitated a warlike column; the massed invasion of the summit replicated its conquest by an earlier generation of the faithful; the crowded occupation of Estella emulated its taking in the 1870s; and the clamorous applause received by the speakers on the platform paralleled the enthusiastic reception given to Carlos VII whenever he had strolled through the same plaza. In this sense, the pilgrims to Montejurra did not placidly experience a mere "annual meeting with Carlist history," as one journalist put it,[91] but actively re-created some of its most glorious episodes in a lively and ceremonially embodied manner. Rather than simply maintaining the memory of these past events, the pilgrims' incorporated practices revivified them and so, like the journalists' articles, tried to deny the passage of time. The physical routines prescribed for dedicated participants acted as types of performative memory, which could be reproduced, with a certain degree of effort, at each staging of Montejurra.[92] The Carlists, after all, were meant to be energetic defenders of their creed and its traditions, and a visitor to the ritual could take their enlivening actions, annually repeated, to be continuing proof of that vitality and commitment.

Partisan journalists acknowledged the active contribution of the participants to the significance of the ceremony. As these writers claimed, the pilgrimage had become so central to the maintenance of the movement and all it stood for that, if the faithful stopped attending, Carlism, and thus the Carlist conception of the country, would be unable to survive. In the words of one correspondent, pilgrims went to Montejurra "every year to hold up the mountain, for if it sank, Spain would sink also."[93]

1. Paco, 1987.

2. Marí and the author, 1987.

3. Milu and his son Marco, 1999.

4. Javi, 1999.

5. La Txus Laita and Marí-José Dallo, Cirauqui fiestas, 1999.

6. "*Requetés*," *Carlos Saénz de Tejada, late 1930s. (Courtesy Carlos Saénz de Tejada)*
The standard literary image of the requetés *was complemented and boosted by a stereotypical visual image of them. Carlos Sáenz de Tejada, perhaps the best-known war illustrator, in his highly stylized romantic drawings, inspired by both surrealism and social realism, created the prototype of these men, portraying them as strong, sure of themselves, and capable of making all the sacrifices necessary to ensure ultimate victory. Drawn against naturalist backgrounds, they seem to live in the landscape, whether that be their home valley or a field of battle (Arcediano and García Díez 1993). Pictorially naturalized within their setting, they and the values they embody are made to seem as timeless as the countryside they are set in. These drawings were extremely popular during the Spanish Civil War and frequently utilized in subsequent decades to illustrate Carlist books, periodicals, and postcards.*

7. *"Con este signo vencerás"* (*"With this sign you will overcome"*), *Gustavo de Maetzu, ca. 1938. (Courtesy Museo de Navarra) Gustavo de Maetzu (1887–1947), a noted Basque modernist painter, spent his last eleven years in Estella. There he developed his interest and love for the history, traditions, and countryside of Navarre, being commissioned by local institutions to produce historicist paintings and murals. This portrayal of a red-bereted* requeté *overshadowed by an old stone cross, set within the local landscape, is typical of his works during this period, several of which commemorate nineteenth-century and Civil War Carlism.*

8. *"Guerras Civiles. Boceto para la Cúpula del Monumento a los Caídos, Pamplona"* (*"Civil Wars. Sketch for the Dome of the Monument to the Fallen, Pamplona"*) *Ramón Stolz Viciano, 1950. (Courtesy Museo de Navarra) This large-scale mural was painted on the inner surface of the dome of the Monument to the Fallen, constructed in a highly prominent position, at the end of the main avenue of the center of Pamplona. Read from right to left, it depicts participants of the various wars that have traversed Navarre since the 1830s: the First and Second Carlist Wars and the Civil War of the 1930s. Carlists of both centuries and their 1930s allies are all portrayed together, contemporaneously, making the same uphill struggle, with a* requeté *at the rock's high point, upholding the cross.*

Since the accession of socialists to the Deputation of Navarre in the 1980s, the monument has been allowed to fall into disrepair and is no longer illuminated after sunset. Today, looking down the avenue at night, all one is aware of is a large blackness.

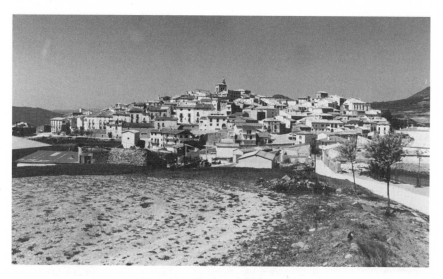

9. *Cirauqui, view from the east, 1998.*

10. *Relaxing at the annual village fiestas, 1911. (Courtesy Antonio Laita)*

11. *The village band at fiesta time, 1912. (Courtesy Antonio Laita)*

12. *El Cojo de Cirauqui in the uniform of a liberal officer, 1870s.*
(Courtesy C. Sánchez de Muniain)

13. *"Cirauqui Todo por los Fueros" ("Cirauqui Everything for the Fueros"), 1870s.*

14. Don Javier and Carlos Hugo, early 1960s. (Courtesy El Diario de Navarra)

15. Pope Paul VI receiving Carlos Hugo and Princess Irene shortly after their wedding, 1964. (Courtesy El Diario de Navarra)

16. *Acting the role of the good Spaniard: Carlos Hugo and María-Teresa at the daily bullfight during the Pamplonan fiesta of Sanfermines. Carlos Hugo wears a red neckerchief, a traditional dress for the fiesta, early 1960s.*
(*Courtesy* El Diario de Navarra)

17. *Princesses Cecilia and María-Teresa at Montejurra, mid-1960s.*
(*Courtesy* El Diario de Navarra)

18. *Flanked by crosses and flags, Princesses Irene and María-Teresa pray at the altar on the summit during a performance of Montejurra, late 1960s.*
(*Courtesy* El Diario de Navarra)

19. Escorted by requetés, *Princess María-Teresa salutes the faithful, at the foot of Montejurra, mid-1960s. (Courtesy* El Diario de Navarra*)*

20. The ascent of Montejurra, mid-1960s. (Courtesy El Diario de Navarra*)*

*21. Celebration of Mass on the summit of Montejurra, mid-1960s.
(Courtesy* El Diario de Navarra)

22. The crowd listening to the afternoon speeches, Plaza de los Fueros, Estella, mid-1960s. (Courtesy El Diario de Navarra*)*

23. The sixtinos *attack the crowd outside the monastery of Irache, 1976.*
(Courtesy El Diario de Navarra*)*

24. Assisting one of the wounded at Irache, 1976. (Courtesy El Diario de Navarra)

25. *A Pamplonan troupe of traditional Basque dancers performing in the main plaza of Cirauqui during the annual fiestas. The building to the right is the town hall; one balcony is decorated with the national, Basque, and municipal flags; the cloth stretched across its railings is the standard of Navarre. The building to the left is the former Carlist Circle of the village, 1998.*

26. *Lighting of the zezensuko (firework bull) at midnight during the fiestas, 1998.*

27. *Overpainting of the village name road sign, changing the Castilian "Cirauqui" to the earlier, Euskera name for it, "Zirauki." The graffitist's "signature" at the lower right of the sign is the symbol for the AEK, the organization for the teaching of Euskera espoused by radical nationalists, 1998.*

28. *Lithograph of General Zumulacárregui by Gustavo de Maeztu, 1940s. (Courtesy Museo Gustavo de Maeztu, Estella). The example of Zumulacárregui has been made to play several roles. Alongside his pictures and murals glorifying the military efforts of Franco's troops, Gustave de Maeztu produced several lithographs and paintings of the Carlist general, whom he saw as a legendary figure of the area, to be dramatically portrayed. His very large painting of Zumulacárregui seated on a white horse is today prominently exhibited by the Town Hall of Pamplona inside the entrance to one of its main administrative buildings.*

Chapter Nine

The Establishment of the Progressives

On 15 December 1968, at a Carlist meeting in the Riojan town of Valvanera, Carlos Hugo deliberately made a highly provocative speech deeply critical of the regime. As he and his advisers had foreseen, Franco reacted by having him expelled from the country. A few days later, his father and two of his sisters were also ordered to leave. Carlists in Pamplona reacted to news of the deportation by spontaneously rioting outside the headquarters of the civil governor. For the first time in many years in a Carlist demonstration, the protagonists did not retreat but stood their ground when the Civil Guard pulled up in their vans. The resulting bloody combat left sixteen guardsmen and many Carlists wounded. Carlos Hugo went to live in Valcarlos (valley of Carlos), a French Pyrenean village next to the border with Navarre—the self-same pass from which, at the end of the Second Carlist War, the fleeing monarch, Carlos VII, had uttered his famous, if unfulfilled, phrase, "¡Volveré!" ("I will return!").[1]

Now in exile, the prince no longer needed to maintain a nonbelligerent policy toward the dictator. His anticipated expulsion had removed any remaining external constraint on the political development of the movement he headed. With his supporters already occupying key posts within the Comunión hierarchy and with many Carlists moving toward the Left, Carlos Hugo could now afford both to criticize the dictatorship and to preach internal reform much more openly, which is what he proceeded to do.

Carlist Evolution: Instruments, Ideology, and Limitations

The main instrument of this ideological evolution was the *cursillos* (short courses), which were staged in Valcarlos. In each of these three-day sessions of intense political discussion, chaired by leading progressives (often Carlos Hugo himself or Zavala), the thirty to forty participants debated the pros and cons of a particular political theme.[2] The pedagogical role of the *cursillos* was furthered by the periodical *Información Mensual (IM)*. Edited by Zavala, and with contributions from leading progressives, it praised all Carlos Hugo's actions and discussed current political themes and events in a critical, highly anticapitalist vein. A supplementary instrument of the Carlist evolution was the detailed questionnaires sent to militants, which required them to specify their political position.[3]

While the discussions in the *cursillos* advanced and developed the party line, they did so in a rather uncoordinated manner and involved only a relatively small number of people. Carlos Hugo and his advisers therefore decided to stage a series of national congresses as a means whereby a more coherent set of reformist policies could be debated and agreed on by a broad section of the movement: members of the Governing Junta, provincial and regional chiefs, and directly voted delegates.

By the end of the first three congresses, held in Valcarlos in December 1970, May 1971, and June 1972, delegates had defined the outlines of the political system they wished to see established. Arguing against capitalist individualism and communist collectivism, they chose as the conceptual linchpins of their proposed system the notions of "social revolution" and *autogestión* (self-management). Land, goods, and the means of production, all of which were controlled by the dominant classes, had to be returned to "society." A social leveling would accompany this ending of economic differentiation; class, as a means of ranking people, would disappear. Come this revolution, "the people" were to be given as much control over their own lives as possible. Workers would participate in all socioeconomic decisions affecting their livelihood. They would not, moreover, participate solely in the democratic management of the factories or businesses where they worked, but in the planning of the national economy as well. People would also take part in the running of their own communities at all levels of representation, from the municipal to the national. Delegates tried to avoid what they saw as the related dangers of overcentralization and radical separatism by agreeing that the country itself would be restructured as a federation of "social republics," with the state becoming but the "communal expression of the other communities, the instrument of global self-management between them." The head of state would be a "socialist monarch" who would maintain his position only if he maintained a pact between the people, represented by political parties, and his dynasty. His main duty was to act as an arbiter, defending pluralism and equality of opportunity against the threat of domination by the central administration, or by the most powerful and prestigious regional communities.[4]

It is deeply unfortunate for the political philosophers of Carlist *progresismo* that the example that inspired them—the policy of self-management practiced in Titoist Yugoslavia—appeared so viable only because most of the facts about the operation of this system were then unknown to Carlos Hugo and his cohort. According to Yugoslav political scientists, self-management simply does not work at the national level, for a variety of damning reasons.

First, what is owned by everybody is owned by nobody. Directors of enterprises regarded themselves as the executors of agreements made by their work-ers' councils. Workers, however, proved to have little interest in managing their firms; their main aim was to gain the highest possible wages compatible with the least responsibility for decision-making. But if directors do not think they are the owners, and workers are uninterested in owning, then there is no one prepared to decide on the risks every enterprise must eventually take.

Second, enterprises run on the lines of self-management led to inflation and economic instability, for the workers always demanded the highest pay, whether or not their businesses were prospering, and their directors felt forced to submit to their demands. The result of higher pay was an increase in expenditure, and the result of that was higher prices. Unlike what occurs in Western European economies, this inflationary process was not checked by competition from other enterprises operating in the same market.

Third, a similar set of administrative problems occurred in the running of the communes (geographically defined units of population). Most people were un-interested in shouldering responsibilities, especially those that potentially laid them open to much blame and little gain, and those who were prepared to take on administrative and executive tasks often carried them out in an ama-teurish and disorganized manner. The cumulative result bordered on chaos.

Fourth, the degree of disorder within communes led to a comparable lack of coordination between them. The consensual compacts that these bodies did manage to make were usually confused in their objectives and were frequently executed in an unsystematic, unproductive fashion.

Fifth, and perhaps most damningly, the abolition of private property might have brought an end to social classes, but only at the cost of creating alterna-tive ways of stratifying society. The old elites based on the possession of land and industry were simply replaced by newly emergent ones based on position within the political, administrative, and managerial hierarchies. There was no easy way to ameliorate this novel form of social inequality, because the polit-ical philosophy of the state denied its very existence. The official ideology of egalitarianism, it appears, benefited only the powerful.[5]

A sixth problem with the idea of self-management, one which Carlos Hugo and his high-minded coterie did not consider in a sufficiently hard-headed manner, was that of regional division. For in countries like Spain and the former Yugoslavia, which include geographically definable concentrations of ethnic communities maintaining a strong sense of identity, it could be ex-tremely difficult indeed for the central government to persuade provincial bodies of the need to reconcile local interests with national ones. Carlos Hugo might have innocently hoped that the process of working together toward the ultimate goal of self-management would generate a sense of solidarity among the citizens of a country, but the rise of militant, popular nationalisms during the latter half of Franco's reign was already suggesting a very different outcome. As suggested by both the war that broke up Yugoslavia and the terrorist campaigns that marked the Spanish transition to democracy, members of ethnic groups may be willing to forego important economic benefits for the sake of securing their identity.

A seventh and final obstacle to the achievement of self-management is similar to that which faced those nineteenth-century Carlists who were bent on introducing a traditionalist form of government. For while all thoroughgoing political philosophies include their own mechanism for the achievement of power, the procedure proposed by the Carlist *autogestionarios* appears as unrealistically optimistic as that of their traditionalist predecessors. In his book, *La vía Carlista al socialismo autogestionario. El proyecto carlista de socialismo democrático (The Carlist Way to Self-Managing Socialism: The Carlist Project of Democratic Socialism)*, Carlos Hugo states that the middle classes will simply be persuaded to give up their privileges in a peaceful manner. Won over by the patent advantages of self-management implemented at all levels and in every sector of society, they will convert without hesitation from an egotistical selfishness to an idealistic communitarianism. This morality—ultimately based on Christian ethics—of good-natured individuals sharing what they had did not take into account the resistance that privileged groups would offer to any imposed reduction of what they considered to be their prerogatives. Any backward look at Carlist history itself would have shown the extreme unlikelihood of people giving up what they already had.

It is perhaps a bit too easy to use hindsight to criticize the past wellintentioned efforts of others. It is important to remember that in the late 1960s and early 1970s the prospect of managing their own affairs may well have greatly excited many Spaniards, who, after all, had by then suffered dictatorship and exclusion from positions of power (however minor) for more than thirty years. Moreover, the almost millenarian tone of the *autogestionarios* was not out of place within contemporary politics when one compares it with the rhetoric of other left-wing groups of the period. Within this inspired company the idea of completely restructuring the state did not seem inappropriately chiliastic nor out of touch with the reality of power within Spain at that time. María-Teresa de Borbón-Parma even entitled one of her books, published shortly after the death of Franco, *El momento actual español cargado de utopia (The Present Moment in Spain Charged with Utopia)*. It opens with the following words:

> We Spaniards of the *pueblos* of Spain are living an extraordinary moment, because it is a moment of rupture. Of rupture with Franquism and, beyond Franquism, with everything that made it possible. . . .

We Spaniards are many, we who have waited many years for this moment and all that it signifies. Not in a passive manner, but constructing the gangplanks that made it possible. And now, whatever our age, we feel young when faced with it. The future begins now.[6]

New Heaven, New Earth?

By this stage leading progressives did not want merely to usher in change, developing just the policies and structure of their movement. In their effort to make Carlism less reminiscent of a horde of gun-toting romantics and much more akin to a tightly controlled modern political organization, they wished also to transform thoroughly Carlists' conceptions of themselves and their association as well.

To that end, the method of entry into the movement was drastically revised. To conservatives, the best way to be Carlist was by birth. "Another way, very befitting of a gentleman," was by baptism of fire. The "coldest" way of joining the movement was by rational choice, which could, however, "take profound root, once the doctrine had been accepted and had inflamed the mind and heart."[7] Following this train of thought, members of the party faithful could dismiss those who had gone over to the side of Don Juan by pointing out that most of them lacked Carlist forefathers.[8] In contrast, for the more radical of the reformers, Carlism was neither a clan nor an inheritance, but an option and a commitment. They did not regard the movement as a closed social group whose membership was decided by birth, but as a more open form of association that people could choose to join. They wanted people who would actively participate in the movement, not those who did nothing more than simply declare, "I'm Carlist until I die!" Thus the progressives came to redefine the very notion of "Carlist." As María-Teresa de Borbón-Parma put it, "To be Carlist is not to offer one's life heroically in a great mystic impulse, but rather to become the instrument that will make Carlism resurge as a popular organized force."[9] A letter published in *Información Mensual* by an Aragonese progressive expressed the same desire for change in definition and disposition in a somewhat more passionate manner:

I'm tired of we Carlists being called "the noble Carlists" or "the noble *requetés.*"

It's not that the adjective "noble" irritates me. But the tone in which people are accustomed to utter this expression suggests that we Carlists charge the first cape put in front of us. Our enemies know this and keep waving capes, very red and very exciting ones, in order to deflect our attention from the *political objective,* which today is fundamental.[10]

One intention behind all the reforms instituted by the progressives was to transform the old Comunión, with its connotations of a backward-glancing Catholicism, into a secularized political party that looked toward the future and was to be called the Partido Carlista. Although the policy of self-management was inspired by the moral values of the Church, progressives now claimed it was no longer necessary for members of the party to be zealously Catholic, or even Christian at all. In a statement that would have shocked their traditionalist forebears, they said an avowed atheist could become a Carlist. But as Cecilia de Borbón-Parma pointed out, while a high percentage of members were lapsed Catholics or nonbelievers, Christian philosophy continued to coexist with, though it did not determine, political ideology within the party.[11]

In the late 1940s, traditionalist hostility to Franco's very mild relaxation of the restrictions on Protestant worship had led to former *requetés* attacking chapels and threatening to disrupt their processions.[12] The liberal reforms of the Second Vatican Council, Carlos Hugo's consistent opposition to the idea of a confessional state, and progressives' criticism of the ecclesiastical hierarchy for its association with the Franquist government, meant that such direct action on the temples of other faiths had become inconceivable by the late 1960s. The imagined threat of a Protestant revival that had successfully, if momentarily, united the otherwise divided Comunión two decades before did not worry the progressives. They were concerned with political action rather than theological debate. Their religious heroes were not those who had sacrificed themselves for mystical ideals, but worker-priests who concerned themselves with the earthly lot of their flock.[13] The more militant of progressives, however, did not simply turn their backs on the past religiosity of Carlism but reacted strongly against it, in a manner that suggested that the example of the *requetés* was far from dead: "To the comfortably well-off, full of money and of hypocritical piousness . . . let them go to Mass, to conferences, and to banquets . . . and to Hell. Fewer masses and more bombs!! Long live Carlos Hugo!!"[14]

The traditionalist motto of DIOS, PATRIA, REY, FUEROS quietly fell into disuse. *Dios* had been put on a side pedestal. *Patria* was gently downplayed, as regional nationalisms—whether Basque, Catalan, or Galician—became more popular and as patriotism came to seem too close to the old Franquist jingoism. The king was now presented as the first among equals. And reformers no longer spoke of the *fueros,* but of "self-determination" for the peoples of Spain.

The outdated slogan, first used in the 1830s, had no place among the categories that constituted the progressives' new world.

The Ousting of the Old

The approval by the majority of those attending the congresses of the new policies and structure helped to consolidate the hegemony of the progressives and to delegitimate the stance of the remaining conservatives. Neocollaborationism had been definitely rejected; the official Carlist organization would no longer stray out of the political opposition to the dictatorship. At the First National Carlist Congress, reformers, employing a tactic they were to use several times, had forestalled potential conservative protest by having a message, ostensibly from Don Javier but in fact written by leading progressives, read out. The import of the missive was to define Carlists as those who, loyal to his dynasty, submitted to the discipline of the organization he headed. Stressing the familial ties both within the Borbón-Parmas and within the movement as a whole, Don Javier's message stated that those who attacked his son directly attacked him and, in consequence, Carlism itself. Those who respected him had to respect his words.

Outmaneuvered, the conservatives were also being physically outnumbered by the increasing ranks of militants. Influential progressives started to dissolve regional committees whose members had not been democratically selected— as was the case with many of the committees. These members were replaced by reformists elected by the militants of their region. Publicly, Carlos Hugo urged aging conservatives to let the Carlist youth take over; privately, Zavala wrote to those (numerous) provincial chiefs who had not attended the first congress, stating bluntly that those who did not distribute Don Javier's message to all the Carlists, and to all those with political interests, within their area should resign. Provincial and regional chiefs were also obliged both to attend *cursillos* over the border and to organize their own in their home areas. Chiefs who refused to do so, and who branded them "brainwashing," were forced to step down. Those conservatives who would not go quietly were summarily dismissed and, in several cases, expelled as well.[15]

Some of the old guard, at first persuaded by Carlos Hugo's early reformism, stayed in the movement until the accumulated changes became too much for them to accept. After the directed move to the Left following Franco's expulsion of Carlos Hugo, the two Carlist *procuradores* for Navarre found they were being treated as personae non gratae by the party. Although they had been among the most active members of the parliamentary antifranquist opposi-

tion, they felt they were being regarded by progressives as refractory reactionaries. In 1971 they refused to stand for reelection because the party executive
had insisted that they agree in writing to their automatic dismissal if, at any
time, it was thought that they were not representing the interests of the movement. In a tense meeting with their king and leading progressives, they argued
that they represented all their constituents, not just people of the same persuasion. They would not be tied to the party alone, and so despite their keen wish
to respect the desire of their beloved monarch, they resigned. Both had enjoyed widespread support and great prestige. As they had warned, neither of
their replacements was elected.[16]

Dictatorial Repression, Carlist Reaction

The regime had once tolerated the Comunión. But by the late 1960s there was
no longer any political reason to do so: the prince had gotten himself exiled by
breaking his gentlemen's agreement with Franco, the neocollaborationists had
left or were leaving the movement, and the progressives continued to propound
antigovernment arguments in an unrelenting manner. No longer prepared to
turn a blind eye to most Carlist activities, the dictatorship now became much
more obstructive: repressing progressives who spoke out at illegal forums, closing their periodicals, and assisting ousted traditionalists who wished to set up
their own counterorganizations. During its most coherent period, this sclerotic
strategy of the aging dictator was known as "Operación Maestrazgo."

In 1969, the ceremonial reinterment of the remains of Vázquez de Mella in
Covadonga was proscribed, policemen raided Princess Irene's office in Madrid, the outspoken editor of *El Pensamiento Navarro* was arrested, and the
political act of Montejurra, which was to have been held in the Plaza de los
Fueros in Estella, was prohibited. Speakers circumvented this ban by giving
their speeches on the mountaintop. María-Teresa, who had entered the country secretly, promised the assembled that "the struggle would continue advancing and that the dynasty she represented would always be present in the
vanguard both within and outside Spain."[17] The day ended with a particularly
violent confrontation between the police and young Carlists still angry at the
expulsion of their leaders. Five days later, the Carlist headquarters in Madrid
was closed, several leaders were hauled in for questioning, and three of the
speakers on the mountaintop were fined.[18]

In 1971 the political act of Montejurra was banned once again. And once
again, the speakers shifted their venue to the summit. Zavala told the crowd
that constitutional guarantees had to be reestablished and that a bill before the
Cortes that proposed amplifying the measures of repression had to be with-

drawn. In speedy response to these latest criticisms, the government removed documents from the Madrid offices of the Junta Nacional de Requetés, closed two of its centers in the capital, and suppressed *Montejurra,* whose owners had already been fined several times before. Zavala had to go into hiding.[19] At the same ceremony two years later, Doña Irene publicly denied a false interview with her, published in the Madrid weekly *Sábado Gráfico,* where she supposedly admitted to a complete lack of interest in Carlism and other Spanish affairs. *Esfuerzo Común,* a Carlist journal produced in Zaragoza, was banned for printing her speech and reporting the background to it. This was not the first time its publication had been interrupted by the forces of the regime. Over the previous two years, its offices had been subject to an official inspection, it had been fined twice, had proceedings brought against it four times, and had been forcibly withdrawn from circulation seven times.[20]

Some impetuous militants reacted against the increasingly intolerant attitude of the dictatorship by taking matters into their own hands. In late 1968, a collection of them, who said they were "ready for anything," staged a secret meeting where they formed Grupos de Acción Carlista (GAC). Envious of the highly successful nationalist guerrillas in Euskadi ta Askatasuna (The Basque Country and Freedom), or ETA, this loosely structured organization of discontented youths carried the party policy of *progresismo* and activism to a point where Carlos Hugo and other leaders could not venture. To foundermembers, the formation of a body dedicated to direct and illegal action was a propagandistic act that would improve the image of Carlism by dramatically helping to rid it of its old right-wing associations. Although they agreed with the "clarification" of Carlist ideology and the modernization of the national organization, some members of GAC did not define themselves anew in an orthodox progressive manner. Instead, they proclaimed the inspiration they drew from the notorious band of guerrillas that was led by a daring but bloodthirsty priest in the Second Carlist War:

> Bad times are coming for all the social republics of Spain. We Carlists know it and have already thought out who is deserving of the sacrifices of our lives.
>
> As in the old days, we Carlists are going to respond. The flag of the priest Santa Cruz has been raised again. Our old enemies know well what that means.
>
> Carlists! Liberty! Everything for the people![21]

The best-known group within GAC was a poorly armed commando, centered in Navarre, that stole photostating machinery for the production of pamphlets, robbed a few banks to finance its operations, and blew up the printing works of *El Pensamiento Navarro,* by then back in the hands of staunch traditionalists who had recently sacked its progressive editor. In the Montejurra of 1970 these proponents of direct action, wielding sticks and bludgeons, led a Carlist crowd in charging the police, overturning their jeeps, and then burning an enormous photo of Franco in front of the assembled multitude.

The Carlist leadership did not approve of GAC's methods. Zavala had many verbal contests with members of the Grupos, whom he called "my students" because so many of them had been politically educated in *cursillos* run by him and other leading Carlists. When one prominent member of the commando told Carlos Hugo and Zavala the day after the *Pensamiento* raid what he and his friends had done, both were very shocked and completely against that type of armed activism. The prince wanted the militant to go immediately and labor in Andalucía as a worker. But he would have none of that.

Although the higher echelons of the party came out against GAC and threatened to expel them if they did not desist, many members viewed its actions with sympathy and offered their assistance if it were asked for. Indirectly the party could exploit the fact of GAC's existence for its own political purposes: because it showed that the commitment of at least some progressives went beyond rhetoric, it helped dispel doubts that Carlism was still solidly traditionalist, and it eased relations between the party and ETA. The Basque nationalist gunmen informed the GAC that it wished to coordinate the units of action of the two organizations into an integrated Basque National Front. But the Carlist commando, it transpired, was too ill-disciplined for the purposes of ETA. And armed GAC activism effectively came to an end on New Year's Eve 1970, when most members of the commando were arrested after bungling an attack on a television transmitter station.[22]

The Rise of a Broad Opposition

While the repressive measures of the dictatorship somewhat hindered the development of the Partido Carlista, its leaders' main cause for worry at this time was not the size of the next fine or the prohibition of their next public act, but the place of the party itself within the rapidly growing ranks of the antifranquist opposition. From its earlier, significant position among democratic organizations, progressive Carlism was coming to be but one group (and not a major one at that) within the spectrum of opposition forces that arose in the dying years of the dictatorship. Many who had previously chosen to support Carlism now aligned with other groups. In the 1950s and early 1960s, most of the undergraduates who had joined the AET had done so because it was then one of the very few student organizations that combated the regime. But by the end of the decade, university unrest had become general, and the AET had to compete for recruits with a variety of other associations. At the same time, within the Basquo-Navarrese clergy, priests who militated for political change preached not the Carlist cause—as their forebears might have done—but the nationalist message.[23] These shifts of alliance by militant students, priests, and other groups made it clear to leading progressives that, despite all their efforts, the party lacked widespread mass support. Carlism, to be politically effective, could not go it alone.

The progressives found a—perhaps unexpected—ally in the Partido Comunista Español (PCE, Spanish Communist Party). Although Carlists and communists had been diametrically opposed in the Civil War, from 1958 on the PCE had pursued a policy of national reconciliation, toning down its anticlericalism and preferring to seek radical reform rather than iconoclastic revolution. Since the mid-1960s, *huguistas* had been in close touch with leading Communists thanks to the contacts made by militants in the MOT who worked together with the Communist agitators running the Comisiones Obreras (CC.OO, Workers' Commissions), the umbrella organization for antifranquist trade unionists.[24] Progressives had to keep their early meetings with the communists secret in order not to upset conservatives within the Comunión. Although these Carlist activists were very much the junior partners in any arrangement with the communists, who were simultaneously forging links with other militant Catholic groups, they jointly tried to foment strikes and to infiltrate the lower ranks of the state-run Organización Sindical (Syndical Organization). In Navarre, which by the late 1960s had became a major center of industrial unrest in the country, Carlist worker-militants worked together with the Liga Comunista Revolucionaria (Revolutionary Communist League), and with the Organización Revolucionaria de Trabajadores (ORT, Workers' Revolutionary Organization), which controlled the CC.OO of the province. In the Basque area, where the communists were poorly represented, they thought it to their advantage to cooperate with the Carlists, whose political force the PCE, like other parties, overestimated.[25]

In the early 1970s orators at Montejurra called repeatedly for the union of all antifranquist forces in a Frente Revolucionario Democrático (Revolutionary Democratic Front). Although opposition groups did not join in this initiative, since they were already making their own separate plans to unite, they did send messages of support. Left to themselves, the Carlists assisted the communists in setting up democratic assemblies, juntas, and round tables *(mesas)* throughout the country. The aim of these temporary bodies was social mobilization for the reestablishment of democracy by grouping together left-wing parties, working-class organizations, and legal associations, though the Carlists and the communists later extended their net further and further in order to include as many moderates as possible. But the political competition for popular support was stiffening, and their joint attempt to set up one of these juntas in the Basque Provinces, the Asamblea Democrática de Gernika (Democratic Assembly of Gernika), did not succeed, while the one they constituted in Navarre failed to win over nationalist groups and the provincially dominant ORT. [26]

In 1973 the Communist Party and influential independents tried to unite the antifranquist opposition by forming the Junta Democrática. The aim of its political program of "democratic rupture" was to bring down the regime through mass demonstrations and a nationwide general strike, followed by the installation of a provisional government and the establishment of a Constituent Cortes that would decide the future political system of the country. The Partido Carlista was invited to join Junta Democrática, but it declined to enter since the Junta was then planning to make Don Juan the president of the provisional political system that would replace the dictatorship. It was not until Don Juan had discredited himself with the Junta by failing to make his promised declaration of total disagreement with his son, Juan Carlos, that the party felt able to enter this loose coalition, in September 1974. But the progressive representatives who attended its meetings soon became dissatisfied with the running of the Junta. In their opinion, it had failed to unite the opposition, was effectively controlled by the communists, did not operate in a democratic manner, showed an increasing lack of initiative, and appeared unable to adapt to the evolving political context.

In July the next year, the Partido Carlista left the Junta to join Plataforma de Convergencia Democrática (Platform of Democratic Convergence), an alternative left-wing front dominated by the Partido Socialista Obrero Español (PSOE, Spanish Workers Socialist Party), which was more disposed than the Junta to enter into dialogue with regime reformists, and which seemed to have a more coherent, serious political program. Santiago Carrillo, the leader of the PCE, slowly came to realize that his policy of strikes toppling the regime would not succeed. As his party quietly dropped the idea of a democratic rupture, and as all parties suffered the unrelentingly repressive measures of the dying dictatorship, both the Junta and the Plataforma put their differences aside, and in March 1976, four months after Franco's death, they amalgamated into Coordinación Democrática (Democratic Coordination), a broad coalition prepared to negotiate with the government.[27]

So, as the country began its transition toward democracy, the Partido Carlista was managing to maintain its own, albeit minor, place within the major group of combined forces pushing for governmental change. In retrospect, this transitional period may be recognized as the political high point of the party within the national context, for the progressives were then still being taken seriously by other groups. Their electoral weakness had yet to be revealed.

Chapter Ten

Montejurra 1976

It is tempting to see in the death of Franco, who finally died a frail old man on 20 November 1975 after being sustained for a fortnight on life-support machines, an appropriate metaphor for the end of his tired and outdated regime. Although it was generally recognized that the Franquist form of government would not survive intact without its dictator, a significant number of Franquists were still prepared to fight any tinkering with the system. As a steadily increasing number of bureaucrats and ministers came to see a future for the country, and for themselves, in negotiation with the opposition over reform toward democracy, unrepentant Franquists saw themselves more and more as besieged defenders of the ultimate redoubt, like Hitler in his Berlin bunker. It appears that some of these men, bent on maintaining as much of their late master's regime as possible, were more than ready to assist Carlist conservatives who wanted to discredit Carlos Hugo and his party and to remake their beloved movement in the old style. And in the first uncertain months of the transition, these unreconstructed traditionalists took advantage of a privileged opportunity to reassert the values they stood for and to regain, literally, the ground they had lost to the progressives.

The Reformation of the Traditionalists

Many die-hard traditionalists, who had been effectively pushed out of the movement into which they had been born, still considered themselves upright Carlists. In their opinion, it was not they but Carlos Hugo and his associates who had betrayed the ancient cause and lost the right to call themselves "Carlists." According to traditionalists, the organization these renegades headed was Carlist only in name; indeed the "Partido Carlista" was a contradiction in terms, since Carlists had always regarded political parties as an imported, non-Spanish source of division. What the progressives styled "revolutionary Carlism" was preposterous and absurd, and a socialist monarchy was inadmissible, for socialism was "enslaving, anti-human, materialist, and atheistic." To these counterrevolutionaries, Carlos Hugo and his followers were but misguided materialists with mundane interests; in contrast, the traditionalists liked to proclaim openly their romanticism and their sense of spirit. To distinguish themselves from their opponents, these reactionaries started to term themselves "pure Carlists" and the progressives "official Carlists."[1]

While many of these traditionalists had wished to see a king of their persuasion installed on the Spanish throne, they were not prepared to keep on compromising their ideals for the sake of promoting a regal but increasingly left-wing family.[2] To them the younger generation of the Borbón-Parmas had betrayed the standard they had been allowed to bear. It was true that Carlos Hugo was a legitimate candidate to the crown in terms of blood, but he was no longer a legitimate one in terms of conduct. Some traditionalists were so disgruntled with his reforms that they disregarded genealogical claims and judged pretenders solely on their behavior. As one of their broadsheets put it, "The loyalty of kings and princes to our doctrines IS THE ONLY TITLE that gives them the right to the loyalty of the people." Thus if Carlos Hugo and his sisters would not fulfill their duties, traditionalists were not beholden to them. In 1975, when Don Javier, by then in his late eighties and recently recovered from a car accident, abdicated in favor of his eldest son, they released a public statement saying that Carlos Hugo was not Carlist because he did not adhere to the principles of DIOS, PATRIA, REY, FUEROS. Zamanillo tried to justify this turning away from the Borbón-Parmas by claiming that legitimism had never been their foremost concern: "Spanish traditionalism," he told a journalist, "has always been more doctrinal than dynastic."[3]

In retaliation for their removal from the movement and in reaction to what they saw as the perversion of its true principles, the more active of these conservatives, at times aided by forces within the regime, began to set up their own associations and to attack those of their former colleagues. In 1967 a small group, dubbing themselves "La Junta Depuradora Carlista" (the Carlist Purificatory Junta), called for the "purifying" of their movement. Claiming to be the "Exterminating Angel" that would watch over Carlism wherever danger existed, the junta demanded the resignation of Zavala and all other leading progressives, the reinstatement of those who had been ousted or expelled, a Carlist prince worthy of the title, and a return to the essential doctrines of traditionalism. Two years later, the collaborationist Miguel Fagoaga, former president of the Vázquez de Mella Circles, staged the initial meeting of the nationwide—though short-lived—Agrupación de Asociaciones Tradicionalistas (Group of Traditionalist Associations). Two years after that, José María de Oriol, the *carlofranquista* minister of justice, assisted by Zamanillo, who had been made secretary of the Cortes, oversaw the creation of a new, conservative Comunión Tradicionalista. In Valencia, where the conservatives were still numerous enough to retain control of the provincial structure of the "official" Comunión, Ramón Forcadell, a local Carlist mayor, headed a separate venture to set up a national organization for former *requetés,* using a traditionalist fraternity, the Hermandad de Maestrazgo (Brotherhood of Maestrazgo), as its base. Valiente, who had been expelled from the Comunión the year before for "disobedience and deviating from the present posture of Carlism" and whom Franco had personally nominated as a *procurador,* became its active leader.[4]

The veterans in this traditionalist camp were very angry at the way the historical role of the *requetés* had been progressively played down, and at the way their organization, the Requeté, had been allowed to fall into decay, or put into the hands of youths who had not done their military service and whose only qualification appeared to be their unmitigated support of Carlos Hugo's *progresismo.* In their broadsheets and open letters, they demanded the reconstitution of their once-proud body and the sacking of "ambitious profiteers and infiltrators."[5] Several wrote to the Marqués de Marchelina, a distinguished veteran whom Carlos Hugo had persuaded to accept the presidency of the Hermandad Nacional de Antiguos Combatientes de Tercios de Requetés (National Brotherhood of Veterans of the Requeté Regiments), criticizing his support of *progresismo.* When it became clear he would not turn against his prince, they tried, unsuccessfully, to have him removed from the post. At the same time, a senior member of the Movimiento wrote to all known conservative members of the Hermandad, urging—similarly unsuccessfully—that the seven Carlist progressives on its head body be dismissed immediately.[6] Some reactionaries were not satisfied with writing letters or adding their signatures to them, but chose to express their views in a more muscular fashion: in May 1971 a group of unidentified persons, dressed as *requetés,* broke into and damaged property of the Catalan monastery of Montserrat, where several months before three hundred intellectuals had gathered to sign a collective letter of protest against the repressive measures of the regime.[7]

The more militaristic among these conservatives were not satisfied with merely creating organizations to counter the progressives. These belligerent veterans considered the rise of mass opposition to the regime so worrying that they called for a new crusade against "communists" and "marxists," who were once again threatening the integrity of Spain. This time these bearers of poisoned doctrines had even infiltrated Carlist organizations, especially AET and MOT. There could be no form of negotiation with these left-wingers, for as the last war had demonstrated, "the only points of contact between Carlists and marxists are the trench and the bayonet." One of their homages to the Mártires de la Tradición ended with the bloodthirsty promise that "we swear to you that we will not rest until we have cleaned your Carlism of all stains, of all traitors, even though we may have to mix our blood with yours."[8]

Progressives, previously content to criticize only their more distant predecessors, were by now openly ridiculing those Carlists who were actively opposed to them, and they classified their former colleagues as a huddle of "ultras," "theocrats," "collaborationists," "opportunists," and saber-rattling "militarists." According to María-Teresa de Borbón-Parma, it was these reactionaries, and not her father, who were responsible for the Comunión's cooperation with the regime in the 1950s and early 1960s. They were to blame for the association of the movement with extreme right-wing, antidemocratic attitudes in the Franquist period. To progressives, these die-hard reactionaries were less pure Carlists than pure Franquists, ones more concerned about upholding the "spirit of 18 July" than the spirit of nineteenth-century popular Carlism; the only type of "tradition" they were concerned to maintain was that of the self-interested infiltrators who, as had so often been the case, wished to use the movement for their own ends. And they had to be publicly denounced as such.[9]

By this time, neither the *huguistas* nor their detractors were trying to keep up a minimal semblance of unity among all Carlists. Instead, they expended effort by insulting one another in different terms: "fascist" versus "communist," "totalitarian" versus "socialist," "integrist" versus "atheist." They were, however, both struggling toward the same end: to call themselves "Carlist" and to be the only ones who could do so. Leaders on both sides believed there was still a broad middle ground of Carlists who could be swayed either way, and for that reason Carlos Hugo, Zavala, and their traditionalist counterparts thought the political contest worth the candle.[10] While members of both factions were busy trying to delegitimate their opponents, progressives liked to pride themselves that at least they had the relative weight of numbers on their side. They believed that the traditionalists' declarations received press coverage thanks only to the assistance of certain right-wing editors. Relatively few people, progressives liked to think, paid much attention to their opponents' retrograde attempt to reassert their almost archaic definition of Carlism and its ceremonial—until, that is, the counterrevolutionaries obtained arms to back their cause.

The Progressive Version of Montejurra

The progressives had not been content with merely ousting their opponents and redefining the nature of the movement. They had also modified its ceremonial calendar, downplaying the traditionalist aspect of annual events, which celebrated the memory of the *requetés*, and introducing El Dia de la Lucha Carlista (The Day of Carlist Struggle), held on 2 October. On this occasion, regional and provincial chiefs were meant to stage political meetings, public acts, and conferences, all with the aim of making known the present line of the progressive leaders.[11]

Montejurra, however, remained the most important annual ceremony of the movement. Its character, though, was now very different from the way it had been staged up to the mid-1960s. The paramilitary parades had been stopped several years before. Priests no longer celebrated Mass in the monastery of Irache for the souls of the insurgent triumvirate, Generals Mola, Sanjurjo, and Varela, nor did they perform the Salve in Estella to the military commanders of the Second Carlist War. Only the older participants accompanied the priest in saying the stations of the cross, and the spoken prayers of those who did had to compete with the singing of popular "protest songs" as well as shouts of "Revolution! Revolution!" or "Long live socialist Spain!"

Leading progressives were keen that Montejurra be seen not as a quaint folkloric ritual of interest only to amateur ethnologists but as an impressively well-run mass political event of relevance to all concerned Spaniards. In their writings, they omitted any reference to the historical geography of the area, ignored the trope of "blood" for the sake of stressing the political nature of the occasion, and made no mention of the Carlist war dead, only a statement of "solidarity with those who preceded us in their aspirations for liberty." [12] To them, Montejurra was to be regarded, above all, as the yearly reunion of a political party, where official speakers commented on recent events, proclaimed the party line, and revealed the party's policy for the immediate future. For progressives, it inaugurated the political New Year, where leaders corrected past errors, brought objectives up to date, and set new goals. [13]

Participants, by listening to the speeches and chatting with others afterward, were meant to be able to take stock of the present political predicament and their party's reaction to it. By consistently turning up for the annual gathering, they were seen to be stating their commitment to the evolving progressive program. Taken en masse, they were to be regarded not as a "communion" of fellow believers but as a *"pueblo"* expressing themselves "authentically." [14] They were "a *pueblo* who wish to be the protagonist of a common destiny, to which all men have a right." [15]

At the same time, progressives were also seen to be renewing the pact between the Carlist people and the Borbón-Parmas. [16] The meeting on the mountaintop was a privileged opportunity for the physical encounter (albeit for many a somewhat distant one) of the *pueblo* with its leaders. For this reason, among others, *progresista* writers were keen to stress the youth of so many of the participants: the Carlist royal family were not in place at the head of the organization simply for reasons of tradition but because the Carlist people, especially their younger, politically more active members, wanted them there.

This reinterpreted form of Montejurra was not meant to be understood as an isolated event within the Carlist calendar. Rather, this politically emotive and invigorating ceremony was meant to serve as a stimulus and a model for activists for the rest of the year. Montejurra was both "a chance to get one's breath and to spur oneself for the daily and darker labor of all the year."[17] The aim was that those attending would receive "a new charge of hope" that would inspire them to continue with their daily tasks.[18] This politically inspiring version of Montejurra was not meant to be anchored to a particular geographical site, at the southerly entrance to Estella, but could be enacted at any time in any part of the country. Thus, the ideal was for progressives to perform a "daily Montejurra in each factory, office, workshop, and in each city or village."[19] As the title to one progressive article put it, "Montejurra 365 Days."[20]

Leading progressives were also well aware that Montejurra was the greatest occasion when Carlists exhibited themselves en masse to outsiders. It was a chance for non-Carlist Spaniards "to see Carlism as it is now and not as they used to see us; they will be able to realize that we are not reactionaries or dreamers but aware of present realities and that we can contribute a lot to the political life of the country."[21] Some used the presence of journalists as a stick to control the crowd, reminding them to behave responsibly because they were being observed and their actions publicized.[22]

The main concern here was that Montejurra not become an occasion for mass demonstration, so providing the authorities with an easy excuse for banning the event. In 1968, an illegal demonstration to protest the expulsion of the Borbón-Parmas, to be held on the eve of the ceremony, was forestalled only by stiff warnings from the Carlist hierarchy and the civil government of Navarre, both published on the front page of *El Pensamiento Navarro*.[23] The next year on the afternoon of the ceremony, a crowd of over 4,000 gathered in the main plaza of Estella. To the massed shouts of antiregime slogans, a portrait of Franco was burned, then trodden underfoot. In the ensuing riot, one member of the Civil Guard fired his pistol and several dozen arrests were made. In Pamplona that evening, a strong police presence thwarted the staging of a further demonstration.[24] In 1970, to prevent recurrence of any such incidents, progressive leaders made repeated, successful calls for discipline and calm. From 1971 on, only the most minor of incidents occurred: that year stones were thrown at a few banks, but the demonstration was dissolved pacifically; the next year, more stones were hurled at banks, and the highway to Logroño was blocked for twenty minutes.[25]

In sum, the community the progressives wished to construct, to celebrate, and to perpetuate at Montejurra was not a backward-looking one, religious in tone, militaristic in manner, and passive in political style, but a forward-looking one, critically informed about current politics, actively engaged as militants, and steered by a left-leaning royal family. If the Carlists of the 1950s had turned a rural gathering held in memory to the dead into a politicoreligious act exalting Carlism, leading progressives of the late 1960s and early

1970s had transformed that into a primarily political (and eventually disciplined) rally focused on opposition to the regime. And they were keen to advertise the fact. *Montejurra* candidly entitled one piece about the 1969 ceremony, "Not Much of a Pilgrimage." A GAC broadsheet was even more blunt: "Who believes in mere romerías?"[26]

Up to the last years of the 1960s, the political part of the ceremony reflected the mixed composition of the leadership, with both loyal conservatives and committed progressives giving speeches. Perhaps the most stark expression of this mishmash occurred in 1968 when messages of support were read out from both Esteban Bilbao, the traditionalist president of the national Cortes, and Santiago Carrillo, the president of the PCE. From the early 1970s, however, fewer and fewer conservative speakers were allowed onto the platform. The speeches given there expressed the increasing dominance of the progressives within the movement: in 1973, the need for decentralizing government was emphatically specified; the following year, speeches stressed the theme of global self-management as the linchpin uniting the ideas of syndical, political, and regional liberties; in 1975, the message from Don Javier and Carlos Hugo that was read out as well as the speech given by María-Teresa underscored the necessity for the coming together of all antifranquist forces.[27] There was to be no more talk from the platform about the virtues of a discriminating collaborationism, or of the glories won by quasicrusaders dying for the sake of a distant god.

The Montejurras of the late 1960s were crowded events assembling many tens of thousands of people. But the numbers attending the event started to drop significantly from 1970 onward. Those Carlists unconvinced by the fundamental shift to progressive politics and unhappy at the decreasingly religious nature of the ceremony ceased to attend. Some parents, remembering the violent demonstrations of some years, stopped taking their children to the event. Perhaps the main reason for the rapid decline in numbers was the fact that the annual gathering was no longer the only public occasion where people could demonstrate their antifranquist attitudes. Politicized democrats were now able to campaign under the banner of their own organizations. They could take part in mass demonstrations in the streets of their own cities: for them there was no need to make the trek to central Navarre to declare their opposition to dictatorship. By the early 1970s, most non-Carlists who attended came from neighboring areas or were close friends of party militants. If the numbers at Montejurra made it an event all the more worth attending, then a noticeable falloff in participants would snowball, making the ceremony rapidly lose any national political importance. Perhaps as many as 100,000 attended in 1969. Three years later, only 15,000 showed up.

The progressives' version of Montejurra did not go undisputed. By now *El*

Pensamiento Navarro was back in the hands of traditionalists, and the articles it published on the performance of the ritual during these years did not mention the solidarity generated among the participants; rather they emphasized the lack of consensus among the crowd. The authors of these pieces claimed that many went for good traditionalist reasons and so were surprised and confused to hear nontraditionalist speeches. These journalists attacked the party and questioned its right to call itself Carlist and to run the ritual in the way its leaders did. According to the reactionary discourse of these reporters, the now customary riots in Estella were an "anti-Montejurra," acted out at 5 P.M., the hour of bullfights. In contrast to this pagan performance, the "authentic" Montejurra was a religious homage to the memory of the Mártires de la Tradición, whose selfless example "true" Carlists still followed. "History" allowed no other reading.[28]

From 1973 on, a host of other traditionalists, acting in the name of revived or new bodies such as the Comunión Tradicionalista, the Hermandad de Maestrazgo, and the Tercios Reales (Royal Regiments) de Castilla and Cataluña, circulated large numbers of pamphlets in the days before Montejurra urging people not to attend. So many were produced that one Carlist privately commented, "Someone has surplus money, without limit, to squander it on this kind of propaganda, which has to be very expensive."[29] In May 1973, for instance, copies of a Cyclostyled flyer, in the name of the "Combatientes de los Tercios de Requetés" (Combatants of the Requeté Regiments), were distributed around *requeté* circles. Entreating *requetés* not to attend Montejurra that year, it attacked progressive organizers for attempting to convert "our dearly beloved memorial to all those who fell for the cause into a symbol of the struggle against those principles that the Carlist people defended with arms in 1936." It also damned organizers for inviting to the event representatives of political parties that had constituted the defeated Frente Popular. Accusing organizers of betraying "our ideas" and selling "our sacred cause," the flyer claimed these progressives were helping marxists to power who, on gaining it, would condemn veteran *requetés* as "war criminals."[30] The anonymous authors of the flyers of the La Junta Depuradora Carlista took a more assertive stance. They urged their readers to attend the ceremony, and to react aggressively, responding to cries of "Long live liberty!" (too marxist for their taste) with shouts of "Long live the *fueros*!," and to cries of "Revolution!" with shouts of "Long live Spain! Long live King Javier!" Above all, the junta urged, true Carlists were to shout the same cry that *requetés* had uttered as they had died: "Long live Christ the King!"[31] For the die-hard traditionalists, the energetic efforts of the treacherous usurpers of "their" ritual could not go unchecked.[32]

Montejurra 1976

Given the continued decline in attendance at Montejurra, and given that the ceremony to be held in May 1976 was the first to be staged since the death of Franco, the leaders of the Partido Carlista were particularly eager for the event that year to be seen as a great success. If Carlism was to remain a noteworthy force within the opposition, it had to demonstrate its power of convocation. Militants were told to hold meetings with their fellows and people sympathetic to the cause, and to explain fully the meaning and the importance of Montejurra; on the day, they were to bring as many as possible to the mountain. At the same time, the secretary-general would hold a press conference on 29 April and would try to ensure that interviews with Carlist leaders were printed in the papers in the following days. "It is vital that we mobilize ourselves to the maximum in order to achieve a massive level of attendance. A level of attendance similar to the last few years would be a failure, since this year conditions are different." Every detail was attended to: which slogans were to be shouted and in which language (Galician, Catalan, Euskera, Valencian, Castilian), and which regional or nationalist flags were to be hoisted. So that the original character of the event would not be completely forgotten and to avoid giving offense to veterans, militants were also told *to learn* the stations of the cross.[33]

It seems that others also wished the celebration of Montejurra that year to be particularly noteworthy. In late April and early May, articles appeared in several newspapers of the extreme right-wing press exhorting people to attend the ceremony. Nineteen seventy-six was to be the year Montejurra would be "won back." People were "duty-bound" to "reconquer" Montejurra for traditionalism. The socialist and philomarxist "so-called Partido Carlista," led by "that strange and foreign citizen Monsieur Hugues," was "essentially an enemy of the sacred principles defended with *requeté* blood." These "Reds, separatists, communists, members of ETA, and fellow travelers" "profaned" and "debased" the Monte de la Tradición (Mountain of Tradition), where they proclaimed "their aversion to the king and to the state." Against this "infamy and outrage," traditionalists would this year regain Montejurra in order to "pray the stations of the cross for our martyrs," to "renew their promises and pacts of loyalty," and to "proclaim the authentic doctrine." The "mystical importance" of Montejurra would be maintained. All these articles were couched in the Manichaean format of an unreformed traditionalism, with its preconciliar Christianity and talk of glory won by bloodletting. The only difference in the use of this customary counterrevolutionary discourse was that this time the perceived foe called themselves Carlist: the "enemy within" had shown itself to be more insidious and more damaging to their legendary movement than the Republicans they had faced beyond the front line. In an ominously muscular tone, one contributor wrote, "I'm going to Montejurra because I always like to go where men go."[34]

In the days immediately preceding Montejurra, talk spread in the area that a hotel near the monastery of Irache had filled with Latin Americans, Italians, and Spaniards from distant provinces brandishing knifes, pistols, and machine guns.[35] Their leader was said to be Don Sixto, whom they treated like a king. He was now being styled the traditionalist pretender, opposed to his elder brother, Carlos Hugo, with whom he had quarreled definitively the previous summer, and to his father, Don Javier, who had publicly excluded him from the dynastic succession.[36] The day before the ceremony, *El Pensamiento Navarro* printed his manifesto on its front page. It proclaimed "the essential principles of Carlism": Catholic confessionality, the organic constitution of society, defense of the *fueros*, and a traditionalist monarchy. On the same day, two young *huguistas* went up to the summit to prepare the loudspeakers for the ceremony. They found the mountaintop already occupied by armed men who threatened them with pistols. On their descent, they met a pair of Civil Guards to whom they reported what they had seen. Instead of receiving assistance, they were immediately arrested and held in jail for the next two days.

On the morning of Sunday, 9 May, progressive Carlists started gathering in the cloisters of the monastery, as they always did at the beginning of the ceremony. But this year, a group of men, carrying steel bars, chains, and gaffs, and accompanied by Don Sixto, Zamanillo, and the sons of Fal Conde, marched out from the hotel to the beat of drummers. Shouting insults, throwing stones, and wielding their truncheons, they attacked the cloistered Carlists, who managed to beat them back. In an altercation between members of the two groups, a *sixtino* pulled out his pistol and shot a man who had called him a coward. He died three days later. The four Civil Guards who had witnessed these events without attempting to interfere were finally forced by insistent Carlists to take action. They physically inserted themselves between the two groups and, with their machine guns pointing at the aggressors, told them not to fire. The *sixtinos* retreated.

The *huguistas* then walked to the foot of Montejurra, watched by more Civil Guards and threatened by more *sixtinos*. In the presence of Doña Irene and Doña María de las Nieves, and later joined by Carlos Hugo, they began their ascent of the mountain. As the head of the crowd neared the summit, they were surprised to find their way blocked by some forty armed men dressed in khaki. Don Sixto, standing amid them and speaking through a loudspeaker, told the halted crowd that he was about to give a speech. His words were answered with boos and shouts of "Carlos Hugo liberty!" The machine gunners opened fire, wounding several and killing one. They then hurried off down a back path. The priest saying the stations of the cross stopped the procession at the tenth station and held Mass there. Then everyone went down the mountain. Members of the ETA in the crowd asked Carlos Hugo if their aid was required, but he turned down the offer. The rest of the day's planned events were canceled. The next day all businesses and shops in Estella closed down, as the funeral for one of the dead was held. Two days later 20,000 attended the memorial service in Pamplona. The killer at the monastery was arrested, as was José Arturo Marquéz de Prado, leader of the traditionalist *requetés* and organizer of the armed band.

Two days after the shooting, an editorial in the extreme right-wing daily *El Alcázar* ended this way: "Last Sunday, responding to provocation . . . a group of men, fewer in number but superior in moral and political strength won back with the price of blood the honor of Montejurra." A note by the Hermandad Nacional de Requetés Veteranos (National Brotherhood of Veteran Requetés), a traditionalist body opposed to the one run by the Marqués de Marchelina argued that they had been provoked into reconverting Montejurra into "the great explosion of faith and patriotism it symbolized" by "the subversive cries, filthy language, and insulting behavior of atheistic separatists who could no longer truly call themselves Carlists."[37]

Montejurra 1976 and National Politics

Despite the aggressive triumphalism of these pieces, the "spiritual reconquest" of Montejurra had, in the eyes of almost everyone else, failed catastrophically. According to progressives, the original aim of Don Sixto had been to scare away the *huguistas* so that his followers and those traditionalists who had heeded his call could perform their own version of Montejurra. Many of these traditionalists were old *estorilinos,* who had accepted the claim of the Alfonsine line to the throne and were prepared, given their implacable opposition to *huguismo,* to have Don Sixto as their figurehead. For them and for Don Sixto, Montejurra 1976 was intended to be the public beginning of a conservative revival within Carlism.

Since late 1975, Don Sixto and Marquéz de Prado had been visiting parts of the country in a recruitment drive, but they had met much opposition and did not gain mass support. Thanks to the covert assistance of other organizations, the die-hard traditionalists they did manage to gather were joined by extreme right-wing activists and foreign fascists. But despite the press campaign with its air of a crusade to "cleanse" the recent history of Montejurra, and despite the offers of free food and transport to carry the faithful to the mountain made by *El Pensamiento Navarro* and by at least two Riojan mayors, the turnout of traditionalists on the day was disappointingly low, and those conservative Carlists who had come in good faith were very put out by the armed aggression they witnessed. An editorial entitled "United in Pain" printed on 11 May in *El Pensamiento Navarro* regretted the violence. It claimed the intention had been to bring Carlists together. "But our flag of unity was trampled on by anticarlist mercenaries": it was time, the editorial stated, that Carlists stopped being used as political puppets by greater powers.

An important question, still not satisfactorily resolved, is to what extent key figures in the government were aware of, and maybe even implicated in, the *sixtinos'* plans. In the condemnatory publications that progressives produced about the murders, they pointed out that a week before the ceremony, José María de Areilza, minister of foreign affairs, had warned the Dutch ambassador in Madrid that he could not guarantee the safety of Doña Irene if she went to Montejurra. Marquéz de Prado, as a leader of the *sixtinos*, had been offered assistance by the Movimiento, which, among other things, provided coaches for the traditionalists. The day before the ceremony, two leading Navarrese Carlists had informed the civil governor of the province about the armed men wandering about the hotel near the monastery. But the official had said he could do nothing unless he received orders to that effect from Madrid. Even the far right–wing press, progressives observed, commented on the extremely uncharacteristic passiveness of the police during the moments of armed aggression. José María Araluce, president of the Gipuzkoan Deputation, and Antonio María de Oriol, then president of the Consejo de Estado (Council of State) and leader of Unión Nacional Española (Spanish National Union) (an extreme right-wing group that financially assisted the *sixtinos*), had both marched in Don Sixto's band on the day of Montejurra. It thus appeared to the progressives that the hired gunmen had indeed distinguished company, as well as powerful friends offstage, when they went into their murderous action. The young activists, who had produced the clandestine booklet *Informe Montejurra '76*, went so far as to claim that Operación Reconquista had been thought up by the cabinet, and that Manuel Fraga, then minister of the interior, together with the director general of the Civil Guard had worked out the strategy, which was to see Don Sixto installed as the figurehead of Carlism.[38]

There is, at present, insufficient direct evidence to substantiate this highly conspiratorial interpretation. It is, however, possible to piece together a somewhat more plausible, though much more open-ended and much less conspiratorial, explanation of the background to the day's events. First, Areilza was not necessarily aware of what exactly was going to happen. It is much more likely that, as a Basque, he had been secretly passed information by the Partido Nacionalista Vasco, warning him that Montejurra that year was likely to be a troubled occasion. As minister of foreign affairs, he would not have wanted to deal with the diplomatic furor that would have arisen if, for instance, a traditionalist had physically struck Doña Irene. Second, since the reorganization of the Ministry of the Interior in the 1960s, effective control of the Civil Guard no longer lay in Madrid but with the regional civil governors. Although Adolfo Suárez and Fraga were, as secretary-general of the Movimiento and minister of the interior, respectively, jointly responsible for the appointment of these functionaries, the rivalry between these two ambitious politicians, both seeking to strengthen their position in the emerging, postfranquist political scene, was then such that they could rarely agree on whom to appoint. Neither wanted to see the other's candidate installed, and so they tended to choose men who were not factionally aligned with either of them, and in whom they did not necessarily have much confidence. Third, according to Rodolfo Martín Villa, then minister of syndicates, the civil governor of Navarre, José Ruiz de Gordoa, forewarned Fraga of what could happen. But he paid no attention. Fourth, Suárez had very little control over local leaders of the Movimiento, while his relations with the incumbent director of the Civil Guard were at the time so bad that the two of them hardly communicated. Alfonso Osorio, then minister of the presidency, says that Suárez rang him on the morning of the event to tell him, in a very surprised tone, of what had happened.[39]

It is thus quite possible that the civil governor of Navarre, knowing that he did not have the ear of his minister, felt unable to exercise sufficient authority over the independent actions of Civil Guards within the province, and thus thought there was little he could do about the machinations of the *sixtinos* and their receiving arms from the Movimiento. Moreover members of the Civil Guard and the Movimiento may well have kept Suárez ignorant of what some of their number were up to. But certain questions remain unanswered: Who was prepared to pay for the hiring of the foreign mercenaries? To what extent did senior members of the Civil Guard actively or passively assist the *sixtinos'* cause? Further, the murder at the monastery of Irache may be seen as the unforeseen, unwanted outcome of an angry encounter between opposed groups, but the spraying of the participants with bullets from the summit was a premeditated, unprovoked act, the political motive of which remains unclear. For if the intention of the *sixtinos* was to unite Carlists, then why had a gunman been allowed to shoot into the crowd, which, while predominantly progressive, also included traditionalists?

It is, of course, possible to imagine that the *sixtinos* who turned up on the day did so out of a variety of motives: some may have genuinely thought that they were going to rally traditionalists and to reassert the primacy of their doctrine over the perversion wrought by progressives; some may have thought that a simple show of aggressive strength would be enough to scare away Carlos

Hugo's supporters; and some individuals may have wished to cause mayhem for reasons foreign to any Carlist cause. It is this last group whose motives are most difficult to fathom.

In the years since the event, senior politicians, when forced to remember the killings, have been ready to accuse almost anyone other than themselves. In the hustings for the general elections of 1983, Fraga and Suárez accused each other of complicity in the affair. Martín Villa, in his memoirs, states that "the responsibility of some authorities, and particularly of some commanders within the Civil Guard, is not small." Fraga, in his memoirs, calls the events "very obscure" and is keen to exonerate both his ministry and the Civil Guard, "who did everything possible to reduce to the minimum the consequences of that tragic clash." Today, people living in villages near Montejurra blame Fraga for what happened.[40]

Fraga, who had been on a political trip to Venezuela during the events, tried on his return to deny the gravity of the killings. He spoke of Montejurra only in personalist terms, downplaying the fatal clash as merely a quarrel between a fraternal pair of Frenchmen: "What is clearly worth condemning is that certain characters of a certain foreign family play politics at the expense of peace in Spain. I can assure you that it will not happen again."[41] He did, however, appreciate the significance of Montejurra sufficiently to bother to take personal, direct command of the investigation into the deaths. But it soon transpired that the government showed little inclination to carry out an exhaustive inquiry or even to keep the gunmen in jail. In early September, the whole council of the Estella town hall resigned because the events remained unclarified. The *sixtinos* arrested were released on bail within seven months and were freed the next year thanks to a general amnesty.[42]

The Demise of the *Sixtinos*

If, as they proclaimed, the intention of those traditionalists in the bunker was to reunite Carlists around the *sixtino* banner, then they failed dramatically. Thanks to the events of that day, the divisions between Carlists of different political color deepened and were gorily advertised, and their "pretender" Don Sixto was expelled from the country. Recognizing the importance of Montejurra within Carlism, they had wished to wrest management of the ceremony and so gain a major means of Carlist self-statement, a prestigious way to strengthen their claim to be the legitimate heirs of the ancient movement. And by failing so ignominiously to win control of the event, this faction's brief bid for power had in effect already ended.

If, as we have seen, the aim of the Navarrese Junta was to stage a pacific but lively celebration of Carlist consensus, then they had been frustrated. Instead, the annual ritual had gained unwanted associations of modern factional violence and fatal incident. In this perversion of the annual ceremony, representatives of opposed factions had not, as they had done in the past, stood side by side on the same platform. Instead they had contested physically the right to present their own conceptions of Carlism, and so had turned the ceremony into a stage on which political difference was bloodily fought out. If the intention of progressives had been to stage a multitudinous Montejurra, which would demonstrate the power of *huguista* Carlism and the rightness of their cause, then they too had failed, because disappointingly few had turned up on the day. Also, their plans for the future had been stymied, because their prince would not soon be allowed to return from exile. Moreover, to those Spaniards who had not yet heard about the political philosophy of self-management, it did not seem, from what they read in the newspapers about the killings, that the Carlists were evolving or clarifying their ideology, but simply living up to their old reputation of forming bands of irregulars who preferred to fight with arms rather than words. In sum, for most Carlists and their observers, the Montejurra of that year was indeed a most memorable event, for the wrong sorts of reasons.

This gory encounter was symbolic, however, of both the current conflicts within Carlism and of the contemporary national scene. The fraternal difference of opinion within the Borbón-Parmas had assumed such dramatic proportions partly because each brother had come to symbolize one side of a bipolar confrontation in the transition: immobilism versus socialist progress. For Don Sixto to head a distinctive Carlist faction, he had had to oppose directly his brother's political views. This had led him into the camp of extreme right-wing activists, a dangerous zone where, it appears, influential antisocialists (who remain unidentified) were prepared to fund his dreams. In this brotherly conflict, resonant with Biblical echoes, the figure of each protagonist exaggerated the public profile of the other. Before, they had been estranged kin; now, they were declared enemies. Progressive publications on the killings portrayed Don Sixto as an uneducated rolling stone who had achieved nothing in his life; whereas the curriculum vitae of Carlos Hugo's life consisted of an impressive list of degrees obtained and of praiseworthy actions displaying his commitment to the movement. Carlos Hugo had wed splendidly; his sibling had still to find a bride. In this bloody political contest, both brothers lost out, a failure that in itself symbolizes the latter, relative success of negotiated change toward democratic government. Meanwhile, the path up Montejurra had gained another monument to the dead, a brass plaque set in stone to the memory of the murdered youth.

Although Suárez, who became president of Spain in July 1976, was keen to work with the opposition over the process of democratization, the government remained intolerant of Carlism, while the spasmodic threat of action by activist traditionalists continued to worry progressive Carlists. In late February 1977 Don Sixto said his men had responded to aggression in Montejurra nine months before: "We hope they won't provoke us this year and will leave us alone."[43] A few days later he "kidnapped" his eighty-eight-year-old father and hid him on the Normandy estate of his brother-in-law Prince Lobkowicz, husband of Doña Francisca. Don Sixto made his aging father sign a statement praising traditionalist Carlism. "Rescued" by Carlos Hugo, Don Javier quickly made a counterdeclaration iterating his political distance from Don Sixto and reaffirming his abdication in favor of his elder son. In a cunning reply the Comunión Tradicionalista issued a statement by Doña Magdalena, Don Javier's wife, in support of Don Sixto and against Carlos Hugo, who, she claimed, had "kidnapped" her husband from his resting place.[44] The mother criticized her educated, dynamic, successful son for the sake of her weaker, younger offspring, who as a beautiful child had been fawned over by his aunts, had not gone to university, had not even completed his training in the Spanish Legion. The royal family was openly divided, with every member politically marked. In April 1968, the cover article of *Montejurra* had been "The Unbribable Dynasty," with studio portraits of the brothers literally backing up their seated father. By the mid-1970s, such an article was inconceivable: Don Sixto had been corrupted by a promise of power, and had enmeshed his eldest sister and his mother in his plots. Carlism could no longer boast of its exemplary family.

Montejurra 1977

Progressives continued to complain of their "systematic persecution" by the government. For the first time ever, both the political *and* religious acts of Montejurra were banned. Over thirty militants were arrested for putting up posters announcing the ceremony, and four meetings in Navarrese towns were proscribed. Frustrated by the prohibition of their ritual and angry that the government had legalized the Comunión Tradicionalista but not the Partido Carlista, 150 Carlists occupied the Deputation in Pamplona and staged an assembly there. On the day itself, police controlled the entrances to Estella; Doña Irene was forcibly driven back to the French border. In order not to provoke too much conflict, a reduced group, watched closely by the police, was allowed to hold an improvised version of the ceremony in the castle of Javier, east Navarre. It was a Montejurra in memory of the previous year's two dead, and of Don Javier, who had died the day before. One speaker told the assembled, "Despite all the difficulties and arbitrary acts, the abuses and the prohibitions, the Partido Carlista said we would be in Montejurra and in Montejurra we are."[45]

They might have been forty miles away from the "sacred mountain," but the 2,000 gathered in the family home of Saint Francis Xavier (the destination of the Javierada) had still come under arduous conditions to a holy, historical site in order to remember their dead and to celebrate their brand of Carlism. If they were unable to perform a definitive Montejurra in its usual geographical setting, they had performatively defined it in another site. If they could not go by the mountain, then they could take Montejurra with them.

Chapter Eleven

The Decline of Carlism

The Partido Carlista was the second political party to apply for legalization and the last to receive it. The Comunión Tradicionalista was legalized without any delay in early 1976. Even the PCE, that hated bogey of the generals, was registered as a political association months before the progressives' organization was finally enrolled. In fact it was not until the general elections of June 1977 had passed that the state legally recognized the followers of the Borbón-Parmas.[1]

Similarly, Carlos Hugo was one of the very last political exiles allowed back into the country. It was only after much negotiation with the government that the prince was given permission to return. On his arrival, in October that year, he emphasized that he posed no threat to the monarchy since his party was not making any dynastic claim. The people of the country, he declared, would decide its form of government; the Carlists were suggesting self-managing socialism only as a worthwhile possibility.[2]

With this act the state ended all restrictions on the party. A popular government had now been voted in, and Juan Carlos had become established as the royal figurehead of the country, helping to steer it through the transitional process away from dictatorship and toward a modern Western democracy. There would be no more repression of the progressives. There was no need. Carlos Hugo had been quite accurate in his comments, perhaps more than he realized: his brand of Carlism no longer posed any threat, either dynastically or even electorally. *Progresismo*, far from becoming a significant force within Spanish politics, was about to enter a period of public decline. Whereas previous chapters discussed the reasons for the creation and gradual rise of *huguismo*, this one charts the course of its rapid decline.

The Disorganization of Progressive Carlism

Carlos Hugo and his associates had wanted to forge a nationwide, democratic, and well-structured political organization out of the old Comunión. Despite their intentions and efforts, however, all they managed to create was a small, inefficacious, ill-organized party, at times barely able to contain its own internal divisions. The progressives may have presented a public face of coherence, unity, and purpose, but what occurred privately, within the party, was very different.

The national leaders regarded the rigorous training of militants as one of the cornerstones in the construction of the party. But many progressives were dissatisfied with the way *cursillos* were organized in Valcarlos. In an assessment of the classes staged there in the summer of 1975, they complained that it was often difficult to estimate the number who would participate in each course. For those who lived in distant provinces, Valcarlos was not easy to reach and, frequently, fewer attended than had been expected. Those who did turn up were not always sufficiently prepared, and their teachers were often unsure at what level to pitch the discussion. Provincial *cursillos* could be even less fruitful: in an account of one held at the Circle in Santander in 1974, its Bilbao organizer stated that of the thirty militants who had been anticipated, only six appeared, and they two hours late; one of them, it soon transpired, had never heard of Carlism until that day. As soon as the course finally got under way, the Circle, to the organizer's great surprise, began to fill with retired Carlists who had come to dine there, as they did every day. Faced with an influx of people who had no appetite for theoretical debate, he decided that the *cursillo,* meant to last two days, should be halted immediately, before it had even completed its first hour.

Part of the function of these courses was to train progressives in the vaunted arts of criticism and self-criticism. But, as senior members of the party recognized, comments made by members of a group on one another could easily be interpreted as personal attacks, which, if not well taken, could lead to people leaving, or being expelled. It also seems that public self-criticism by a militant of his, or her, own political defects to fellow members of a group was infrequently performed. Like many of the plans for the party's structure, it was more talked about than executed.[3]

Militants, who had been trained above all in political philosophy and in the theory of political action, had also to learn, sometimes painfully, how to adapt their style to the particular group they were dealing with. Those Madrid Carlists who tried to muster support in the youth clubs of their area came to realize, as one of them confessed, that "the youth movement is not a movement of philosophers, but of people who like music and are concerned about problems such as drugs and sex." Some militants who entered these clubs sought to politicize them too directly and too quickly, and became embroiled in ideological confrontations with other groups within them. Where the Carlist infiltrators did succeed in raising the consciousness of members, the club often became so political that other youths were disinclined to join. The party executive stressed that militants were to remind themselves constantly why minors were attracted to these clubs in the first place.[4]

The *cursillos* were not just poorly organized or sometimes ill attended. There were also too few of them, leading to a dearth of properly instructed militants. In fact the number of militants as a whole, whether trained in courses or not, was worrisomely low, and had become even lower because of recent departures. By June 1977, in all the Canary Islands there was a grand total of four militants; in Burgos there were five; in Andalucía there were perhaps as few as twenty-five; while in Galicia and Bizkaia there were fewer than forty apiece. Although Carlos Hugo boasted on his return of there being 25,000 militants, the files in the party archives suggest that there were then fewer than seven hundred registered militants throughout the country, and even that figure is misleadingly high since it includes men past the age of retirement and youths who, while once active, had since given up fighting for the cause. The militants in each of the provincial branches were assisted by a greater number of "affiliates," but they were generally regarded as lacking the political training necessary to advance the party locally in a systematic manner. Only in areas such as Madrid, Navarre, and Gipuzkoa were there enough militants for the provincial branches to set up specialized sections such as workers', students', and professionals' fronts.[5] The majority of the politically active in the *huguista* rank and file were, moreover, relatively young, and youthful militants were considered unsuitable for certain tasks.[6] The party executive stated that it wished to have a greater number of "mature" militants, but it did not seem to know how to recruit them. The social origin of those who did militate was a further cause of concern. In many cities, the single largest source of militants was the universities; only a minority of activists came from urban proletarian homes—an embarrassing fact for an organization that now styled itself as a workers' party.

All these problems, whether arithmetical, demographic, or social, were compounded by a lack of money. Although the party was headed by a great landowning family, its efforts were constantly hamstrung by a shortage of funds. Many Carlists did not always pay their subscriptions, and both local chiefs and the national executive had to appeal repeatedly to its members for more cash. When in early 1978 a local militant was made the political secretary of the section for Malaga, he discovered to his surprise that it had been able to pay its annual dues to the party only thanks to the continued, but secret, generosity of one well-to-do activist. In these straitened circumstances, it is unsurprising that one of the tasks set in *cursillos* for budding leaders was how to regalvanize a provincial section of the party whose coffer was empty.[7]

The response of the party to the challenge of the general elections of 1977 starkly revealed the combined effect of all these various deficiencies and weaknesses. Progressives could have legally presented themselves as independent candidates, but in most areas they chose not to do so. The reasons many provincial branches gave for not participating included poverty, paucity of personnel, inadequate organization to mount an effective electoral campaign, insufficient support from the leaders of the party, the progressives' lack of a public image known across the country, and little coordination between provincial branches as well as between them and the national executive. Some branches were unable to collect the 500 signatures needed before an independent could stand; some did not even try. Of those candidates who did present themselves, not one was elected: those who stood in Palencia and Valladolid won fewer than a thousand votes apiece, both coming in last in their constituencies; the representative for Navarre came in tenth out of thirteen candidates, while the vote obtained in Castellón was, in the words of two provincial chiefs, "ridiculous"; the candidate for Gipuzkoa had not even lasted the course, withdrawing before polling day.[8] For the first time in almost a century there were to be no Carlists in a democratically elected Cortes.

In Navarre, too many parties with left-wing nationalist policies had presented themselves, to the detriment of all their candidates. In early 1977 the Carlists tried to create a bloc with similar-minded Basque parties. Since the Basque organizations had little support within Navarre, they were at first keen to ally with the progressives, whose power in the province they grossly overestimated. But no agreement could be reached in time for the elections.[9] To progressives throughout the country, this unexpectedly poor showing at the polls came as a great disappointment; they had hoped for far better returns in the traditional heartland of the movement. To progressives in Navarre itself, these results were taken as confirming the end of Carlism's former predominance in the province.[10] A local newsmagazine, commenting on the elections, headed one section, "Carlism: The Lost Hegemony."

Provincial progressives reacted to this electoral ignominy by criticizing the national leadership in the strongest terms, the branch for Valladolid and Segovia even calling for the resignation of the more senior leaders of the party.[11] One of the provincials' most serious comments concerned the perceived failure of their superiors to produce a coherent political line geared to the immediate predicament of the country. Grand statements about Carlist ideology made at congresses were insufficient when having to deal with the ever-shifting reality of national politics during the transition. For instance, regional chiefs needed to know which parties to form local coalitions with, and on what conditions. These provincial critics also complained that their national leaders rarely stirred out of Madrid, and that many of the proposed superordinate structures of the party were either nugatory or nonexistent. Carlos Hugo and his cohort, they noted, were clearly more adept at planning a suitable framework for their movement than they were at putting their schemes into effect. This inability to construct a functioning, nationwide organization, plus the fact that Zavala's critics regarded his desire for discipline as bordering on the dictatorial at times, could make the party leaders' words about internal democracy and self-management at all levels sound particularly hollow. One clique of Basque progressives went so far as to deride their secretary-general as "an authoritarian manipulator whose absolute power and increasing influence over our leader Carlos Hugo is converting him into a neo-Stalinist despot."[12]

Faced with mounting criticism, the national executive tried to reimpose order by invalidating an assembly of Madrid progressives that, in its opinion, had not been correctly convoked. It also ejected those critics who voiced their comments publicly, and those whose critiques were regarded as questioning the very nature of the party's program and structure previously agreed on at the congresses.[13] Many others, disheartened by the turn of events, simply left.

The Return of Carlos Hugo

The national leadership tried to quell any further internal dissent and to reverse the flagging fortunes of the party by staging a Fourth National Congress in late October 1977, by publicizing the work of Carlos Hugo, and by attempting to revitalize the ceremony of Montejurra. With the prospect of more general elections once the constituent Cortes now meeting had produced a national constitution, the party needed to prepare itself for the coming electoral challenge. It could not afford to fail at the polls again.

The congress was presided over by Carlos Hugo, who had returned from exile the day before. The main aim of this gathering was to reaffirm the commitment of the party to a socialist form of self-management. From now on, those activists who disagreed with this political program would have to resign or be automatically expelled. Publicly, the party presented itself at the close of the congress as a well-structured organization with a clear goal. Privately, in an *Informe a los militantes,* Zavala confessed that the public image of the party as a *partido de masas* did not correspond to its inner reality; nonetheless, he argued, the image was necessary for the sake of political survival. He admitted that many militants were now disillusioned and apathetic, that they felt they had little influence over any decisions made within the party, and that the poor showing at the polls had left them demoralized and envious of others' success. In the process, they had become overcritical and suspicious of their superiors' motives. Instead of helping to unite the party, they were now helping to paralyze it. Zavala's simple cure for all these ills was a call to action: if militants, casting aside their mistrust, fulfilled their duties and participated fully in the activities of their movement, the party would re-form as a truly democratic, coherent organization, one capable of advancing the socialist cause and winning votes.[14] The effectiveness of Zavala's words would be judged by the party's results at the next general election.

In spring 1978, the party tried to relaunch Montejurra as a mass rally and to overcome the unwanted associations it had gained in the last two years by staging the event as both a pacific political assembly and as a grand fiesta. The posters and stickers advertising the occasion were done not in the usual stark red, white, and black but with gaily colored montages of Spain's regional flags. The night before the ceremony, singers from different regions of the country joined in a public Fiesta de Solidaridad de los Pueblos (Festival of Solidarity of the Pueblos), held in a Pamplona stadium. This imaginative attempt to enliven Montejurra and to boost attendance by putting on an expensive musical jamboree failed, however, to halt the decline in numbers. Only four thousand turned up on the day.[15]

Carlos Hugo, now that he was once again a Spanish resident, attempted to restimulate his followers by visiting Carlist centers throughout the country, and by publicizing his *La vía carlista al socialismo autogestionario*.[16] Carlos Hugo's book may have helped his image as a socially concerned politician who had thought long and hard about the problems of Spanish society, but its publication came several years too late to have any positive political effect. Although it was the product of years of discussion in *cursillos* and party meetings, this bulky but simply written political tract was more a tombstone to the efforts of the progressives than, as originally hoped, the herald of a new dawn. In the referenda for political reform and for the constitution, held in December 1976 and December 1978, respectively, and in the first general elections of 1977, the great majority of voters manifested their clear preference for a negotiated transition to a constitutional democracy over a radical jump into the unknown. Edifying dreams of recasting the state were being forgotten for the sake of instituting specific political reforms. In this evolving political climate, the Carlist utopianism of socialist self-management came to seem gravely out of step with the pragmatism of the Spanish electorate.

Progresismo in Navarre

The party continued to propound its policy of a thoroughgoing federalism as the ideal frame for the postfranquist state. Unlike the more outspoken nationalist parties, however, it did not question the integrity of Spain itself, and it argued against those that advanced what it termed "isolationist separatisms." Progressives wanted to federate Spain, not to balkanize it. Imitating the strategy employed by larger parties, provincial branches of the party were reorganized as semiautonomous bodies corresponding to the "historic regions" of the country. As an acknowledgement of the rising concern to reassert the value of local languages, some of these bodies were renamed accordingly: for example, the Partit Carlí de Catalunya; in Navarre, progressives joined with their Basque brethren in Bizkaia, Álava, and Gipuzkoa to form the Euskadiko Karlista Alderdia (EKA, Basque Carlist Party). The aim of the nationwide organization, which fought against any electoral regulations that encouraged a two-party system, was that these regional bodies would ally, on an equal footing, with other socialist parties in their area. Such coalitions would ward off the danger of the party being "colonized" by the large, very well-organized PSOE, which had already absorbed other groups to its left.

In the Basque area, however, the situation was somewhat more complex. Publicly, leading Navarrese progressives claimed that they had done so badly at the polls because the provincial section of the party had not participated as fully as it could have, because several of its electoral meetings had been prohibited, and because it had been legally unable to present itself under its own name. It is unlikely, however, that many Navarrese of voting age did not recognize "Agrupación Electoral Montejurra," with its silhouetted symbol of the mountain, as the progressives' temporary title. Their leading candidate, Mariano Zufia, was, moreover, an already well-known figure in Navarrese politics; in April he and other local progressives had occupied the Foral Deputation to publicize the unwarranted delay in the legalization of the party.[17] Privately, in their internal documents, members of the EKA recognized that their poor electoral results were partly a consequence of their overidentification with the radical Basque Left. Since Basque groups had, in recent years, been in the vanguard of the antifranquist opposition, and since Basque progressives had, according to the leaders of the EKA, suffered "a sort of inferiority complex" because of their movement's former, close association with the regime in the area, the regional section of the party had taken up the Basque cause to a degree that obscured the distinctiveness of its own political program: federalist and socialist self-management.

The best move for the EKA, as far as its tacticians were concerned, was to mark out its own particular political space and to stop participating in convocations composed exclusively of parties on the radical Basque Left. In 1978 EKA spokesmen began to assert that they did not support ETA, which they criticized as antidemocratic in its methods, and that they would not ally with any of the pro-ETA nationalist groups. Although Carlos Hugo personally did reach the political point of condoning armed reaction when the violence of the state became too oppressive, no leading member of the EKA thought the present predicament anywhere near that grave.[18]

The local political situation was complicated further by questions over the future status of Navarre. Leading nationalists demanded the integration of the province into an autonomous Basque region. These irredentist claims were vigorously opposed by *navarristas*, right-wing Navarrese who, lauding the distinctiveness of their own province, wished it to be declared an autonomous area of its own. Any prospect of a negotiated solution to this question appeared to be a distant one, since the bloody combination of Basque terrorist violence and continued repression by the forces of order within the area was beginning to harden local attitudes along a nationalist-*navarrista* divide. By December 1977 the tortuous negotiations over the powers to be transferred to the planned Basque Autonomous Area had reached an impasse thanks to the *navarristas'* sustained opposition. To break the deadlock, the Partido Nacionalista Vasco (PNV, center-right Basque Nationalist Party) and the PSOE agreed to the *navarristas'* demand that integration of the province could be neither assumed nor imposed; the Navarrese had to decide their own future in a referendum. Since the PSOE then held the electoral balance of power in the province, between left-wing and nationalist groups versus right-wing and regionalist ones, the socialists' shift on the issue effectively ended any hope of incorporation being quickly accepted by a legislature. ETA, in contrast, argued that Navarre was by definition part of Euskadi and that therefore the question could not be answered by a plebiscite. In late November a commando killed a police commander in Pamplona, and in early January there were two further incidents, resulting in the death of an inspector of police and two gunmen. In reaction to these events, the PNV and the PSOE went even further in their stipulations by arguing against holding the referendum in a climate of violence; the Navarrese electorate would not be asked to declare their opinion on the matter while ETA sought to influence them by killing its opponents. Since the gunmen showed no signs of laying down their arms, this latest condition pushed the idea of even staging a plebiscite far beyond the immediate political future—as many angry nationalists well realized.

In the meantime the EKA, like the PSOE, had become aware of the relatively little support within Navarre for its incorporation into the Basque Country. The leaders of the EKA, who had previously fully supported the calls for Navarrese incorporation, now openly backed the two conditions set by the PSOE and started to work closely with their local representatives in the negotiations over the status of Navarre. Having moved away from the more intransigent of the nationalist groups, the EKA began to distance itself from even the moderate PNV, because of their differing views over the constitutional referendum. Since the constitution failed to recognize fully Basque aspirations for autonomy, all nationalist parties urged their members to abstain or to vote no in the plebiscite; in contrast, the Partido Carlista, as a nationwide organization with interests wider than just those of the Basque Country, joined the campaign for an affirmative vote.[19] Quite clearly, in this sort of highly charged political context, a regional branch of the party, such as the EKA, could not be both patriotic and fully nationalistic at the same time. It had to make choices.

In the following January, the EKA stopped participating in meetings of Basque parties about the possibility of forming an electoral coalition: the nationalists were no longer so keen on an alliance, since the previous elections had revealed the weakness of Navarrese support for progressive Carlism, while the EKA publicly considered that the exclusively nationalist approach of the other parties was "not adjusted to the reality and objectivity that the Navarrese people need in these moments."[20] Despite the party's wish that regional sections join local coalitions, progressives in the Basque area had decided that, for the sake of their political survival, it was best to go it alone.

Carlist Failure at the Polls

Navarrese progressives might have carped at Basque politicos for being out of touch with reality, but as the results of the general elections (held on 1 March 1979) showed, it was not the nationalists but the Carlists who were out of step. Even though the party, now a legal organization, had time to prepare for the electoral contest, in every province—except Navarre—in which it participated in the hustings, it was among the least successful parties, and in some cases was the least successful, winning even fewer votes than that other survival from the Civil War, the Falange Español Auténtico. The party had, it is true, concentrated most of its efforts on five of its candidates, but even so, not one of them was elected: in Murcia and Tarragona, they polled just 0.4 and 0.6 percent of the vote, respectively; in Melilla (the smallest constituency in the country) and in Gipuzkoa, they performed marginally better, winning 1.1 and 1.23 percent; in Navarre, the party's area of greatest strength, its candidate had managed to win only 7.6 percent.[21] Depressed progressives were forced to ask themselves: why had they fared so badly?

One cause was the party's recent change in its political program. In mid-1978 the results of a specially commissioned survey suggested that the party was seen as preferring to oppose government policies rather than propose workable alternatives. It was regarded as being at times too "strident." A number of progressives had voiced the same criticism in the working assemblies held throughout the country during the same period: these pragmatists wanted a less idealist, more realizable set of policies. Since the earlier elections had shown that many leftists with radical sympathies chose not to vote for extremist parties for fear of precipitating another civil war, the party executive decided to moderate its program and to give up the idea of a "radical break" with the previous regime for the sake of a peaceful, gradual process toward democracy. The ideal of self-managing socialism, though approved by the Fourth National Congress in late 1977 and iterated by Carlos Hugo and Zavala at Montejurra in 1978, had not even been mentioned in the campaign. Zavala tried to justify this sort of opportunism by claiming that politicos needed to play dirty:

> Those who advance excuses, in order not to stain themselves, are falling into the worst kind of dirtiness. Those who avoid these risks are the critics of the party, those who from marginal positions pretend to be in the party yet are its greatest detractors. In truth they are not committed to its ideology. . . .
> We prefer to stain ourselves. . . . There will always be time to wash oneself, to correct and rectify our direction, because we always have the same objective: the struggle for socialist self-management.[22]

While this sort of strategic thinking would have made good electoral sense in a party whose members were used to the pragmatic necessity of adapting their policies to the needs of the political moment, it was not very appropriate for an organization many of whose most active members prided themselves on the distinctive ideology they had helped develop over the preceding ten years. Some of these proud Carlists thought such a sudden shift in policy for electoral ends unacceptably opportunist. Some began to wonder whether it was worth maintaining the party as an end in itself, whether the simple aim of political survival justified such an abrupt change of some of its goals. One Navarrese former militant told me that he had realized it was time to leave when, in a private discussion with Carlos Hugo, the prince had mentioned the possibility of allying with the Unión de Centro Democrático (UCD, Union of the Democratic Center), the center-right coalition of government, for the sake of winning a few seats. The local wing of PSOE accepted him immediately.

During this period, between the Fourth National Congress and the general elections, those who had originally entered Carlism during the reign of Franco for political reasons deserted it for the same reasons; to them, it had become clear that the party had no effective future. The politically ambitious born into Carlist families went to join other organizations for similar reasons; they wanted to work in parties or trade unions that had the promise of political clout. Basque militants, unhappy with the party's support of the constitution and its change of policy toward the question of Navarrese integration, switched allegiance to more radical, nationalist groups; some of the more activist members, expelled from the party, quietly entered ETA.[23]

Desertion to other parties thinned the ranks of militants, and the majority of those remaining had little political ambition. As one provincial leader of a now moribund section stated in his letter of resignation to Zavala,

> Pepe, I tell you sincerely that in these moments I feel frustrated and an enormous failure, although no one knows better than I myself that since I joined the party in 1973 I have lived for nothing else, even to the point of having spent all my savings as well as those of my wife, and of not having gone to a cinema, a recital, etc, for more than three years (except for two films I saw in Madrid so as not to get bored while waiting for some meeting or another to begin). I have no wish to cry or to complain of anything since everything I did or do was of my own free will. But a moment comes when I ask myself if it is worthwhile to do all this without being able to rely on the help of anybody.[24]

By April 1978, the local organization of the party had effectively ceased to function in Andalucía, Aragón, Asturias, Extremadura, and Galicia. In May, the political secretary for Seville and its province informed his superiors in Madrid that the party in his area was now

> reduced to a minimal level of expression; it is not heard, it is not known, it is not met with. The last unitary action in which it made any noise, but without the least profit, has been its organization and participation in the Day of Andalucía. Since that act we have been totally silent and inactive, meetings of the most committed militants and affiliates becoming more and more infrequent, before stopping altogether two months ago. . . . The party in Andalucía has disappointed the people, the working class, and all those companions on the Left who once valued us as a serious party with a certain power of convocation and organization.[25]

Militants in many areas, pessimistic of their party's electoral chances, were patently unenthusiastic and did not give the party much help in the campaign. Most had to be asked, in some cases persuaded, to stand as candidates in the 1979 elections. The party executive had wanted to present its representatives in all fifty-two constituencies, but it succeeded in finding candidates for only thirty-seven of them. As the party executive admitted in an internal document, the infrastructure provided during the elections by this largely demoralized political workforce "had been minimal, deficit, and inoperative."[26]

A further reason for the party's electoral ignominy was that, despite the consistent efforts by Carlos Hugo and like-minded militants, many Spaniards still thought of the Carlists as ferocious *requetés* fighting on the side of Franco for the sake of the Church. Many were still unsure whether the party was monarchist or not. Political groups on the Left may have appreciated the internal transformation of Carlism and accepted it as a further party within their ranks, but in the popular view, Carlism was still firmly wedded to its traditionalist past. People remembered the years of collaboration and of traditionalists in the cabinet. They had not forgotten that Carlist symbols had been used for ceremonial purposes by the regime since the war: in February 1937, the "Oriamendi" had been made a national hymn, the red beret had become part of the Movimiento uniform, and the Carlist flag with the Cross of Saint Andrew had been included in the regime's stock of banners.[27] The party executive, well aware of these problems of image, had a few years previously decided to hide its connections with the Frente Obrero Sindicalista (FOS, Syndicalist Workers' Front), which it had created and secretly funded, so that people could not possibly associate this workers' front with any remnant of unreformed traditionalism. Carlos Carnicero, a member of Carlos Hugo's cabinet, says that it was during a coach journey from Bilbao to Madrid just before the 1979 elections when he suddenly realized that his party had no hope: chatting with three fellow passengers—a hairdresser, a nurse, and a dentist—he discovered none of them had any idea that Carlism had moved away from the Right.[28]

Party leaders argued that a lack of international support and of money had also hindered their efforts. Unlike the PSOE, the Liberals, the Christian Democrats, and the Communists, who had all been assisted by their respective internationals, the Partido Carlista had no rich foreign backers to call on. For the 1979 campaign the Borbón-Parmas had donated 70 million pesetas of their own money, while the party had raised another 10 million from conscientious members. It also secured several loans. However, these arrived late, delaying the release of much of the party's publicity. Even if all this money had arrived on time, it was still relatively little compared to the electoral budgets of other parties, which could be as much as seven times larger. The postelectoral debt, of over 30 million pesetas, with which the party was left was paid off only by the sale of part of its patrimony. The party had spent most of its budget on mounting effective campaigns in those five constituencies (Murcia, Tarragona, Gipuzkoa, Melilla, and Navarre) where either Carlism had traditionally been strong, the provincial branches were well organized, or the particular candidate was popular locally. But as the results showed, none of these conditions was sufficient to get Carlist candidates into the Cortes. Many of the party's otherwise potential supporters thought it had "missed the train of the transition": since no Carlist representatives had been able to participate in the parliamentary debates over the constitution, these potential supporters had come to disregard the party as a viable political force. Voting strategically, they preferred to support left-wing parties that stood a better chance of seeing their candidates elected. In Navarre, the political situation had become so polarized between nationalists and *navarristas*, with the PSOE occupying an uneasy middle ground, that there was no political space for a small center-left party that supported only mildly nationalist demands. Although the Navarre branch of the party had promoted their candidate, Carlos Hugo, as an already experienced politician with an impeccably well-rounded education and character, and though the number of votes cast for his brand of Carlism rose from 8,423 (3.8 percent) in the previous elections to 19,522 (7.6 percent), that was still about 4,000 votes short of getting their president elected as a deputy.

A closer look at the polls in Navarre reveals that few city dwellers voted Carlist and that there were high returns only in Tierra Estella and in the areas that flanked the highway from the valley of Pamplona to Viana, the town in the southwestern corner of the province.[29] In other words, the party fared well only in municipalities of longstanding Carlist support. This suggests that the electorate faithful to the party were villagers who tended to vote for Carlism more out of tradition than for specific political reasons. Thus, it appears that by 1979 the main source of the party's electoral strength was those rural folk who were not prepared to compromise their notion of Carlist identity, no matter whether their candidates had failed at the polls in the previous elections, no matter whether their national leaders propounded self-managing socialism or some milder set of policies. On this basis, *progresismo,* as a political philosophy, had failed to change fundamentally the nature of provincial Carlism. What progressive leaders had seen at times as the dead weight of tradition stifling change within their ranks was now proving to be the saving grace of what remained of their ancient movement.

The Departure of Carlos Hugo

The party's definitive and undeniable electoral failure precipitated an internal crisis, above all between the executive in Madrid and the progressives in Navarre. When Carlos Hugo's political cabinet proposed dissolving the party, Navarrese leaders objected most strongly. As they said, they did not regard Carlism so "coldly." People whose sense of self was so bound up with the movement were not going "to close the shop." No matter how few of their representatives were elected, they were not going to forsake the identity they had inherited and still valued so highly. Zavala and his associates thought otherwise. They saw no point in working for an organization that appeared to have no political future, and in October they resigned en bloc.[30]

Two months before, Carlos Hugo had rejected proposals made by Navarrese Carlists that he be given more executive power and so be obliged to preside over more committees. The Navarrese thought this a way to unify the party. But their prince wanted a more honorary post, one with fewer ties.

Since the elections he had become more distant and, according to those close to him, had taken on a sadder visage. He was attending far fewer meetings than before, and his appearance at Montejurra that year, which was staged as a quieter, Navarrese event rather than as a grand one of national scale, was not celebrated with any of the usual fanfare.[31] Three days after the resignation of his cabinet, he had all militants sent a detailed questionnaire asking for their opinions on the evolution of the party and its political future, with a view to its possible reorganization. In its résumé of the contemporary situation, the questionnaire stated that the principal and most evident consequence of the electoral results was the disappearance from the present political scene of the Carlists as a party; the media were ignoring the party, which was characterized by "inactivity, apathy, absence."[32] Navarrese militants thought many of the questions loaded, implying that they should disband as a party. Many regarded the survey, which had not been approved by party committees, as a maneuver by their president to outflank the executive and chose not to fill it in. Carlos Hugo's ploy failed. Since the Navarrese proposals about his position were to be put forward at the next congress, he decided to retain the initiative by appearing unexpectedly at the federal council of the party on the morning before the gathering. He curtly presented his resignation, and then walked out.[33] Some members cried during the afternoon meeting of the council. Their king had gone.

Although the party kept the presidency vacant in the hope he might reconsider, Carlos Hugo did not return to the fold. Instead, together with his close former advisers, he established a center in Madrid for the study of socioeconomic problems facing Spanish politicians. But the venture lacked money, and it closed within a year.[34] Irene separated from her husband and returned to Holland and to Protestantism; Carlos Hugo left the country; María-Teresa became a university lecturer in politics; and their former associates found jobs, most in branches of journalism.

The Borbón-Parmas had iterated that they were not making any dynastic claim, yet the regal bloodline of Carlos Hugo was one of the two original struts of his authority. Although he had tried to resolve the apparent contradiction of a populist prince by his concept of a "socialist monarch," and though he had gotten the party at its fourth congress to *vote* him in as president, the poles of royalty and thoroughgoing democracy had still sometimes clashed. In many meetings, he and his sisters had chatted informally in a most unregal, friendly manner with Carlist villagers. But at the same time he was the only person in the movement who was always addressed by the honorary title of "Don," while members of his political cabinet, when dealing with outsiders who wished to speak with the prince, would refer to him as "His Highness." The party may not have pushed the claim of the Borbón-Parmas to the Spanish

throne, but Carlos Hugo was careful to emphasize that he could never renounce his inheritance: whatever happened in politics, he remained a Borbón
prince and the bearer of the Carlist crown. Many prominent progressives in
Navarre had not wanted Carlos Hugo to present himself in the 1979 elections.
Aware of the fact that many Carlist villagers still regarded him in predominantly regal terms, they argued that if he lost he would *quemarse* (burn himself
out). A king could electioneer in the street only once and retain any majesty.
Carlos Hugo clearly agreed by abandoning the cause after his defeat. The unusual spectacle of a prince in parliament was not to be.[35]

If Carlos Hugo occupied a central space in Carlism, then his departure was
a critical loss for the already badly flagging movement. For the first time ever,
Carlism both lacked a regal leader and had no prospect of gaining one. Without a Borbón at its helm, the cause lost much of its distinctiveness and its
liveliness. Carlos Hugo's divorce the following year only added to members'
disillusion. He could no longer claim to evince "the traditional virtues par
excellence";[36] the progressive rank and file had lost a leader who had personified the values they held dear. Die-hard Carlists believed that "true" followers
of the cause maintained their faith until death. Carlos Hugo had gotten out
when it had suited him for reasons of political expediency. He was not called
a *chaquetero* (turncoat) since he had not switched sides. But he was seen as a
traitor, and his desertion was all the more grave given the publicity it received
and the apical position he occupied within the party. Some traditionalists
thought his departure proved that he was not a "true" Carlist in the first place,
for a real prince of the line would never have walked out on his people. One
Navarrese leader of the party confessed to me that he could not understand
how Carlos Hugo and his wife could give up Carlism so easily. Even though
Doña Irene is so rich she "has money coming out of her nose," he said her
commitment and that of her husband was indisputable. They had worked too
hard for too long for their dedication to be questioned. How then, he won-
dered, could they have left the cause?

One educated conservative Carlist, waxing emotional at the end of our discussion, repeatedly affirmed that the movement would have survived had it
not been for the interference of Carlos Hugo and his sisters. It would have
been a minor, but strong, force within the Navarrese opposition, combating
the specter of Basque nationalism. To him, the Borbón-Parmas had first damaged and then destroyed the cause. The Carlists had been deceived by Franco
in the war and then by Carlos Hugo afterward. The antics of an "adventurer"
had smashed the ancient movement he had lived and fought for.

In the Montejurra of 1987, the secretary-general of the party remembered in
his speech the fine character of Don Javier on the tenth anniversary of his
death, then added that his son "doesn't count." No one in the crowd even

murmured disagreement. True Carlists remain Carlists forever, turncoats have no shame, and a king who turns away from his people is the greatest disappointment of all.

Postelectoral Carlism

This royal decapitation worsened the political prospects of the movement, which progressively polled fewer and fewer votes. In the municipal elections, held the month after the general elections, the Partido Carlista gained a mere 7 of the 264 mayorships in Navarre; only one of its candidates was voted onto the Foral Council of the province.[37] With such a reduced base of support, the party could no longer afford to campaign alone in national hustings.[38] It did not participate in the general elections of 1982, and in the elections to the Foral Parliament held the following year, its percentage of the Navarrese vote dropped from 4.79 percent to 2.55 percent.[39] By the 1980s, the party had become so small that its regional organizations, such as the EKA, stopped acting as separate bodies and spoke only in the name of the whole party. Just before the 1986 general elections, the party felt the need to join forces with other groups in a coalition, Izquierda Unida (United Left), which was dominated by the Communist Party. But the alliance fared badly at the elections and the Carlists, complaining that the Communists paid no heed to their opinions, abandoned the coalition within a year of having joined.[40] In 1987 the party did not put forward any candidates for the Foral Parliament, while neither of the two remaining Carlist mayors in Navarre chose to stand for reelection. Even in Estella, former jewel in the Carlist crown, the party felt it had not enough support to justify presenting municipal candidates.[41] By that date Carlism had no elected representatives outside a few Navarrese town halls, where isolated stalwarts continued to labor in the name of their movement. Since 1989, the party has presented itself in elections to the European Parliament, as the constituencies are much larger and thus there is a greater chance of agglomerating the vote of the faithful. But the results have still been miserable.

Former Carlists now working in other parties say that the feeling of allegiance to Carlist tradition was so strong for some militants that they stubbornly refused to see that there was no political space for the party on the electoral stage. Although their hopes were in vain, they kept on actively militating until they "burned themselves out." Mariano Zufia, secretary-general of the EKA during the transition, said to me in 1984 that the party could not simply disappear by merging with another, larger party: he had fought as a *requeté*; he and his sons had all been jailed for their beliefs; all of that could not just be given up. At a congress held in 1987 in Pamplona and attended by fewer than a hundred delegates, the retiring leaders had great difficulty persuading people to become candidates for the executive posts of responsibility. A motion that the party should dissolve itself was defeated only after some discussion; the majority felt that though their organization had no real political future, it could not be disbanded.[42]

If resilient Carlists cannot give up the party because of their sense of the past, they are at the same time dogged by that past, for some traditionalists have proved to be as steadfast as their former brethren. During the years of the transition, these diehards were divided into a number of small groups, all the products of a series of schisms with Don Javier or Carlos Hugo: the Regency of Estella, the Comunión Tradicionalista, the Comunión Carlista Legitimista, the Unión Carlista, and the Comunión Católico-Monarquica Española.[43] Most of these groups were headed by prominent members of the old Comunión, or by their sons. In the early 1980s, representatives of these various groups started to meet to discuss the possibility of merging. At a Congress of Carlist Unity held outside Madrid in 1986, they agreed to re-form as a unitary organization, to be called the "Comunión Tradicionalista Carlista." Among other activities, this reconstituted Comunión publishes its own journal, *Acción Carlista,* stages national congresses every two or three years, and holds its own annual ritual gatherings in Montserrat and in Isusquiza, Bizkaia, which in the 1980s were being attended by about the same number of people as were turning up at Montejurra. Upholding the idea of a monarch who would rule over a confessional state and respect regional *fueros,* these traditionalists have frequently criticized the actions of the party, and were particularly scathing of its association with the Communists in Izquierda Unida.[44] They have not forgotten the glorious days of *requetés* trouncing the hated Red horde, and they are not going to let those in the party forget it either.

In the late 1980s, this renovated Comunión started to become much more active. Graffiti in the name of the organization began to appear in Pamplona and along Navarrese highways. During this period, as notorious ultraconservatives left it for other bodies, the Comunión also managed to shed much of the extreme rightist image that had clung to it from some of its forebears. In 1994 it presented itself in the elections to the European Parliament, spending about $40,000 on its campaign. In Navarre it polled 473 votes (0.21 percent of all votes cast) and in the country as a whole 5,226 votes (0.03 percent). In comparison, the Partido Carlista won 583 votes in Navarre (0.59 percent of all votes cast) and 82,410 votes nationally (0.2 percent). These results suggest that if the Partido Carlista can be regarded as primarily a testimonial organization, then the present-day Comunión must be regarded as maintaining an even more precarious toehold on contemporary politics.

Chapter Twelve

Village Carlism: 1939–1987

Carlos Hugo versus Valiente, Zavala versus Zamanillo: both of these opposed pairs had their own historiographies of the Carlist movement, whose modern history they also helped to create. Both had nationwide visions and dealt with politicians of national importance. While the evolution of the movement they steered is refracted in the historical course of Carlism in Cirauqui, a study of what happened in this sort of rural context serves to reveal some of the particular inflections the movement could be given by modern villagers, who dealt only with one another and local politicos. In the village, both progressives and their opponents have their own accounts of Carlism, their own ways of evaluating its supporters, and their own visions of its future, or of its lack of one. And given that the cause now hardly exists outside of a few *pueblos* such as Cirauqui, examination of these villagers' ideas, attitudes, and acts is all the more revealing about the impoverished state of present-day Carlism.

To understand the development of this localized Carlism, however, it needs to be placed within its various, evolving village contexts. For if until the Civil War the social life of Cirauqui had undergone relatively little fundamental change since the advent of Carlism, during the last decades of the dictatorship and the first one of the transition, villagers experienced a series of radical transformations—economic, political, religious, social, and cultural—that would alter profoundly and thoroughly the nature of their joint existence.[1] As new forms of livelihood and association, together with new conceptions of kinship duty and identity, began to emerge and then to dominate, what had once been central started to become peripheral. What had once seemed unimportant now took on tones of the greatest significance. Within this process, the Carlism of Cirauqui was to enjoy a remarkable Indian summer, only to be followed by a precipitous decline.

Life under Franco

Even before the final triumph of Franco's forces, the rule of the dictatorship had already been firmly established throughout Navarre and the surrounding provinces. In Cirauqui, there would be no more free elections for several decades. Placemen substituted democratically elected representatives. The civil governor of Navarre appointed the mayor, who, at the end of his term of office, would be asked to name three or four possible successors, one of whom would be selected. Councillors were chosen according to the idiosyncratic electoral system of the regime's "organic democracy."

Members of the town hall and other local officials became the active agents of Franquist repression. Those who had been on the Left, and were now out of prison, were discriminated against, both negatively and positively, in a myriad of obstructive ways, both major and petty. Anyone applying for a municipal post was screened politically, and only those whose commitment to the regime was unquestionable were considered seriously. Villagers admit that during the "years of hunger" in the 1940s, both some on the Left and some on the Right stole garden produce. But it was usually the leftists, not the rightists, who were punished for their thefts. Leftists who indulged in riotous behavior tended to receive much heavier fines or sentences than similarly indulgent rightists. As one veteran of the Right put it to me, in those days, leftist villagers "had to keep quiet." During the annual selection of who would be allowed to cut which trees on the commons for firewood, those villagers on the Right would always get the trees with the best wood and those on the Left the worst. According to aging leftists, these sorts of repressive measure could occur in almost any sphere of public business until about 1950.

Although the degree of repression began to ease somewhat from that time on, it left a lasting sense of bitterness among some of its victims. Villagers told me how a number of their older neighbors, who had been young men in the first decades of the regime, would at times voice their great frustration at never having been councillors, at never having been able "to do things" because their political leanings were even slightly suspect. One man, whose father had been jailed for several years for having voted for a Republican party, several times bewailed to me how he had never been given a position of responsibility either in the army (during his military service) or in the village. He would then often complain about how very heavy the fines levied by the police were in those straitened times. His resentful protests usually ended with the heartfelt exclamation, "You can't imagine what a dictatorship is like if you haven't lived under one!"

After the war, political difference was very muted. After all, officially it no longer existed. The only particular political group whose members openly expressed their affiliation was the Carlists. *Requetés* wore their red berets on Sundays and continued to celebrate their fiestas, which now included the annual pilgrimage to Montejurra. In 1944 the Carlists of the village decided to buy a house in the main plaza as a permanent home for their Circle. Some Carlists claim that any man in the village could drink in the club and that leftists did go there. But some aging socialists who, as adults, suffered the wartime and immediate postwar repression, say they never set foot inside its doors. For people of this generation, one's politics was masked, but not forgotten. In contrast, the now late-middle-aged sons of veteran leftists, who were boys during the war, state that, in the absence of political discussion and of any formalized political activity, one slowly learned to forget. Villagers of this age range even contracted marriages across the political lines—for instance, the daughters of steadfast Carlists wedding the sons of unrepentant Republicans who had been imprisoned for their beliefs.[2]

During this postwar period the effective, and unchallenged, rulers of the village were the mayor and the priests, and to a lesser degree the municipal secretary and the town councillors. Except for the priests, who came from outside Cirauqui, almost all the other officeholders were members of the more well-to-do classes within the village. Thus it is with some justification that leftist villagers today state that during those decades the governance of Cirauqui was a rule of its poor by its rich.

Several times a year these officeholders ritually manifested the congruence of their interests. All members of the town hall would ceremonially attend a series of church services: the formal procession around the village on the Feast of Corpus Christi, the Mass celebrated on the feast day of the village's patron, Saint Román, and the Salve held the night before, the *setenarios* (the seven sermons given on consecutive days the week before Holy Week by an outside priest hired by the town hall), and a variety of religious events during Easter itself. In the church, the mayor and councillors had their own pew, which they shared with the judge and seven members of the Civil Guard (who were stationed in the village until the 1950s). On the Feast of Corpus Christi and Easter Sunday, members of the town hall were invited to wine and biscuits in the parochial center. Also, on the feast days of Saint Roman and Saint Catalina, the priests would invite all the *fuerzas vivas* (living forces; i.e., the officeholders) of Cirauqui to join them in throwing chestnuts from the roof of the center to the villagers gathered below and to dine with them later. After the Mass held during the village's annual *romería*, the town hall would invite the priests to lunch with them in the hermitage; on Maundy Thursday, after the morning services, the town hall would invite the priests, the judge, and the commander of the guardsmen to eat with them. Here, concelebration and commensality were meant to signify, and to reinforce, the commonality of this governing elite's concerns and interests.

Mayors saw as one of their key duties the securing of money from the Deputation for the improvement of the village. The incumbent between 1948 to 1954 had the electrical network of the village updated and initiated the paving of its streets: till then, the streets had been covered irregularly with stones, creating holes so deep that cars could not drive over them. He also had a track for tractors constructed, which stretched from the village itself to the boundaries of the municipality. His successor oversaw the completion of the paving, had the main water source, then sited 800 meters away from the village, brought up to its edge, and put together the official petition to the Deputation for a new primary school and a house for the village doctor, both of which were built during the incumbency of his replacement. The mayor from 1970 to 1979 had the main plaza of the village resurfaced, tracks to fields renovated, the street lighting fixed, and the facade of the town hall restored.

Besides the mayors, the other great motivators of village projects were the parish priests, and the most significant of these in the postwar period was a man whom I shall call Don Bonifacio. Stationed in Cirauqui from 1958 to 1978, Don Bonifacio is remembered by his supporters as "a man of extraordinary stature," who initiated and oversaw the establishment of a series of projects beneficial to the village. To his detractors, he exemplified, in a religious mode, the authoritarian values of the regime they hated. Don Bonifacio could thus be seen as an embodiment of the regime writ small, in both its socially positive and negative aspects, and, with the aging of the dictatorship, as a man increasingly out of step with the times.

In the mid-1960s, he supervised the creation of an agricultural cooperative and shortly afterward a granary. Their main aims were to help the needy, sometimes at the expense of the rich. For their members, they provided seed and fertilizer at prices less than the market rate, bought their crops at highly competitive rates, and rented out tractors and harvesters, so saving the needy from having to enter into potentially exploitative reciprocal arrangements with farmers wealthy enough to have their own machinery. Using money left to the parish by a wealthy villager, Don Bonifacio also organized the purchase of land on the edge of Cirauqui, which was then flattened for use as a soccer field. Perhaps his most controversial project was persuading a pair of German businessmen to set up a small factory for the making of hinges and small pieces of plastic. Originally it was hoped the factory, which opened in 1970, would create 100 jobs, 85 percent of them for villagers. However, while the production of the plastic entailed the hiring of many hands, it also entailed a large, constant supply of water. Within three years, it was clear the water supply to the village was insufficient for these needs. So the Germans controlling that side of the business closed it down and left, throwing many people out of work and causing widespread discontent. It reopened later but offered fewer jobs.

Some opponents of Don Bonifacio complained that he was the most powerful person in the village and was able to get the incumbent mayor to do his bidding. But, according to one former mayor, while he and councillors were happy to work with Don Bonifacio on projects he initiated of benefit to the village, he usually had relatively little to do with the town hall. At times the mayor and councillors even turned a deaf ear if Don Bonifacio protested against a popular project. For instance, when he complained against the proposed construction of a swimming pool, because sunbathers would display too much of their flesh, the town hall politely listened to his comments but did not act on them.

His opponents claim he inspired fear rather than respect. They complained of the ways he tried to control the lives of others according to his own, conservative interpretation of Christianity. For instance, he had the distribution of the diocesan weekly within the village stopped because, he said, "it sowed confusion." His critics claim he did this only because the periodical did not follow a conservative line. According to them, Don Bonifacio also exploited the confessional for reactionary ends. Furthermore, now middle-aged women remember that in his weekly meetings with girls of the village, he made it clear he wanted them to remain "virgins and saints." During dances, he would try to get the municipal constable to prevent young couples from dancing too closely. Don Bonifacio very strongly advocated a highly traditional sense of family. It is said that if a mother, unsure whether to treat her children more liberally, went to discuss the matter with him, he would make her feel guilty instead of encouraging a more open dialogue between the generations. This closed-mind approach could lead to acute conflicts within families over topics such as how free a rein to give children, and what hour daughters had to return from evening fiestas. Even Don Bonifacio's supporters admit that he "was stuck in his own times," never changing out of his black garb and almost never entering a village bar.

As these critics point out, when Don Bonifacio could not get what he wanted pacifically, he was, like the regime itself, prepared to act violently. For instance, he laid down that women attending Mass had to wear veils and stockings. In the mid-1960s he had an independent-minded woman forcibly ejected from church for entering with her legs bare. To her cries of "Bastard! Bastard!" members of the faithful physically removed her from her pew and carried her up the aisle. The year before, a detachment of soldiers had briefly visited the village. That night they organized a dance in the main plaza. Don Bonifacio told the mayor to stop the event. When he saw that he would not, he went down to the plaza and recriminated him publicly, calling him a straw man, lacking personality. The soldiers decided to leave.

The Rise of Opposition

When asked about the recent past, villagers emphasize that by the late 1950s Cirauqui was literally crumbling. Although the years of hunger had passed and government requisitioning of crops had ended, the incomes of many were still very low and unemployment was rife. The houses in the village, some centuries old, were not being restored, some were not even being maintained, and new ones were not being built. The village was beginning to empty as people left to seek work elsewhere. Paradoxically, it was this rural emigration that was to assist the regeneration of the village.

The first wave of migrants occurred in the 1950s as Bilbao underwent a new phase of industrial growth. The second and more sustained wave started in the 1960s when the Foral Deputation decided to initiate the belated industrialization of Navarre, focusing growth on the capital, Pamplona, and four regional centers. This change in the nature of villagers' employment accelerated in the late 1960s as the state embarked on the tardy development of its secondary school and university systems. Until then, the only way most young villagers could receive an education beyond the primary level was by entering a seminary. But with the construction of public schools by the government, scholastically capable youths whose fathers tilled the soil at home became able to seek jobs as white-collar workers in urban centers. The number of students at seminaries dropped precipitously: for example, in the Pamplonan seminary, the total number fell from 292 in 1968 to 10 in 1970, a drop of 97 percent.

These new kinds and new patterns of villagers' employment would radically change the nature of life in Cirauqui. The increase in many people's salaries and the gradual rise in the educational standard of younger villagers helped to level somewhat the social hierarchy. The doctor was no longer the only person in the village with a degree, and the position of the parish priest as a privileged, educated intermediary between the village and the world beyond was increasingly threatened. Workers and their families living in Bilbao or other distant centers became seasonal returnees, coming back to Cirauqui for traditional festivities, part of the summer, and the occasional weekend. Those with jobs in Pamplona or its environs either lived there and returned on weekends or commuted daily from the village. Some of these new generations of nonagricultural workers began to invest the surplus cash their jobs generated in the restoration of their familial homes or in the purchase of a flat in one of the small blocks of flats that developers had constructed at the edge of the village. Cirauqui began to smarten up.

Since these migrants, employed mainly in factories, earned better wages for fewer hours of work than agricultural laborers or smallholders, the number of villagers living off the land began to decline. The mechanization of agriculture, which had started in Cirauqui in the 1950s when the larger landowners began to invest in tractors and harvesters, reduced the need for well-to-do farmers to hire extra labor. By the 1960s, the traditional dawn labor market, where *jornaleros* would gather in the main plaza to see if the rich would employ them that day, had become but a memory. The farmers had gotten machinery and the landless jobs elsewhere. As large-scale farming became more commercially efficient, smallholding as a way of life started to make less and less economic sense. The worsening marriage prospects of smallholders hastened the demise of this mode of production, as women became ever more reluctant to tie themselves for life to a form of domestic economy that demanded almost as much of wives as it did of their husbands. Young men began to seek actively other forms of employment, even if they were set to inherit enough land to live off. By the late 1970s, only three kinds of people were left working the land: a small band (never more than seven) of larger landowners, who had enough to make their venture profitable; a steadily declining number of older smallholders, who were unprepared to change their livelihood; and a relatively large group of those in receipt of government pensions, which acted in effect as state subsidies to these small-time agriculturalists. Some salaried employees maintained the smallholdings of their aging parents, working these holdings in the evenings and on weekends. But this they usually did more as a hobby than as a significant source of income.

The sum consequence of these changes was that the population of the village was coming to be structured seasonally. In winter, Cirauqui was home to the decreasing band of agriculturalists, a few store owners, and rising proportions of commuters and pensioners; it was a quiet time, and villagers started to regard this annual period as one during which their village edged on the sad, even the moribund. Summer was a much livelier time, when the population might more than double as residents were joined by returnees and their families. One major effect of these changes was that villagers were no longer commonly committed to the land. The economy was being transformed and diversified, and the nature of people's links to the village and to one another was changing profoundly. Thus any idea of "the village" as a working, albeit fractious, agglomeration of indigenous coresidents was no longer reproduced ineluctably by the once customary socioeconomic practices of resident villagers. Instead, "the village" was fast becoming a constructed ideal, which people wished to strive to achieve, of a near-idyllic place where one could live in a healthy manner away from the pressures and pollution of the city, a place to which one was linked by history, blood, and, at the very least, occasional residence.

In this steadily evolving context of fundamental change, Carlism, if it was to remain politically viable and meaningful to its village supporters, needed to be recast in renovated, nontraditionalist terms.[3] In the late 1960s, young Carlists in Cirauqui, frustrated by the continuation of the regime and desirous for change, began quietly to meet, away from the somnolent Circle frequented by their fathers, to discuss the ideas propagated by progressives. This generation of villagers, then in their late teens and early twenties, had not known the disruptive years of the Republic nor the immediate aftermath of the Civil War. Rather, they were reaching maturity at a time when the opportunities for further education and salaried jobs were steadily increasing, as were the possibilities of working-class protest, with mass strikes becoming ever more common throughout the province. At the same time, various sectors of civil society were beginning to talk publicly of the need for openness and alternatives to the present system. Franco, now in his late seventies, could not live forever, nor, it seemed, could his brand of dictatorship. ETA, active primarily in the Basque Country and Navarre, had established itself in the vanguard of the opposition, and even Carlists had instituted their own versions of armed activism. The young Carlists, aware of these developments, wished to discuss what they collectively should do, and how they should act.

Most of them had already heard something about *progresismo* from the speeches at Montejurra, to which their parents had taken them; some had learned more by attending the visits of Carlos Hugo or one of his sisters to nearby villages, ones famed for their Carlism, and by joining Multhiko Alaiak, a Carlist-dominated *peña* (club providing various forms of social activities) in the center of Pamplona. The horizons of several of these young Carlists had been broadened by their experience outside the village: one, then still a monk, had first become aware of the nature and extent of social problems while working in Bilbao; another had made friends with radical progressives while studying at a seminary. These village youths passed word about the meetings to those of their peers whom they already knew were keen for political reform. They would assemble regularly in the houses of one or another of them to talk about the contemporary situation in the country, and in the village. These discussions mixed the theoretical and the practical: they debated both the pros and cons of different forms of national government and what concrete measures could be taken in Cirauqui itself. Two young progressives from Pamplona, prominent in the provincial organization of the party, visited the village occasionally in order to keep these youths up to date on the new currents passing through the movement and on the developments in policy.

These young Carlists did not tell their elders what they were up to: they thought the elders would not be interested. They believed that traditionalist Carlist villagers would find too alien the new political language they were rapidly acquiring. In their opinion, terms such as "socialism," "socialist monarchy," "self-management," "participatory democracy," and *"asambleas"* (where all attending were allowed to speak and to vote) were integral parts of a political vision far distant from that held by their seniors. When one of them gave refuge to a member of the GAC in the attic of the large house he was managing, they kept the fact strictly secret from older Carlists. The dynamism of these youthful activists, who would, come the transition, be ready to participate in demonstrations (such as the occupation of the Deputation) beyond the bounds of the village, came to contrast strongly with the lassitude of their fathers. So few Carlists of the older generations now bothered to attend the Circle that it was difficult to find a caretaker to manage it. In 1973, the building was leased to a non-Carlist, who ran it as a cafe-bar. The number of villagers visiting the locale immediately began to rise, anti-Carlists not being put off by the large but fading sign, "Circulo Carlista de Cirauqui," left hanging high on its facade.

The more dedicated of the village's young Carlists attended a *cursillo* in Valcarlos, though one of them later complained to me that the organizers seemed more interested in showing them how to be effective local militants than in training them how to assume positions of greater responsibility. It was her impression that the more important posts within the provincial branch of the party were being saved for other people. These budding militants also took part in clandestine meetings of the party staged in Estellan and Pamplonan churches. Since these gatherings were illegal, they had to be disguised as religious discussion groups: Mass would be said at the beginning, and an open Bible left on the altar during the political debate in case the police appeared, as they sometimes did.

It was this clutch of young Carlists, joined by a few like-minded contemporaries, who realized that if directed change was to come to Cirauqui, they would have to initiate it themselves. Their task was indirectly aided by villagers participating in the strikes, for their news and views of these conflicts helped to generate a local, critical consciousness about social and economic problems. In June 1970 the Carlist activists staged a very well-attended meeting of the village youth to discuss their collective concerns and anxieties. This led one member of the group to attempt to stimulate further debate by having a critical analysis of the village published in a provincial newspaper.[4] In it he spoke of the worries of the village youth, who felt increasingly alienated from the traditional forms of practicing the Christian faith and who needed a cultural center, with a library and sports facilities, to give them something to do. Don Bonifacio later admitted to the man that this public criticism had "devastated" him. Otherwise, the article appears to have had little more effect than to advertise the concerns of some about the state of the village. At Christmas the next year, the man wrote an open letter to Don Bonifacio in which he systematically criticized his narrow-minded, static Catholicism, which was blind to the conciliar reforms and out of touch with the changing realities of villagers. Don Bonifacio's clerical conception of the Church, the man charged, left no space for the laity except as subjects or recipients of his messages, while the young people of the village were increasingly disappointed and disoriented, partly because he did not organize any activities for them, such as youth Masses, Christian educational courses, or working groups.[5] Like his article, the man's letter seems to have had little effect. Don Bonifacio did not change his pastoral style.

The group came to realize that a different approach was needed. Since, in their opinion, the political consciousness of most villagers was still so low, the best way of motivating change and carrying the people with them as they went was not yet to engage in open political proselytizing, which would have alienated more than it would have attracted, but to embark on popular, highly participatory projects. These projects, both festive and recreational, would embody, practice, and publicly demonstrate their progressive ideal of democratic self-management. But first, to get these projects under way, they felt it necessary to contest openly, and in a sustained manner, the position of the village's leading reactionary.

Challenging Don Bonifacio

By 1975 an inner group of the young Carlists, five strong, had developed their political analysis of the village a little more than the others. They realized that they needed someone capable of bringing together and consolidating the somewhat diffuse political currents emerging within Cirauqui. They had also realized that a confrontation between the forces of change and stasis was imminent and that it was best to ensure that it occurred within a religious frame, because it would be very hard to change anything without first breaking Don Bonifacio's grip on many of his parishioners.

The person they thought best to spearhead this change was Juan María Valencia, a young missionary from the village then at home on leave. Having such a prestigious reformer as leader, they believed, would attract many people to their side. Valencia understood the role they wanted him to play. He regarded the strategy as risky, given that he was back for only a few months. But since he had helped similarly minded groups in South America, he felt honor-bound to do the same in his hometown and so chose to join them.

They began by holding informal meetings in his family's house about the situation in the village. These gatherings made many villagers uneasy, since people normally met in bars and meetings held elsewhere had an air of the conspiratorial. This caused tension. In the bars people entered heated debates, defending or criticizing the group's actions. To be able to debate matters in a more relaxed setting, the group decided to spend a Saturday night in a shepherd's cabin on a nearby mountain range. There they discussed what to do, how to express or share their concerns about the village. They agreed, as a first step, to stage a march. On their return on Sunday, they found many villagers unhappy, wondering what plot exactly the group was hatching. But many of the village youth were already prepared to back them. When, shortly afterward, the group proposed a march to the hermitage in a nearby range of hills, they were accompanied by about 80 percent (about fifty persons) of all village youth. The day passed well, with the celebration of Mass, prayers, a communal lunch, and games.

To Don Bonifacio, the patent success of the march suggested that he was losing religious control of the village. So he began openly criticizing Valencia, for not donning vestments when celebrating Mass at the hermitage and for not wearing a cassock when giving Holy Communion to the sick. Although he allowed Valencia to concelebrate Mass, he refused to grant him access to the pulpit. Privately, he would dispute aspects of theology with him, giving his reply in the next sermon, even though his points passed over most of the congregation. These actions caused much bad feeling, especially the prohibition on him preaching, as Valencia was much liked by many of his fellow villagers.

The climax of this mounting conflict came at Easter, which the group regarded as an opportunity to stimulate the meeting of village youth, who otherwise had little to do during Holy Week. They decided to hold a democratic assembly in the village school on Palm Sunday. But no one would give them the key: the mayor said the teacher had it, the teacher the cleaners, the cleaners the mayor. They finally gained entrance when one lad broke a window. This assembly was the first time that the village youth had ever voted in their lives. In the course of an intensive debate, they agreed to put on an alternative Holy Week, by holding alternative assemblies to those that Don Bonifacio would stage at the same time in the church. In order not to make the conflict worse, they also agreed to put on extra assemblies, at another time, open to all and with invited speakers. Rumors then spread that Don Bonifacio, in his annual Easter-time meeting with the town hall, had persuaded the mayor and councillors that it was necessary to summon the Civil Guard to suppress this "revolt." This led to much conflict within families, since parents did not want to see their children arrested. Under such pressure, the group cancelled the alternative assemblies.

Come Easter Wednesday, Valencia visited his opponent in the parish center and told him he ought to tell him to his face what he was saying about him and others. In the ensuing confrontation, Don Bonifacio called the missionary "a camouflaged communist," in South America "preparing the ground [*hacer la cama gorda*] for Russia." In reply, Valencia called Opus Dei, the reactionary Catholic organization to which he thought Don Bonifacio belonged, "refined capitalism," a "historic justification of bourgeois hegemony." "You do not have the right to subject the village to the ideology of Opus," he charged, arguing that a parish priest ought to provide more versions of the faith. Otherwise, he was guilty of a "subtle inquisition."

On Maundy Thursday, the day the first assembly was to have been held, a squad of Civil Guards arrived as Mass began. These paramilitary police, ignorant that the assembly had been cancelled, toured the village looking for the meeting place. Not finding anything, they entered the church during the service. They stood for a few minutes by the main door, then left. In reaction to this threatening move and to the increasing tension they could feel in the village, many youths expressed their rejection of Don Bonifacio by attending the remaining Easter services in the church of the neighboring village.

That Saturday, Easter Eve, seventy-three villagers signed an open letter strongly criticizing the summoning of the armed police and Don Bonifacio's "out of date and abstract" approach. Proclaiming their solidarity with Valencia, they ended the letter with a call for a genuine, profound reconciliation, for "the Reconciled Man is the New Man announced and loved by Jesus."[6]

When Valencia returned to Ecuador the following week, an immediate cause of the friction disappeared. However, the conflictive process had a series of lasting effects. For it demonstrated publicly the existence of a widespread desire for democratic change, the ability of villagers to act together effectively and independently of the controlling forces in the village, and the lengths to which those forces were ready to go to remain in position. It also displayed in a highly dramatic manner that many villagers were no longer prepared to accept Don Bonifacio's hegemony in an unquestioning manner. In Cirauqui, the days of overly authoritarian parish priests were numbered.

Fiestas

The conflict between Valenica and Don Bonifacio provided the huddle of activists and the young villagers sympathetic to their concerns with a brief, intensive period of political activity. To consolidate this progress and to raise people's consciousness further, the energetic activists chose to stimulate participation in the most important social event in the Cirauqui calendar: its weeklong fiestas. The municipal Comisión para las Fiestas (Committee for the Fiestas), unlike almost all other committees set up by the town hall, traditionally included some of the younger members of the village. Since youth were the most active and exuberant revelers in the seven days of fun, it was best to have some of them on the committee helping to decide how the municipal budget for the event was to be divided. Taking advantage of this annual opportunity to display their organizing ability, the new, younger members of the committee effectively decided much of what was to be included in the fiestas.

Their first initiative was to stage, within the weeklong program of fiesta events, El Día del Pueblo (The Day of the Village). El Día consisted of a communal lunch in the main plaza. The Comisión para las Fiestas provided wine and bread free, and groups of people brought their own stews. The idea proved very popular and it grew rapidly, with many people participating the second year it was held. Owners of bars bordering the plaza also joined in, providing free spirits and cigars. Even though they might not have agreed politically with the activists, they realized the initiative was good for business. The meal ended with dancing, followed by the band leading a joyful procession on a round of the village. The activists intended El Día to be nonpolitical. They saw it primarily as a way to bring people together, to bring life to the village. El Día is today a fully integrated, highly popular part of the fiestas, attended by almost all villagers not too infirm to walk up to the plaza.

Another equally lasting, equally significant initiative of the activists was the setting up of a *barraca*. This is a temporary structure, a corrugated iron hut erected specially for the period of fiestas at one edge of the plaza. The activists, aided by a large number of volunteers, ran it as a bar, selling drinks at slightly cheaper prices than any of the three permanent bars bordering the plaza. On the counter was placed a pot for donations toward the assistance of imprisoned members of ETA, especially one who had first cousins in the village and had been jailed for supposedly killing a policeman during a shoot-out between terrorists and the Civil Guard. Also, the bartenders sold political stickers, as a further source of income for the prisoners and as a mode of political identification for politicized revelers to wear. The group, and many associated with them, explicitly saw the *barraca* as a form and example of their ideal of popular self-financing self-management. To them, this temporary bar, which was a great social and economic success, was a concrete rejection of authoritarian Franquist institutions, among which they included the town hall.

Members of the group and sympathizers sitting on the Comisión para las Fiestas developed its program greatly: for instance, creating El Día de los Mayores, when a communal meal was held in the plaza for older villagers, and El Día del Niño, when special events were put on for young children, such as puppet shows or the screening of cartoons. They also put on a variety of competitions, for the best shot at clay pigeon, for the best maker of stews for El Día del Pueblo, and, particularly popular, for the best masked skits. Some of the committee's innovations had greater aims than the purely recreational and were staged in order to raise people's consciousness. For example, members of the committee organized the holding of competitions of "traditional" Basque rural sports (woodchopping, stone-lifting, weight-carrying, tug-of-war) and the performance of folkloric Basque dances, performed by semiprofessional groups from Pamplona, northern Navarre, or beyond. Some years they got the committee to hire Basque nationalist singers or musicians using traditional Basque instruments; some years they read out communal messages sent to the imprisoned ETA member and any telegrams received from him. Members of the group saw these events as efforts to recuperate the "lost" Basque identity of the village, and to create and maintain an oppositional stance to the continuing regime. They were ways of reminding villagers, even during the festive period, of the historical and political nature of their collective present condition.

The Transition to Democracy

Most left-wing villagers today in their late forties or fifties look back on the years of the transition as an intoxicating period when, for the first time, they were able to express their political views freely and without fear of damaging consequences. But people did not suddenly begin talking politics publicly as soon as Franco died. They slowly started to discuss issues of the day more and more openly, as they became increasingly confident that they could do so. By that stage, in the village bars, the most politically committed were quite prepared to shout support for "their" side whenever it was mentioned on the television. One of the earliest casualties of this new outspokenness was Don Bonifacio. In the small hours of one night during the fiestas of 1978, a group of alcohol-emboldened villagers sang beneath his balcony, "Leave! Leave!" He did, the next day, returning a few weeks later only to collect his belongings. His replacement, a much younger man, wore no habit, entered bars freely, and did not hide his openness to new ideas.

Differences of ideological opinion that had been masked during the time of the regime could now be publicly stated, as politics became a prime topic of conversation wherever people gathered. Nationally, the fragile coalition of interests that had held together the antifranquist opposition fragmented into an almost bewildering diversity of parties, ranging from the large and well organized to the minuscule and ephemeral. The consequence in Cirauqui was that the previously united opponents of the regime began to divide openly, along the lines of party affiliation.

In the general elections of 1977, in which over 82 percent of the Cirauqui electorate participated, the Carlists, standing as Agrupación Electoral Montejurra, won 32 percent of the vote, so emerging as the largest single political group in the village. In only two other villages throughout the whole of Navarre did the Carlists gain a higher proportion of the vote. Otherwise, the vote was split across the political spectrum. The right-wing Alianza Foral Navarra won 19 percent of the vote, the center-right Unión de Centro Democrático

(UCD) 18 percent, the center-left Partido Socialista Obrero Español (PSOE) 5 percent, and the left-wing Unión Navarra de Izquierdas (UNAI) 7 percent, the remaining 18.5 percent of the vote being divided among seven other parties. In the following general elections, held on 1 March 1979, the Carlists, this time standing as the EKA, slightly increased their share of the vote. On a slightly lower turnout (76.5 percent), they won 35 percent of all votes cast, a figure bettered in only three other villages of the province. The right-wing Unión del Pueblo Navarro (UPN) won 18 percent, the UCD 18 percent, the PSOE 11 percent, the centrist Nacionalistas Vascos 7 percent, the left-wing nationalists Herri Batasuna (HB) 8 percent, and the UNAI 4 percent.[7]

It is difficult to assess the reasons for the slight increase (3 percent) in the Carlist vote, since so many parties had disappeared in the interim, and since a number of new ones had arisen. It is probable that the EKA, which in these elections had been much more organized than when they had campaigned under the banner of Agrupación Electoral Montejurra, won a little support from those who had previously voted for some of the variety of left-wing groups that had not re-presented themselves in the later general elections. What is more significant, however, is that while the vote for the UCD remained the same and the supporters of Alianza Foral Navarra simply switched allegiance to Unión del Pueblo Navarro, the demise of the small left-wing groups appears to have benefited both the PSOE, which had confirmed its existence as a major statewide party in the elections of 1977, and the Basque Nationalists, who in this election emerged as a significant political force in Navarre.

A further reason why it is difficult to be more exact about the causes for change in the voting patterns is that, as several late-middle-aged villagers pointed out to me, they and a number of their neighbors were in 1977 still relatively ignorant about the nature of differences between different political parties. One, now a confirmed supporter of the Right, had in that year voted PSOE because an in-law was a distant kinsman of its leader, Felipe González. Only later did he realize what socialists stood for. Villagers also underline the influence of Don Bonifacio in the first hustings. Several old women referred to him for guidance about voting, while from the pulpit and during performances of the Rosary, he urged parishioners to vote for the Right and damned left-wing groups as "communists!" Also, it is important to note that several people did not exercise their franchise because they continued to fear the potential consequences. Some older villagers did not vote because they had been imprisoned in the war for their beliefs, while another did not because his father had been shot in the rear guard.

By the time of the next general elections, held in 1983 and won by the PSOE, the Partido Carlista had disappeared from the national political scene. In Cirauqui, the PSOE won the most votes (36 percent), followed by the UPN

(22 percent) and HB (11 percent), with two other center-right parties gaining 10 percent in total and two other nationalist parties picking up 11 percent between them. What these results suggest is that most of those who had previously voted for the Partido Carlista now gave their support either to the PSOE or to nationalist forces, which, in total, had gained as many votes in Cirauqui as had the Right.

Comparing the results of the general elections in the village with those to the Foral Parliament of the province allows us to gain a finer-grained idea of the political evolution of Cirauqui. While in the 1979 elections to the provincial chamber, the Partido Carlista won only 4.8 percent of the provincial vote, in Cirauqui it gained 28 percent—a percentage bettered only by the Carlists of one other Navarrese village. Otherwise the vote was mainly split between the left-wing nationalist coalition Agrupación Tierra Estella (ATE) (29 percent), the UPN (20 percent), the UCD (12 percent), and the PSOE (10 percent). The pattern of voting here suggests both the increasing local importance given to nationalism and the organizing power of the ATE within Navarre. In the 1983 elections to the local parliament, the Carlists put forward a well-known and well-respected local candidate who won 25 percent of the vote in the village—the third-highest proportion gained by the party in any Navarrese electoral district. The other proportions were the UPN 20 percent, the right-wing Alianza Popular 5 percent, the PSOE 20 percent, HB 17 percent, with three other nationalist parties picking up, between them, 12 percent. These results demonstrate that even by as late as 1983, when the Partido Carlista had departed from the national stage, a very substantial proportion of villagers continued to regard Carlism as a viable alternative, at least within the provincial ambit. These results also confirm the establishment by then of nationalism as one of the most potent forces within provincial politics.

The most socially divisive elections, however, were neither the general nor the provincial ones, but those to the town hall, held in April 1979. For the first time, antifranquist villagers had the chance of becoming councillors, or even mayor, of their own municipality. In the general and foral elections villagers had voted for candidates from their province but not from their locality; in these local hustings they were choosing kin, in-laws, or people they knew well, and the decisions of those whom they elected would affect them directly. The leftists and nationalists in Cirauqui, who were increasing in number and were increasingly well organized, presented their list of representatives as Candidatura Asamblearia, while the progressives put forward a Candidatura Popular, and the conservatives in the village an Agrupación de Agricultores. The left-wing Basquist coalition, which was backed above all by members of the politically active youth of the village, won three seats; the right-wing alliance, which was generally seen to be supported by those who worked the land and who were convinced antinationalists, won two; the progressives also won two seats. It seems the progressives had not been able to assemble a list of impressive candidates, as some of the more energetic and more politically engaged among them had begun to move away from the party, usually toward the left-wing nationalist coalition.

In the ensuing discussions, the nationalists and the progressives could not come to an agreement over the distribution of posts. So the Carlists accepted the rightists' offer of the mayorship in return for joint control of the municipal council. The nationalists, in reaction to their exclusion from power, came to regard their former progressive colleagues as renegades to be reviled. Open meetings of the town council became a focus for their discontent. With no rules about who was to speak when, these meetings tended to become very lengthy, with members of the public intervening when they wished, for as long as they wished. Meetings that began at 8 P.M. might still be in session at midnight, with half of the agenda yet to discuss. At times, meetings became very stormy, nationalist villagers shouting their opposition to municipal proposals. On at least one occasion the disorder reached such a level that the municipal constable had to remove some people physically from the chamber.[8] Sometimes, the mayor felt forced to end the session prematurely. As he later lamented to me, some sessions were "pure madness." Others perceived them differently. When I asked one radical nationalist, now in her sixties, about these meetings, she spontaneously exclaimed, "What a pleasure they were! What a chance to vent one's feelings! After so many years of silence, what a pleasure!"

To restore some order to the proceedings, the mayor had a resolution passed that forbade members of the public from intervening in a motion until councillors had debated and voted on it.[9] This effectively stifled the sort of debate that many earlier participants had enjoyed. Some radical nationalists regarded this as censorship of the people and, after protesting, stopped attending. Meetings gradually became much less lively, as fewer people bothered to turn up.

Over the next few years, more and more progressives, discouraged by their party's public failure and disillusioned by its change in policies, became politically disenchanted and shifted their electoral allegiance to other groups. In the preparations for the next municipal elections, held in 1983, the remaining progressives showed little enthusiasm for presenting themselves again, and managed only to confect a joint ticket with local supporters of the PSOE a day before the deadline. The left-wing Basquist coalition made the mistake of heading its slate with a particularly hard-line radical nationalist, who had already served time for his politically motivated actions. This time, the right-wing alliance, calling themselves "Agrupación Independiente," were much more organized, placing two energetic men at the top of their list, one a middle-ranking farmer in his early forties, the other a creative artist in his late thirties. In the elections, the Agrupación gained 239 votes and five of the seats; the left-wing nationalists won 84 votes and thus one seat. The remaining seat went to the socialist heading the Carlist-PSOE alliance, who received 47 votes. In other words the village, which in the first years of the transition had consistently returned one of the highest proportions of votes to the progressives in the province, and the country, had by 1983 a town hall empty of Carlists.

The progressives of Cirauqui did not stand again. They knew there was no point. Too many had stopped working for the cause, too many villagers saw it as a spent political cause, with the provincial branch of the party having control of only a few town halls, with a few councillors in other municipalities, and a single representative in the parliament of Navarre (who was not reelected). In 1994, only twenty-two villagers voted for the party in the elections to the European Parliament, making it the fifth political force in Cirauqui and a long way behind any of the main parties. Today, the most active of those in the village who still call themselves Carlist do no more than attend Montejurra, the occasional political dinner staged by the party, and an annual feast on the estate of a rich Navarrese member. There is little more they can do.

The Demise of Carlism

The extraordinarily good results obtained by the Carlists in Cirauqui in the general and foral elections of the first years of the transition—among the most impressive results for the party in the whole of the Spanish state—are testimony both to the enduring legacy of Carlism within the village and to the exemplary, revitalizing activity of some of its younger members. These outstanding successes make the subsequent, rapid decline of the local vote for the party all the more striking. It is thus appropriate here to ask: In what, exactly, did the Carlisms of the village activists and their elders consist? And what sort of Carlism has survived the passing of *huguismo?*

To the question, "Are you Carlist?" people in their late fifties or older (whether veteran *requetés* or not) often reply, "Until my death!" They are Carlist and will remain so. The majority of people who answer in this way are men, ones who do not wish to devalue their war experiences nor those of their parents and grandparents. In contrast, a smaller number of women make the same statement of lifelong commitment, and most of them, it appears, maintain the memory of the movement for the sake of their late fathers, whose memory they revere. Understanding Carlism in genealogical terms, these men and women have assumed their familial inheritance and will not let it go until their own demise. The Carlism of these aging members of the movement varies: some are unrenounced traditionalists; some accepted Carlos Hugo's *progresismo* to varying degrees. But most of them, whatever their contemporary party political leanings, say it does not matter whom they now vote for: they still *feel* themselves Carlist. Several argued to me that former Carlist politicians who today occupy prominent posts in other parties still regard themselves as Carlists. "It's something," they stressed, "you feel inside."

One young villager, the son of a Carlist though not one himself, tried to explain to me this essentialist, emotive attitude of his parental generation. He said that a simple economic, political, or social analysis would be sufficient for the study of other parties, but that it would not be enough for understanding Carlism because people were Carlist for a reason more profound, more psychological: this was "the spark." He went on, "People nowadays who say they're Carlist are people who don't want to break with something. It's a tradition, a root within their family. Carlism has no ideology. Other parties have ideologies and their ideologies can be compared. But not Carlism. Carlism's like a puddle. It stands on its own. Other parties aren't like that." Unlike other parties, Carlism could not be contained within the usual institutional parameters; it stood out on its own, incomparable, unconventional.

Members of the Carlist generation who actively participated in the "renaissance" of the movement in Cirauqui in the late 1960s and 1970s are prepared to recognize the soundness of this sort of analysis. However, those among them who have since moved over to other parties, whether on the Left or the Right, seem uncomfortable with its logical consequences, as though the familial nature of rural Carlism threatened to undercut the validity of their political convictions in those days. As far as they are concerned or wished me to understand, they did not assemble in one anothers' houses for the sake of maintaining an identity handed down by their parents, but for the sake of fomenting change.

Some of these former Carlists no longer wish even to speak of the movement, and deny that they had any connection whatsoever with it. When I pointed out to one man who was claiming never to have been a Carlist that I had seen his name on the list of new members in the minutes of the Circle's meetings, he hurriedly tried to brush the fact aside by saying he had joined only for social reasons. When I spoke to another, who—villagers stated—had been an active Carlist and whose father had been instrumental in the establishment of the village's Circle, he strongly denied any connection with the movement. He acknowledged that his father had been involved in the creation of the Circle but claimed that he had done so only to assist his Carlist friends in meeting the legal requirement of a certain number of signatures to found the club. Other villagers attribute these denials partly to former Carlists' disappointment with the party's failure at the polls. Their hopes were dashed, their work for the movement came to nothing, and they do not want to be reminded of the loss.

An additional reason ascribed by non-Carlists for these former Carlists' denials of their previous allegiance is the popular image within Navarre of Carlism as a movement whose time has passed. By the mid-1980s, to most Navarrese, Carlism had only historical, not contemporary relevance. A school-teacher from a nearby village was very keen to persuade me that it was not worthwhile to study Carlism; it served only a folkloric function nowadays. Villagers could state with some pride that their forefathers had taken to arms to defend their ideas against the state, but Carlism, he claimed, no longer amounted to anything else. There were more profitable political topics to in-vestigate nowadays. His friends, who had been listening to his arguments, judged that he was embarrassed; he did not want the modern history of Navarre remembered in terms of a seemingly anachronistic movement that mixed politics with a pretender and genealogical steadfastness.

Many former progressive activists in Cirauqui had become committed to Basque nationalism during their period of militancy and chose to leave the party when its support for nationalist goals faltered. When I discussed the recent political history of the village with some of them, they quickly brushed aside their progressive past and derided Carlos Hugo's political philosophy as a hodgepodge thrown together from various ideological sources. They no longer wish to be associated with the movement in any way and are now spared the ungrateful task of justifying monarchic populism to left-wing skeptics. One villager, neither a Carlist nor a nationalist, told me he thought these former Carlists were so ready to denigrate *progresismo* partly in order to underline their present commitment to a different ideology. They do not want their belief in a fully autonomous Basque state questioned by fellow nationalists.

The revivified form of Carlism that appeared in Cirauqui in the last decade of Franquism had as broad a social base as the Comunión had there during the Republic. The progressives in the village included some of its biggest land-owners, and some of its smallest, as well as lawyers, teachers, office workers, bricklayers, and the unemployed. While it seems that those villagers who es-poused the progressives' cause cannot be categorized conveniently in terms of social class, it is noticeable that very few of those who eventually went over to radical nationalism hold particularly well-paid professional positions and not one tills large tracts of land. It can be stated, however, that those who did not leave the movement come, like their Carlist forebears, from a broad social range. Thus what remains of progressive Carlism in Cirauqui is just as difficult to specify in terms of social class as was its predecessor decades before.

Those of the next generation in the village from Carlist families show no interest in the movement. Now in their thirties, they were too young to be politically concerned during the first years of the transition. Unlike those inhabitants ten years or so older than them, who fomented so much activity in Cirauqui in the 1970s, members of this generation are among the most politically apathetic in the village. Although most of them participate in the organization and running of some village events, they do not attempt to politicize these acts. To them, Carlism is something to do with their parents and their parents' idea of the past. When I discussed the recent history of the cause with their parents, they immediately looked bored and often left the room. They did not want to know. Others of their generation simply do not know. Some, aware of my work, said to me that they had occasionally heard of El Cojo and that he came from Cirauqui but that they knew nothing more about him. They wanted me, an outsider, to tell them who he was and what he had done. One young Pamplonan, who passed much time in Cirauqui with her kin who lived there, and who later married into the village, one day confessed her ignorance to me and then asked, "What *was* Carlism, Jeremy?"

When I discussed Carlism with one man in his sixties, he mentioned to me that none of his sons had followed him. He did not complain about the fact, though it clearly pained him. That the Carlist tradition of his family would end with his death seemed almost a form of disrespect to his ancestors, a betrayal of their efforts. One reason why the sons and daughters of Carlists have been able to shrug off their families' legacy with apparent ease is that traditional forms of inheritance have become generally less important to the younger generations of villagers. The increased educational opportunities available to the schoolchildren of Cirauqui since the late 1960s meant that many of them were no longer economically reliant on their parents. They did not need to follow their fathers into the fields but could get jobs in factories or offices in Estella or Pamplona. A father might still teach his sons what he had learned of agricultural methods, but in the majority of cases he was no longer preparing them for their future working life. The transmission of his knowledge of the countryside thus passed from being a preparation for the adult life of his successors to being merely the transmission of the agricultural customs of the area—in other words, a means by which his sons could understand how their father worked, and why. For children who went on to university, their parents' way of life became almost a form of folklorism. Thanks to their scholastic education, adult offspring could start to teach their parents things rather than being exclusively taught by them. These sorts of intergenerational changes, together with the associated decline of previously accepted forms of authority, whether in domestic, religious, or civil spheres, enabled many younger members of Cirauqui to be much more independent than their parents had been at their age, and to place far less emphasis on their inheritance, whether of land or of Carlist allegiance. Moreover, the reduced notion of respect maintained by people in these younger generations no longer includes automatically adopting the same political identity as their fathers. They can vote for whom they wish, without too many qualms.[10]

Villagers antipathetic to Carlism agree with older Carlists' idea of lifelong constancy. But they agree with this notion only for the sake of censuring the evolution of the movement. Wielding a traditionalist definition of Carlists, these critics ask how supporters of the extreme Right could turn toward the radical Left. In their opinion, only *chaqueteros* can change so much. Progressives might claim that despite their ideological development, they have still retained their Carlist identity, but their opponents will have none of it. Those middle-aged or elderly Carlist villagers who did not follow Carlos Hugo in his shift to the utopian Left acquiesce in this judgement, and they can be very damning of what the progressives did to a movement that once meant so much. To them, the work of Carlos Hugo and his cohort is only to be condemned; as one, remembering the *requetés'* wartime exploits in the Basque Country, said to me, "The party wants Navarre to join with Euskadi, so that the children of those they fucked can now fuck them."

Local right-wing critics may damn progressives for their earlier dalliance with radical Basque movements, but the very few Carlists now in their late forties or fifties who are still loyal members today vigorously repudiate their past nationalist sympathies. In 1977, one column of the massive Marcha de la Libertad (March of Liberty), which demanded an amnesty for all political prisoners (especially nationalist ones), had paused for a night at Cirauqui, where they had been readily fed and housed by, among others, progressives. But today those self-same progressives tend to refer to this event only to emphasize how far they have moved politically and how distant they have now become from radical nationalists. As far as they are concerned, the day when they hung *ikurriñas* (Basque flags) over their balconies to celebrate the arrival in the village of the marchers is long past. The radical nationalists in Cirauqui, in turn, disparage these deserters from their camp by classing them with former *requeté* conservatives as *"fachas"*—a general term of left-wing political abuse, which originally signified "fascist."

At times, the more politically committed of villagers, whatever their age or ideological inclination, will try to straitjacket families over generations by rubbishing those of their opponents who have not heeded what their parents did, or what happened to them. Socialist villagers can make highly deprecatory comments about neighbors or kin who today vote for right-wing parties though their Republican fathers or in-laws were shot or imprisoned in the war. Similarly, right-wing villagers may complain that the mature children of *reque-*

tés who did not act well in the war should not be too vociferous in the adversarial politics they propound, because they are "stained." According to these rhetorical strategies, the sins of the fathers are visited on the children. Like the local saying that the son of a Carlist is a supporter of Herri Batasuna (discussed in the next chapter), these remarks and accusations demonstrate that at least some villagers still believe that both positive and negative aspects of political affiliation can be inherited.

One consequence of the steadfastness of elderly Carlist villagers is their stated belief that the movement could always revive. It could still return to its former strength. To use their own cliché, Carlism is like the Guadalquivir River: it runs its course, travels underground for a stretch, then resurfaces as strong as ever. Skeptics today may think Carlism has effectively disappeared; in contrast, the unyielding faithful "know" that though it may no longer be very evident, it retains subterranean force. On this account, they have good reason to be constant in their beliefs unto death.

The Rise of Basque Nationalism

In Cirauqui, the renovated Carlism of the progressives failed within a few years of the dictator's death. In stark contrast to this decline, and equally striking, was the rapid rise of Basque nationalism within the municipality.

The village electoral results tell one version of this tale. In the 1977 general elections, nationalist parties failed to win more than 3 percent of the vote; two years later their proportion of the vote was up to 15 percent and in 1983 to 22 percent. Their proportion in the foral elections of 1979 and 1983 was even more impressive, in each case 29 percent of the village vote. What is so revealing, and what helps to explain this remarkable rise, is that the majority of these proportions went to radical left-wing forms of nationalism. In fact, since the late 1970s throughout Navarre nationalism as a political force has been predominantly of the radical left-wing varieties: Herri Batasuna, Euskadiko Eskerra, and Auzolan, all products, at different stages, of the evolution of ETA. The reasons for the popularity in Navarre of radical, as opposed to moderate, nationalism are complex and still little studied. What appears to have happened is that as the statewide organizations of the radical left wing, which had been so effective in the early and mid-1970s, began to lose support, the majority of those Navarrese beyond the center-left switched allegiance to similarly radical but nationalist parties. The workers' parties they had once supported had singularly failed to impress the electorate and threatened to disappear, while nationalism generally appeared to be on the rise; so these left-wing Navarrese were able to remain within an electorally viable vanguard of root-and-branch change by voting for radical versions of nationalism. Paradoxically, it was some of the statewide organizations, such as the Partido Carlista, that helped to prepare the ground for this change, for by recognizing the legitimacy of at least mild nationalist claims within their policies, they helped to create and maintain a nationalist consciousness. Some parties even organized themselves into geographical subunits on the basis of nationalist claims. For example (as mentioned earlier), the Partido Carlista formed the EKA, composed of the provinces of Gipuzkoa, Bizkaia, Álava, and Navarre.

It might also be argued that radical nationalism offered young village activists a new, almost utopian form of identity at a time in Cirauqui of fundamental change in almost all domains: social, economic, political, and cultural. If the Spanish frame had been discredited, because of its old associations with Franquism and its newer ones with the center-right, the novel socialist Basque frame provided its supporters with the comforting vision of a small nation-state, with a distinctive society, economy, politics, and culture. With external forces steadily eroding the time-honored ways of village life, this brand of the Basquist creed suggested a new set of regional certainties from which contemporary villagers could stand and interpret the world. According to this almost psychological explanation, radical nationalism allowed its followers to site themselves in a mental landscape where all were equal, the village integrated with the city, and everything bent on a common Basque project.

The Politics of Village Nationalism

The political force of local left-wing nationalism was demonstrated at the first municipal elections when its Candidatura Asamblearia won more seats than either of the other groups. Although some nationalist villagers stopped attending meetings of the town hall because of the new restrictions on intervening, the nationalists on the council continued to remain active. For example, they consistently presented motions in support of current nationalist demands and, at the time of the fiestas, a motion to have the ribbon of the Spanish national colors removed from the municipal flag.[11] Also, every Sunday morning, those running the Comisión de Cultura (Committee for Culture) laid out for the children of the village a series of games, such as chess, under the gallery of the town hall. In its chamber, they would set up a Ping-Pong table and a library.

The liveliness of local nationalism was demonstrated by the regular assemblies, organized by nationalist activists within the village and attended by up to seventy people, to discuss matters of municipal import. Arguing that "the best mayor is the *pueblo* itself," they staged these meetings so that the *pueblo* could play an active part in the course of its history. Perhaps the largest single project on which these activists worked was the construction of a swimming pool for the village. In the mid-1970s a group of young activists, mainly Carlists, had thought up the project, as a way to provide village youth with something to do. They felt they had to initiate it themselves, since the town hall then seemed almost totally preoccupied with agricultural concerns. The project soon won widespread support, with many people donating money and their labor. The broadly cooperative nature of the endeavor led many of its participants to see it as a genuinely popular enterprise, significantly independent of the municipal authorities. Several members of the newly elected town hall showed surprisingly little initial interest in the project, as though they did not wish to increase their burdens, while its organizers, mindful of their autonomy, did not seek municipal subsidies as energetically as they might have done. As a consequence, when the leaders of the project became identifiably nationalist, the project came to be seen by those villagers who resisted change as an enterprise of the village Left, and thus to be opposed for that political reason. Once this perception had become established among a reactionary sector of the population, it became that much more difficult for the controllers of the town hall to assist the project, had they even wished to. The end result was that a significant enterprise, of potential benefit to almost the whole community, came to be seen as the preserve of left-wing nationalism, thus deepening, rather than alleviating, division within the village.

The depth of that division was starkly displayed in 1983 at the next municipal elections, when the center-right won five seats and the nationalists only one. Meetings of this town hall frequently served only to increase animosity along the political lines, with the sole nationalist councillor at times fiercely debating particular issues with the mayor.[12] Partly because they were so poorly represented on the council, the radical nationalists tried to boost popular debate on matters of local import by producing a bulletin-magazine. But according to some villagers, *Aitzibita*, by providing detailed and strongly worded critiques of the workings of the town hall, did more to exacerbate division than to stimulate discussion.[13] In 1983 the center-right councillors tried to heal the rift by inviting a well-known group of nationalist musicians to play in the fiestas. But many village nationalists rejected this advance and refused to attend the event, while a dispute during the concert between a bar owner and two nationalists ended in violence, leading to many nationalists boycotting the bar for several years. Staging the event had only worsened the divide.[14] During this general period, the confrontation between nationalists and their opponents could sometimes turn even more threatening, on two occasions to the brandishing of pistols.

From the mid-1980s on, the electoral allegiance of villagers hardly changed, until the mid-1990s when the vote for radical nationalism started to decline. In the municipal elections of 1987, 1991, and 1995 the centrist coalition gained, respectively, 57 percent, 56 percent, and 68 percent, while in the same contests the radicals won, respectively, 37 percent, 36 percent, and 28 percent. In the general elections, the vote for the UPN climbed steadily from 27 percent in 1986 to 38 percent in 1996, while the PSOE share of the vote declined, to 27 percent in 1996. At first, the HB vote rose, to 20 percent in 1986 and 21 percent in 1989. But, as occurred in many other constituencies, it then began to drop sharply, to 15 percent in 1991 and 12 percent in 1995. It seems HB lost local voters to Izquierda Unida, the nationwide left-wing coalition, and to Eusko Alkartasuna, a moderate nationalist party that broke away from the PNV. More and more villagers, once sympathetic to armed radicalism, appear to be turning their political attention elsewhere.

As local support for Herri Batasuna has declined, a certain rapprochement between protagonists of the local nationalist and non-nationalist blocs has become increasingly evident. With the exception of a single incident (described below), which occurred during his first days in office, the mayor elected in 1987 managed to run a much less divided town hall. He achieved this by not antagonizing radical nationalist councillors and by acceding to some demands of theirs, such as the (illegal) hoisting of the Basque flag during the village fiestas. As one *batasunero* put it to me, "It is in his interest to let us fly it, as we are prepared to do things for the village." The next mayor went even further to emphasize the shift from the old schemas of power; he wished to end the symbolic confluence of the municipal and ecclesiastical forces within the village. On the feast day of Cirauqui's patron, Saint Román, when the town hall en bloc traditionally joined the priest in leading the formal procession around the village, the mayor chose to stay in bed. The swimming pool also ceased to be a source of politically aligned conflict when urgent repairs were suddenly needed. In return for partial control of its management, the town hall agreed to take over partial responsibility for its funding. Telling evidence of the much less heated nature of local politics in the 1990s is that hardly anyone now goes to meetings of the town hall these days, and that people who would have avoided one another fifteen years previously for ideological reasons now may even be seen joking together.

The Culture of Village Nationalism

The activists wished not only to see radical nationalist policies implemented in the town hall but to foment the establishment of Basque culture within the village. One way they substantiated this was by setting up a course in Euskera. Evening classes were given four times a week by a young villager who had learned the language from a returned refugee. About twenty attended. Some displayed their commitment to the nationalist cause by learning to play instruments seen as traditionally Basque, such as the bagpipes and the *txistu* (Euskera for flute). Some began to dress in the politically appropriate style, sporting berets and *kaikus* (knitted waistcoats bearing designs seen as "traditionally Basque"). Attempts were also made to institute Basque celebrations, such as the *olentzero,* a mythical charcoal maker who, in December, plays a role similar to that of Father Christmas. Nationalist villagers regarded these efforts, like the performances in the annual village fiestas of Basque singers, dances, and sports, as ways to revive, and to remind other villagers of, the Basque legacy of Cirauqui.

Although it is most likely that Euskera was still being spoken in the village in the late eighteenth century, I could find no oral memory of its use. There are, however, still many Basque words in the Castilian dialect spoken by the people of Cirauqui: for instance, in some of the card games they play, the foods they eat, and the expressions they use.[15] A large number of these terms are now being lost, since so many of them are associated with agricultural practices and the raising of livestock. Many of the toponyms for places or plots of land within the municipality are also in Euskera, and dedicated nationalists within the village set themselves the task of compiling them—under threat of disappearance because of the *concentración parcelaria* (reorganization of arable land into larger plots). They also like to point out that the original name of the village is in Euskera, as shown by the ancient plaque beneath the municipal coat of arms set into the facade of the town hall: "Soy de la ilustre vila de Zirauki."

It is easy to regard these various efforts as but more examples of "the invention of tradition."[16] The Euskera learned by nationalist villagers today is not the dialect spoken by their ancestors but a new, expanded dialect, *batua,* created in the 1970s and reliant on words from the seven dialects of the language still extant. It is not possible to know whether festivities such as the *olentzero* were in fact once celebrated in Cirauqui. It is dubious whether sports such as competitive woodchopping, more associated with mountainous areas, were formerly performed in the village. Thus these events, though cloaked in the trappings of tradition, should be seen as less the selective revival of supposedly traditional occurrences and more as part of the latter-day creation of a modern Basque culture. Since other villages in other areas within the Basque ambit have also begun to "restage" such festivities and sports, the contemporary content of fiestas in Cirauqui now tends toward a common Basquist standard. In other words, these village fiestas, meant to celebrate the local community, now do so within a common Basquist frame.

It is important to place these events within a broader context, for nationalists were not just busy inventing a distinctive past but a distinctive Basque form of modernity as well. They wished to be seen as both the heirs of a laudable past and also as up-to-date as their contemporaries in other lands.[17] Villagers practicing the *txistu* may also buy the latest record of a band playing *el rock radical vasco* (radical Basque rock). They might participate in competitions of traditional sports, while at the same time following the fortunes of Basque football teams in the national league, once renowned for their own "Basque" playing style.[18] During the spring and summer, they may spend most of their weekends in one kind of festive nationalist event or another, whether a collective camp, a mass marathon, or a recital by Basque troubadours *(bertsolaris)*.[19] Fiestas in Cirauqui became as likely to include woodchoppers as a race of *goitiberas* (an urban Basque version of bobsled). Thus, the created Basque culture in the village is not static but continues to evolve.

The dynamic nature of this modern culture is underlined by the fact that though certain forms of this re-creation may disappear, others are introduced. For instance, though the evening classes in Euskera ended in the mid-1980s, a significant number of nationalist parents now make the economic sacrifice of paying for their children to go to an *ikastola* (a school where Euskera is the medium of communication) in Estella. Similarly, the fiestas may not always include Basque rural sports, but the program these days may well be produced in a bilingual version, while certain events may be presided over by bilingual presenters.

One consequence of all these efforts—municipal, recreational, and linguistic—is that the major political and cultural division within the village was no longer between the Left and the Right, between Carlists and non-Carlists, between Franquists and non-Franquists, but between nationalists and non-nationalists. The majority of debates about politics or culture that arise among villagers today gyrate about this Basque axis and not any of the others. One result of this process is that Carlism has moved or been moved to the very margins of village life. As the local asked me, "What *was* Carlism, Jeremy?"

La Guerra de las Banderas

If the steadfast see Carlism as like the Guadalquivir River, one way in which it may unexpectedly reappear was displayed in 1987 during "La Guerra de las Banderas" (The War of the Flags), which occurred during the village fiestas. A month before, a new set of councillors had been voted in: three were members of a left-wing Basquist coalition, and the other four represented centrist or right-wing interests. The left-wingers presented a motion at a meeting of the town council that the *ikurriña* be flown alongside the national, Navarrese, and village flags that were traditionally hoisted from the balcony on the town hall on the opening day of the festivities. Since it was (and still is) illegal to fly the Basque flag next to the banners of the country and of the autonomous province of Navarre at official events, the motion, after a brief heated debate, failed. The left-wingers were particularly disappointed because they had thought the two more moderate members of their opponents were going to vote with them. The flag had been hoisted in the fiestas staged during the tenure of the first postfranquist town hall. Nothing had happened then, the police had not arrived, no one had been arrested. So why, the left-wingers asked themselves, were the two more moderate councillors not prepared to take a very slight risk now?

Nine nights later, on the eve of the fiestas, a clutch of the left-wing nationalists spent several hours up ladders, decorating all the cables that crossed the village streets with Basque flags. At the following midday, a councillor stepped out onto one of the municipal balconies and, in the traditional manner, opened the fiestas by lighting a firework rocket. As it exploded in the sky, two of the nationalist councillors suddenly appeared at the adjacent balcony and affixed an *ikurriña* to its railings, to the cheers of some of the crowd. No one touched this banner, but the next morning people awoke to find that someone had tied a crude homemade version of the Carlist flag to another one of the municipal balconies. They later learned that a late-middle-aged Carlist, irritated by the sight of the *ikurriña*, had asked the mayor for permission to raise the ensign of his movement.

Some left-wing nationalists were annoyed at what they interpreted as a belittling of their gesture. According to the angrily worded broadsheet nationalists distributed next day in the village, the 44 percent of the village electorate that had voted for their side supported the idea of Cirauqui as part of the Basque nation. Therefore they should be allowed to fly their banner.[20] In contrast, the Carlist flag represented only a residual minority and thus had no right to be fluttering over the main plaza. One antibasquist progressive argued to me, in defense of his movement's ensign, that the *ikurriña* should not have been raised because it was "stained" with the blood spilled by terrorists; but as a companion of his, also a progressive, pointed out, the Carlist flag was similarly "stained." Some villagers thought certain of the banners looked like rags. Some thought the situation was beginning to edge on the ridiculous.

In this colorful contest, the symbols of Carlism had been resurrected and exhibited publicly for the first time in several years in order to combat the nationalists' claimed need for representation. In other words, what was publicly left of Carlism in Cirauqui had become merely a supplementary form of subvillage identity, to be exploited only in rare times of political need and, even then, not to be taken very seriously by the majority.

Chapter Thirteen

The Legacies of Carlism to Basque Nationalism

The Partido Carlista may today stand low on the political profile of northern Spain, but many Basques do not doubt the continuing relevance of Carlism's legacies. For instance, it is a common perception in the area that Basque nationalism grew out of Carlism; in particular, many think that modern, armed radical nationalism is heavily indebted to Carlist antecedents. The possible connections between these movements is a broad, intricate topic that deserves its own book-length treatment. Here I wish only to signal the complexity and contemporary pertinence of the theme, not to indulge in precipitate generalizations or hasty pseudo-conclusions. In this chapter I will merely sketch the outlines of the topic: to register nationalist images of Carlism, to elucidate the uses to which they are put, to catalog local explanations for the connections, and to assess the coherence of those explanations.

That Carlism played a central role throughout the course of the nineteenth century in the Basque area is not in dispute.[1] What can be disputed, however, is the ways that role should be interpreted and portrayed. One frequent mode of nationalist interpretation is similar to that of the progressive historians: praise of popular Carlism and criticism of its elites' machinations. Here, the Carlist uprisings are to be seen as "the people in arms," as the committed, popular rejection of threats posed by centralizing forces, while the linking of their demands with the call for a traditional monarchy is to be regarded as the unfortunate consequence of the locals' need for royal leaders, whose interests extended far beyond the Basque ambit. On this reading of the past, popular Basque Carlism was crypto- or proto-nationalist, while "the terms 'carlismo,' 'carlista' and 'carlistada' can be applied, without distinction, to any political initiative which implies collaboration of Basque forces with Spanish ones."[2] For example, in 1987 when a leader of the radical nationalists wanted to criticize the PNV for making a pact with the PSOE, he compared it with the "Abrazo de Vergara" (Embrace of Vergara), the infamous end to the First Carlist War when the military commandeers of both sides publicly embraced, which was regarded as a betrayal by many of the Carlist mass. The leader of the radicals called the modern pact "unnatural, treacherous, which makes us see that the PNV follow the same steps as Carlism, which first betrayed (the people) and then dissolved itself."[3] According to this logic, this "neo-Carlist" pact threatened to be the first stage of the PNV's demise.

Antinationalist attitudes about Carlism and its putative successors were starkly revealed during the "peace process" of the late 1990s in the Basque Country. When, in 1998, the main moderate nationalist parties formed, for the first time ever, an informal alliance with HB, antinationalists immediately expressed fears that the lining up of this new Basque bloc against the Madrid government was a retrograde step, calling to mind the old opposition of Carlists against centralists. To these antinationalists, modern nationalists are but Carlists under the skin. The key difference is that, unlike nineteenth-century Carlists who laid siege to Bilbao, their latter-day successors have won control of the city.[4] Alfonso Guerra, leading member of PSOE and former vice-president of Spain, was quite explicit about what he thought was here going on: the PNV, he said, "has returned to its old ways, and its old ways are the most rancid Carlism. All Basque nationalism is absolutely Carlist; not just pre-constitutional, but premodern, which is what the Carlism of the Basque Country has always been."[5] To one commentator, these remarks were the opening of a "media-based Carlist war." He went on, "Will we be capable of resolving the conflict better than a hundred years ago? Or, for the umpteenth time, will we see the 'reds' and the 'blacks'?"[6]

Non-Carlists may also represent the movement or its ideology in much more personal, more individual terms. In his polemical and best-selling account of Basque nationalism, *El Bucle Melancólico,* the Basque literary historian and antinationalist commentator Jon Juaristi argues that Carlism is still alive in the very heart of the PNV. According to him, Xabier Arzalluz, the long-reigning president of the PNV, and son of a *requeté,* upholds the common nationalist belief that Carlism was an ethnically Basque movement, whose primary program was the defense of the *fueros.* But where Arzalluz differs from most nationalists, who believe Carlist foralism was overtaken at the turn of the century when nationalism proper surfaced as a separate political force, is in believing that the ideas of Carlism were still "correct" in this century and have been so "until recently" (Arzalluz's own words). For Arzalluz, the mistake Carlists made was not rising up against the Republic (which had divided Basques), but rising up *together with Franco.* Once the *requetés* realized they had won the war only to lose the peace, they realigned themselves with fellow Basques in opposition to the central regime. Thus, on Juaristi's reading, Arzalluz is best classed, not as the most senior nationalist in the whole of the Basque area, but as "the last Carlist."[7]

For some, this personal association of Carlism and Basqueness can be carried to a more abstract, or more profound level. Thus the influential Basque sculptor Jorge Oteiza, whose existentialist writings on Basqueness can tend toward the mystical, has portrayed contemporary Basques as having two grandparents: one Carlist, one liberal. He characterizes the Carlist ancestor as embodying the Basque trait of a "rapid, instantaneous instinct, to contest reality and resolve the instant." The conjunction of this Carlist trait of "intense emotion or enthusiasm" with the liberal one of "limitation" constitutes for him the irreconcilable mixture typical of Basque thought. He develops his idea in a military mode:

> Carlism is no more than an irrational and defensive constant of our cultural inheritance, and for the simple fact of being Basque, everything Basque is Carlist. In our conservative left hand, immobile like a shield, we conserve and maintain our tradition. Our left hand is Carlist. The sword evolves and lives in our right hand, which we have not learned to live with with a truly liberal intelligence. . . . What a Basque cannot be is solely Carlist, a Basque cut down the middle.[8]

The Basque intellectual and radical nationalist José de Arteche has echoed Oteiza's general sentiment in his own writings: "At the bottom of everything Basque, whatever it be, is what we call Carlism. It is necessary to give some name to this *querencia* [beloved instinct]. The latest version of that Carlism is ETA."[9]

For many radical nationalists, the legacy of Carlism is a highly ambiguous one. Some have been quite prepared to equate nineteenth-century Carlism and ETA, though normally without recourse to the "instinctual" element posited by Arteche. The thread these radicals draw is primarily a politicomilitary one, which runs from the Carlist Basque insurgents of the 1830s and 1870s to the *gudaris* (members of the Basque divisions within the Republican army) of the late 1930s to the *etarras* of our times. In the words of three radical nationalists:

> [T]he Carlist battalions, essentially Basques, organized themselves to the cry of "Long live the Fueros!" . . . The First Carlist War was for the Basques of the south [i.e., Basque Spain] a fight of national defense against the Castilian imperialism of the central power. Those of the north [i.e., Basque France] helped them actively, passing them arms, sheltering the refugees.
>
> In 1936 the Basque Carlists believed they were still defending their liberties. This made them fight against their *abertzale* brothers who fought for a modern, national version of the *fueros*.[10]

If in the middle of the nineteenth century the situation of Basque culture in the north of the Basque Country was catastrophic, it was even much worse in the south of the Basque Country, where they saw themselves obliged to enter into a war that even today has not finished, to defend Basque identity.[11]

We could say, if it was worth comparing, that the Hundred Years War is reduced, when placed beside ours [i.e., the Basque struggle], to the category of a mere skirmish on a summer afternoon. . . . Euskadi, which is neither imperialist nor oppressive of other peoples, reacts historically with great violence in defense of its own. In the nineteenth century, armed response has occurred twice in Euskadi (the Carlist Wars). In what has so far passed of the twentieth century, armed response has occurred twice again, namely: first in '36 and then in the present. That of today is the one of longest duration of the four mentioned.[12]

Telesforo Monzón, a minister in the Basque government during the Civil War and a forceful leader of the radical nationalists in the 1970s, used to speak openly of his movement's Carlist heritage. In 1979, he declared that the Basques had been fighting the same war for one hundred and fifty years. To him, both Carlist wars, the Civil War, and the continuing campaign of ETA were all part of the struggle for the restoration of Basque sovereignty.[13] Radical nationalists have also quoted, with approval, the commentaries of Juan José Rosón, minister of the interior during the transition: "In reality the terrorist phenomenon is not clear, given that in 1873 events took place in the Basque Country and Navarre that have recurred in 1980 in an identical manner, and even the terminology then used is the same as that of today."[14]

Besides making broad generalities about the connections between ancient Carlism and modern ETA, radical nationalists have at times focused on specific Carlist personalities. In particular, two local Carlist leaders of the nineteenth century are frequently singled out for praise: Zumalacárregui, the famously successful Basque Carlist general in the first war, and Santa Cruz, the notorious guerrilla-priest of the second war. To my knowledge, no radical nationalist has ever criticized either of these characters in print. On the contrary, in the summer of 1986, *Egin*, the Herri Batasuna newspaper, ran a series of lengthy articles recounting in detail the priest's wartime exploits.

The drawing of this chronological thread, of battles fought on Basque fields, serves to give historical depth to the modern struggle. It is a manner of underlining the popular nature of the radicals' fight, and thus of legitimating it. In other words, the underlying historicist logic here is: the people have risen up in the past, and it is the people who are rising up now; therefore, if the people were right to rise up in the past, then we are right to do so today. The eulogies to Zumalacárregui and Santa Cruz act in a similar, though more individualist mode: these two men serve as historical figures to emulate, as role models meant to inspire modern-day urban guerrillas. They are nineteenth-century exemplars for twentieth-century times. For instance, Eustakio Mendizabal, popularly known as "Txikia," one of the most charismatic of the early leaders of ETA, kept a biography of Santa Cruz among his books and, according to a fellow-in-arms, "was well acquainted with Zumalacárregui and opted for his tactics; not for his strategy but for his tactics. Zumalacárregui was the first to use guerrilla warfare in organic relation with the regular army." [15]

Many radical nationalists, however, are very uneasy about much of the Carlist legacy and wish to distance themselves from it as much as possible. Thus from the late 1970s on, radical politicians started openly to use *"carlista"* as a metaphor for the irrational, reactionary, integrist, antisocialist, and absurdly old-fashioned. They no longer had to consider the party as a potential ally and could afford to caricature its past for their own purposes. In 1986 when *Egin,* the radical nationalists' newspaper, complained about the militaristic tone of the newly formed Basque Autonomous Police, it said that both "their formal and their day-to-day uniforms are inspired by those of the Carlist armies, the theocratic and absolutist faction of the Basque people." [16]

Although many members of Herri Batasuna tend to regard large sections of the Carlist legacy ambiguously, both villagers and local commentators on Basque society are quick to point out a series of parallels between popular Carlism and modern-day radical nationalism. It was in Cirauqui that I first heard the common saying, usually uttered by critics of both Carlism and Herri Batasuna, that "Hijo de carlista batasunero es" ("The child of a Carlist is a *batasunero"*). These local critics of political extremism, whether of the Left or the Right, point out that many *batasuneros* are the offspring of *requeté* fathers. Using a quasibiological argument, they claim that these modern-day radicals (and the terrorist gunmen whose actions the radicals never condemn) have inherited the sanguinary characteristics of their fathers. They are seen to be as hot-blooded, stubborn, violent, fanatical, and intolerant as those who in 1936 went off to fight "the Reds." Although it is a striking fact that some of the most politically active radical nationalists in Cirauqui *are* the offspring of staunch Carlists, it is also true that some of the other, equally energetic, *batasuneros* in the village do not come from Carlist families, and that the adult children of many other Carlists in the village today vote for other parties, such as the socialists of the PSOE, or the center-right *navarristas* of the UPN. The common saying, based on an overly simplifying connection made by moderate villagers between two disliked forms of political activity, obscures the variety of response among the sons and daughters of Carlists to the changed political context of their day. It is but another way for villagers to apply a familial perspective on local political activity, another means for them to understand the life of their *pueblo* in genealogical terms.

In contrast, the hypotheses proffered by local commentators about the Carlist legacy of radical nationalists are less genetic in basis than psychological and social. Victor Manuel Arbeloa, son of a Carlist, noted historian, and a PSOE MEP (member of the European parliament) for Navarre, has suggested that "Hijo de carlista batasunero es" may well be true. In the 1940s, he argues, many Carlists, frustrated and disillusioned, came to reject the regime they had helped to install. This antigovernmental attitude they may well have transmitted to their children, along with the bellicose traditions of their Carlism. Javier Astrain, a former progressive and Navarrese politician, has tried to make the connection in terms of a common truculent utopianism. He contends that the Carlists of former decades, like many *batasuneros* today, were unflinching idealists who preferred struggle to triumph. Luciano Rincón, the Bilbao writer and journalist, has highlighted the religious training (and, by implication, the religious zeal) of members of both groups. To him, an important section of radical nationalism is made up of "old clerics and veteran ex-seminarians who hung up their habits in order to 'throw themselves up the mountain' just like their ancestors in the Carlist Wars." Reyes Berruezo, a former progressive and former deputy to the Cortes for the Navarrese wing of the PSOE, has focused on the way that Herri Batasuna today, like Carlism in its own time, is the only political organization with its own way of life, where members, if they so choose, can "live within" the party, creating their social world almost totally within a *batasunero* ambit.[17]

All these hypotheses are suggestive, though some are very difficult to corroborate. It is clear, however, that all of them register telling aspects of Herri Batasuna. First, it is well known that a significant number of local former priests and former seminarians did join HB, where some of them have gone on to play leading roles. However, given that HB appears to be reluctant to acknowledge this fact and that a definitive, nonpartisan social history of the party has yet to be written, the degree of sacerdotal influence within it cannot yet be satisfactorily ascertained. Second, it is easy to demonstrate that radical nationalist groups stage a remarkably broad range of social activities. Indeed they do so to such an extent that *batasuneros* may, without too much difficulty, constitute their own society within the wider Basque society. Third, it is the case that their interpretations of the sociopolitical world are, at their most extreme, structured in a starkly Manichaean manner, where truths, to which they claim access, are stacked up against lies, which are maintained by their deluded or self-seeking opponents. Fourth, sociologists of HB have confirmed that for many of its members their identity is performatively defined in terms of political action. For a radical, especially a young radical, to act is to be. The danger here of course is that political violence may then become an end in itself, a merely very potent way of unifying members. In these settings, loyalty to the group may be so intense that it becomes not just a central but an almost inalienable part of one's personality.[18]

Bearing all this in mind, it is not difficult to catalog a series of parallels between the most developed versions of pre-progressive Carlism and modern radical nationalism: the influence of priests, the almost religiously fanatic zeal, the simplified interpretation of the world, the possession of absolute truths, the centrality of violence, the dismissal of democracy, and group identity as the core of one's being. Yet compiling this kind of list is facile and runs the grave risks of cloaking as much as it uncovers, of inventing new kinds of tradition instead of seeking for more subtle kinds of explanation. For what the list masks is the complex variety of each movement, and what it ignores are their potential similarities with other political organizations. Like the villagers' use of "Hijo de carlista batasunero es," it is a mode of straitjacketing each into a particular characterization for the purposes of an interest-laden comparison. Moreover, this intellectual shaping of each into a common mold becomes a way to pass silently over the internal diversity of both Carlism and radical nationalism. Their important differences are sidelined for the sake of a mutually dismissive correspondence: what was bad about Carlism has been reproduced in HB; what is to be deplored in radical nationalism comes out of Carlism.

Deconstructing the supposed connection is a relatively simple task. First, there are many strands within HB: marxism, Trotskyism, anarchism, and so on. Carlism is only one of the strands woven into it, and extremists upholding any of the other strands could just as easily be classed as antidemocratic evangelists totally dedicated to their cause. Second, though both Carlists and radical nationalists have spoken of their respective political communities as a *"pueblo,"* the internal structure of each is very different. That of the Carlists has been stereotyped in essentially transgenerational terms with the familial hearth, in a *rural* setting, as the prime site of ideological transmission. In contrast, the *batasunero pueblo* is defined predominantly in terms of common exploitation and common political action, with the urban street as the prime site for the display of ideological commitment. It is quite possible that some now veteran radicals inherited an antigovernmental bellicosity from their *requeté* parents. But as one analyst of HB argues, "The reference points within which those aged thirty or less get stirred up do not re-echo a thrill inherited and assumed like a legacy of generations. It is a designer agitation."[19] Third, though it is the case that young urban *batasuneros* can live almost exclusively within their own subculture, the same was not quite so true for Carlists. Although they might have had their own Circles in which to socialize, because most lived in villages (as opposed to cities) they had to participate alongside their non-Carlist neighbors in a variety of local activities, such as church services, religious fraternities, and the annual fiestas. And at that level of sociality, their sense of lived political community would be only slightly greater than that of PNV nationalists, who have their own *batzokis* (clubhouses) and their own round of annual celebrations.

For the comparison to be effective and convincing, what is needed is not a dovetailing set of similarities but the isolation of key common processes and conditions that will *generate* the host of resemblances in each of the two movements. In the meantime, putting together a single "mind-set" for both Carlist and radical nationalist extremists and associating that with a loosely connected collection of social variables may tell us more about analysts' capacity for superficial comparison than anything else. The same commentary would also apply to any argument that, over the centuries, locals have maintained some kind of "deep structure," of which militant Carlism and radical nationalism are but manifestations at different historical moments. Thus, until the successful identification of a generative explanation (which I personally doubt), all we can state is that many locals themselves—whether villagers, politicians, or academics—do perceive some connection, however vague or loosely formulated, between Carlism and radical nationalism. Of course, making the connection is also an evaluation of the two movements and, usually, a strongly negative one.

The Partido Carlista has not been quiet about the attempts to make connections between their movement and nationalism. At times it has reacted strongly. In 1980 there was a heated exchange in the Foral Parliament of Navarre when radical and moderate nationalists argued that since certain famous Carlists of the last century had, in their day, been regarded as terrorists, those in ETA today should be praised, not damned. Carlist progressives in the chamber retorted vigorously that such a comparison was inadmissible.[20] They did not want their view of local history sullied by association with the gunmen. Progressives have also protested the rewriting of recent history by Basque politicians keen to damn the chances of their political opponents. For example, in his report on the 1977 general elections, the leader of the Álavan progressives complained that members of the PNV were openly stating they would prefer to ally with the Communists than with the Carlists, whom they blamed for the extension of the Civil War into the Basque Country: "as if they themselves had fired only lollipops and biscuits from their trenches. It would seem so, since they consider the Carlists responsible for all the dead."

The general problem for contemporary Carlists here is that, despite their best efforts to control the image and understanding of their movement, its past is part of common history and, as such, open to examination and representation by anyone interested in that past. But this past dogs the party in a second way. Because Carlism was so much more significant politically during its first hundred years than during its later period, any portrayal of the movement, whether by modern novelists or travel writers, emphasizes its traditionalist period at the total expense of its subsequent *progresismo*. For example, the best-selling Basque writer Bernardo Atxaga in his novel *Un espía llamado Sara* presents Zumalacárregui and his officers of the first war as a group of cynical killers infiltrated by traitors. Almost all the writings of Pablo Antoñana, a veteran Navarrese writer, revel in a rich evocation of the local past, especially its Carlist conflicts. In recent years the Foral Deputation, in a bid to boost a sense of provincial culture, has subsidized the publication or, in some cases, the republication of Antoñana's works. The latest is his *Relato cruento*, which stresses the familial connections between participants in the first, second, and civil wars. In his travelogue *Sobre la marcha*, the much younger Navarrese writer Eduardo Gil Bera uses the first war expedition of the Carlist General Miguel Gómez as the frame and constant reference for his own itinerary.[21] In marked contrast to this continuing fascination in the local exotic, there is, to my knowledge, no literary work that makes any reference, however meager, to the progressives. The pacific efforts of Carlos Hugo and his people do not excite the same novelistic passions.

The essentially backward-looking view of Carlism as a movement of the ignorant or the bigoted, which led to nationalism, is repeated by those politically interested who regard the movement from outside the Basque ambit. For instance, a recent editorial in the Falange bulletin *Nosotros* was headed by Pío Baroja's notorious comment, "Carlism is cured by reading and nationalism by traveling."[22] After the killing by ETA of a Madrid professor in 1996, one contributor to the Web site magazine of the University of Salamanca students wrote: "Basque nationalism, the moderate as much as the radical, drinks from the same sources. These are (a) the conservation of the foral privilege, incompatible with the modern state and with the self-same concept of equality; and (b) a utopian, ascientific and amoral racism. The first has been defended not only by the present nationalists, but also by that cancer that Spain suffered in the past century and which called itself Carlism (by the way, do you remember in what band the Carlists were in the Civil War?)."[23]

This sense of Carlism as something primarily of the past is a general attitude that may be reinforced even by local journalists. In 1986, a socialist deputy tried to justify the lack of support for the PSOE in nationalist areas by claiming that his party had lost "in the Carlist dominions." A Navarrese columnist sharply rebuked him and argued that the parliamentarian's vision of the country was clearly based on the nineteenth, not the twentieth, century. To the journalist, Carlism was part of the old Spanish image, of a turbulent country bedeviled by rebellions, slaughters, and civil wars, and only enlivened by song, music, and dance (preferably flamenco).[24] To such people, the only interest Carlism has today is anthropological.

What all the above suggest is that the legacy of Carlism is neither stable nor unitary. Interpretation of its nature and worth is not the exclusive privilege of any one group, but changes from political position to political position: from the good to the bad, the constructive to the destructive, the ideologically suggestive to the fanatically narrow-minded. At times, the play of Carlist images seems like the movement of a kaleidoscope—one slight turn and a bright new pattern emerges. Today's Partido Carlista may regard itself as the main direct successor of the original movement, but that gives it no intellectual copyright over the Carlist inheritance. It has no monopoly over the interpretation of its past. In this sense, the party is saddled with a history it cannot control, and that others may have reason to exploit for their own ends. Given these conditions, perhaps the only conclusion that can be made here is that the legacies of Carlism will continue to be sites of contest. They will remain labile, plural, and open ended.

Epilogue

Montejurra 1986

About three hundred people went to Montejurra in 1986. The great majority were Navarrese or Basques; only a handful came from further afield. Some complained quietly about the poor turnout: "There aren't even four cats," one said. They noted the lack of policemen—five Civil Guards directing the traffic—as a sign that Carlism was no longer considered dangerous. At ten o'clock in the morning about one hundred started to go up the mountain, though only ten to fifteen of the faithful followed the priest in saying the stations of the cross. Walking slowly, pausing occasionally to admire the view and to catch one's breath, it took half an hour to reach the peak.

By the start of the Mass, the mountaintop was merely littered with people. In his sermon on the summit, the priest remembered those Carlists, such as his father, who had not come because they were too old to climb Montejurra. In the political act, held at midday at the foot of the mountain, Carlist representatives spoke from a cart decorated with the name, slogans, and symbols of the party. The loudest claps were reserved for a call to remember the martyrs of the Montejurra of 1976; for an Aragonese Carlist who said his father, grandfather, and great-grandfather had all fought for the cause; for a speaker who said that Carlism with its long history and tradition is still the same; and for an impassioned speech against the writer of a letter published in *El Diario de Navarra* a few days before, which criticized the party for allying with the Communists in Izquierda Unida for electoral ends. The new leader of the Carlist youth organization spoke of plans for future activities. (What he and his huddle of peers later discussed was the possibility of putting on a series of friendly football matches.) At the end of the speeches, the people listening cried "Vivas!" to the party and to Montejurra. Among the small crowd, a few youngish men off to one side giggled and joked during the speeches. An irritated, older neighbor told them sharply to have respect and asked why none of them were wearing the customary red headgear. "Are you people," he said out loud, "ashamed of the red beret?"

A party stall sold drinks, hot snacks, remaindered progressive books, and outdated stickers for past events. People relaxed and chatted with old friends, before going into the shade to cook their lunch. The seven Carlists from Cirauqui joined with those from the next two villages to cook and to share their meal of lamb stew, barbecued chops, salad, fruit, and wine. At the end of the meal, coffee, *pacharán,* and cigars were passed around. Carlist leaders went from fire to fire, chatting jocularly to each group of commensales for a few minutes, maybe drinking a little of their wine from a goatskin forced into their hands, before passing on to the next group. After lunch, a little excitement and noise was generated by a raffle and children's games. By 5:30 P.M., most had left. Some went straight home. Others continued in the company of their fellows in the large but somewhat empty Carlist Circle of Estella, before, perhaps, joining the evening promenade by the townspeople along the streets of the Old Quarter.

The ritual of Montejurra started as a pilgrimage of bereaved Navarrese who wished to remember ritually their late beloved. In the mid-1950s, it was made into a mass Carlist gathering. By the mid-1960s, it was predominantly a political rally, attended by Carlists and other opponents of Franco. In 1976, it briefly won unwanted fame as an arena for armed aggression. Since the late 1970s, it has become a small, primarily regional ceremony. Although it retains a minor political aspect, Montejurra is now a pseudofamilial gathering of old friends and acquaintances who will not let their Carlist identity die. Since grand rallies or massed gatherings of the faithful are now mere side events in the calendars of major parties (otherwise filled with television appearances and photo opportunities), the continuing importance of Montejurra to the Partido Carlista serves only to underline its political marginality. As the opportunities for progressives to express publicly their allegiance gradually decrease—they are too few to stage a demonstration or mount a protest—Montejurra emerges as almost their sole means of collective self-assertion. It is a rare, remaining proof of the continued existence of their brand of Carlism. Since the role of their political party is now purely testimonial, participating in the event becomes more plainly a public affirmation of belonging to the movement. For when else, these days, can they put on their red berets?

The ritual form of Montejurra has remained the same, though the functions it serves have changed several times over the course of five decades. The main reason for this structural persistence is that there is no need for change. Both postwar traditionalists and their progressive successors were able to use the ceremony for their own ends. They did not need to tinker with its basic form, though they altered its scale and its social composition. Participants today, by keeping to the same ceremonial structure, can state that they are preserving the Carlist tradition of their family by maintaining the tradition of Montejurra. That ceremonial tradition itself fits into the long-established context of *romerías,* whose structure Montejurra broadly imitates. Changing the form of Montejurra without very good reason would threaten its nature as a Carlist tradition and go against the ceremonial conventions of the country. Of course, the idea of what constitutes Carlism has evolved greatly, but those who attend Montejurra these days can still claim, on grounds of historical continuity and historicism, that they are respecting the memory of their forefathers because they are sustaining the life of Carlism.

The number of participants remains strikingly low, but the party does not consider ending its annual performance. Since the Comunión Tradicionalista Carlista continues to hold annual ceremonies in the Basque area in honor of one or another Carlist anniversary, party leaders are worried that if they stop staging their event, the Comunión might "win back" Montejurra. Because of this threat, the party cannot give up holding the yearly ritual. No matter how small attendance becomes, they must go on.

In 1965, the *juanista* Theo Aronson described the previous year's Montejurra in rousing terms, but ended on a contrastive note: "When the last of the great crowd had gone and the only sound to be heard was the clanking of the bells as the goats once more took possession of the rocky pathway, one was left with the suspicion that one had perhaps witnessed an act of homage to the most lost of all lost causes."[1] Taking my cue from Aronson, I could end this book in an elegiac mode, with Montejurra as the scene of the Carlists' last stand against the aggressive forces of change. But the fact that the ceremony is still staged annually, over thirty years after Aronson penned his account, suggests that the Montejurras performed today can be viewed both as a coda for the movement *and* as creative activity celebrating Carlist continuity.

To most onlookers, Montejurra may seem the final redoubt of an ever-diminishing group, but to others it can appear as a willful act of resistance by Carlists who believe that an event under their control is worth maintaining. To these Carlists, their movement can continue to exist as a meaningful community even if it is now outside the boundaries of conventional party politics in Spain. The existence of an opposed band (the Comunión), which may well wish to commandeer the mountain for its own ceremonial purposes, helps to justify celebrants' belief in the value of what they perform. Just because many people, some Carlists included, think that the movement is dying, does not mean that they are necessarily right. Montejurra is as much about life as it is about death.

Appendix I

The survey details the holdings of everyone, whether a villager of Cirauqui or an outsider, owning taxable goods in the village. The taxable goods are the following: tilled land, vineyards, olive groves, and olive groves with rows of vines planted between them (these four sorts of goods were each categorized into six classes, of declining quality); market gardens (three classes); houses (five classes); barns (two classes); yards (within or outside the village); livestock (workhorses, working mules, asses, mares, bovines); businesses. By computer analysis of the survey results, supplemented by data from the 1879 census of the village, it is possible to gain some idea of who owned what and how much in Cirauqui at that time.

It is necessary to state immediately that, for a variety of reasons, analysis of the cadastral survey can give only an approximation, at best, of the socioeconomic structure of Cirauqui. We lack much relevant information: for instance, about the number of villagers who worked for others, as laborers or servants, or who sharecropped others' land. The survey tells us nothing about how many members of Cirauqui possessed land, and how much, in neighboring villages. Also, it classes people as individuals; it is thus impossible, without recourse to supplementary data, to derive some idea of family holdings, of groups of siblings or close kin who worked cooperatively. Furthermore, the numerical data produced by the analysis are deceptively precise, since landowners, who had to declare the extent and quality of their holdings (which had been measured by surveyors or engineers), frequently undervalued them and underestimated their bounds, when not actually concealing the existence of holdings.[1] It might, of course, be argued that since this temptation to understate the value of one's possessions was general, it should have little effect on the *comparative* analysis of villagers' holdings.

Despite these lacunae and caveats, it is still well worth reporting the results of the analysis, since the survey remains the major single source of detailed information about the structure of the village during this period, while data from the 1879 census can give us suggestive insights concerning aspects of the social structure about which the survey is silent. The survey and census do not enable us to draw as exact and comprehensive an analysis as we might wish, but that does not mean they should be left unanalyzed. Since this computer-based analysis is, to my knowledge, the first carried out on a cadastral survey of a Navarrese or Basque village, it may also be justified by the methodological example it provides for historians and anthropologists of the area.

Once the total tax paid by the villagers had been calculated, it was possible to plot a graph (figure 3) depicting the cumulative distribution of the total tax paid by the villagers, ranked from those paying the least tax to those paying the most. The most striking observation that can be made from looking at the graph is that the majority of tax is paid by a small minority: 60 percent of the taxpaying villagers provide less than 11 percent of the villagers' total tax bill, while the richest 20 percent pay more than 71 percent of it. In order to obtain a finer-grained idea of the division of wealth, it was necessary to divide the population of villagers who owned taxable goods (374 individuals) into deciles: ten classes, each of 37 individuals (four deciles had 38), grouped according to the amount of tax they paid. Thus, decile 1 was composed of those 37 individuals who paid the least tax and decile 10 of those 37 individuals who paid the most.

Analyzing the data according to the contributions made by each decile to the total tax paid on each taxable good (figures 4–40) serves to underline the dominance of the "higher" deciles in the majority of kinds of taxable goods, especially in those goods of higher quality. Members of decile 10 paid over 72 percent of the total tax bill for first-class tilled land. Members of deciles 9 and 10 together paid over 75 percent and over 47 percent of the bill, respectively, for second- and third-class tilled land. Also, they owned all the market gardens (except for a few held by members of decile 2), as well as at least 45 percent of each class of vineyard, paying over 93 percent, 86 percent, and 72 percent of the total tax bill, respectively, for first-, second-, and third-class vineyards. Similarly, in the case of olive groves, members of these two deciles owned at least 71 percent of each class, except the fifth class, of which they owned 53 percent. Their ownership of mixed olive groves and vineyards was even more extreme, with them paying at least 78 percent of the total tax bill for each class, and over 90 percent for first-, second-, and sixth-class mixed plots. They paid over 53 percent of the bill for housing, over 88 percent of that for barns, and over 90 percent of that for yards, whether within or outside the village. As for livestock, they possessed all the mares owned by villagers and almost all the bovines. Finally, they paid over 69 percent of the tax bill for businesses held by villagers.

Looking across the deciles at the total tax bill for each good enables us to obtain a comparative idea of the relative ownership, by decile, of different goods within Cirauqui, and so to underscore the economic dominance of its greatest taxpayers. But if instead we look at the total tax bill paid by each decile (figures 41–50) and analyze a sequence of these bills, it is possible to gain a somewhat more exact idea of the economic behavior of particular deciles, from the poorest to richest. Comparing all ten of figures 41 to 50, it seems that the aim of the poorest was to obtain tilled land, usually of low quality, an animal to help work it, and a place to live. Of the 37 members of decile 1, all but one owned some land (all very small plots with poor soil), seven had a mule or an ass, and four a small house. For those immediately above decile 1, the aim appears to have been to obtain more tilled land and, if possible, to acquire a plot for vines. Of the members of decile 2, 85 percent owned tilled land, almost all of low quality and with an average holding of 2.05 hectares.

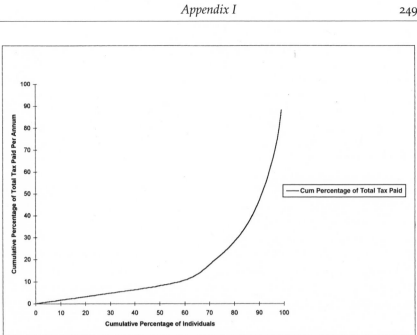

Fig. 3. Distribution of Total Tax Paid Per Individual

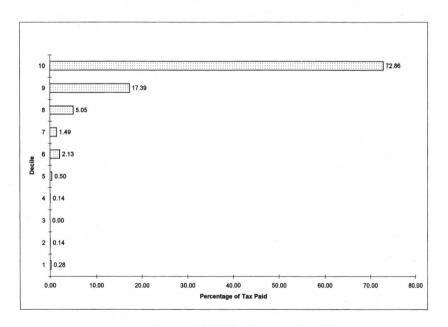

Fig. 4. Tax Paid on Tilled Land, First Class

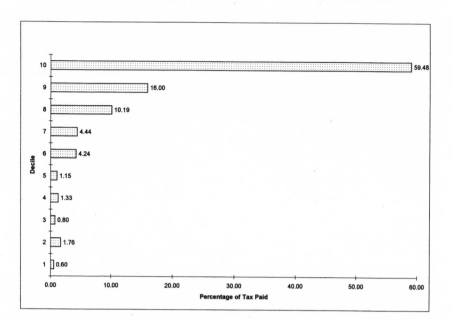

Fig. 5. Tax Paid on Tilled Land, Second Class

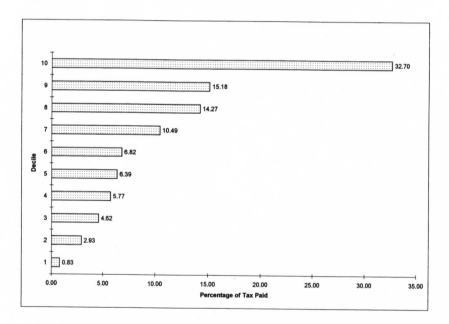

Fig. 6. Tax Paid on Tilled Land, Third Class

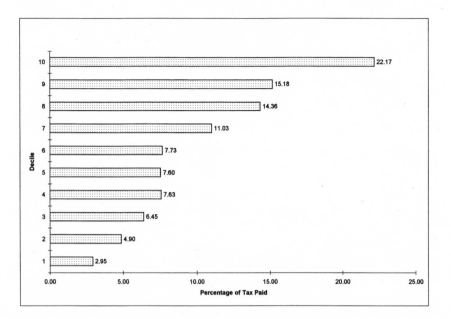

Fig. 7. Tax Paid on Tilled Land, Fourth Class

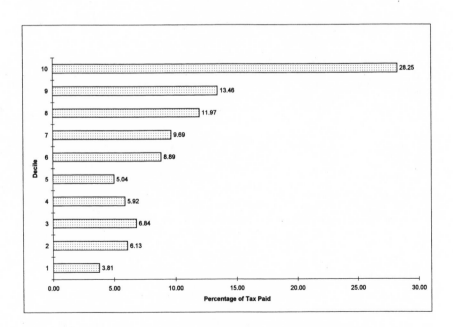

Fig. 8. Tax Paid on Tilled Land, Sixth Class

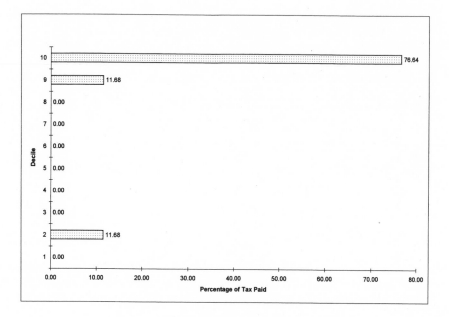

Fig. 9. Tax Paid on Market Gardens

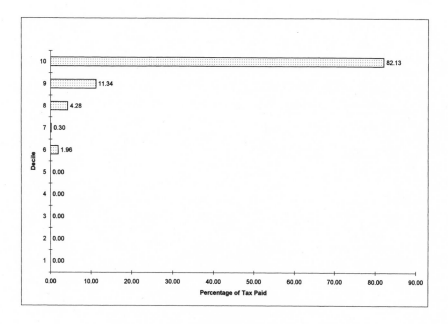

Fig. 10. Tax Paid on Vineyards, First Class

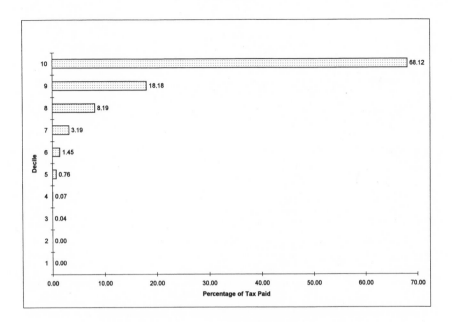

Fig. 11. Tax Paid on Vineyards, Second Class

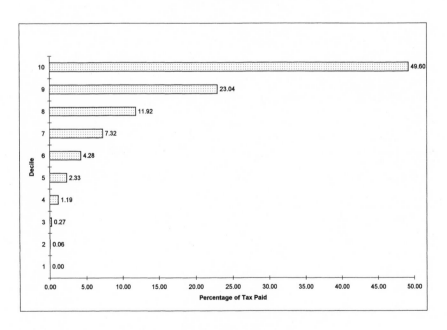

Fig. 12. Tax Paid on Vineyards, Third Class

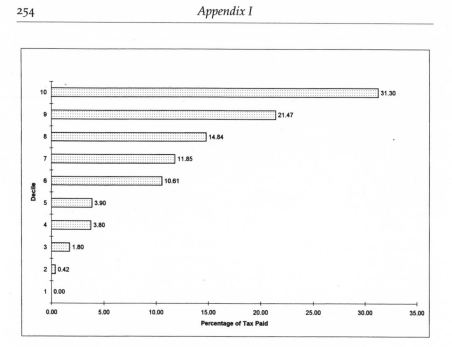

Fig. 13. Tax Paid on Vineyards, Fourth Class

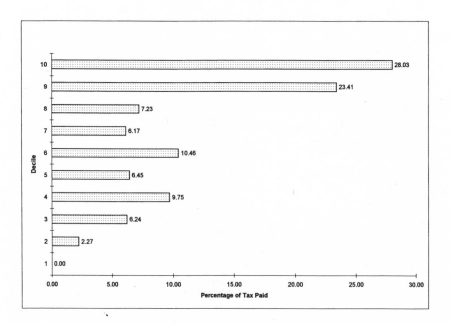

Fig. 14. Tax Paid on Vineyards, Fifth Class

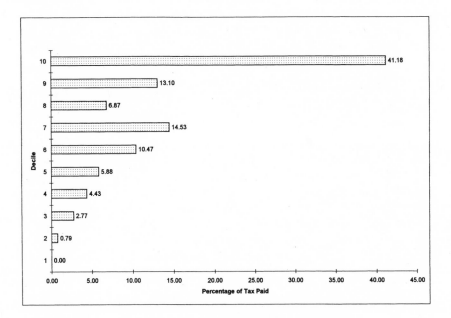

Fig. 15. Tax Paid on Vineyards, Sixth Class

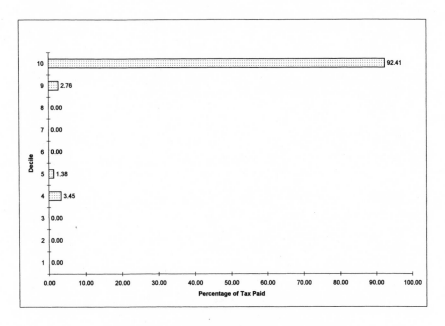

Fig. 16. Tax Paid on Olive Groves, First Class

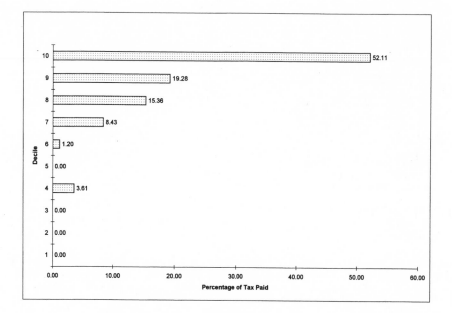

Fig. 17. Tax Paid on Olive Groves, Second Class

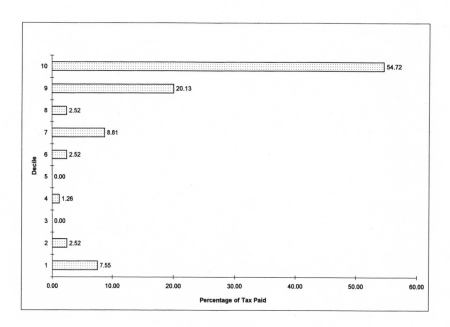

Fig. 18. Tax Paid on Olive Groves, Third Class

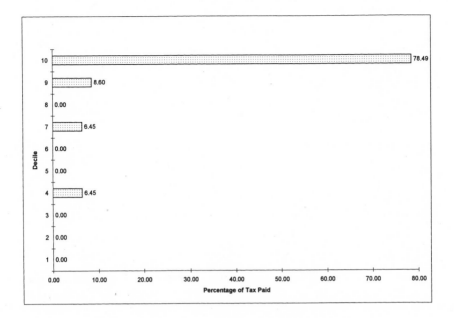

Fig. 19. Tax Paid on Olive Groves, Fourth Class

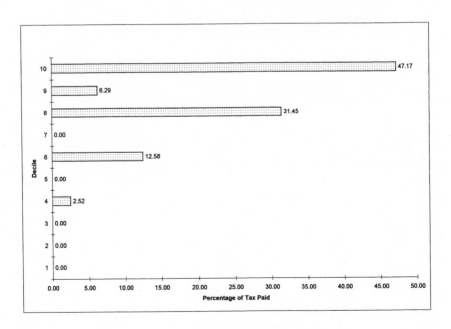

Fig. 20. Tax Paid on Olive Groves, Fifth Class

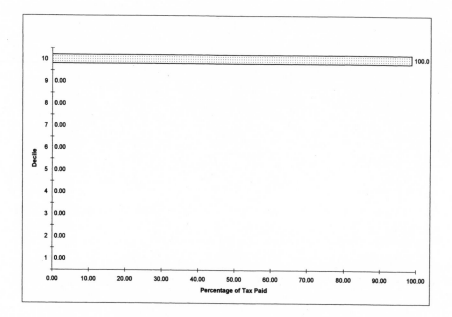

Fig. 21. Tax Paid on Olive Groves, Sixth Class

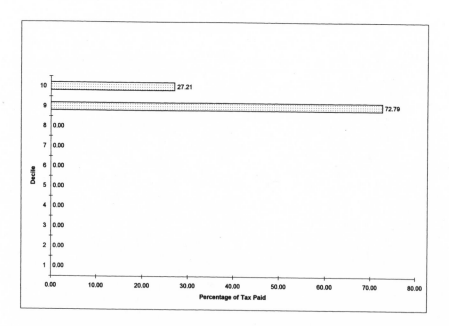

Fig. 22. Tax Paid on Mixed Vineyards and Olive Groves, First Class

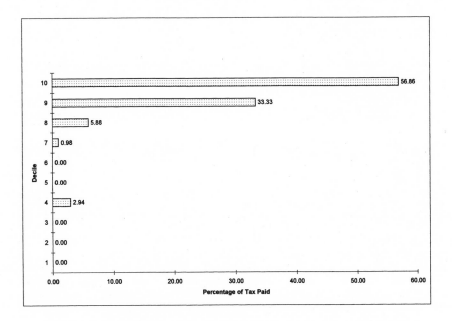

Fig. 23. Tax Paid on Mixed Vineyards and Olive Groves, Second Class

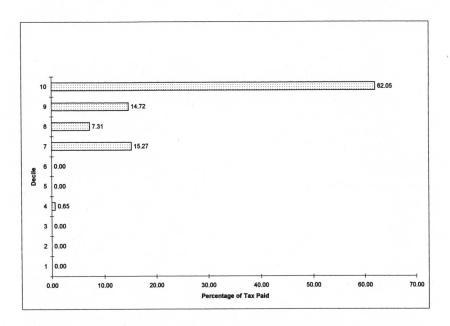

Fig. 24. Tax Paid on Mixed Vineyards and Olive Groves, Third Class

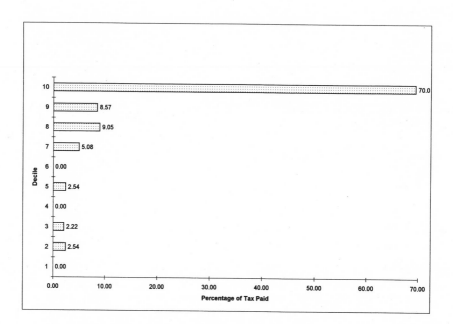

Fig. 25. Tax Paid on Mixed Vineyards and Olive Groves, Fourth Class

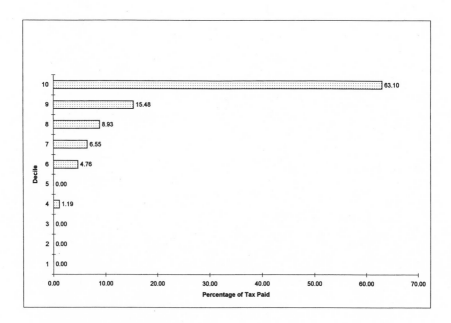

Fig. 26. Tax Paid on Mixed Vineyards and Olive Groves, Fifth Class

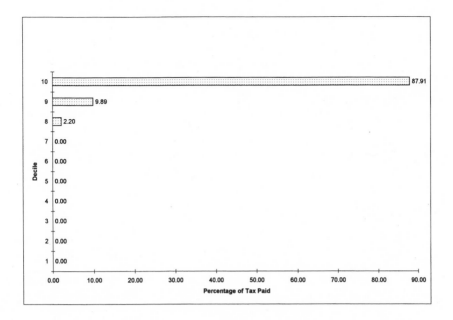

Fig. 27. Tax Paid on Mixed Vineyards and Olive Groves, Sixth Class

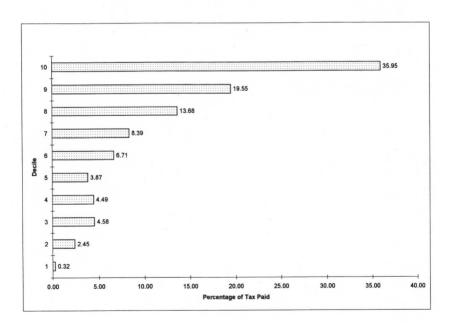

Fig. 28. Tax Paid on Houses

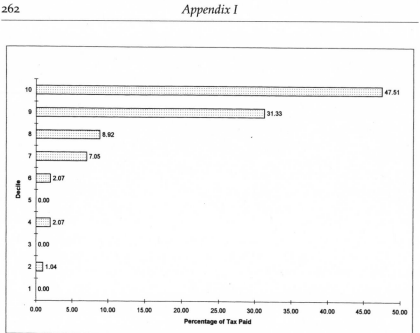

Fig. 29. Tax Paid on Barns

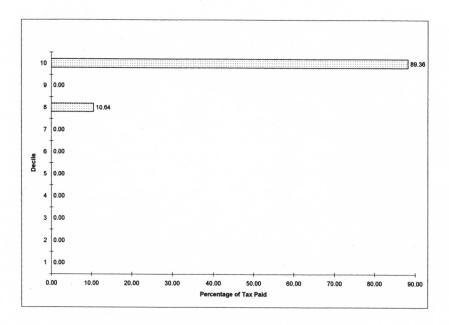

Fig. 30. Tax Paid on Yards Within the Village

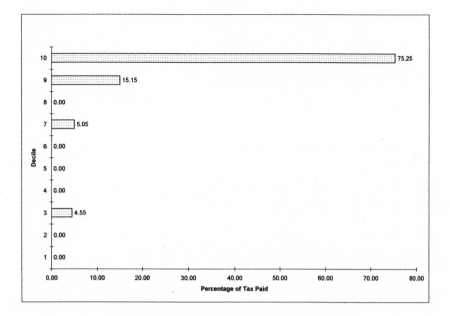

Fig. 31. Tax Paid on Yards Outside the Village

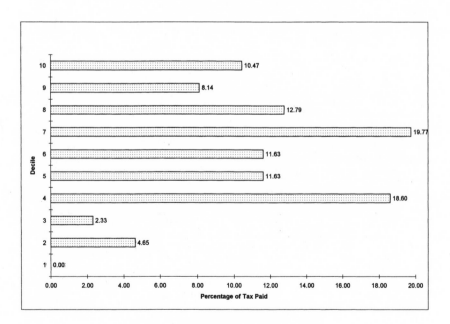

Fig. 32. Tax Paid on Working Horses

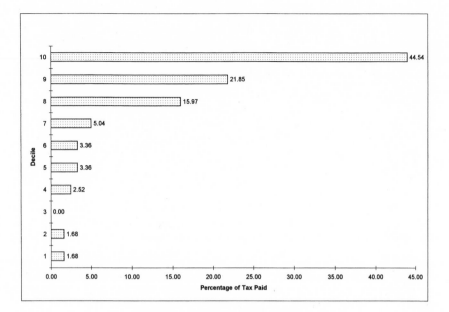

Fig. 33. Tax Paid on Working Mules

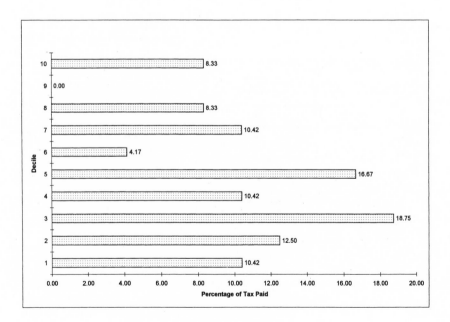

Fig. 34. Tax Paid on Asses

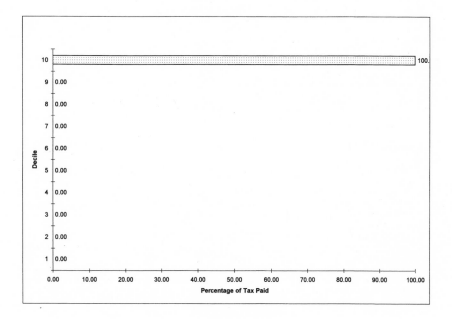

Fig. 35. Tax Paid on Mares

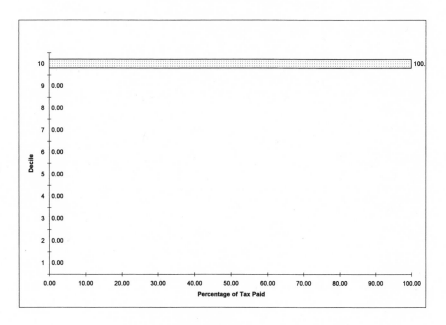

Fig. 36. Tax Paid on Bovines Aged 1-3 Years

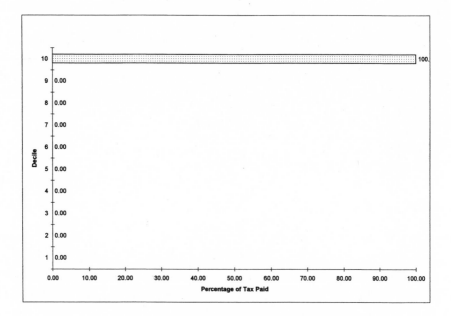

Fig. 37. Tax Paid on Bovines, Native Species

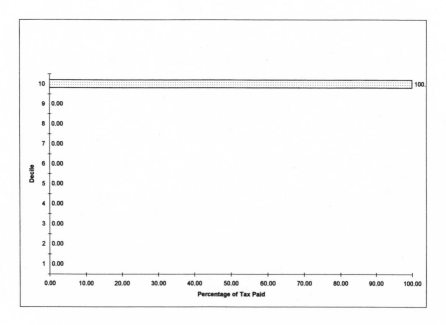

Fig. 38. Tax Paid on Bovines, Swiss and Breton Species

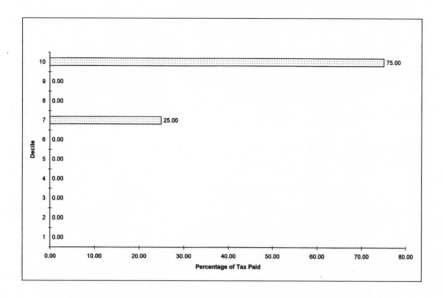

Fig. 39. Tax Paid on Bovines, Working and Breeding

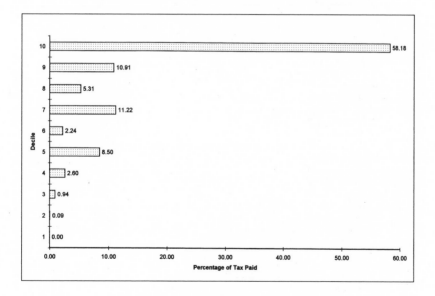

Fig. 40. Tax Paid on Business

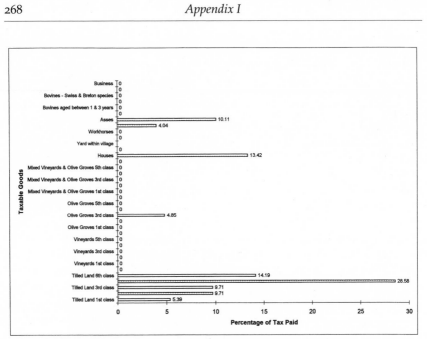

Fig. 41. Tax Paid by Taxable Goods, Decile 1

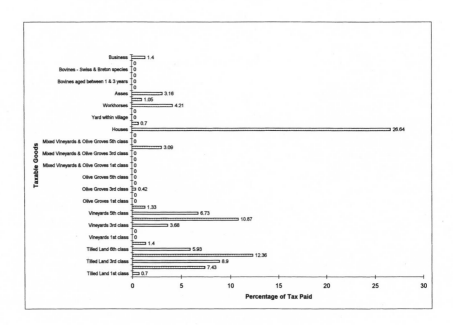

Fig. 42. Tax Paid by Taxable Goods, Decile 2

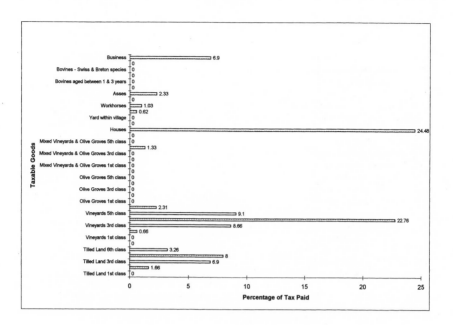

Fig. 43. Tax Paid by Taxable Goods, Decile 3

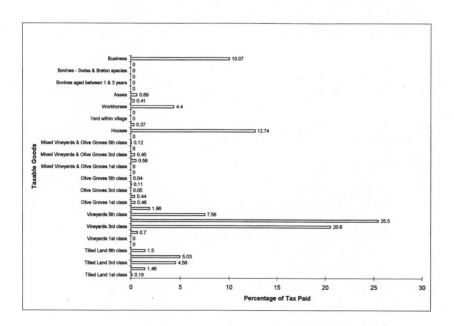

Fig. 44. Tax Paid by Taxable Goods, Decile 4

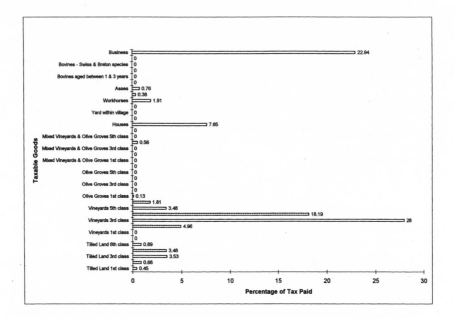

Fig. 45. Tax Paid by Taxable Goods, Decile 5

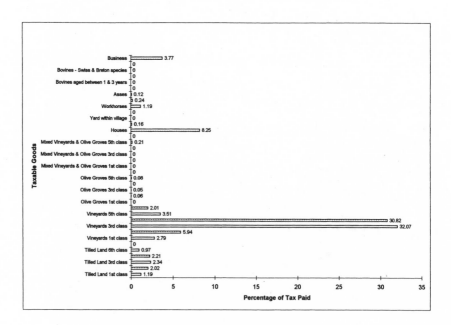

Fig. 46. Tax Paid by Taxable Goods, Decile 6

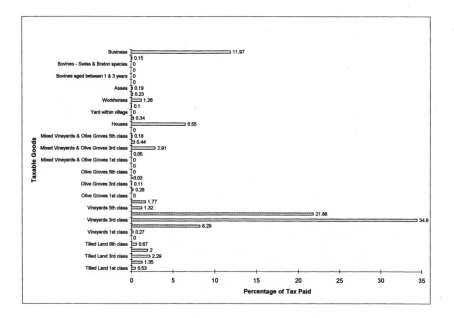

Fig. 47. Tax Paid by Taxable Goods, Decile 7

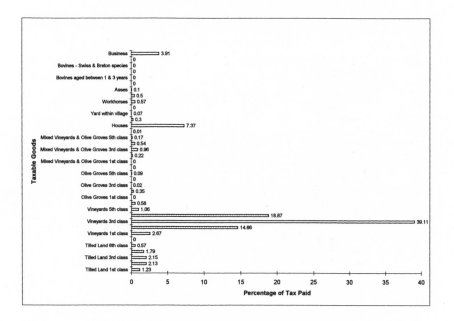

Fig. 48. Tax Paid by Taxable Goods, Decile 8

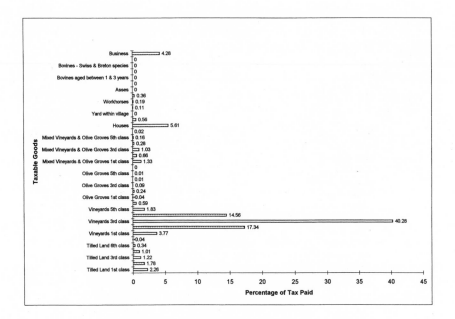

Fig. 49. Tax Paid by Taxable Goods, Decile 9

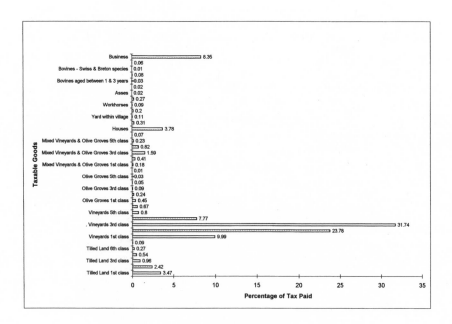

Fig. 50. Tax Paid by Taxable Goods, Decile 10

Thirty-one percent owned very small vineyards, all of low quality, and with an average size of 0.125 hectares; 34 percent of them had a house (two-thirds of those being of the lowest quality); 31 percent had a work animal.

Moving up this tax-ranked scale a little, the aim of most of the only very slightly more wealthy was to gain tilled land of better quality, and if possible more land in general, as well as to obtain somewhat larger vineyards. Among members of decile 5 for instance, 78 percent owned land, of mixed quality, with an average holding of 2.33 hectares; 70 percent owned vineyards, most of medium to poor quality, with an average holding of 0.76 hectares. Compared to decile 2, a greater proportion of the members of decile 5 (51 percent) had a house, and many of them of better quality (third- or fourth-class); similarly, a greater percentage (43 percent) had a work animal. It appears from the data that the majority of villagers in deciles 3 to 6 attempted to diversify their resources rather than concentrate their wealth in any one good. For example, among the members of decile 5, there are only two villagers who owned tilled land who did not also own a vineyard, and one of those two generated income by cobbling. The main exception to this generalization about diversifying resources was most of the artisans and petty traders of the village, many of whom appear to have relied completely on practicing their craft or plying their trade. Thus, of the ten artisans and tradespeople in decile 5, seven of them owned no land, houses, or animals, while of the other three, two owned comparatively little land and the third simply sold some fruit and vegetables as a way to supplement her income.

An analysis of the holdings of the members of decile 8 suggests that the somewhat more wealthy villagers of Cirauqui acted in a similar economic manner to their poorer neighbors, by attempting to diversify their resources. All members of this decile, except one, owned tilled land, a significant proportion of which was of good to medium quality, the average individual holding being 4.55 hectares. All owned vineyards, the majority of their holdings being of good to medium quality, with an average individual holding of 2.57 hectares. In contrast to the members of decile 5, only one of whom owned an olive grove, fifteen members (39 percent) of decile 8 owned olive groves and/or groves with lines of vines planted between them, the average holdings of each being 0.31 hectares and 0.44 hectares, respectively. All but four owned houses, the majority of medium quality; seven owned barns, and twenty-six owned one, if not two, work animals. The only "land-poor" members of this decile are the craftsmen and tradespeople: a blacksmith, the owner of a chocolate shop, a tavern keeper, and two grocers.

The economic behavior of the members of decile 10 tends to confirm, in a heightened manner, the strategies pursued by the other, less wealthy villagers, that is, diversification rather than specialization. All owned tilled land, some of them large stretches of it, the average individual holding being 12.9 hectares. All possessed land of the best quality, though individual holdings of it exceeded 3 hectares in only three cases. All owned vineyards, of diverse quality, from the best to the poorest, the average individual holding being 9.7 hectares. All but six owned olive groves and/or groves with lines of vines planted between them, the average holdings of each being 0.86 hectares and 0.79 hectares, respectively. All had houses, the majority of best to medium quality; some were landlords, possessing up to ten houses each. Two-thirds owned barns, and five of them more than one. Eleven (29 percent) owned yards, and (once again) some of them more than one. All but five had one, if not several, work animals. Twenty-one also ran businesses, seventeen of them as distillers of crude brandy. As well as distilling, some had other trades or occupations: pressing oil or grapes, cutting people's hair, or acting as pharmacist for the surrounding area. Only three members of this, the richest decile, developed their businesses rather than invest much of their wealth in land: Cirauqui's two millers and one villager who distilled brandy, made candles, and ran a chocolate shop.

(The keying in of the data and its analysis were carried out by Ms. Gill Turner, using an spss program.)

Appendix II

APPROXIMATE NUMBERS ATTENDING MONTEJURRA, 1939–1989

1939	Approx. 10,000
1941	Two coachloads from Pamplona[1]
1954	>11,000; approx. 5,000[2]
1955	>5,000[3]
1956	>12,000[4]
1957	25,000 to 30,000[5]
1959	40,000[6]
1960	45,000[7]
1962	40,000 to 50,000; 60,000; 390 coaches, 629 cars, 55 motorbikes, special trains[8]
1963	60,000; 80,000; 18,000 communions in Irache[9]
1964	60,000 to 120,000; 60,000 to 70,000; >50,000; approx. 100,000[10]
1965	>100,000; 100,000[11]
1966	>100,000; 150,000[12]
1967	"20 percent more people than 1966"; "biggest ever"[13]
1969	"Biggest ever"[14]
1970	"Fewer than previous years"[15]
1971	"Notable decline in the number of people"[16]
1972	15,000[17]
1973	"Even fewer people"[18]
1974	5,000 to 6,000[19]
1975	Approx. 3,500[20]
1977	(Held in Javier) approx. 2,000[21]
1978	5,000; 4,000[22]
1979	2,000[23]
1980	2,000[24]
1986	300[25]
1987	200[26]
1989	300[27]

275

Notes

1. Sherzer 1987: 296.

CHAPTER ONE. INTRODUCTION

1. On the social composition of early Carlism, see Barreiro Fernández 1976; Ardit Lucas 1977: 299–305; Castroviejo Bolibar 1977; Asín Remírez de Esparza 1983; Asensio Rubio 1987; Asín and Bullón 1987; Asín Remírez de Esparza 1988; Fernández 1988, 1990; Millán 1990; Shubert 1990: 93–95; Bullón de Mendoza y Gómez de Valugera 1991a; La Parra López 1991; Mundet i Gifre 1991; Clara 1992; Rubio Ruiz 1992; Vallverdu i Marti 1992; Rújula López 1995.

2. Río Aldaz 1987, 1991, La Torre 1991.

3. Andrés-Gallego 1987: 207.

4. There is an ever-growing literature on the social composition of Carlism in the provinces of Bizkaia, Gipuzkoa, Álava, and Navarre. See, for instance, Aróstegui Sánchez 1970; Real Cuesta 1985; Rodríguez de Coro 1986; Garralda 1986; Imbuluzqueta Alcasena 1988; Rodríguez Ranz 1988; Barahona 1989; Pan-Montojo 1990; Agirreazkuenaga 1990; Gurrutxaga 1990; Fernández Sebastian 1991; Lázaro Torres 1991; Vidal-Abarca López 1991.

5. Carr 1966: 187.

6. Sesmero Cutanda 1991.

7. Bullón de Mendoza y Gómez de Valugera 1995.

8. Clemente 1990: 53–57.

9. Garmendia 1984: 74, 295–300, 383. On the early evolution of Carlist political thought, see also Wilhelmsen 1995.

10. Real Cuesta 1985: 17–19.

11. Lannon 1986: 83; 1987: 36–44.

12. Los liberales son de manteca
    y sus fusiles de mierda seca
    y los carlistas son de tocino
    y sus fusiles de acero fino
    (Esparza 1988: 32)

13. Garmendia 1984: 301.

14. Real Cuesta 1985: 128–32.

15. Blinkhorn 1975: 20–27. On the various forms of traditionalism, within and without Carlism, see Vázquez de Prado and Caspistegui 1991.

16. Blinkhorn 1975: 30–31.

17. Real Cuesta 1985: 80; Clemente 1990: 75–76.

18. Prats i Salas 1990. From 1905 to 1914, however, Carlism enjoyed a brief resurgence in Barcelona as a radical current within the movement concerned with the lot of the proletariat, gaining adherents prepared to fight anarchist terrorists and thugs from Alejandro Lerroux's anticlerical Radical Party. See Winston 1985, esp. pp. 65–107.

19. "Antes se acabarán las chispas en las fraguas que los carlistas en Navarra." Larronde 1977; Elorza 1978; Corcuera Atienza 1979; *Navarra Hoy,* 25 August 1990; García-Sanz Marcotegui 1994.

20. Mina Apat 1985.

21. Fuente Langas 1994.

22. Blinkhorn 1975: 32, 39–40; Mina Apat 1985; Luengo Teixidor 1991: 32–42.

23. Pascual 1986: 39. On the rise of Carlism in Andalucía, see Alvarez Rey 1990; on the revival of the Requeté and on Fal Conde's staging, throughout Carlist Spain, of great parades of intimidatory intent, see Calleja and Aróstegui 1995.

24. In Fraser 1979: 64–65.

CHAPTER TWO. REPRESENTING THE *REQUETÉS*

1. *Boletín Oficial del Estado,* no. 390, Dec. 411, 8 November 1937.

2. Franco's bestowal of the decoration was so generally perceived as recognition of the *requeté* war effort that in 1939 he tried to reduce tension between the Comunión and the Falange by awarding the Cross of Saint Ferdinand to Valladolid, a Falangist stronghold.

As a further sign of his gratitude to, and of his respect for, the Carlist militia, Franco even wore a red beret (distinctively Carlist headgear) during his official visit to Pamplona. Of course, such praise might only have been intended to mollify Carlists rightly suspicious that the insurgent militia was not going to usher in the traditionalist utopia the *requetés* were fighting for. In the same way, Franco's stipulation that only *requetés* could be members of his personal bodyguard was viewed as a folkloric concession to ward off Carlist criticism.

The term *"requeté"* itself comes from an eponymous regiment, famed for the valor of its troops, who fought in the First Carlist War. On the origin and development of the term, see García Serrano 1964: 494–97; Burgo 1978a: 839–40; Aróstegui Sánchez 1988.

3. Fussell 1975; Rutherford 1978; Extramiana 1983; Gil 1990; Thomas 1990: 12.

4. Nagore Yarnoz 1982.

5. Nonell Brú 1965: 11.

6. López-Sanz 1966: 9.

7. J. Lezaun, "Nuestro provincianismo," *Punto y Hora,* 12–19 July 1979, p. 15; López Atxurra 1990: 73–75. In one example of the genre, the First Carlist War in the Basque Country is presented as Navarrese, not Basques, fighting the "revolu-

tionary" liberals. The immediate response of the *requetés* to Franco's uprising was "a unaminous impulse without peer in the history of Spain." The "unequalled contribution" of Navarre, with its "total selflessness," was a message "to the world." Indeed, according to this author, it was Navarre that "decided the triumph of the crusade" (Gurpide Beope 1943: 145–47).

8. On the *novela social,* see Jordan 1990.

9. Herzberger 1995: 23.

10. A further difference between the two militias was that the Falange accepted anyone within its ranks, while the Requeté, with very few exceptions, was composed only of Carlists and their known friends. A significant proportion of the exceptions appear to have been anticommunist or militantly Catholic foreigners who wished to fight against the Republican forces but were not, by law, allowed to enter the regular army.

11. Cia Navascués 1941: 126; Redondo and Zavala 1957: 67; López-Sanz 1963: 94; 1966: 147; Etayo 1990: 84; Thomas 1990: 74. While authors claim that after battles *requetés* were not prodded by fury into eliminating prisoners, López-Sanz is forced to admit that the record of neither side in the war is "unstained" (1963: 96–97, 127). In Navarre, that "stain" includes the more than 2,700 shot in the rear guard during the first months of the uprising. In fact the *requetés* showed their mettle from the very first day of the war. There were several "incidents" in the Plaza de Castillo of Pamplona during the afternoon of 18 July 1936, and at the end of one altercation the *requetés* killed their young opponent (Flandes Aldeyturriaga 1988: 142). On the number of deaths in Navarre, see Altaffaylla Kultur Taldea 1986; Jimeno Jurio 1988. On the involvement of certain Navarrese priests in these killings, and for an example of *requetés* stealing from a chaplain, see Saralegui Lorea 1991.

Carlist writers also fail to mention that some *requetés* strongly suspected that Franco and his generals were using them as cannon fodder. As these soldiers put it, "We're not Senegalese"—a slighting reference to the Moroccan battalions within the Nationalist army who were deployed as shock troops and suffered a very high level of fatalities. The troops were in fact from northwest Africa, not Senegal, but the epithet stuck. (Cf. Santa Cruz, 18(1): 109 n; 20: 26 n.)

12. Pérez de Olaguer 1937: 70; López-Sanz 1963: 150, 159.

13. López-Sanz 1963: 180, 184. See also Redondo and Zavala 1957; Revilla Cebrecos 1975: 47.

14. Baleztena and Astiz 1944: 73; López-Sanz 1963: 169, 225, 232, 236. These Carlist authors, keen to concentrate on the saintly behavior of the *requetés,* make light of almost any hardship the soldiers had to bear. Indeed the *requetés,* like the Falangists, were better fed and militarily supplied than other units within the insurgent army.

15. López-Sanz 1963: 150, 182, 220; García Escudero 1975: 148, quoted in Sánchez 1987: 153; the nurse's quotation comes from Fraser 1979: 311. Antonio Molle Lazo, twenty-one years old, from Cadiz, a *requeté* in the regiment of Nuestra Señora de la Merced, was killed in the first months of the war. "After suffering great tortures and mutilations on his body while in opposition to the blasphemies and insults of

his enemies, he responded with shouts of the most blessed heroism, 'Long live Christ the King! Long live Spain!'" (from a holy card asking for prayers toward his beatification. See also Sánchez Carracedo 1940; Sarabia 1940).

16. Santa Cruz 1979–1992, vol. 5: 238; Frazer 1979: 312.

17. Cia Navascués 1941: 75; López-Sanz 1963: 94, 103.

18. Cia Navascués 1941: 136, 232; López-Sanz 1963: 205.

19. Kemp 1957: 80, 92; 1990: 48, 58; Urra Lusarreta 1957; Caro Baroja 1980: 238; Sánchez 1987: 107.

20. Cia Navascués 1941: 134; García Sanchiz 1943: 42; *El Pensamiento Navarro* (hereafter *PN*), 8 May 1954, p. 8; 9 May 1954, p. 10; López-Sanz 1963: 97. For a paean to the crosses of the Carlist regiments, see *PN*, 5 May 1957, p. 8.

21. López-Sanz 1963: 152. For further examples of soldier's salvation from otherwise certain death by the direct intervention of God, see López-Sanz 1963: 180–84.

22. "Los nietos del Cid," Romero Raizábal 1938: 279–80; López-Sanz 1966: 180. To García Sanchiz, "the requetés fought in flights of archangels, with neither cruelty nor greed, communing before combat, praying at its end. . . . They did not fight: they split, as in the Apocalypse, the cup of the Lord's ire" (1943: 36).

23. Cia Navascués 1941: 144; López-Sanz 1963; 1966; Domenech Puig 1956; Reig Tapia 1988. Some of those fighting on the other side had a similarly apocalyptic and Manichaean vision of the war (see Sperber 1974).

24. Carlos Quinto, como el Cid,
vuelve, muerto, a batallar.
Tomás de Zumalacárregui,
el buen soldado leal,
de su herida en Begoña
ha conseguido sanar.
Al lado de sus nietos,
abuelos y padres, van
los bisabuelos de Estella,
las sombras de San Marcial.
Todos se meten en filas,
¡ay, mi Dios que manantial! . . .
General Emilio Mola,
llevas un siglo detras:
¡que es como llevar delante,
cautiva, la Eternidad!
(By José María Peman, quoted in Aróstegui Sánchez 1988: 11)

25. Romero Raizábal 1938: 293–96.

26. "Romance de los tres sitios de Bilbao," Casariego 1945: 39–40.

27. García Sanchiz 1943: 42; López-Sanz 1966 passim; Resa 1968: 1; Burgo 1970: 29.

28. Fussell 1988: 222–31; 1989.

29. Casariego 1975.

30. Claramunt 1937: 9.

31. Carlos Cruz Rodríguez, quoted in García Serrano 1964: 493–94.

32. Etayo 1990: 38; Lee 1991: 90–91.

33. Blinkhorn 1984: 79. On the Carlists' successful petition to Mussolini for arms and training, see Lizarza Iribarren 1953: 45–49; Burgo 1970: 517–20; Saz Campos 1986: 66–73.

34. Aróstegui 1988.

35. Aróstegui 1991: 64–65.

36. García Serrano 1964: 499.

37. "Cálzame las alpargatas, dáme la boina, dáme el fusil, / Que voy a matar mas Rojos que flores tiene el mes de April." "*Rojo*" was a modern substitute for "*guiri*" in this traditional Carlist song (García Serrano 1992: 66–69).

38. Claramunt 1937: 11, 34.

39. Pérez de Olaguer 1937: 77–78; García Sanchiz 1943: 40; Ministerio de Cultura 1989.

40. The history of the Margaritas has yet to be written, though there is an illuminating section on their development in Navarre in Pascual 1988: 299–302. See also Fernández and Roda 1998: 183–84. It is significant that in Álava in the 1910s, Carlists opposed to what they saw as the self-interested machinations of the movement's provincial elite presented their own slate of candidates in local elections. Considering themselves representatives of a popular, authentic, simple, self-sacrificial Carlism, forever loyal to its principles, members of this faction called themselves "*los margaritos*," after Doña Margarita, whose supposed "simplicity" was taken to personify their understanding of Carlism (Real Cuesta 1991: 92).

41. Codón Fernández 1959.

42. García Sanchiz 1943: 7; López-Sanz 1963: 20, 160, 184; 1966: 24; Resa 1968: 37.

43. Yo quiero subir al cielo
    escalón por escalón
    para darle un abrazo
    a don Jaime de Borbón (López-Sanz 1963: 229)

44. López-Sanz 1966: 5, 24; Prayer book of the Hermandad de la Vía-Crucis de Montejurra; *Montejurra* 25: 21, 23; Christian 1972: 132, 177–78; Nicholls 1989. The quote is from Antoñana 1990: 18–19. On the paternal associations of the Carlist idea of monarchy in the First Carlist War, see Pan-Montojo 1990: 147.

45. Pérez de Olaguer 1937: 84; Romero Raizábal 1952: 35–41; *PN*, 12 May 1954, p. 10; López-Sanz 1963: 158, 229; Resa 1968: 12. There is a sculpture of the Hernandorena trio in the Carlist Museum in Pamplona. One seventy-four-year-old *requeté* is reported to have transferred himself from the Bilbao front to that of Madrid because the heavy rain in the Basque Country affected his health (Pérez de Olaguer 1937: 147–54).

46. Resa 1968: 8. These are the first lines of the "Oriamendi," the Carlist anthem:
    Por Dios, por la Patria y el Rey
    lucharon nuestros padres,
    y por Dios, por la Patria y el Rey
    lucharemos nosotros tambien.

47. Resa 1968: 12.

48. López-Sanz 1963: 162; Resa 1968: 19.

49. López-Sanz 1963: 14, 28, 148, 166; 1966: 91; *PN,* 3 May 1964, p. 20; *Montejurra* 11; *Diccionario de la lengua española.* For further examples, see Pérez de Olaguer 1937: 97, and García Sanchiz 1943: 42.

50. López-Sanz 1963: 171, 173, 183; 1966: 114; Barreiro Fernández 1976: 165; Burgo 1978a: 123. Similar events are described in Pérez de Olaguer 1937: 75, 157–63. For another Basque example of the political exploitation of particular kinds of berets as partisan headgear, see Pablo 1995: 57–58.

51. *PN,* 4 May 1965, p. 16; Marqués de Marchelina, "La ofrenda al Apóstol," *Montejurra* 12.

52. Cia Navascués 1941: 104–7.

53. Kemp 1957: 103. It was thanks to the *requetés* that the success of the insurrection in Navarre had been so speedy and so complete, and that the initial bridgeheads of the insurgents in Aragón, Gipuzkoa, and especially Madrid had been maintained. For a surprisingly honest assessment, by a socialist, of the strategic contribution of the *requetés* in the early days of the war, see "El tributo pagado por los carlistas," *La Lucha de Clases,* Bilbao, 28 May 1937 (reprinted in Garmendia 1975: 83–84).

CHAPTER THREE. VILLAGE CARLISM

1. Kemp 1957: 26.

2. *Católogo Monumental de Navarra* 1984: 409–26; Iriarte and Chocarro 1990.

3. One of the earliest references to the area comes from a French pilgrim who made the journey in the twelfth century. He and his companions stopped by the river to let their horses drink. There

we met two Navarrese sitting on the bank, sharpening their knives, used to skin pilgrims' horses that had drunk that water and died. In answer to our questions, they lied that it was good to drink. Because of this, we watered our horses there and straight away two of them died, which the pair immediately skinned. (Picaud 1951)

4. Haranburu 1983, vol. 2: 272.

5. Floristán Imízcoz 1982: 296–97; Martín Duque 1986, vol. 2: 169–70, 208.

6. Floristán Imízcoz 1982: 289–91; Martín Duque 1986, vol. 2: 172, 208.

7. Padrón 1879, caja 96, AMC. The occupation of one man was given as "proletarian." Analysis of the occupational composition of Cirauqui is complicated by the fact that an unspecified (presumably small) number of widows who worked their late husbands' holdings (*viuda labradoras*) are included in the number of *labradores.* Also, the list does not include the number of local women who worked as servants for the more wealthy.

8. This unequal access of locals to land was common throughout Navarre: see, e.g., Gerónimo de Uztariz-en Lur Lantaldea 1991.

9. Real Cuesta 1991: 90–92.

10. Some of this land had already been sold once before. For example, in 1842, the town hall of Cirauqui sold by reversion contract ten *corralizas* (farms, or stock-yards), which, once recovered, were sold again in 1864 and 1869 (Floristán Imízcoz 1993: 291 n. 18).

11. *¡¡Trabajadores!! Organo de la UGT en Navarra,* 7 October 1932; Donézar 1975: 292, 295; Floristán Imízcoz 1982: 96, 289–90, 296–97; Haranburu 1983, vol. 2: 270; Martín Duque 1986, vol. 1: 208.

12. Azcona y Diaz de Rada 1938, qtd. in Burgo 1978a: 840. See also Furley 1876: 100.

13. Idoate 1966: 324–27.

14. *Enciclopedia General* 1976, vol. 7: 186.

15. Secretaría correspondencia, caja 72, AMC. In the first week of April that year the town hall informed the military governor that a "horrible and outrageous act" had been committed in the village. But no further details are given.

16. Secretaría correspondencia, caja 72, AMC. For plans of the fort of San Isidro, see nos. 467 and 527, Servicio Geográfico del Ejercito, AGN; Martinena Ruíz 1989: 191, 194.

17. Dorregaray's first message to the leader of the Voluntarios in Cirauqui and his reply are reproduced in Montoya 1874: 70–72. Information on the massacre comes from a transcript from Hoja Matriz de Servicios, Arma de Caballería, AGM, in López Andono 1990: 8; transcript of manuscript, *La II Guerra Carlista,* by "Gorriti of Puente," in the author's possession; Pirala 1877, vol. 4: 449; Ferrer 1954, vol. 25: 79–80; García-Sanz Marcotegui 1985: 111–21. The quotation comes from "Parte detallado que el Jefe de la fuerza de voluntarios de la Republica de Cirauqui pasa al Sr. Gobernador civil de la provincia, sobre los horribles asesinatos perpetrados por el grueso de las facciones el dia 13 de la fecha," in Montoya 1874: 73–80. Gorriti insists that he personally witnessed the events at Cirauqui "from the first to the last, and no one can contradict me."

18. Transcript of manuscript, *La II Guerra Carlista,* by "Gorriti of Puente," in the author's possession.

19. Legajo "Quintas 1871–1879," caja 88, AMC; legajo "1875. Diputación. Relaciones de ayudas a emigrados AD 11 y 29 septiembre 1875," no. 40, AADN.

20. Legajo "1877–78. Guerras Carlistas. Expedientes sobre indemnizaciones. Denegaciones. Estella," AADN.

21. Transcript of manuscript, *La II Guerra Carlista,* by "Gorriti of Puente," in the author's possession; Nuñez de Cepeda, in López Andono 1990: 6; Rodríguez de Coro 1991a: 114.

22. "Libro de actos de lealtad tradicionalista de Cirauqui," APCN.

23. "Juzgado de Cirauqui sentencias," 1932, nos. 16 and 17; 1933, no. 1, caja 14, AMC. For another example of political insults leading to a fight, see "Juzgado de Cirauqui juicios verbales," 1936, no.3, caja 15, AMC.

24. Lapeskera 1993: 90.

25. 1933, no. 191, AJE; Sentencias, 22 August 1933, caja 14, AMC; "Libro de actas del ayuntamiento de Cirauqui," 21 August 1933; *La Voz de Navarra*, 17 March 1934; Majuelo Gil 1989: 216.

26. 1933, nos. 69, 84, 130; 1934, nos. 276 and 294; 1935, nos. 2 and 149, AJE.

27. *¡¡Trabajadores!!*, 26 January, 23 February 1934; 1934, no. 12, AJE; Altaffaylla Kultur Taldea 1986: 401; Majuelo 1989: 231.

28. "Libro de actas . . . ," 1934, 8 April, 22 April, 6 May, AMC; Altaffaylla Kultur Taldea 1986: 401.

29. For examples of violent crimes, and one case of incest, committed in Cirauqui at the beginning of the twentieth century, see Lapeskera 1993: 88–91.

30. Legajo 1980, causa no. 50, Sala de lo Penal, AATP. Unfortunately, while this archive includes a docket of all the cases dealt with in 1914, the papers dealing with the riot in Cirauqui have not been filed. García-Sanz Marcotegui 1984: 36 n. 4 lists a series of violent disputes between Carlists and their opponents, and of politically provocative acts committed by Carlists, which occurred between 1914 and 1923, and which were judged at the provincial court in Pamplona.

31. Majuelo Gil 1989; Blinkhorn 1991.

32. The election, on 26 April 1936, was held to vote for the *compromisarios* (delegates), who together with the deputies in the Cortes would elect the next president of the Republic (Mañas Leache and Urabayen Mihura 1988).

33. For details of the killings, see Altaffaylla Kultur Taldea 1986: 402–3.

34. This female pressure was nothing new. In the First Carlist War, a liberal officer in Navarre observed that the women of the towns "pour out abuse on the heads of those whom they see withdrawing (from the Carlist ranks), obliging them in this way to return to their companies" (Bonet 1835: 7, qtd. in Coverdale 1984: 296). In the second war, according to the contemporary commentator and Estellan Carlist Cesareo Montoya, "women animated the timid, aroused the lukewarm, and insulted the indifferent" (qtd. in Antoñana 1990: 31). The data from which the military statistics are derived come from Pascual 1988.

35. Legajo 21, carpeta 3, Junta General de Navarra, AGN; list of subscribers to the *Gaceta de Oñate* (the official bulletin of Don Carlos), Fondo "Carlistas" de la Real Academia de la Historia; Bonet 1835. I thank J. Pan-Montojo for these references.

36. "Quintas 1871–1879," caja 88, AMC; "Legajo de socorros de presentados carlistas y emigrados 1875–76," Serie Guerras Carlistas, AADN.

37. Legajo "1877–78. Guerras Carlistas. Expedientes sobre indemnizaciones. Denegaciones. Estella," AADN.

38. *El Pensamiento Navarro* (hereafter *PN*), 7 March 1906, qtd. in García-Sanz Marcotegui 1992: 33 n. 47.

39. Quoted in Zaratiegui Labiano 1996: 190. On people within the electoral district of Estella deciding whom they would vote for depending on the favors they were promised, see García-Sanz Marcotegui 1990a: 458–59.

40. García-Sanz Marcotegui 1990b: 21.

41. For details of all elections in Cirauqui between March 1871 and June 1931,

see cajas 71, 91, 125, 141, 166, 181, 210, AMC. Of all the national and provincial elections held during this period, the only ones mentioned in the text are those where I have been able to ascertain the political affiliation of all the candidates. For some details on these candidates, see Pérez Goyena 1962, vol. 8: 58, 80, 87, 176, 241, 250, 256, 487, 572; 1964, vol. 9: 143, 273, 466; García-Sanz Marcotegui 1992. The politics of Navarre during this period have been very little studied; the only relevant works of note are Mina Apat 1985 and García-Sanz Marcotegui 1992.

42. Virto Ibañez 1987; Serrano Moreno 1989: 761; caja 210, AMC.

43. "El Carlismo," two programs of *Espacios y tiempos*, Radio Nacional Española, broadcast in Navarre, March 1987.

44. "Santa Visita Pastoral de Ilzarbe," caja 205, no. 29, AAP.

45. Caja 283, no. 99, AAP; Apesteguia 1988: 42–43.

46. Caja 302, no. 235, AAP.

47. Caja A/13, no. 119 (1820), AAP; Fraser 1979: 125. Catholicism saturated the provincial way of life. To Carlists of central Navarre, soaking a gory blanket to make a bloody solution, as the *requetés* restoring the church at Villanueva de Argecilla had done, was an act with symbolic precedent: according to legend in that area, wine, not water, wetted the cement for the building of several churches— homes of the mystical transformation of Communion wine into the blood of God. A further example of the association of stone with the lasting power of blood are the stains supposedly left on the walls by the corpses of the murdered Voluntarios.

48. Caja 175, no. 125, AAP; caja 179, no. 126, AAP; national statistics from *Guia de la Iglesia en España* 1967: 19, 61–124; survey by R. Duocastella in *Social Compass* 12 (December 1965); both quoted in Lannon 1987: 10, 92. On the social origin and sacerdotal training of the Navarrese clergy in the first decades of the twentieth century, see Pazos 1990.

49. Caja 29, no. 41, AAP; caja 38, no. 45, AAP; caja 39, no. 32, AAP; "Quintas," caja 88, AMC.

50. "Libro de actas," 1931, AMC; Altaffaylla Kultur Taldea 1986: 401. Christian interprets the phenomenon of moving crucifixes, which occurred in the years following the First World War in—among other places—the Navarrese villages of Piedramillera and Mañeru as indirect reactions to Catholic villagers' sense of their church being under siege from aggressively atheistic left-wing groups. The apparitions of Mary in 1931 in Mendigorría (a parish contiguous to that of Cirauqui) and in Ezquioga, Gipuzkoa, may be partially understood in the same sociopolitical manner (see Christian 1987, 1992, 1996).

51. This overlaying of the memory of the later war on that of the earlier one appears to be a phenomenon general to the Basque area. Coverdale notes that the surviving folk material on the First Carlist War is quite small: only a few songs have been collected by local ethnologists. At the beginning of the twentieth century, the novelist Pío Baroja found the memory of the first war alive only among men who had actually lived through it. He did not come across any living oral tradition about this war among the younger generation (Coverdale 1984: 301 n. 31).

52. Even Paul Preston (1990: 10, 24), the distinguished, usually temperate, British

historian of Spain, refers to the Comunión as "maniacally anti-modern," to the
Requeté as a "fanatical militia," and to Carlists in general as "troglodytic."

53. Dos Carlistas juntos bien, tres y bronca seguro.

Siempre amigos de la pólvora.

Los Carlistas andan por los montes como los conejos
y no se atreven a salir porque están llenos de piojos.

El Carlista es un animal de cresta roja,
pasta en los montes de Navarra.
Cuando comulga ataca al hombre.
Y al grito de "¡Viva Cristo-Rey!"
ataca a todo Dios.

According to Antoñana (1990: 18), Carlos VII was known by his Madrid detractors
as "King of the *Alcornoques*" [cork oaks, blockheads], "King of the Forests," and
"King of the Jungles."

54. Urabayen 1988 (1924): 86.

55. The child who inherited the land was usually burdened for many years with
obligatory payments to his siblings to compensate them for their landless inheritance. Parents would divide their land equally among their children only if all of
them had married heirs or heiresses. For further details on modes of inheritance in
Cirauqui, see MacClancy 1991.

56. Basques used to throw a handful of salt into the fire when a bad sign was
observed (Caro Baroja [1949] 1971: 301); the ashes from the New Year fire were
thought to have healing properties; and to prevent bad spirits descending into the
house via the chimney, Basques made a cross in the ashes (Arraiza 1930). See also
Azurmendi 1988. On the central role of ashes in ritual form and function in Basque
culture, see Zulaika 1987, 1988: 330–32.

57. In the nearby valley of the Amescoas, twenty kilometers to the west of Cirauqui, most people used to stipulate in their wills that part of their estate was to
be spent on Masses and responsories performed for the sake of their souls. According to Luciano Lapuente Martínez, the native ethnographer of the Amescoas, bereaved kin were scrupulous about fulfilling the religious wishes of the dead. He
emphasizes how much the locals used to enjoy performing responsories over the
tombs of the dead. On important dates in the liturgical calendar, at the end of High
Mass, the priest would come down from the altar and sing a responsory in the
center of the church. He would then visit the tombs where women had lit candles
for responsories.

On the two days dedicated to the memory of the dead, All Souls' Day and the
Day of Saint Lazarus (the Monday of Holy Week), the whole village attended
Mass. At the end of the service, the priest gave out bread, which housewives
had offered up, to the children and adolescents of the village. Afterward, people
prayed responsories over the tombs of members of their nuclear and trunk families. They had also spent all the preceding afternoon performing the same prayers
over the remains of their dead kin (Lapuente Martínez 1971: 146–48).

58. The native ethnographers of San Martín de Unx, a village thirty kilometers to the southeast of Cirauqui, emphasize the importance of the family home as a concrete reminder of their dead:

> The house . . . is the ambit within which those kin now dead spent their lives and who left within its walls part of their spirit. If on the walls of the house hang photographs (of that primitive "studio" type) of the parents or grandparents, it is not by chance, but because the house still belongs to them in some sense. . . . When the memory of the deceased is truly accepted, one tries at every moment to improve the house, to keep it clean, because one's ancestors lived in it and, it is thought, that is what they would have done (Zubiaur and Zubiaur 1980: 104).

59. Lhande Heguy 1975 (1907): 73. In a similar fashion, Carlists could argue that their movement merited respect *because* of its age (e.g., Rego Nieto 1985: 77).

60. It is possible that this statement of familial steadfastness was heightened by contrast with those Carlist families in the neighboring provinces of Bizkaia and Gipuzkoa who had converted to Basque nationalism in the late nineteenth and early twentieth centuries.

61. When the red beret was placed on the head of Prince Felix Lichnowsky, a Prussian general who had come to participate in the Carlist campaign of the 1870s, "it appeared to him a solemn initation was being carried out" (Burgo 1985: 11). Don Cayetano, *requeté* brother of Don Javier, the Carlist pretender, was buried with his red beret on (*Montejurra* 15). In 1987, the Partido Carlista paid tribute to an old soldier who had climbed Montejurra every year that he was physically capable. In a simple ceremony, he was officially presented with a specially embroidered red beret.

62. Valle 1985: 131–34; Larrañaga and Pérez 1988: 23–29. In a rural parish of Santander in the 1960s, women assumed "control of all affairs pertaining to the spiritual well-being of the household," while men's "relationship to the divine was generally less affective and more instrumental" (Christian 1972: 134, 171).

63. Don Cayetano, the *requeté* brother of Don Javier, hung round his neck a gold relic containing a splinter of the true cross, given him by his mother and which his father had worn in battle during the Second Carlist War (Santa Cruz 1979–1992, vol. 2: 34).

Detentes became so popular that a small market in them arose. During 1938 and 1939, an advertisement for the sale of metal versions was placed in issues of the religious periodical *El Mensajero del Corazón de Jesus*: "Lithographically colored metal *detentes*, of equal size to the enclosed engraving, bordered with the national colors, provided with a safety pin. Extremely valuable for making a public display of enthusiastic love for the most loved Heart and for claiming its protection in the frontline and in the rearguard" (qtd. in Sánchez Erauskin 1994: 57 n. 9).

In the "Album Carlista," an illustrated scrapbook kept by a Navarrese during the Second Carlist War (today stored in the Archivo General de Navarra) is the detente of a Carlist soldier killed in action with a bloody bullet hole through it.

64. On the Mother of God as a role model for Spanish women, see Kenny 1962: 79; Larrañaga and Pérez 1988: 29–33; Martín Gaite 1987: 107–8. Caro Baroja emphasizes the importance that devotion to the Virgin in her diverse avatars has had in Spain (1969: 123).

Many *requeté* regiments had a Marian image embroidered into their flag. The men of each unit venerated their chosen manifestation of the Virgin who, in turn, protected them; in some cases, the particular Marian image was strongly associated with the area from which the regiment drew its men. Even the personal standard of the pretender in the First Carlist War had an image of the Sorrowing Virgin, embroidered by his wife (*PN,* 11 May 1954, pp. 8, 10). On the military mobilization of the Marian cult by Primo de Rivera and Franco, see Perry and Echevarria 1988: 163–68, 203–19.

65. *Montejurra* 11: 19.

66. 1940: 165.

67. In his novel *¡Llevaban su sangre!,* the Navarrese writer López-Sanz employs the term for those "big poofters [*mariposones*] and fickle persons [*veletas,* lit. 'weathercocks'] who dance to the tune of political changes" (1966: 32).

68. In the late nineteenth century in Navarrese politics, those who switched sides (e.g., oscillating from integrism to Carlism and through to conservatism and back again) were chided as "mestizos" (people of mixed race) (García-Sanz Marcotegui 1992). The choice of this particular metaphor underlines the efforts of locals to naturalize the cultural, to portray political allegiance in biological terms. For if commitment to a party was regarded as pure and as lasting as membership in a definable "race," then a person who switched parties was as impure and as despicable as mestizos were then seen to be.

CHAPTER FOUR. POSTWAR CARLISM

1. José Angel Zubiaur, interview by author, Pamplona, 24 September 1990.

2. Carlist disenchantment with unification grew as their representation within the FET diminished: they were given eleven of the fifty seats on the First National Council of the Movimiento, but their numbers were not increased when the Second National Council was expanded to a membership of ninety. With the Germanophile Falange in the ascendant as the Axis Powers appeared to win battle after battle, informal encounters in cities between groups of Carlists and Falangists were frequently uneasy and sometimes turned violent. *Requetés* were irritated by the standardization of militia dress: in the Victory Parade held in Madrid to celebrate the end of the Civil War, they were particularly bitter about the order to march in blue shirts, the uniform of the Falange. In official ceremonies, Carlists who did not make the obligatory fascist salute during the hymns sung at the end of the proceedings were often set upon by righteous Falangists. Religious gatherings staged by *requetés* were frequently followed by brief, spontaneous demonstrations, then fistfights with Falangists waiting outside the church or nearby, and finally the in-

tervention of the police (López Rodó 1977: 28; Marquine Barrio 1982). For further examples of violent encounters between Carlists and Falangists, see Santa Cruz 1979–1992, vol. 1: 114, 124; vol. 4: 106–11; vol. 5: 220, 229, 237; vol. 7: 72–73; Heine 1983; Cubero Sánchez 1991: 19–20; Preston 1993: 334.

In August 1942, the clash between the two forces took a more deadly turn and had much wider consequences. On the ninth of that month, six thousand Carlists gathered in Tolosa, Gipuzkoa, to commemorate the liberation of the city: many spent the whole day of celebration, not in church, but skirmishing with members of the Falange. Eight days later, General José Enrique Varela, minister of war and a traditionalist sympathizer, attended a special Mass in the basilica of Begoña in Bilbao for the souls of *requetés* who had died in the war. As the Carlists left the church, shouting "Long live the King!" and anti-Franco slogans, Falangists threw two grenades into the crowd, wounding a dozen people. After order had been restored, Varela visited the secret Circle within the city, and found the Carlists there busy handing out pistols. He argued with them that military leaders in the country were always ready to overlook *requeté* activities and to intercede on their behalf, so long as they did not take up arms. The men left the pistols in their places.

Franco responded to this incident, which provoked the first serious crisis of his regime, by administering his brand of Solomonic justice: in order to maintain the balance of "families" within his government, he dismissed representatives of the two groups involved. Both Varela and Ramón Serrano Súñer, Franco's brother-in-law and secretary-general of the FET, were sacked. The exact intentions of the grenade throwers remain obscure, but most Falangists understood their action as a critique of traditionalist monarchism and of Franco's insufficiently pro-Axis line; Varela publicly interpreted it as a Falangist attack on the army. Although one of the perpetrators of the incident was executed, senior Carlists were resentful that the rest were amnestied soon afterward. In reaction to these events, many of them, including Rodezno, resigned from their posts in the Movimiento (López Rodó 1977: 28; Santa Cruz 1979–1992, vol. 4: 122–24, 134; Heine 1983: 280; Ellwood 1987: 84–90; Preston 1993: 465–66).

3. Santa Cruz 1979–1992, vol. 10: 133.

4. Santa Cruz 1979–1992, vol. 13: 32; 14: 150.

5. For examples of the traditionalist collaborationists' opposition to the implementation of fascist policies, see López Rodó 1977: 31, 128–32, 133–35, 516–19, 559–61; Arrese 1982: 171–81; Payne 1987: 260, 447–48; Toquero 1989: 267.

6. Equipo Mundo 1970: 63–64, 107–10, 233–36, 389–92; López Rodó 1977: 19; Miguel 1978: 173.

7. It is noteworthy that outside of Navarre and the Basque Country, Carlists were given relatively few posts in the new nationwide hierarchies. The Navarrese deputies to their own Foral Deputation and to the Cortes for the Franquist period are listed in Floristán Imízcoz 1986, vol. 2: 125.

8. Cubero Sánchez 1991: 9–11.

9. Alfonso Carlos, in a letter to Esteban Bilbao written shortly before the death of the aged pretender, stated that he had chosen Don Javier as regent because of

his exemplary character and because he was, according to Alfonso Carlos's reading of Carlist genealogy, the rightful heir, after Alfonso Carlos himself, to the Carlist claim to the Spanish throne (sections of the letter are quoted in an interview with Esteban Bilbao in *La Actualidad Española*, no. 883 [5 December 1968]).

10. C. de Borbón-Parma 1997.

11. Bourbon-Parma 1949. On 5 May 1957, at the very same time that his eldest son, Hugues, was speaking at the annual Carlist ceremony of Montejurra "in the name of my father the King," Don Javier was attending a gathering in France organized by Le Souvenir Vendeen, where he spoke "in the name of the Most Christian Royalty of France" (Santa Cruz 1979–1992, vol. 18 [I]: 77). For the *carlosocta-vista* reaction to his presence there, see ¡*Carlistas!*, September 1957.

12. Santa Cruz 1979–1992, vol. 11: 158–62.

13. Santa Cruz 1979–1992, vol. 9: 50; 17: 224–27.

14. Romero Raizábal 1972; Blinkhorn 1975: 230, 301; Clemente 1977: 127–31.

15. Santa Cruz 1979–1992, vol. 2: 5–8.

16. Santa Cruz 1979–1992, vol. 6: 151–57.

17. Burgo 1970: 450–62; Blinkhorn 1975: 85–88, 228ff.; Santa Cruz 1979–1992, vol. 4: 87–88; vol. 5: 132; vol. 6: 5, 40; vol. 7: 9, 17; vol. 8: 5–10; Cubero Sánchez 1991: 8.

18. Melgar 1964: 142, 146; Burgo 1970: 450–62; López Rodó 1977: 35, 64; Arrese 1982: 172; Toquero 1988: 238–41; 1989: 175–78.

19. Burgo 1970: 444–46, 484–86; "Con las manos arriba y bandera blanca," *Montejurra* 58 (February 1971): 4; Dionisio Ridruejo, qtd. by Clemente in *Montejurra* 56 (December 1970): 56; Clemente 1977: 35; Arrese 1982: 154, 173; Heine 1983: 281–83. For statements of the *carlosoctavista* political program, see Cora y Lira 1953; Clemente 1977: 185–93.

20. Romero Raizábal 1936: 95. Some *carlosoctavistas* argued that his genealogical claim to the Carlist crown was much stronger than that of Don Javier. Jaime del Burgo, for instance, has argued that Carlos V, as the first Carlist king, established a new dynasty, one separate from that of his brother Ferdinand VII, in the same way that Phillip V had established the Spanish Borbón dynasty by separating himself from the French line of Louis XIV. When Alfonso Carlos died, the legitimate inheritance therefore passed, not to any descendant of Carlos V's siblings (such as Don Javier), but to the late pretender's closest living kin, Doña Blanca, mother of Carlos VIII, sister of Jaime III, and brother's daughter of Alfonso Carlos.

21. Santa Cruz 1979–1992, vol. 5: 5–23; vol. 6: 128–50; vol. 9: 299; vol. 12: 175.

22. Heine estimates that by the end of the 1940s, the political weight of the *carlosoctavistas* was similar to that of the *falcondista* and collaborationist sectors of Carlism (1983: 282). Of course, many of the *carlosoctavistas were* collaborators.

23. On the 1945 incident, see Villanueva 1997. One traditionalist told me that in the early 1950s in Madrid, he and his *falcondista* friends would spend their Saturdays hunting *carlosoctavistas* to beat up. See also Heine 1983: 282–83.

As happened in Pamplona, the only Circle open in Barcelona was officially closed after an armed skirmish between Carlists and the police (Cubero Sánchez · 1990).

24. Santa Cruz 1979–1992, vol. 11: 34–49.

25. Santa Cruz 1979–1992, vol. 9: 179–84, 228.

26. Santa Cruz 1979–1992, vol. 11: 45, 97–98; vol. 12: 93–94.

27. Burgo 1970: 462; Santa Cruz 1979–1992, vol. 11: 117, 134–37, 153; vol. 12: 101.

28. Santa Cruz 1979–1992, vol. 11: 6, 157.

29. Melgar 1964: 147–48; Burgo 1970: 465–66; Santa Cruz 1979–1992, vol. 12: 33–46, 121; vol. 13: 71–79; vol. 14: 5–37, 106–7.

30. Payne 1987: 349–55.

31. The threat, though distant, could at times appear very real: in 1944, 10,000 Communist *maquis* had briefly entered the country via the Aran valley, and sporadic guerrilla activity continued until the early 1950s. Don Javier also did his bit from his base in Paris. Any information he collected from his trawl of chancelleries about maneuvers against Spain was sent to Carlists who transmitted it on to the Generalísimo via friends in the army.

32. Santa Cruz 1979–1992, vol. 6: 119, 124–25; vol. 7: 48, 65, 100, 207; vol. 8: 141, 168, 173; vol. 9: 35, 77; vol. 10: 7–15.

33. "Declaración del Principe Regente don Javier de Borbón-Parma al Generalíssimo don Francisco Franco Bahamonde," 7 May 1947, in Clemente 1977: 294–95; López Rodó 1977: 90.

34. Santa Cruz 1979–1992, vol. 9: 156.

35. Santa Cruz 1979–1992, vol. 10: 41.

36. Fusi 1987: 66–68; Payne 1987: 372–80; Santa Cruz 1979–1992, vol. 9: 82–83, 108, 156.

37. Shortly after the meeting, Franco, writing in the Falangist newspaper *Arriba*, took the most unusual step of openly criticizing the Comunión. Prominent Carlists in Navarre and Gipuzkoa, surprised and upset by the article, wrote official notes against the meeting. Even though the leadership of the Comunión did take the step of publishing an open note criticizing the meeting, fears persisted among *javieristas* that their pretender would renounce his rights in favor of Don Juan.

38. Santa Cruz 1979–1992, vol. 10: 162; vol. 11: 180; vol. 12: 106, 192; vol. 13: 52, 69, 90, 187; vol. 17: 238. On the attempts to advance the cause of Carlos VIII's brothers, see *El Diario de Navarra*, 1 April 1964; Burgo 1970: 470; Preciado 1975; López Rodó 1977: 302–3, 623–26. As late as 1958, the leaders of the *carlosoctavista* wing, which promoted the claim of "Carlos IX," the Archduke Antonio, brother of the late pretender, still felt their cause had sufficient promise for it to be worth continuing to publish two periodicals, *¡Firmes!* and *¡Carlistas!*, as well as to set up a new Carlist association, the Amigos de Vázquez de Mella (Santa Cruz 1979–1992, vol. 19 [II]: 205, 213; vol. 20: 124). It seems, remarkably, that there are still some *carlosoctavistas* today: see, for example, "The Real King of the Spanish Tradition. Carlos VIII (1943–1953)" on the Web site http://caltrap.bbsnet.com/realking.htm. On the bizarre history of the bogus pretender "Carlos X," the self-styled Duque

de Santiago de Compostela, see "An unknown Carlist pretender" on http://caltrap.bbsnet.com/annexiii.htm.

39. Burgo 1970: 446–70.

40. Burgo 1970: 476.

41. Santa Cruz 1979–1992, vol. 17: 140. A copy of Zamanillo's personal testimony of the sacking of Fal Conde is reproduced in Echevarría 1986: 183–85.

42. Toquero 1989: 241, 249.

CHAPTER FIVE. THE RISE OF THE PROGRESSIVES

1. Lannon 1987: 248–52. For Don Javier's views on the postconciliar position of the Church in Spain, see *La Iglesia Católica en España. Informe sobre la situación actual. Dirigido al Presidente de la Conferencia Episcopal Española, por Don Javier de Borbón Parma*, March 1974 (copy of this pamphlet in APCT).

2. At a meeting of the National Council in Madrid in January 1956, Don Javier, cornered by adamant Basque Carlists, had publicly accepted the legitimate succession to the Spanish monarchy, to the great irritation of Iturmendi and his cohort, who had arranged Don Javier's entry into the country on the understanding that he was going to relieve himself of much of his Carlist commitments. José Maria Valiente tried to assuage the ruffled *carlofranquistas* by writing a note for Don Javier disclaiming his declaration (Burgo 1970: 477–78).

3. *Sivattistas* were not going to be led by a pretender who had sacked Sivatte and had betrayed the original "spirit of 18 July" by telling his people to cooperate with the degenerate regime and the hated Movimiento. "Proclama a los Españoles," Regencia de Estella, April 1958; *Tiempos Criticos*, no. 36 (June 1958); Santa Cruz 1979–1992, vol. 20: 7.

4. Melgar 1964: 146–51; López Rodó 1977: 128, 139, 149, 152; Santa Cruz 1979–1992, vol. 19 (II): 245–318. The exclamation is quoted in Aronson 1966: 222.

5. Blinkhorn 1990: 191–92.

6. López Rodó 1977: 201.

7. Santa Cruz 1979–1992, vol. 20: 87.

8. *Times* (London), 11 March 1955, p. 6; 11 March 1960, p. 11.

9. Lavardín 1976: 45–47. In February 1961, Valiente and Zamanillo helped to squash a maneuver against the regime by the College of Lawyers (Salgado-Araujo 1976: 312).

10. At the meeting, Franco gave his consent to the dissemination of Carlist propaganda and to the opening of Vázquez de Mella Circles. The following year he included five Carlists among the 97 *procuradores* he nominated to the Cortes. He also permitted the creation of the Hermandad Nacional de Antiguos Combatientes de los Tercios de Requetés (National Brotherhood of the Veterans of the Requeté Regiments).

11. P. J. Zabala, "Evolución Carlista," *Montejurra* 60 (April 1971): 12; Clemente

1977: 44, 211; 1990: 131. The most active groups were based in the university towns of Santander, Logroño, Zaragoza, Madrid, Barcelona, and the Basque Country. The Santander students produced their own journal, *Azada y Asta*, and the Madrid students *La Encina*.

12. Letter of the AET delegate for Madrid to Secretaría General, Comunión Tradicionalista, 3 May 1965; "Actividades de la AET," Delegación Provincial, Madrid, AET, 1966, APCT; Cubero Sánchez 1990.

13. For example, he received extensive coverage in the national press when it was "revealed" he was working down an Asturian mine for a month. He also learned to parachute, making a record number of jumps in two days.

14. Two of them fulfilled the then-obligatory Social Service, and Cecilia assisted for two weeks in a lepers' colony. María-Teresa worked alongside her aiding flood victims in Cataluña, then went to Navarre in order to tour systematically the loyal villages of the province while ostensibly studying at the local university.

15. *Montejurra* 11 (November 1965): 15–17; 34 (February 1968): i–ii; López Rodó 1991: 29.

16. "Nota verbal presentada a S.A.R. El Principe de Asturias, por el Secretario General de la Comunión, el dia 16 de Noviembre de 1966," Secretario General, Comunión Tradicionalista, APCT.

17. Salgado-Araujo 1976: 252, 359, 420, 515; López Rodó 1977: 198, 201; 1991: 19; Preston 1993: 701. In the early 1960s, Carlos Hugo received assistance from the general secretariat of the Movimiento. When a supporter of Juan Carlos asked its leader to explain his motives, he replied, "We have to keep options open; in this way we can do Franco a great service" (qtd. in Powell 1990: 34). One Carlist of Cirauqui, now in his late sixties, told me that at one performance of Montejurra in the mid-1960s, he met a group of men who said they had been drinking in a bar earlier that day in Bilbao when a friend had asked them if they wished to go to Montejurra, as there was a coach waiting. During the trip they were provided with red berets.

Jaime del Burgo (*Montejurra* 58 [February 1971]: 4) has also claimed that *javieristas* received "subventions, help, and protection" from the Movimiento.

18. A. Ruiz de Gallareta, interview by author, Madrid, 28 September 1990; *Boina Roja* no. 45 (March 1959), no. 50 (August 1959). Doña Pilar de Borbón, Juan Carlos's elder sister, had been thought of as a possible partner for Carlos Hugo. Both Franco and the family of Don Juan welcomed the idea, seeing a marriage between the two branches of the Borbóns as a felicitous resolution of the dynastic dispute. But it was known that many Carlists would have been strongly against their prince marrying one of the representatives of the hated liberal monarchy. More to the point, Carlos Hugo was already courting his future bride by the time an informal meeting was arranged between him and Doña Pilar.

19. *Times* (London), 8 February, p. 8; 10 February, p. 10; 11 February, p. 8; 8 April, p. 14 (all 1964). Although Queen Juliana tried to keep her daughter in the line of succession, Carlos Hugo refused to accept the conditions set by the Dutch cabinet that he renounce all other dynastic interests, become a Dutch citizen, live in Hol-

land, and bring up their future children in the country. Since many Dutch disapproved so strongly of Franco's Spain, the cabinet was unable to drop any of its demands. Irene acknowledged the political deadlock, and agreed to give up her rights to the throne. For details of, and editorials on, this constitutional crisis, see *Algemeen Dagblad*, 25 March; 3 April, p. 5; 20 April; 25 May; *De Govi-en Eemlander*, 1 April; 3 April, p. 1; 14 April; 20 April; *De Telegraaf*, 10 February; 12 February; 27 February; 6 March; 9 March; 2 April, p. 5; 25 April; *De Volksrant*, 11 February; 12 February; 13 February; 7 March; 4 April, p. 1; 20 April, p. 1; *Nieuws van de dag*, 6 April (all 1964). Spanish translations of all these Dutch articles are in APCT. For a *juanista* account of the controversy in Holland over the marriage arrangements, see Aronson 1966: 223.

20. Circular Secretaría General no. 42, 24 July 1964, Secretaría General, Comunión Tradicionalista, APCT; Fraga Iribarne 1980: 102. For examples of the anti-Carlist articles written by *juanistas*, see *ABC*, 9 February, 18 February 1963.

21. Salgado-Araujo 1976: 412; Fraga Iribarne 1980: 125. In July 1965, during the preparations for a reshuffle of the cabinet, Franco considered appointing Zamanillo as minister of justice. But when Carrero Blanco objected, calling Zamanillo a *"hugonote,"* Franco agreed and appointed instead the *carlofranquista* suggested by Carrero Blanco, Antonio María de Oriol (López Rodó 1990: 532). It seems Franco's cabinet listened to his plea. For example, Adolfo Suárez, then director general of Spanish radio and television, later president of the country during the transition to democracy, promoted the cause of Juan Carlos and ensured that Carlos Hugo did not appear on television (Soriano 1995: 130).

22. Carlos Hugo's personal staff, interview by author, Igúzquiza, 25 October 1988.

23. Franco might have been prepared to tolerate the prince for political reasons, but his police would not tolerate outspoken Carlist critics of his regime: in 1965, the more vituperative speakers at the annual Carlist ceremonies at Villareal de los Infantes and at Durango were all fined. In February the following year, police forcibly closed the National Carlist Congress then being held; four months later, the ceremony at Villareal was banned—those Carlists who still turned up spent the day fighting the police (*Le Monde*, 14 February 1966; Cubero Sánchez 1990).

24. For example, see the reply by *Boina Roja* (a journal of the intransigents) in January 1959 to the anticonfessionalist stance of the young activists in their periodical *Azada y Asta* no. 3 (1958).

25. *Times* (London), 11 March 1961, p. 7.

26. Santa Cruz 1979–1992, vol. 25 (II): 423–25. From the information I have been able to gather, the Juntas, which survived into the 1970s, do not appear to have been very active politically.

27. Although the progressives portrayed themselves as clear-sighted activists pitted against refractory and aging conservatives, they were ready to work together when necessary. For instance, the progressives were at times prepared to defend the official posture adopted by the Comunión regarding collaboration as a temporary tactic, a disposable means to certain political ends. During the winter

of 1958, Valiente, Zamanillo, and a group of hardworking Carlist youths spoke at gatherings throughout the country in a largely successful attempt to reaffirm the Borbón-Parmas as the leaders of the Comunión. Three years later, Carlist youth participated in the huge ceremony at Burgos attended by Franco, celebrating his twenty-five years in power. They then asked him to visit Navarre as a sign that he had not yet decided definitively in favor of Juan Carlos. But Franco did not take up their offer.

28. Lavardín 1976: 143–48; Santa Cruz 1979–1992, vol. 25 (II): 339–420.

29. The *Ideario*, couched in the standard style of an unreconstructed traditionalism, propounded the establishment of an integrist monarchy presiding over a corporative parliament, which granted little power to the regions. As far as the authors were concerned, there was no good political reason for ideological deviation from prewar principles.

The *requeté* document *La Gran Verdad sobre España. El 18 de Julio en peligro* argued that the increasingly evident liberalizing tendencies in the government, and in society in general, had to be countered by all those—whether Carlist, Falangist, or regular soldiers—who had participated in the "Crusade."

30. A group of students promptly replied to the *Ideario* with an *Esquema doctrinal*, which promoted progressive ideas of a popular monarchy in a democratic state, an independent Church, the legalization of political parties and workers' syndicates, and equality of opportunity. On the *Ideario* and the *Esquema doctrinal*, see Clemente 1977: 206–27.

31. Cubero Sánchez 1990.

32. J. M. Zavala and M-T. de Borbón-Parma, interview by author, Madrid, 4 September 1991.

33. For a detailed critique of the congress, see the letter of the leading Catalan Carlist, José Vives, to Valiente, February 1966, APCT.

34. On the proposed content of the speeches at the Montejurra of that year, see *Informe CE–1966 (Sugerencias)*, APCT. Massó and the other former secretaries publicly criticized the return to neocollaborationism in May in an open letter, and in *¿Que Pasa?*, no. 202 (11 November 1967). Two issues later, its editor printed the response of Zavala, by then secretary-general, to their article, and added his own counterresponse (copy of the open letter in APCT).

35. In sharp contrast to his message on the eve of previous plebiscites, Don Javier told his subjects to vote "Yes" in the referendum over the Ley Orgánica del Estado (Organic Law of the State). In his message for the Montejurra of 1967, he asked God to enlighten Franco, and in an indirect reference to the members of the AET and MOT then participating in the student strikes and workers' protests, he urged Carlists to play a full part in Spanish public life without transgressing the bounds of legality.

36. On the work of these Carlist deputies, key members of the "Cortes transhumantes" (the group of thirteen antifranquist deputies), see *Montejurra* 36 (April 1968): 10, 22; 42 (October 1968): 6–7; 48 (September–October 1969): 22; 54 (September–October 1970): 10–13; 55 (November 1970): 4–16; Miranda Rubio 1994.

37. Comunicación no. 1, Junta Suprema, Comunión Tradicionalista, January 1968; López Rodó 1977: 267.

38. Perhaps he thought the relations between Franco and those pressing the Alfonsist claim were then so bad that it was worth disappointing the more progressive among Carlists for the possibility, however distant, of seeing his son installed.

39. María-Teresa de Borbón-Parma, interview by author, Madrid, 5 September 1990; Preston 1993: 739. On 22 July 1969, at an official ceremony in the Cortes, where Franco designated Juan Carlos as the future king of Spain, the prince stated, "I belong, by direct line, to the Spanish Royal House, and in my family, by the designs of Providence, the two branches have united." For at least one *estorlino*, this statement and the official designation demonstrated that the *estorlinos* had been right in 1957 to pledge their allegiance to Don Juan, the father of Juan Carlos. (See the letter by Bernando de Salazar in *Mundo,* 19 June 1971, reprinted in Garmendia 1975: 86–89.)

CHAPTER SIX. KINGS AND COMMON PHRASES

1. Brook Shepherd 1968, 1991; Bogle 1990; C. de Borbón-Parma 1997: 246. On Don Javier's links with France, see Santa Cruz 1979–1992, vol. 20: 171–85. In 1911, Don Javier participated in an armed incursion into northern Portugal in an attempt to restore the recently deposed Braganzas, the family of his mother. Ten years later, he and his elder brother, Sixtus, acted as intermediaries in the negotiations between the French prime minister, Aristide Briaud, and the deposed Austro-Hungarian emperor Charles, their sister's husband, in his second restoration attempt. In the First World War, Sixtus and Don Javier wanted to join the French army, but a law of 1889 forbade all members of the former royal family from military service. Don Javier had in many ways a remarkable past, but he was not the most remarkable of his family, being clearly outshone by Sixtus, the most intelligent and energetic of his siblings. Their First World War peace plan was primarily the work of his brother, and historians refer to this diplomatic episode as "the Sixtus affair."

2. *Ordenanza del Requeté; ¡Montejurra! Ha dicho el principe,* pamphlet distributed at Montejurra 1966, APCT.

3. Carlos Hugo de Borbón-Parma, "Carta del principe," *Información Mensual,* November 1965, p. 1.

4. Pereda de la Reguera 1964: 110; Anon 1967; *Esfuerzo Común* 126 (March 1971): 3; *Montejurra* 22: 9; 23: 6–9; 27 (June 1967): 18; 28 (July 1967): 12–13; 31 (December 1967): 15–18, 20–21; 32 (November 1967): 8–15; 39–40: 8–11; 44: 8. While *huguista* journalists were at times prepared to claim their prince had gained a doctorate while studying at Merton College, Oxford University, he in fact spent only three terms in the town, as an associate student of Campion Hall, a Jesuit hall of residence associated with the university.

5. Members of his personal staff nicknamed María-Teresa "Doña Inflexibil-

ity," María de las Nieves "Doña Good Sense," and Cecilia "Doña Warmth and Friendliness."

6. Williamson 1986; Nairn 1988: 27.

7. Nairn 1988: 45.

8. Fraga Iribarne 1980: 100.

9. Pereda de la Reguera's *Carlos y Irene* (1964) is an unstinting panegyric to the characters of the newly wed couple.

10. Letter quoted in Santa Cruz 1979–1992, vol. 19 (II): 55.

11. "Don Carlos en Lisboa. Glosas a un discurso," *Montejurra* 34 (November 1968): 12–13. For examples of joint letters to Don Javier written by groups of traditionalists seeking to persuade him to return to a more conservative position, see Vila San Juan 1993: 251–58.

Some of these private meetings could be very stormy. Santa Cruz (1979–1992, vol. 28: 40) recounts the meeting in 1966 between a prestigious traditionalist leader, Don Antonio Garzón, and Don Javier and Carlos Hugo:

> Once the three were seated, Don Antonio Garzón asked Don Carlos Hugo if he would say, in front of the king, whether it were true or not that he, Don Carlos Hugo, had said that Carlism and he were socialist. . . . He did not deny it: he was evasive and playful. "Don Javier was furious," Garzón related. Garzón cut him short: "Yes or no!" Don Carlos Hugo and Don Javier continued to be evasive and lively, neither agreeing nor disagreeing. "Yes or no!" Don Antonio Garzón repeated three times. Until finally he stood up and said, "I no longer have any doubt that His Highness is socialist," and walked out.

12. Letter from Luis Martínez Erro to Luis Ruiz Hernández, 9 June 1968, caja "Navarre," APCT.

13. Rego Nieto 1985: 47, 52–53.

14. Lavardín 1976: 245.

15. M-T. de Borbón-Parma 1979: 79.

16. A. Goñi, "Presencia," *Montejurra* 60: 8–10.

17. *Montejurra* 18: 8; 25: 20; 29: 9. Also, *Montejurra* 37: 22.

18. Unamuno [1897] 1940: 24; López Rodó 1977: 211. Carlos VII was both the husband of Carlos Hugo's paternal grandfather's sister, and the brother of his father's mother's sister's husband. When in 1931, Alfonso, Carlos VII's younger brother, agreed to accept the Carlist crown, he immediately added "Carlos" to his Christian names (Zavala 1976: 24–25).

At the Montejurra of 1957, Hugues was referred to as "Carlos Javier." Later, he called himself variously "Carlos María Isidro," "Carlos," "Carlos Hugo," and "Hugo Carlos." It was not until 1962 that he decided definitively on "Carlos Hugo" and had this change made legal (Santa Cruz 1979–1992, vol. 24: 62).

19. *Le Berry Republicain,* 23 February 1970, pp. 1, 6; *Le Nouvelle Republique,* 23 February 1970; copies of the speeches given at the presentation by Don Javier, a representative of Carlist youth, the secretary-general of the Comunión, and Carlos Hugo can be found in APCT; *Montejurra* 56: 10–11.

20. *Montejurra* 25: 21, 23.

21. Nicholls 1989: 123.

22. MacClancy 1991: 126–27. Christian, describing the changes he has witnessed in a Cantabrian mountain valley between 1968 and 1988, states, "I think I see more tender husbands and loving fathers" (Christian 1989: 189).

23. *Montejurra* 18: 25; 20: 1; 48: 23.

24. Raimundo de Miguel, "Monarquía Popular," *Montejurra* 23: 2–4; Romero Raizábal 1968: 18.

25. P. R. Garisoain, "Don Javier, ¡Aqui Estamos!," *Montejurra* 33: 33.

26. *El Pensamiento Navarro*, 3 May 1970, p. 10.

27. "Discurso de un miembro de la Junta Suprema en Lignieres," 22 February 1970, APCT.

28. "Discurso pronunciado en Montejurra por un representante del Carlismo," 1970, APCT.

29. My analysis of *"pueblo"* is inspired by those of Pitt-Rivers [1954] 1971 and Garmendia 1984: 333, 337–38. See also Gambra 1983: 167.

30. From *Tiempos Criticos,* qtd. in Bryan 1965.

31. Unsigned speech made on the day of the Mártires de la Tradición, 1971, APCT.

32. P. J. Zabala, "Tradición y legitimidad," *Montejurra* 7 (23–30 May 1965): 2–5; Fonseca 1972.

33. P. N. C., "Tradición y tiempo," *Montejurra* 38 (June 1968): 17.

34. Both comments of Carlos Hugo were used to head *Boletín Informativo. Jefatura Regional Carlista de Castilla la Nueva.* See also the article "La tradición y el tiempo" in its issue of 15 January 1966.

35. The quote is from an interview with J. M. Zavala in *Indice* 1961, qtd. in Lavardín 1976: 101. For traditionalist commentaries on the notion of "tradition," see Miguel 1969; Gambra 1983: 137.

36. See, for example, "Discurso pronunciado en Montejurra por un representante del Carlismo," 1970, APCT; Gambra 1983: 198–206.

CHAPTER SEVEN. PAST MASTERS

1. Marx 1929, qtd. in Clemente 1977: 11.

2. That progressive historiography is still today part of the lived reality of at least some progressives is suggested by the contributions made in 1998 by "Eudo," a Carlist well steeped in this version of his movement's past, to an Internet discussion list on contemporary politics in the Basque Country. See, e.g., http://www.pais-vasco.com/foro/politica/0484. Moreover, Josep Clemente and María-Teresa de Borbón continue to write on Carlist history in a progressive mode (e.g., M-T. de Borbón-Parma 1989; Clemente 1990).

3. C. H. de Borbón-Parma 1976: 11.

4. Clemente 1977: 13–14, 29.

5. Clemente 1979: 25–50. Substantially similar but briefer versions of Carlist history are given in Clemente, "Apuntes para una historia del Carlismo Catalan: Los Carlistas Catalanes en el Siglo XIX segun el Profesor Vicens Vives," *Montejurra*, 27 (June 1967): 16–17; C. H. de Borbón-Parma 1976: 9–18; M-T. de Borbón-Parma 1977: 55–58; 1979: 3–41; Clemente and Costa 1976: 11–17; Zavala 1976: 5–41. The most complete progressive version of Carlist history from 1900 to 1928 is "Guia política del Carlismo" by E. Olcina and J. C. Clemente in center-page supplements to *Montejurra*, numbers 49, 50 (January 1970), 51, 53, and 56.

6. Qtd. in M-T. de Borbón-Parma 1979: 29–30.

7. From Ferrer 1958, vol. 23: 245–46, qtd. in Clemente 1977: 12–13. Clemente did not include those passages from Ferrer where he mentions that Carlos VII's lieutenants thought it would be inappropriate for their pretender to meet with the labor leader. As an upright traditionalist, Ferrer tries to explain this unusual meeting by stating, "It is not necessary to say that there could not have been any agreement with Don Carlos, but this event is worthy of attention because it indicates the great international respect that Carlos VII enjoyed" (Ferrer vol. 23: 245, qtd. in Clemente 1977: 12–13).

8. Clemente 1978: 19; M-T. de Borbón-Parma 1979: 32.

9. Unamuno 1917: 152.

10. *Manifest del poble de La Garriga*, 25 January 1849, Biblioteca de Cataluña, (46.71) VAR II (original emphasis), qtd. in Borbón-Parma 1979: 29.

11. Zavala 1976: 7.

12. *Esquema doctrinal* (1964) qtd. in Clemente 1977: 213; Clemente 1977: 14. See also Artur Juncosa Carbonell's introduction to Clemente 1978. On a more biological note, Zabala (1977: 16) claimed that the early Carlists' "instinct" of self-defense prevented them giving up the "characteristic values of a primary socialism."

13. For information on this point with respect to the Basque phase of the First Carlist War, see Coverdale 1984: 303.

14. Coverdale 1984: 299–301.

15. Blinkhorn 1979: 39–40.

16. Information in this paragraph comes from Garmendia 1984: 279–94.

17. Information in this paragraph comes from Winston 1985. According to Winston, Don Jaime supported but certainly did not found the *sindicatos*. Its president made the pretender an honorary member of the new organization—"perhaps the only case of a royal trade unionist on record" (Winston 1985: 112).

18. *New York Daily Tribune*, 18 August and 4 September 1854, republished in Marx and Engels 1939: 123. Viriathus is the most renowned of the Iberian leaders who fought against the invading forces of the Roman Empire.

19. Unamuno 1916, vol. 1: 216; 1917, vol. 6: 153.

20. Unamuno 1966: 998.

21. Blinkhorn 1975: 41.

CHAPTER EIGHT. MONTEJURRA

1. *El Pensamiento Navarro* (hereafter *PN*), 4 May 1939, p. 6; 8 May 1966, p. 13.

2. *PN*, 8 May 1966, p. 13; *Montejurra*, 25: 17.

3. "Libro de actas del Ayuntamiento de Ayegui," 1 May 1940, AMA.

4. Baleztena and Astiz 1944: 78–82; *PN*, 2 May 1971, p. 3; 2 May 1976, p. 1.

5. *PN*, 2 May 1953, p. 1. The only fulsome account I was able to find about the pilgrimage in this period is in Baleztena and Astiz 1944: 78–81.

6. *El Diario de Navarra* (hereafter *DN*), 11 May 1954, p. 7; *PN*, 11 May 1954, pp. 1, 10, 12.

7. *DN*, 3 May 1964, p. 1. For the change in numbers attending Montejurra over the years, see appendix 2.

8. *DN*, 3 May 1964, p. 1; 10 May 1966, p. 24; *PN*, 4 May 1965, p. 1.

9. *DN*, 16 May 1961, p. 7; *PN*, 7 May 1963, p. 16. In 1965, 3,470 *requetés* (1,000 of them from Navarre) marched past their leaders. Two years later, only 350 turned up in their uniforms (Caspistegui Gorasurreta 1995: 396 n. 55).

10. *PN*, 5 May 1956, p. 10; 7 May 1957, p. 10; 12 May 1959, p. 12; 10 May 1960, p. 4.

11. *DN*, 10 May 1960, p. 4; *PN*, 8 May 1962, p. 10; *Montejurra* 37: 25.

12. *DN*, 6 May 1958, p. 7; 10 May 1960, p. 4.

13. *PN*, 4 May 1965; 5 May 1966.

14. *PN*, 5 May 1966, p. 1; *Montejurra* 26: 13.

15. Lisón Tolosana 1980. On *romerías*, see also Christian 1972, Lisón Tolosana 1983, Corbin and Corbin 1987: 121–24. On Navarrese *romerías* in the 1940s, see Baleztena and Astiz 1944.

16. Larrion n.d.: 3.

17. Turner 1974: 189. See also Morinis 1992: 4–5.

18. Ferrer 1941–1960, vol. 8: 225–27.

19. C. H. de Borbón-Parma 1977: 65.

20. *Montejurra* 25: 85–89; Holt 1967: 250.

21. Iribarren 1946: 3; Jimeno Jurio 1990: 41.

22. *DN*, 3 March 1940, p. 3; 5 March 1940, p. 1; 12 March 1940, p. 1; 10 March 1942, pp. 6–7; 6 March 1945, p. 3; 10 March 1945, p. 2; *Montejurra* 5: 8.

23. Baleztena and Astiz 1944: 74, 83–92; Larrion n.d.: 16.

24. Sánchez Erauskin 1994: 38–40.

25. Lauzurica 1939: 399, qtd. in Sánchez Erauskin 1994: 27–28.

26. Politicizing Catholic ritual had long been part of Carlist strategy. For instance, in 1876 some leading Carlists, totally opposed to any form of liberal Catholicism and keen to rekindle the movement within months of the second war's end, organized a popular pilgrimage to Rome. It drew 7,000 people from all over the country. The next year a similar excursion was halted only by the combined action of the government, powerful politicians, and senior ecclesiastics. But even this influential alliance of liberals could not prevent, in 1878, the celebration by integrists of a large number of very well-attended local *romerías* (Real Cuesta 1985: 11).

27. Letter of Joaquin Bilbao Luna to Sixto Barranco, 9 April 1964, APCT. Other recently created events in the postwar Carlist ritual calendar included ceremonies in Zaragoza in March; in Villareal de los Infantes, Castellón, in June; in Covadonga, Asturias, and Haro, Logroño, in July; in Caminareal, Teruel, and Isarquina, Álava, in September; and in Bilbao in November (*Esfuerzo Común* 65 [July 1965]: 9).

28. On mass Carlist rituals in Cataluña during the Second Republic, see Calleja and Aróstegui 1995: 48–49.

29. The ceremony on the Navarrese mountaintop became so renowned within Carlism that it was used as a metaphor for other, lesser events. The annual pilgrimage to a hermitage on the slopes of the Sierra Mariola, southern Valencia, in honor of the Carlist soldiers who died there in a battle in 1873 is locally known as "the Montejurra of the Levant" (*Montejurra* 6 [April 1965]: 11).

30. The forces of the regime might also try to reduce the numbers at Montejurra by prohibiting all soldiers, whether in uniform or not, from attending (Caspistegui Gorasurreta 1995: 419).

31. *PN*, 11 May 1954, p. 8.

32. *PN*, 10 May 1955, p. 12.

33. *Montejurra* 17: 27; *PN*, 7 May 1954, p. 6; 11 May 1954, p. 12.

34. For a Carlist eulogy of the "Holy City" of Estella, written during its occupation in the Second Carlist War, see Montoya 1874: 11–12.

35. Burgo 1939; Unamuno [1897] 1940: 112.

36. *PN*, 13 May 1954, p. 6; 6 May 1962, p. 14; SAB, "Montejurra es el Carlismo, Estoril el Liberalismo," *Montejurra* 17: 27. The modern Carlist writers' style of description of Montejurra was not novel: for a similarly dramatic literary exploitation of the mountain's physical nature and geographical position by a partisan author during the Second Carlist War, see Montoya 1874: 8.

37. *PN*, 8 May 1954, p. 8; 12 May 1959, p. 12.

38. For a list of examples, see Leatherbarrow 1987.

39. Unamuno [1897] 1940: 246–47. On the symbolism of making high places, especially once fortified ones, the destination of pilgrimages, see Nolan and Nolan 1989: 318–20.

40. *PN*, 9 May 1954, p. 10.

41. SAB, "Montejurra es el Carlismo, Estoril el Liberalismo," *Montejurra* 17: 27.

42. Ferrer 1941–1960, vol. 8: 231.

43. Baleztena and Astiz 1944: 73.

44. *PN*, 4 May 1939, p. 6.

45. *PN*, 4 May 1939, p. 6; 2 May 1948, p. 6; 8 May 1954, p. 8; Baleztena and Astiz 1944: 90.

46. *PN*, 10 May 1955, p. 1.

47. *PN*, 4 May 1941, p. 1; 3 May 1942, p. 1; 10 May 1955, p. 12; *Montejurra* 25: 4; J. A. Zubiaur, interview by author, Pamplona, n.d.

48. *PN*, 11 May 1954, p. 10; *PN*, 4 May 1939, p. 6; 4 May 1941, p. 1; 11 May 1954, p. 10; 8 May 1962, p. 10. Indeed, for one writer, the pilgrimage did not start at Irache "but begins in any part of Spain where there is a *requeté*. From that place he

commences the ascension of the mountain, and from that place he later remembers the day of May, the day of Montejurra" (*DN*, 12 May 1959, p. 12).

49. *PN*, 2 May 1963, p. 18.

50. *PN*, 30 April 1942, p. 1; 9 May 1954, p. 10; 11 May 1954, p. 10; 10 May 1955, p. 10.

51. On the difference between pilgrimages that are couched in a discourse of sacrifice and penance and those that are couched in a discourse of miracles, see Eade and Sallnow 1991: 17.

52. *PN*, 8 May 1954, p. 8.

53. *PN*, 2 May 1941, p. 4; 2 May 1948, p. 6; 11 May 1954, pp. 8, 10; 12 May 1954, p. 6; *DN*, 6 May 1942, p. 1; *Montejurra* 17: 21.

54. *Montejurra* 25: 17 (original emphasis).

55. *Montejurra* 10: 16; E. Paningua, "Montejurra," *Los Sitios*, 15 May 1966; reprinted in *Montejurra* 17: 21.

56. *PN*, 3 May 1942, p. 1; 9 May 1954, p. 10; 12 May 1954, p. 6; 7 May 1957, p. 12; *Montejurra* 17: 20.

57. Lavardín 1976: 31.

58. *PN*, 14 May 1961, p. 12. The "fire" of faith, enthusiasm, and emotion lit on the summit were, it was stated, replicated in the devout fire of each Carlist hearth where the events of the day were discussed (*PN*, 12 May 1954, p. 6).

59. *Vía Crucis Montejurra*, Pamplona 1957.

60. *PN*, 10 May 1955, p. 12; "Itinerario de Montejurra," *PN*, 12 May 1959, p. 12.

61. *DN*, 10 May 1955, p. 4; 2 May 1967, p. 24; *PN*, 4 May 1956, p. 1; 8 May 1959, p. 1; 9 May 1959, p. 1; 8 May 1966, p. 8. See also Miguel Veyrat 1973, *Carta abierta a un monárquico de siempre*; reprinted in Garmendia 1975: 91–93.

62. *DN*, 7 May 1963, p. 16; *PN*, 9 May 1959, p. 1; 4 May 1965, p. 8. On the *romería de las madres navarras* as the forging of many families into a single one, see Baleztena and Astiz 1944: 81.

63. *PN*, 1 May 1954, p. 10; 3 May 1955, p. 12; 7 May 1957, p. 12.

64. *Montejurra* 17: 11, 13, 21.

65. *PN*, 10 March 1940, p. 6.

66. *Montejurra* 24: 27.

67. *PN*, 1 May 1956, p. 1; 2 May 1956, p. 1; 5 May 1956, p. 1; 10 May 1959, p. 12; 15 May 1966, p. 1.

68. Qtd. in M-T. de Borbón-Parma 1997: 70.

69. Aliatar, "El Monte de Fe," *Montejurra* 25: 4.

70. Villagers now in their forties who were brought up in non-Carlist households said to me how excluded they felt from this annual fiesta in their hometown. One radical nationalist, and virulently anti-Carlist, now in her sixties, said how much those who had been maltreated by the Franquist forces in the war and its aftermath hated the night before Montejurra, when the streets of their village were occupied by those who had participated in their repression, when all they could do was complain behind closed doors.

71. Connerton 1989: 43.

72. Lavardín 1976: 57–59; López Rodó 1977: 138; the quote comes from *Tiempos Criticos*, cited in Bryan 1965. When I asked one of the founders of the Hermandad de los Caballeros Voluntarios de la Cruz, which organizes the September pilgrimage to Montejurra, whether political speeches were included in the day's events, he smiled at me and said, "No. We all think the same."

73. Lavardín 1976: 94–95; M-T. de Borbón-Parma 1979: 86–87.

74. *DN*, 7 May 1963, p. 16; *PN*, 7 May 1963, p. 16; Lavardín 1976: 153–56.

75. *PN*, 5 May 1964, p. 16; Lavardín 1976: 232.

76. *PN*, 4 May 1965, p. 8; Lavardín 1976: 256–57; Clemente 1977: 46–55; M-T. de Borbón-Parma 1979: 87.

77. *Montejurra* 17; Lavardín 1976: 268; M-T. de Borbón-Parma 1979: 88–89.

78. *DN*, 2 May 1967, p. 24; *Montejurra* 26: 12–19; Lavardín 1976: 277–78.

79. M-T. de Borbón-Parma and J. M. Zavala, interview by author, Madrid, 5 September 1990.

80. Sallnow 1987: 7.

81. On Turner's approach to pilgrimage, and on those of his commentators, see Turner 1967, 1969, 1974, 1975, 1978; Lane 1981; Sallnow 1981, 1987; Geertz 1983; Graburn 1983; Hertz 1983; Morinis 1984; Daniel 1987; Abélès 1988; Neville 1987; Eade and Sallnow 1991.

82. Vázquez de Prada Tiffe and Ruíz Garrido 1995: 240.

83. Santa Cruz 1979–1992, vol. 22 (I): 169.

84. Caspistegui Gorasurreta 1995: 387 n. 18.

85. Caspistegui Gorasurreta 1995: 428.

86. J. M. Zavala and M-T. de Borbón-Parma, interview by author, Madrid, 5 September 1990. On the reaction of *carlosoctavistas* to the first appearance of Carlos Hugo at Montejurra, see the letter of Antonio Lizarza quoted in Santa Cruz 1979–1990, vol. 19(II): 217.

The various incidents listed in this paragraph are the only ones of which I have knowledge. There may well have been more.

87. *DN*, 8 May 1962, p. 12; 7 May 1963, p. 16; *PN*, 4 May 1965, p. 1; Lavardín 1976: 72, 128, 156; López Rodó 1990: 330.

88. *PN*, 10 May 1966, p. 10. Lavardín 1976: 268. Carlists who still attend Montejurra today like to mention the Scot's presence, as though it shows that their movement had international support. None of them appeared to know that in 1950 European legitimist organizations had sent representatives to the ritual nor that a group of French traditionalists had attended in 1968 (*Montejurra* 37 [May 1968]: 30–31; Santa Cruz 1979–1990, vol. 12: 24 n).

89. Anderson 1983.

90. On the self-referential quality of nationalist rituals, see Breuilly 1982: 344; Smith 1991: 77–78.

91. *Montejurra* 17: 24.

92. On the role of incorporated practices within ritual, see Connerton 1989.

93. *Montejurra* 16: 20.

CHAPTER NINE. THE ESTABLISHMENT OF THE PROGRESSIVES

1. On this event, see MacClancy 1989. In Bilbao, the police could disperse the demonstration against the expulsion only by firing into the air (Cubero Sánchez 1990).

In Valcarlos, Carlos Hugo could convene meetings with Carlists from Navarre, the Basque Country, and neighboring provinces. For short periods he would also stay in Perpignan or northern Portugal, where he could meet with Carlists from Cataluña and northwestern Spain, respectively.

2. Themes for discussion included the political, social, and economic situation of Spain; the reality of Carlism; ideologies; military uprising; the Church; the army; youth; the media; mysticism and Carlist philosophy; syndicalism; regionalism; freedom and political representation; power and sovereignty; power in Spain; the leader; propaganda; the bridgeheads of the party. "Plan de cursillos," n.d.; "Cursillos para dirigentes de la Juventud Carlista," n.d., caja "Cursillos," APCT.

3. M-T. de Borbón-Parma 1979: 98–121.

4. The Carlist representatives at the congresses agreed not only on the policies their movement should propound but on the structure of their organization as well. The majority of delegates, who supported the internal changes the progressives were already instituting, affirmed that the base of the party was to be made up of popular assemblies of militants who would debate and suggest amendments to papers on ideology and strategy proposed by the Gabinete Ideológico of the party. At the next level were to come regional assemblies, composed of delegates who would attend the National Congress, where each would put forward the decisions of the people they represented. At the apex of the movement was the Junta Suprema, composed of six members and presided over by Carlos Hugo on behalf of his father. This clutch of progressives, which was able to meet frequently, reported to the Governing Junta, a larger body that, because it included all eighteen regional chiefs, was convened much less regularly. All leaders were to be elected except for regional chiefs, who were to be chosen by the party executive from a list prepared by provincial chiefs. In an effort to end amateurism, the diverse and demanding duties of militants and other officeholders were explicitly laid out ("Acta de la reunion de constitución del Gabinete Ideológico del Carlismo," 31 May 1970; "Organización Interna," January 1971; "Proyecto de Asambleas Populares Carlistas," September 1971; "Carta a los jefes regionales y provinciales. Asunto: Asambleas Populares Carlistas," December 1971; "Acta de la Reunion celebrada el 22-7-72," Gabinete Ideológico, APCT).

5. Golubovic 1991; Simmie 1991; Smidovnik 1991. On "self-management" as a political concept, see Gurmendez 1978 and Mate 1978; on its place within the ideology of the French Left during the late 1960s and 1970s, see Bell and Criddle 1984.

6. M-T. de Borbón-Parma 1977: 11.

7. "Tradición y transmisión," *Montejurra* 10: 4.

8. *Montejurra* 10: 10.

9. M-T. de Borbón-Parma 1979: 81.

10. "Carta de un carlista aragonés," *Información Mensual* (hereafter *IM*), November 1965, p. 2 (original emphasis).

11. C. de Borbón-Parma 1977: 29. See also the interview with the Princess Irene in *Punto y Hora,* no. 6.

12. Santa Cruz 1979–1992, vol. 1: 107; vol. 9: 239–49; vol. 10: 27.

13. "Puntos importante para exponer ante la Jerarquía y que sirvan de base de discusión," n.d. (early 1970s), caja "Iglesia," APCT; "La Iglesia Católica en España. Informe sobre la situación actual. Dirigido al Presidente de la Conferencia Episcopal Española, por Don Javier de Borbón Parma," March 1974, APCT.

14. Cyclostyled pamphlet produced by the Dirección Regional en el País Valenciano de las Juventudes Carlistas in protest against the meeting held by the pro-regime Junta Provincial de la Comunión Tradicionalista, n.d., APCT.

15. P. J. Zavala, "Paso a la juventud," *Montejurra* 30: 2–3; *Montejurra* 33: 28; Carta a los jefes provinciales, J. M. Zavala, 19 December 1971, APCT. On the dispute in 1968 between progressives and their opponents over the election of the provincial chief for Valencia, see "¿Y los derechos del pueblo?" (Cyclostyled broadsheet), Valencia, 10 July 1968, and the letter of Luis Pérez Domingo to Zavala, 14 November 1968, APCT. For different views on the public dispute five years later over the dismissal of Pascual Agramunt, blind war hero and then provincial chief of Valencia, see *Aparisi Guijarro* 12 (March 1973), 13 (December 1973), and "Informe sobre el cese como Jefe Provincial de Valencia y posterior expulsión del Partido Carlista de don Pascual Agramunt Matutano," La Junta Provincial de la Comunión Tradicionalista de Valencia, 26 August 1973, caja "Valencia," APCT.

16. M. Zufia, interview by author, Pamplona, 27 April 1987; J. A. Zubiaur, interview by author, Pamplona, 24 September 1990; Zubiaur n.d.

17. Telegramas y cartas cruzados entre el excmo. Sr. Gobernador Civil de Asturias y el presidente de la Hermandad Nacional de Antiguos Combatientes de Tercios de Requetés, Hermandad Nacional de ACTR, February 1969, APCT; *Times* (London), 14 February 1969, p. 6; Clemente 1977: 261; Eriz 1986: 63–72.

18. *Montejurra* 41 (September 1968): 28. At the demonstration following Montejurra, a platoon of Civil Guards rescued a plainclothes policeman who had been cornered, by firing shots into the air. But the crowd would not disperse, and demanded the release of a youth who had been detained. Fifteen minutes later he was released and the guardsmen marched off to the sound of jeers, Carlist hymns, and choruses of "Franco is a traitor!" *Times* (London), 5 May 1969, p. 5; 12 May 1969, p. 1.

19. Jauregui and Vega 1984: 258–59.

20. Clemente 1977: 268–69. It is worth remembering that the repressive measures of the regime were not directed solely at left-wing Carlists. In 1974, the indomitable Mauricio de Sivatte was arrested and fined for his strongly worded criticisms of the government at the Aplec of Montserrat organized by the Regency of Estella (*Diario de Barcelona,* 23 June 1974, *Informaciones,* 25 June 1974, *Fuerza Nueva,* 8 June 1974).

21. GAC broadsheet, n.d., APCT.

22. *Montejurra* 41 (September 1968): 29; 46 (May 1969): 20; 52: 8, 13; 57 (January 1971): 15; "¡De Las Fuerzas Activas Revolucionarias Carlistas!," FARC, APCT. On "El affaire de *'El Pensamiento Navarro,'*" see *Montejurra* 53 (June–July 1970): 12–16; on the history of GAC, see MacClancy 1989. The last operation performed by the two remaining GAC guerrillas occurred on the morning of Montejurra in 1971 when they stormed the offices of a Pamplona radio station and transmitted a message about the proposed federation of the peoples of Spain. Juan Querejeta, one of the leading members of the GAC commando, remembered,

> We established relations with ETA from the very beginning. Teo Uriarte, who was one of our contacts, used to say to me that our organization was just a game, that we were the prodigal sons of Franquism, and that the regime would never take us seriously. When I was arrested, in the attack on the Berberana transmitter, one of the first things that passed through my head was: Well, now Teo won't be able to say that they treat us with benevolence. I looked forward to meeting him in prison in order to remind him of his words. (qtd. in Juaristi 1989: 87)

23. On the movement from Carlism to Basque nationalism within the Basque clergy, see García de Cortazar and Lorenzo Espinosa 1988: 252–57. On the political division between older conservatives and younger activists within the Navarrese clergy, see Iztueta 1981: 180–202. Symbolic of this politically engaged ecclesiastical group is Bishop Antonio Añoveros, a former *requeté* chaplain heavily influenced by conciliar reform, who in 1971 was suddenly forced to take a long vacation for having delivered a sermon sympathetic to the Basque nationalist cause.

24. The first Comisiones Obreras (CC.OO) constituted in Madrid used to frequent a Carlist Circle there (Jauregui and Vega 1984: 258). The Carlists were also the first to lend their premises to the Unión Militar Democrático (UMD, Democratic Military Union), the illegal association of antifascist lieutenants. Carlist officers were put in contact with members of the UMD and told to help them as much as possible. The UMD also passed military maps to the Polisario freedom fighters in the Spanish Sahara via the Carlists.

25. Carrillo 1983: 36; Sanz 1986: 110, 119. On the workers' movement in Navarre, see "Ortzi" 1978: 397–400; Santamaría Blasco 1988; Iriarte 1995: 92–95, 104–5. In late 1971, a group of radical Navarrese progressives joined with local members of the Liga Comunista Revolucionaria in strongly criticizing the ORT and trying to dislodge it from its commanding position within the provincial CC.OO. The attempt failed, mainly for lack of sufficient support.

26. Sanz 1986: 175.

27. "Nota verbal comunicada per el Partido Carlista a la titulada 'Junta Democrática de España' con fecha de Junio de 1974," Partido Carlista, APCT; "Nota oficial de la Junta de Gobierno del Partido Carlista sobre la incorporación del mismo a la Junta Democrática de España," Partido Carlista, 15 September 1974, APCT; "Instrucciones en torno a la nota oficial de la Junta de Gobierno sobre la Junta Democrática de España," 21 September 1974, APCT; "Informe. La Junta Democrá-

tica de España y sus relaciones con el Partido Carlista," *Orientación Política,* Partido Carlista, March 1975, APCT; Preston 1986: 74–75, 85.

CHAPTER TEN. MONTEJURRA 1976

1. *El Pensamiento Navarro* (hereafter *PN*), 5 May 1972, p. 1. It seems that in the nineteenth century a good number of foreigners, such as the author Joseph Conrad, joined the Carlist army precisely because of its romanticism (on Conrad's involvement in Carlism, see Gurko 1962: 21–26). For well-publicized criticisms by the *sivattistas* of the progressive arrogation of "Carlist," see *ABC,* 3 February 1976, p. 8; *El Correo Catalan,* 3 February 1976, p. 23; *El Noticiero Universal,* 3 February 1976, p. 5; *Solidaridad Nacional,* 3 February 1976, p. 5; *Tele/eXpress,* 3 February 1976, p. 6; *Diario de Burgos,* 4 February 1976, p. 4.

2. In 1968, Valiente, who had recently resigned from his post in the Comunión, told Franco, "The traditionalists will attack you by day, but not by night. Whatever Your Excellency decides about the succession, do it while you are still alive; the authentic traditionalists will accept it." To Franco's comment, "Why do they not accept Juan Carlos? He is worth a lot; I brought him up myself," Valiente replied, "Say it, Your Excellency, in an authorized manner and the traditionalists will respect it" (López Rodó 1991: 279).

3. "La Familia Real Carlista," n.d., Cyclostyle, copy in APCT (original caps); interview with Zamanillo, *La Verdad. Diario regional del sureste,* 11 March 1969, p. 1.

Although Zamanillo's claim made an unintended parallel to the progressives' rewriting of history, most *antihuguistas* strongly disagreed with their reinterpretation of the past. Both the "Cartas" and "Navarra" files in the APCT contain letters written in the late 1960s and the early 1970s to the editor of *Montejurra,* complaining about Olcina and Clemente's articles on Carlist history.

4. "Nota confidencial," 26 December 1967, "A todos los Carlistas," 1 March 1968, "Carta abierta a Don Juan Palomino," 25 February 1968, "Junta Depuradora Carlista," 4 March 1967, caja "Junta Depuradora Carlista," APCT; *Comunicación No. 1,* Junta Suprema, Comunión Tradicionalista, January 1968, APCT; *Ya,* 20 October 1969, pp. 14–15; 11 May 1971; *Mundo,* 29 May 1971, pp. 23–24.

5. Note to the secretary-general of the Comunión by the regional chief of the Comunión, Elda (Alicante), about the visit of General Luis Ruíz Hernández, 14 September 1967; letter of General Luis Ruiz Hernández to Don Javier, 30 November 1967; "La desaparación del Requeté de Madrid," Los Requetés de Madrid, n.d.; "Carta Abierta a los Carlistas," Jefatura Provincial del Requeté de Madrid, 10 April 1968; "Dios, Patria, Fueros y Rey Javier," Jefatura del Requeté del Reino de Valencia, 20 March 1973; copies of all these documents in caja "Propaganda," APCT.

In 1964, veterans had been very angry with the leadership of the Comunión for prohibiting any military display (including battle dress) at the Montejurra of that year. (On this prohibition, see "Concentración de Montejurra," 18 April 1964; "Concentración en Montejurra (II)," 22 April 1964, Secretaría National, AET, APCT).

6. Letter to the Marqués de Marchelina, Los Ex-Combatientes Carlistas, 10 February 1968; "Carta abierta al Marqués de Marchelina," La Junta Depuradora Carlista, n.d.; "Nota para la prensa. Falsa Asamblea de la Hermandad de Antiguos Combatientes de Tercios de Requetés," Secretaría, Partido Carlista, 4 March 1975; copies of all three documents in APCT.

7. *El Correo Catalan,* 11 May 1971; *Times* (London), 12 May 1971, p. 5. Some progressive Carlists liked to be as threatening as their conservative opponents. In 1968, the GAC wrote to all members of the Carlist Circle in Burgos, commanding them to send letters to the secretary-general in Madrid demanding the resignation of its president. The GAC missive ended, "It may be that you are among those disgusting fence-sitters, who sell themselves for the sake of a post. If that be so, and you do not obey our order, something that we will know, we want you to know and to be aware that you have confronted GAC" (copy of this letter, n.d., in APCT).

8. Letter of Enriques Montanes to the Jefe Provincial de Leon, 1 February 1968, copy in APCT; P. A., "Un Carlismo Socialista?" *Montejurra* 53 (June–July 1970): 11; "A los Martires en 1973," Jefatura del Requeté del Reino de Valencia, March 1973, APCT; *Pueblo,* 18 April 1974, 29 August 1975; *Ya,* 19 April 1974; *Fuerza Nueva,* 20 April 1974; *Informaciones,* 29 July 1975; *Pueblo,* 29 July 1975; *Blanco y Negro,* 2 August 1975, 27 August 1975; *Brujula,* 8 August 1975; *ABC,* 29 August 1975; *El Ideal Gallego,* 29 August 1975. In an appropriate appeal to the importance of tradition, some of these traditionalists also argued that governments could not be decided by elections, for the dead were given no vote. The past generations, who had upheld tradition, would not have been consulted.

9. Letter to members of the Hermandad Nacional de Antiguos Combatientes de Tercios de Madrid, Marqués de Marchelina, 5 February 1968, APCT; "El Integrismo Tradicionalista, extrema derecha del Franquismo," *Información Mensual,* July 1975; M-T. de Borbón-Parma 1979: 193.

10. See Vilarrubias 1975, for an extended yet impassioned argument to Carlist youth to mend their progressive ways.

11. "A los Jefes Regionales y Provinciales del Carlismo. Asunto: Dia de la Lucha Carlista, Censo y Asambleas Populares," Secretaría General, Partido Carlista, 30 November 1971, APCT.

12. "Encuesta sobre Montejurra," *Esfuerzo Común* (hereafter *EC*), no. 144 (1 May 1972): 21.

13. "Encuesta sobre Montejurra," *EC,* no. 144 (1 May 1972): 20.

14. "Encuesta sobre Montejurra," *EC,* no. 144 (1 May 1972): 22.

15. "Tres opiniones sobre Montejurra," *EC,* no. 166–67 (15 April 1973): 49.

16. "Encuesta sobre Montejurra," *EC,* no. 144 (1 May 1972): 21.

17. "Encuesta sobre Montejurra," *EC,* no. 144 (1 May 1972): 22.

18. "Tres opiniones sobre Montejurra," *EC,* no. 166–67 (15 April 1973): 48–50.

19. "Encuesta sobre Montejurra," *EC,* no. 144 (1 May 1972): 20.

20. *EC,* no. 189 (15 May 1974).

21. "Encuesta sobre Montejurra," *EC,* no. 144 (1 May 1972): 21.

22. "Montejurra 1970," *EC,* no. 117 (June 1970): 9.

23. *PN,* 2 May 1968; 4 May 1968, p. 1.

24. *PN,* 6 May 1969, p. 10.

25. Caspistegui Gorasurreta 1995: 436.

26. "Montejurra '72," GAC, copy in APCT.

27. M-T. de Borbón-Parma 1979: 159, 176–78, 189–90.

28. See coverage of Montejurra by *PN* from 1971 to 1975, especially 5 May 1972, p. 1; 9 May 1972, p. 20; 3 May 1974, p. 1. These conservatives were also annoyed that the "chaplain" of Montejurra, the traditionalist Don Joaquin Vitriain, had been replaced by a younger priest, one more open to *progresismo.*

See also "Montejurra '72, resumen anual de una catástrofe," *¿Qué Pasa?,* 20 May 1972, reprinted in Garmendia 1975: 95–98.

29. Letter from A. Izal to A. C. Fal, 8 May 1973, qtd. in Capistegui Gorasurreta 1995: 438 n. 232.

30. "Montejurra—73," Combatientes de los Tercios de Requetés, Cyclostyled flyer, copy in CDHCPV.

31. "A todos los Carlistas," La Junta Depuradora Carlista, n.d., copy in APCT.

32. In the days before Montejurra 1975, rumors circulated that violent young traditionalists would attempt to disrupt the ceremony. But nothing untoward occurred on the day (Caspistegui Gorasurreta 1995: 440).

33. "Montejurra '76. Normas para el desarollo del acto," Servicio del Orden, Partido Carlista, April 1976; *Informe,* no. 4 (14 April 1976), Partido Carlista, APCT.

34. *El Alcázar,* 5 May 1976; *Brujula* 32 (23–30 May 1976); *Fuerza Nueva,* no. 483 (10 April 1976); no. 488 (15 April 1976); no. 489 (22 May 1976); *El Noticiero Universal,* 11 May 1976; *PN,* 13 April 1976; 23 April 1976; 24 April 1976; 30 April 1976; 8 May 1976.

35. This account of Montejurra 1976 relies on fieldwork interviews, Clemente and Costa 1976, *Informe Montejurra '76, Punto y Hora* (hereafter *PH),* 4 (16–31 May 1976), and "Carlistas a tiros en Montejurra," *Diario 16,* 16 June 1989, Historia de la transición, pp. 258–70.

36. "Don Sixto de Borbón Parma, Separado del Carlismo," Servicio de Prensa, Partido Carlista, 19 November 1975, APCT.

37. *El Alcázar,* 15 May 1976.

38. *Informe Montejurra '76,* 1976; Clemente and Costa 1976.

39. Osorio 1980: 95; Martín Villa 1984: 30. I am very grateful to Charles Powell for providing information about the political background to Montejurra 1976.

40. Martín Villa 1984: 30; Eriz 1986: 212; Fraga Iribarne 1987: 47. Fraga is well aware that Basque and Navarrese Carlists hold him to blame for what occurred. (See his comments about the demonstrations mounted against him in these areas by Carlists [Fraga Iribarne 1987].)

The plot of this story has thickened recently, thanks to "revelations" about the dangerous rivalries at that time between different government departments. A leaked secret report made by the Civil Guard in September 1979 claims that Cesid (the secret service of the Spanish state) stopped an investigation into Jean Pierre Cherid. Cherid was a French mercenary who directed the Batallón Vasco Español

(Basquo-Spanish Battalion) (a very shadowy, clandestine organization in whose name were committed several violent crimes, including murders, against Basque Nationalists in the early years of the transition). Armed with a wooden pole, he was among the *sixtinos* at Montejurra 1976. Relations between the Civil Guard and Cesid were so bad that GOSSI, a special group within the Guard, carried out a number of attacks against Cesid installations. General José Sáenz de Santamaría, then director of the guard, stated in September 1998 that "the dirty-war crimes of the stage of UCD [Unión de Centro Democrático, then the party of government] have still not been revealed" (*El Mundo,* 5 September 1998). One implication of this labyrinthine tale of dark dealings and fatal consequence is that the actions of Cherid and others were being funded by sectors from within the government: by whom exactly, for what period, and for what reasons remain unclear.

41. *El Diario de Navarra* (hereafter *DN*), 12 May 1976; *Informaciones,* 15 May 1976.

42. *DN,* 11 November 1976: 28; *Diario 16,* 19 November 1977. José María Araluce, together with four of his bodyguards, was shot dead by an ETA-M commando in October 1976.

43. *DN,* 23 February 1977, p. 1.

44. "Comunicado del Partido Carlista sobre el secuestro de Don Javier de Borbón," Servicio de Prensa, Partido Carlista, 5 March 1977, APCT; *DN,* 5 March 1977, p. 5; 9 March 1977, p. 3; *Punto y Hora* 27 (17–23 March 1977): 10.

45. *PH,* no. 28 (April 1977): 4; "Los Carlistas, en casa," no. 34 (4–11 May 1977): 10–13; "La Javierada Carlista," no. 35 (12–18 May 1977): 6–8.

CHAPTER ELEVEN. THE DECLINE OF CARLISM

1. *El Diario de Navarra* (hereafter *DN*), 10 July 1977: 1; *El País,* 10 July 1997; *Ya,* 10 July 1977.

2. *El País,* 19 July 1977; *Costa Blanca,* 23 August 1977; *Arriba,* 29 October 1977; *Diario 16,* 31 December 1977.

3. "Autocrítica 1974," Partido Carlista de Vizcaya; "Cursillo de Santander," 16 December 1974; "Informe. Cursillos 1975"; "Informe de las visitas a las comarcas de Alicante," Partido Carlista de Valencia, August 1976; "Como debemos hacer uso de la crítica y autocrítica," n.d., APCT. On the lack of organization among regional chiefs, see the letter of J. M. Zavala to Jefaturas Regionales, 10 November 1970, APCT.

4. "El trabajo en los clubs juveniles," ed. Las Juventudes Carlistas del País Valenciano, September 1973, APCT.

5. "Contestaciones al 'Informe sobre la situación del Partido,'" Partido Carlista de Álava, de Andalucía, de Burgos, de Canarias, de Galicia, de Madrid, de Navarra, de Vizcaya, July 1977, APCT. "Informe General del Partido en Baleares-Pitinsas desde la ultima reunión de Consejo Federal," November 1978, APCT.

The role of the MOT had been overshadowed by newly arisen alternative workers' organizations, and it was incorporated into Comisiones Obreras (CC.OO). As a replacement, the Partido Carlista created the Frente Obrero Sindicalista (FOS), which was to be a workers' front separate from CC.OO and which would promote the progressives' ideal of self-management. So that potential recruits would not be put off by the historical association of Carlism with the regime, the party claimed to have no connections with the FOS. Besides progressive militants, the membership of FOS came to include Marxists, assemblarians, and anarchists. While its trained militants were relatively few in number, they were instrumental in starting strikes in certain Navarrese and Castellón factories.

The FOS, though supposedly independent of the Partido Carlista, did in fact receive secret directives from its leaders. By 1975 the internal debate within the FOS executive over whether or not to maintain these clandestine links became so divisive that the party withdrew its funding. The resulting cash crisis forced the FOS to integrate within CC.OO: in effect, the FOS had dissolved itself. One consequence of the way the FOS was founded was that at the very time the Navarrese labor force was gaining a justified reputation as one of the most politicized in Spain, those local progressive workers who were participating in the struggle were unable to do so under their own banner. Thus *huguista* Carlism failed to reap any direct political benefits from the continued agitation in the factories of the province. On the contrary, it was notable only by its apparent absence. To prevent the same mistakes occurring again, the new Frente Obrero Carlista (FOC, Carlist Workers' Front) set up to succeed the FOS was, from its inception, openly declared to be an integral part of the party. But its creation came too late to halt the decline of progressive worker-militants.

6. Some student regional leaders complained of a lack of seriousness among their members, who would not turn up for meetings ("Reunión de los Grupos de lucha en bachiller del Partido Carlista de Vizcaya y Navarra. Marzo de 1964," APCT).

7. "Cursillos. Tema 4. Organización de una provincia," Partido Carlista, n.d.; "Informe económico," Secretario Político Provincial, Malaga, APCT.

8. "Análisis global de nuestra participación en las elecciones," J-F. Martin de Aguilera and E. Diez Monsalve, n.d. (1977), APCT.

9. Arregi 1981: 261–302. In 1975 the Carlists were still considered sufficiently influential by other groups that they were able to convoke a meeting of the anti-franquist opposition to discuss their proposal of uniting the political forces in the Basque region. The gathering was attended by representatives of the PSOE, the military and politicomilitary factions of ETA, Basque Christian Democrats, and a variety of radical Basque and left-wing groups. But nothing came of the proposal. The groups attending were too diverse politically for them to agree on anything substantial, and none saw anything to gain in giving the Carlists the initiative.

10. "Comunicado del Comite de Dirección del Partido Carlista de Euskadi (EKA)," EKA, 24 April 1977, APCT.

11. "Análisis global de nuestra participación en las elecciones," J-F. Martin de Aguilera and E. Diez Monsalve, n.d. (1977), APCT.

12. "Primer comunicado del colectivo socialista de EKA," April 1978, APCT.

"Acuerdo tomado por la Asamblea de Militantes del Partido Carlista de Madrid celebrada el dia 23 de Junio 1977," Jefe Provincial del Partido Carlista, Madrid, June 1997, APCT.

Zavala's directives about the way to hold *cursillos,* which were meant to last three days, from 9:00 A.M. to 2:00 P.M. and 4:00 P.M. to 9:00 P.M., included rules that participants were not to leave the room without the express permission of the director of the *cursillo,* and that the plan and program of work of each course could not be changed, even by its director, without the written authorization of Zavala himself. The directives also recommended that participants should, at every moment, comply with the corresponding rules or norms: "These rules or norms will serve to orient participants so that they do not deviate from the line established by the political, doctrinal, and ideological directives." "Reglamentos de cursillos," Secretaría General, Partido Carlista, n.d., APCT.

13. Statements by J. M. Sabater Salvador, Secretaría General, Partido Carlista, 15 and 16 January 1978; "Dossier sobre la invalidación de la asamblea del Partido Carlista de Madrid por el Consejo Federal de Dirección, en su reunión de los dias 14 y 15 de enero, con aportación de todos los documentos, acuerdos y hechos relativos al caso," Consejo Federal, 16 January 1978; "Informe sobre la reunión del Consejo Federal de Dirección celebrada el dia 18 de febrero de 1978," Secretaría General, February 1978; "Informe y acuerdos de la reunión del Consejo Federal del Partido Carlista celebrada durante los dias 11 y 12 de Marzo de 1978," Secretaría General, March 1978; APCT.

14. "Enmienda a la totalidad del proyecto de linea política del Partido Carlista, presentada por el Partido Carlista de Euskadi (E.K.A.)," EKA, October 1977; "Comunicado del consejo Federal de Dirección a todos los militantes del Partido," Secretaría General, Partido Carlista, December 1977; "Informe a los militantes. Situación real y programa de desarollo del Partido Carlista," Secretario General Federal, Partido Carlista, March 1978; APCT.

15. "Montejurra '78. Instrucciones a todos los miembros del Consejo Federal," Secretaría de Organización, Partido Carlista, n.d. (1978), APCT; *DN,* 9 May 1978, p. 16; *Egin,* 9 May 1978, pp. 6, 8.

16. *El Pueblo Gallego,* 9 November 1977; *Actualidad Política,* 28 November 1977; *Pueblo,* 7 December 1977; *Diario Regional,* Valladolid, 8 December 1977; *Las Provincias,* 16 December 1977; *Egin,* 24 January 1978; *Mundo Diario,* 27 January 1978; *Solidaridad Nacional,* 28 January 1978.

17. "Declaración del Comite de Dirección del Consejo Consultativo del Partido de Euskadi (EKA)," EKA, 27 April 1977, APCT.

18. "Informe de Vizcaya sobre la situación política de la izquierda vasca y alternativas por mandato del Consejo Nacional de EKA," Comité Político, 8 December 1977, APCT; *DN,* 24 January 1978, p. 13; 29 April 1978, p. 4; *Denok Batean,* March 1978, 2; *Egin,* 5 November 1978, 10; *Izquierda Vasca,* EKA, n.d. (1978), APCT. In 1973, a trio of leading Basque Carlists met with members of ETA in Bayona. The gunmen wanted the Carlists to join in the armed struggle, but the progressive activists refused, saying the situation did not yet justify such measures.

19. *DN*, 2 November 1978, p. 5; *Egin*, 4 October 1978, p. 5; 10 October 1978, p. 10; "Constitución '78. Consolidar la democracia para construir el socialismo," Partido Carlista, n.d. (1978); "Constitución 78 y referendum," Partido Carlista, n.d. (1978), APCT.

20. EKA statement quoted in *DN*, 14 January 1979, p. 17.

21. *El País*, 3 March 1979. The party had not fielded candidates in the provinces of Badajoz, Cáceres, Ceuta, Córdoba, La Coruña, Guadalajara, Jaén, Oviedo, Salamanca, Segovia, Seville, Soria, Toledo, Valladolid, and Zamora. Nationally, the party gained less than 0.125 percent of the vote (52,338 votes).

22. "Informe a los militantes. Situación real y programa de desarollo del Partido Carlista," Secretario General Federal, Partido Carlista, March 1978, APCT.

23. "Informe y acuerdos de la reunión ordinaria del Consejo Nacional de Dirección del Partido Carlista celebrada el 16 y 17/12/78," Secretaría de Relaciones Políticas, Partido Carlista, 21 December 1978, APCT. C. Catalan, interview by author, Pamplona, 30 April 1987; J. Querejeta, interview by author, Fuenterrabía, 7 September 1987.

24. Letter to J. M. Zavala from F. Pérez Puerto, Secretario del Partido Carlista de Andalucía, 7 August 1977, APCT.

25. "Primer comunicado del colectiva socialista de EKA," April 1978; "Análisis de la realidad del PCA en Sevilla y provincia, en Julio 1978," Partido Carlista de Andalucía, May 1978, APCT.

26. "Informe del Comité Ejecutivo sobre las elecciones generales del 1 de Marzo de 1979," Comité Ejecutivo Federal, Partido Carlista, March 1979, APCT.

27. Although during the Franquist period progressives tended not to use the Cross of Saint Andrew as a symbol of the movement because of its association with the Movimiento, in 1972 militants attending the Second Nationalist Carlist Congress proposed, and had passed, a motion that it be revived as an emblem of Carlism (C. de Borbón-Parma 1977: 7).

28. Leading Carlists had long been aware of the image held of their movement by non-Carlists, both within Spain and beyond. In the preparations for the Montejurra of 1964, the national secretary of the AET warned his members that one prestigious English newspaper was representing the ceremony as one of "torchlight processions, wildly reactionary speeches in an atmosphere of typically Fascist mysticism" ("Concentración de Montejurra," 18 April 1964, Secretaría Nacional, AET, APCT).

29. Gobierno de Navarra 1979a.

30. The same tension between national leaders who thought of Carlism in almost exclusively tactical terms and provincial ones who had a much broader concept of Carlist identity also manifested itself in December 1969 when five of the GAC commando were arrested during their raid on a TV transmitter. The progressives in the capital gave them no support at all, despite protests from the movement's Navarrese and Gipuzkoan deputies. This pair of conservatives argued that whatever these misguided youths had done, they were still Carlists, and ones, moreover, in need of legal aid, which they proceeded to provide.

31. "Montejurra '79," Secretaría de Organización, Partido Carlista, 20 April 1979, APCT.

32. "Encuesta a los militantes del Partido Carlista," copy in the author's possession.

33. "Declaración de Carlos Hugo de Borbón Parma al Consejo Federal de Dirección del Partido Carlista," 24 November 1979, APCT.

34. The only publication of their Centro Europeo de Estudios Socioeconómicos was the pamphlet *CEES. Una propuesta para el debate,* Madrid, May 1980.

35. He would not have been the first Borbón prince to enter a parliament. In the 1960s, Otto of Habsburg and Borbón-Parma, heir of the last emperor of Austria-Hungary and son of Don Javier's sister the Empress Zita, moved toward liberalism and Christian Democracy. Renouncing his claim to the throne in order to return to Austria, he became first the president of a monarchist party in an unsuccessful bid to become head of state via the democratic process, and later his country's leading representative in the European Parliament at Strasbourg (Santa Cruz 1979–1992, vol. 13: 104–7; Brook-Shepherd 1991).

36. *Montejurra* 18: 8.

37. Gobierno de Navarra 1979b.

38. "Informe sobre las jornadas de trabajo. Julio de 1980, Santesteban (Navarra)," Secretaría General, Partido Carlista, August 1980, APCT.

39. Gobierno de Navarra 1979b, 1983.

40. *Navarra Hoy* (hereafter *NH*), 12 May 1986, p. 7; 17 May 1986, p. 10; 29 April 1987, p. 7.

41. *NH,* 3 May 1987, p. 9; 7 June 1987, p. 13; Gobierno de Navarra 1987.

42. *NH,* 16 February 1987, p. 5.

43. Among the more short-lived groups were Acción Publica del Regionalismo, put together in 1975 by Valiente and Zamanillo, the Unión Social Monárquica assembled the same year by Forcadell from his supporters within the Hermandad de Maestrazgo, and Unión Nacional, constituted in 1976 and whose members included Valiente and Antonio María de Oriol. Valiente's final political move was to take his followers with him when he entered the right-wing nationwide party Alianza Popular, then headed by Fraga (Fraga Iribarne 1987: 88; López Rodó 1993: 108, 218).

44. *NH,* 29 October 1985, p. 8; 18 January 1986, p. 9; 8 June 1986, p. 8; 17 June 1986, p. 19; *Egin,* 30 September 1986, p. 7; *DN,* 9 May 1986, p. 26. The most fulsome statement of their political philosophy is given in *Carlismo Otra Vez* (Comunión Tradicionalista Carlista 1989). The Gipuzkoan branch of the renovated Comunión publishes *Fuerista,* while *Boletín "Fal Conde"* is produced by Granadan traditionalists.

When the party asked for the return of those of its newspapers, magazines, radio stations, and centers that had been confiscated by the government during the years of the regime, the Comunión immediately contested the petition, arguing that it was the only legitimate Carlist organization and therefore the only rightful owner of the expropriated property (*NH,* 17 January 1978, p. 4). There was a similar, long-running dispute between members of the two bodies over possession of the objects once displayed in the Navarrese Museo de Recuerdos Históricos de la Tradición.

CHAPTER TWELVE. VILLAGE CARLISM: 1939–1987

1. On the nature and evolution of these transformations within Navarre as a whole, see Mendaza Clemente 1994, Echeverría Zabalza 1994.

2. In the first days of the uprising, in one village of the Ribera, the supporters of the insurgency shot or imprisoned the local male Republicans; then they rounded up the female sympathizers of the government, shaved their heads, and paraded them around the streets. After they had been sufficiently mocked, someone suggested that they be raped, but some of the young men protested, on the grounds that they might later wish to marry them. (On this incident, see Altaffaylla Kultur Taldea 1986.)

3. For an overview of social and ideological change in Navarre during this general period, see Pérez-Agote 1989.

4. "La juventud se define. Cultura y deporte además de trabajo," *El Diario de Navarra,* 20 June 1970.

5. Photocopy of the letter in the author's possession.

6. Photocopy in author's possession.

7. The PCE won 1 percent, and four votes were declared invalid. Electoral figures for both elections come from Gobierno de Navarra 1977, 1979a.

8. See, e.g., "Libro de actas del ayuntamiento de Cirauqui," 5 September 1980.

9. "Libro de actas del ayuntamiento de Cirauqui," 17 August 1979.

10. MacClancy 1991.

11. See, e.g., "Libro de actas del ayuntamiento de Cirauqui," 5 September 1980, 4 September 1981, 8 October 1981, 27 August 1982, 17 December 1982. The nationalists could, however, receive support from other councillors. On 25 April 1981, the town hall held an extraordinary meeting where it passed unanimously a motion expressing "its most energetic protest against the arrest of [one of the nationalist councillors] as arbitrary and unjustified." On 20 May 1982, it agreed, by five votes to two, to donate money to an organization dedicated to the teaching of Euskera; on 25 February 1983, it agreed unanimously to make a further donation to the same end.

12. See, e.g., "Libro de actas del ayuntamiento de Cirauqui," 1 July 1983, 4 November 1983, 4 June 1985.

13. The first issue was published on 30 June 1983; the sixth (and last) on 31 December 1986. Copies in the author's possession.

14. The possibility of violence against left-wing nationalist youth in the village had been dramatically demonstrated the previous November when two off-duty members of the Foral Police had taken violent control of a bar on the edge of the village patronized by youths from Cirauqui and neighboring villages. During the

two hours they occupied the bar, they beat up several of its clients, treated disparagingly any books they found dealing with Euskera, and insulted the two young female villagers running the bar as *"abertzale* [Basque patriot] prostitutes." Eighty-six villagers signed a petition denouncing the event, but a motion to the same effect, presented by the nationalists at an extraordinary meeting of the town hall on 7 December, was not approved. On this incident, its consequences and the debate it provoked, see *Deia,* 8 February 1983; *Egin* 3, 5, 7, 9, 10, 15 December 1982; 26 January; 8, 18 February; 1 March; 15, 21, 29 April; 4 May 1983; *Navarra Hoy,* 4, 9, 10, 11, 12, 13, 14, 16, 17, 18 December 1982; 26 January 1983; *El País,* 5 December 1982.

15. Udalaren Euskara Zerbitzua 1995.

16. Hobsbawm and Ranger 1982.

17. Urla 1993.

18. MacClancy 1996.

19. MacClancy 1993.

20. "¿Bien del pueblo or intolerancia?," Candidatura Asamblearia Independiente de Cirauqui; September 1987. Copy in author's possession.

CHAPTER THIRTEEN. THE LEGACIES OF CARLISM
TO BASQUE NATIONALISM

1. For assessments by Basque historians and intellectuals of the connections between Carlism and early Basque nationalism, see, for example, Beltza 1978; Corcuera Atienza 1979: 52–58; Garmendia 1984: 431–39; Real Cuesta 1991: 86–87, 178; García-Sanz Marcotegui 1995.

2. Juaristi 1997: 330.

3. *Egin,* 7 March 1987, p. 7.

4. *El Mundo,* 12 November 1998, p. 10; 28 March 1999, p. 20.

5. *El Mundo,* 26 January 1999, p. 8.

6. *El Mundo,* 28 January 1999, p. 2. In June 1999, during the debate in the Cortes on the state of the nation, Iñaki Anasagasti, pnv spokesperson in the chamber, attacked the government for its inactivity in the peace process, for its failure to help solve what he called *"el largo contencioso"* (the long dispute), which had started with the Carlist Wars. He was promptly criticized by an antinationalist journalist for his "whining Carlism" (*El Mundo,* 23 April 1999, p. 3; 24 April 1999, p. 14). For further examples of antinationalists criticizing the association of traditional Carlism and modern Basque nationalism, see *El Mundo,* 8 January 2000, p. 5; 14 February 2000, p. 6; 15 May 2000, p. 12; 18 May 2000, p. 4.

7. Juaristi 1997: 326–44. For further analysis of Arzalluz's attitudes toward Carlism, see Urquijo 1998: 86–89.

8. Oteiza 1984: 321.

9. Arteche 1967: 15. Beltza deals exclusively with the role of Carlism in the origins of Basque nationalism.

10. Davant 1987: 41–42.

11. Apalategi 1987: 81. The significance of the book from which these three quotes come was underlined in 1999 by a local journalist in his commentary on the intentions of the Basque bloc participating in the peace process (*El Mundo,* 26 January 1999, p. 4).

12. Castells 1987: 219.

13. Monzón n.d.: 78, 95, qtd. in Gilmour 1985. See also Juaristi 1999: 178.

14. *Deia,* 20 April 1982; qtd. in Castells 1987: 219.

15. Qtd. in Aulestia 1998: 40. See also Urquijo 1998: 101–2; Juaristi 1999: 72–73, 160, 198, 214.

16. *Egin,* 30 October 1986, p. 10. See also *Navarra Hoy* (hereafter *NH*), 24 October 1986, p. 14; *Egin,* 19 August 1986, p. 4.

17. Rincón 1985: 78. The comments by Arbeloa, Astrain, and Berruezo are all personal communications.

18. MacClancy 1993; Arriaga Landeta 1997; Aulestia 1998: 64.

19. Aulestia 1998: 99–100.

20. *Egin,* 1 August 1980, p. 7.

21. Antoñana 1996; Atxaga 1996; Gil Bera 1996.

22. *Nosotros. Revista de análisis político de FE-JONS,* no. 18 (March 1997), http://www.falange.es/nosotros/nosotros18/editora.htm.

23. Letter by E. Battaner, 15 February 1996, to *Ciberespacio Charro* II, no. 8, University of Salamanca, http://judas.usal.es/cech/numeros/cech8.

24. *NH,* 18 March 1986, p. 431; Aronson 1966: 224.

EPILOGUE: MONTEJURRA 1986

1. Aronson 1966: 224.

APPENDIX I. COMPUTER ANALYSIS OF THE
1897 CADASTRAL SURVEY OF CIRAUQUI

1. Santamaría et al. 1992: 339.

APPENDIX II. APPROXIMATE NUMBERS ATTENDING
MONTEJURRA, 1939–1989

1. *El Pensamiento Navarra* (hereafter *PN*), 4 May 1941.
2. *PN,* 11 May 1954, p. 1; *El Diario de Navarra* (hereafter *DN*), 11 May 1954, p. 7.
3. *PN,* 10 May 1955, p. 12.
4. *PN,* 8 May 1956, p. 12.
5. *PN,* 7 May 1957, p. 10.

6. *Times* (London), 12 May 1959, p. 10.

7. *Times* (London), 10 May 1960, p. 11.

8. *PN*, 8 May 1962, p. 12; *Arriba*, 8 May 1962.

9. *DN*, 7 May 1963, p. 16; *PN*, 7 May 1963, p. 16; *Montejurra*, 29 June 1963.

10. *Times* (London), 4 May 1964, p. 12; *DN*, 5 May 1964, p. 16; *PN*, 5 May 1964; Lavardín 1976: 232.

11. *PN*, 6 May 1965; Lavardín 1976: 254.

12. *Montejurra* 17 (1966); Lavardín 1976: 268.

13. *PN*, 5 May 1967.

14. *PN*, 6 May 1969.

15. *DN*, 5 May 1970, p. 28.

16. *DN*, 4 May 1971, p. 28.

17. *DN*, 9 May 1972, p. 24.

18. *DN*, 8 May 1973, p. 14.

19. *DN*, 7 May 1974, p. 28.

20. *DN*, 6 May 1975, p. 28.

21. *DN*, 10 May 1977, p. 32.

22. *Egin*, 9 May 1978, p. 6; *DN*, 9 May 1978, p. 16.

23. *DN*, 8 May 1979, p. 18.

24. *DN*, 6 May 1980, p. 18.

25. *Navarra Hoy*, 12 May 1986, p. 7.

26. *Navarra Hoy*, 11 May 1987, p. 5.

27. *El Correo Espanol–El Pueblo Vasco*, 8 May 1989, p. 13.

Bibliography

ARCHIVES

AAD	Archivo Administrativo de la Diputación, Navarre
AAP	Archivo del Arzobispado de Pamplona
AATP	Archivo de la Audiencia Territorial de Pamplona
AGM	Archivo General Militar, Segovia
AGN	Archivo General de Navarra
AJE	Archivo Judicial de Estella
AMA	Archivo Municipal de Ayegui
AMC	Archivo Municipal de Cirauqui
APC	Archivo Parroquial de Cirauqui
APCN	Archivo del Partido Carlista, Navarre
APCT	Archivo del Partido Carlista, Tolosa
CDHCPV	Centro de Documentación de Historia Contemporánea del País Vasco, San Sebastián

PERIODICALS

El Diario de Navarra (DN) 1939–1989
Esfuerzo Común (EC) 1963–1973
Montejurra
Navarra Hoy (NH)
Punto y Hora (PH)
El Pensamiento Navarro (PN) 1939–1976

BOOKS AND ARTICLES

Abélès, Marc. 1988. "Modern Political Ritual. Ethnography of an Inauguration and a Pilgrimage by President Mitterand." *Current Anthropology* 29 (3 June): 391–404. First published in *Les Temps Modernes*, March 1987.

Agirreazkuenaga, Joseba. 1990. "La via armada como método de intervención política. Analisis del pronunciamiento carlista (1833)." In *150 años del convenio de Bergara y de la ley del 25-X-1839*, edited by Joseba Agirreazkuenaga and José Ramon Urquijo Goitia, 177–226. Colección Fondo Histórico. Vitoria: Parlamento Vasco.

Agirreazkuenaga, Joseba, and José Ramon Urquijo Goitia, eds. 1990. *150 años del convenio de Bergara y de la ley del 25-X-1839.* Colección Fondo Histórico. Vitoria: Parlamento Vasco.

Altaffaylla Kultur Taldea, ed. 1986. *Navarra 1936. "De la esperanza al terror."* Tafalla: Altaffaylla Kultur Taldea.

Alvarez Rey, Leandro. 1990. "El Carlismo en Andalucia durante la Segunda República (1931–1936)." In *Sevilla, 36: Sublevación fascista y represion* by A. Braojos Garrida, L. Alvarez Rey, and F. Espinosa Maestre. Seville: Muñoz Moya y Montraveta.

Anderson, Benedict. 1983. *Imagined Communities: Reflections on the Origin and Spread of Nationalism.* London: Verso.

Andrés-Gallego, José. 1987. "Génesis de la Navarra contemporánea." *Principe de Viana* XLVIII, anejo 6, Primer Congreso General de la Historía de Navarra, 1: Ponencias, 195–234.

Antoñana, Pablo. 1990. *Noticias de la Segunda Guerra Carlista.* Panorama, no. 16. Pamplona: Gobierno de Navarra, Departamento de Educación y Cultura.

———. 1996. *Relato cruento.* Pamplona: Pamiela. First published 1978, Pamplona: Caja de Ahorros Municipal de Pamplona.

Apalategi, Jokin. 1987. "Euskadi. Algunos rasgos esenciales de su historia cultural euskaldun." In *Euskadi en Guerra,* edited by Jean Louis Davant et al., 61–107. Bayonne: Ekin.

Apesteguia, Goya. 1988. *Un poco de Cirauqui.* Cirauqui.

Arcediano, Santiago, and José Antonio García Díez. 1993. *Carlos Sáenz de Tejada.* Vitoria: Fundación Caja de Ahorros de Vitoria y Álava.

Ardit Lucas, Manuel. 1977. *Revolución Liberal y Revuelta campesina. Un ensayo sobre la desintegración del régimen feudal en el País Valenciano (1793–1840).* Barcelona: Ariel.

Aronson, Theo. 1966. *Royal Vendetta: The Throne of Spain, 1829–1966.* London: Oldbourne.

Aróstegui Sánchez, Julio. 1970. *El Carlismo Álavés y la Guerra Civil de 1870–1876.* Vitoria: Diputación Foral de Álava.

———. 1988. "La tradición militar del carlismo y el origen del requeté." *Aportes* 8: 3–23.

———. 1991. *Los combatientes Carlistas en la Guerra Civil Española, 1936–1939.* Vol. 1. Madrid: Fundación Hernando de Larramendi.

Arraiza, Francisco. 1930. *La cocina navarra.* Vergara: Congreso de Estudios Vascos.

Arregi, Natxo. 1981. *Memorias del KAS.* Donostia: Hordago.

Arrese, José Luis de. 1982. *Una etapa constituyente.* Barcelona: Planeta.

Arriaga Landeta, Mikel. 1997. *. . . y nosotros que éramos de HB . . . Sociología de una heterodoxia abertzale.* San Sebastián: Haranburu.

Arteche, José de. 1967. *Discusión en Bidartea.* Zarauz: Itxaropena.

Asensio Rubio, Manuela. 1987. *El Carlismo en la provincia de Ciudad Real, 1833–1876.* Ciudad Real: Diputación de Ciudad Real.

Asín Remírez de Esparza, Francisco Javier. 1983. *El Carlismo Aragonés, 1833–40.* Zaragoza: Librería General.

————. 1988. "El Carlismo en la primera guerra. La importancia de los estudios regionales y la necesaria revisión de algunas cuestiones." *Principe de Viana* XLIX, anejo 9, Primer Congreso General de Historia de Navarra, 4: Communicaciones, 265–78.

Asín Remírez de Esparza, Francisco Javier, and Alfonso Bullón de Mendoza y Gómez de Valugera. 1987. *Carlismo y sociedad 1833–1840*. Zaragoza: Librería General.

Atxaga, Bernardo. 1996. *Un espía llamdo Sara*. Madrid: Acento.

Aulestia, Kepa. 1998. *HB. Crónica de un delirio*. Madrid: Temas de Hoy.

Azcona y Diaz de Rada, J. M. 1938. "El Batallón del Requeté, Tercero de Navarra." *El Diario Vasco* (San Sebastián), 14 May.

Azurmendi, M. 1988. *Los fuegos de los simbolos. Artificios sagrados del imaginario en la cultura vasca tradicional*. San Sebastián: Baroja.

Baleztena, Dolores. 1957. *Cancionero Popular Carlista*. Pamplona: Gómez.

Baleztena, Dolores, and Miguel Angel Astiz. 1944. *Romerías Navarras*. Pamplona.

Barahona, Renato. 1989. *Vizcaya on the Eve of Carlism: Politics and Society, 1800–1833*. Reno: University of Nevada Press.

Barreiro Fernández, José Ramón. 1976. *El Carlismo Gallego*. Santiago de Compostela: Pico Sacro.

Bell, David Scott, and Byron Criddle. 1984. *The French Socialist Party: Resurgence and Victory*. Oxford: Clarendon Press.

Beltza [Emilio López de Adán]. 1978. *Del Carlismo al nacionalismo burgués*. San Sebastián: Txertoa.

Billig, Michael. 1992. *Talking of the Royal Family*. London: Routledge.

Binns, Christopher. 1979. "The Changing Face of Power: Revolution and Accommodation in the Development of the Soviet Ceremonial System." *Man*, n.s., 14: 585–606.

Blinkhorn, Martin. 1972. "Ideology and Schism in Spanish Traditionalism." *Iberian Studies* 1: 16–24.

————. 1975. *Carlism and Crisis in Spain, 1931–1939*. Cambridge: Cambridge University Press.

————. 1979. *Carlismo y contrarrevolución en España, 1931–1939*. Barcelona: Grijalbo.

————. 1984. "War on Two Fronts: Politics and Society in Navarre 1931–6." In *Revolution and War in Spain, 1931–1939*, edited by Paul Preston, 58–84. London: Methuen.

————. 1990. "Elites in Search of Masses: The Traditionalist Communion and the Carlist Party, 1937–82." In *Elites and Power in Twentieth-Century Spain*, edited by Francis Lannon and Paul Preston, 179–201. Oxford: Clarendon Press.

————. 1991. "Land and Power in Arcadia: Navarre in the Early Twentieth Century." In *Landownership and Power in Modern Europe*, edited by R. Gibson and M. Blinkhorn, 216–34. London: Harper Collins.

Bloch, Maurice. 1986. *From Blessing to Violence: History and Ideology in the Circumcision Ritual of the Merina of Madagascar*. Cambridge: Cambridge University Press.

Bogacz, T. 1986. "'A Tyranny of Words': Language, Poetry and Antimodernism in England in the First World War." *Journal of Modern History* 58: 642–68.

Bogle, Joanna, and James Bogle. 1990. *A Heart for Europe: The Lives of Emperor Charles and Empress Zita of Austria-Hungary.* Leominster: Fowler Wright.

Bonet, L. 1835. *Apuntes sobre la guerra de Navarra extractando la topografía del país, que favorece los movimientos de la facción. Caracter de sus habitantes para protegerla. Elementos que ha tendio por su formación, y los que tiene para su sostenimiento y fuerzas de que se compone en esta fecha; con una sucinta idea del sistema de campaña, y de los medios que siendo adoptados, podrán acaso terminarla.* Valladolid: Aparicio.

Borbón-Parma, Carlos Hugo de. 1976. *¿Que es el Carlismo?* Barcelona: La Gaya Ciencia.

———. 1977. *La via Carlista al socialismo autogestionario. El proyecta carlista de socialismo democratico.* Barcelona: Grijalbo.

Borbón-Parma, Cecilia de. 1977. *Diccionario del Carlismo.* Barcelona: Dopesa.

———. 1997. "Nuestro padre, don Javier." In *don Javier, una vida al servicio de la libertad,* by M-T. de Borbón-Parma et al., 237–50. Barcelona: Plaza & Janés.

Borbón-Parma, María-Teresa de. 1977. *El momento actual español cargado de utopia.* Madrid: Cuadernos para el diálogo.

———. 1979. *La clarificación del Partido Carlista.* Madrid: EASA.

———. 1989. "El Carlismo entre 1881 y 1889." In *Centenario del Código Civil,* edited by Francisco Rico Pérez, 465–75. Madrid: Universidad Popular Enrique Tierno Galvan.

———. 1997. "Memoria de mi padre." In *Don Javier, una vida al servicio de la libertad,* by M-T. de Borbón-Parma et al., 49–76. Barcelona: Plaza & Janés.

Borbón-Parma, María-Teresa, Josep Carles Clemente, and Joaquín Cubero Sánchez. 1997. *Don Javier, una vida al servicio de la libertad.* Barcelona: Plaza & Janés.

Bourbon-Parma, François Xavier de. 1949. *Les accords secrets Franco-Anglais de décembre de 1940.* Paris: Plon.

Brenan, Gerald. 1943. *The Spanish Labyrinth: An Account of the Social and Political Background of the Spanish Civil War.* Cambridge: Cambridge University Press.

Breuilly, John. 1982. *Nationalism and the State.* Manchester: Manchester University Press.

Brook Shepherd, Gordon. 1968. *The Last Habsburg.* London: Weidenfeld and Nicolson.

———. 1991. *The Last Empress: The Life and Times of Zita of Austria-Hungary, 1892– 1989.* London: Harper Collins.

Bryan, G. 1965. "The Red Berets: The Persistent Vitality of Carlism." *The Tablet* (London), 19 June, 683–84.

Bullón de Mendoza y Gómez de Valugera, Alfonso. 1988. "Nuevas notas sobre el Carlismo y los Fueros." *Principe de Viana* XLIX, anejo 9, Primer Congreso General de Historia de Navarra, 4: Communicaciones, 291–97.

———. 1991a. "El Carlismo Extremeño." In *Los Carlistas, 1800–1876,* edited by Francisco Rodríguez de Coro, 229–43. Vitoria: Fundación Sancho el Sabio.

———. 1991b. "Carlismo y Sociedad." In *Los Carlistas, 1800–1876*, edited by Francisco Rodríguez de Coro, 119–42. Vitoria: Fundación Sancho el Sabio.

———. 1995. *La Primera Guerra Carlista*. Madrid: Actas.

Burgo, Jaime del. 1939. *Veteranos de la Causa*. San Sebastián: Española.

———. 1970. *Conspiración y Guerra Civil*. Madrid: Alfaguara.

———. 1978a. *Bibliografía del siglo XIX. Guerras Carlistas, luchas politicas*. Pamplona.

———. 1978b. *Navarra*. Serie: España es asi. Leon: Nebrija.

———. 1985. *De la España romantica. Lances y aventuras de un General Prusiano (1837–1848)*. Pamplona: Gobierno de Navarra.

Calleja, Eduardo, and Julio Aróstegui. 1995. "La tradición recuperada. El requeté Carlista y la insurrección." *Historia Contemporanea* 11: 29–53.

Carnicero, Carlos, et al. 1977. *Asamblea Federal del Frente Obrero del Partido Carlista*. Madrid: Akal.

Caro Baroja, Julio. 1969. *Ensayo sobre la literature de Cordel*. Madrid: Revista del Occidente.

———. [1949] 1971. *Los Vascos*. Madrid: ISTMO.

———. 1980. *Introducción a una historia contemporánea del anticlericalismo español*. Madrid: ISTMO.

Carr, Raymond. 1966. *Spain, 1808–1939*. Oxford: Oxford University Press.

Carrillo, Santiago. 1983. *Memoria de la transición*. Barcelona: Grijalbo.

Casariego, Jesús Evaristo. 1945. *Romances modernos de toros, guerra y caza*. Madrid: Masia Alonso.

———. 1975. *La historia triste de Fernando y Belisa*. Oviedo.

Caspistegui Gorasurreta, Francisco Javier. 1995. "El Carlismo Navarro en la posguerra." Diss., Universidad de Navarra.

Castells, Miguel. 1987. "Represion generalizada en Euskadi y respuesta global." In *Euskadi en guerra*, edited by Jean Louis Davant et al., 153–221. Bayonne: Ekin.

Castroviejo Bolibar, María Francisca. 1977. *Aproximación sociologica al carlismo gallego*. Madrid: Akal.

CEES (Centro Europeo de Estudios Socioeconómicos). 1980. *Una propuesta para El Debate*. Madrid.

Christian, William A. 1972. *Person and God in a Spanish Valley*. New York and London: Seminar Press.

———. 1987. "Tapping and Defining New Power: The First Month of Visions at Ezquioga, July 1931." *American Ethnologist* 14, no. 1: 140–66.

———. 1989. *Person and God in a Spanish Valley*. Rev. ed. Princeton, N.J.: Princeton University Press.

———. 1992. *Moving Crucifixes in Modern Spain*. Princeton, N.J.: Princeton University Press.

———. 1996. *Visionaries: The Spanish Republic and the Reign of Christ*. Berkeley: University of California Press.

Cia Navascués, P. 1941. *Memorias del Tercio de Montejurra por su capellán*. Pamplona: La Acción Social.

Clara, Josep. 1992. "Sobre el carlisme a la demarcacio de Girona." In *El carlisme I la seva base social,* edited by Josep María Sole i Sabate, 215–26. Barcelona: Llibres de l'Index.

Claramunt, J. 1937. *El teniente Arizcun.* Burgos: Española.

Clemente, Josep Carles. 1969. *Hablando en Madrid.* Barcelona: Grijalbo.

———. 1977. *Historia del Carlismo contemporáneo, 1935–1972.* Barcelona: Grijalbo.

———. 1978. *Nosotros los Carlistas.* Madrid: Cambio 16.

———. 1979. *Los origenes del carlismo.* Madrid: EASA.

———. 1990. *El Carlismo. Historia de una disidencia social (1833–1976).* Barcelona: Ariel.

Clemente, Josep Carles, and C. S. Costa. 1976. *Montejurra 76. Encrucijada politica.* Barcelona: Grijalbo.

Codón Fernández, José María. 1959. *La familia en el pensamiento de la Tradición.* Madrid: Ediciones del Congreso de la Familia Española, fascículo XXXI.

Comunión Tradicionalista Carlista. 1989. *Carlismo otra vez.* Madrid: Servicio de Documentación y Publicaciones.

Connerton, Paul. 1989. *How Societies Remember.* Cambridge: Cambridge University Press.

Cora y Lira, J. de. 1953. *Carlos VIII. Monarca Tradicionalista. Pensamiento religioso, e ideario politico y social del actual representante de la Dinastia Legitima española.* Madrid: ¡Volveré!

Corbin, John R., and Marie P. Corbin. 1987. *Urbane Thought: Culture and Class in an Andalusian City.* Aldershot: Gower.

Corcuera Atienza, Javier. 1979. *Orígenes, ideologia y organización del nacionalismo vasco, 1876–1904.* Madrid: Siglo Vientiuno.

Coverdale, John F. 1984. *The Basque Phase of Spain's First Carlist War.* Princeton, N.J.: Princeton University Press.

Cubero Sánchez, Joaquín. 1990. "El Partido Carlista. Oposición al Estado Franquista y evolución ideológica (1968–1975)." In *La oposición al régimen de Franco. Estado de la cuestión y metodología de la investigación,* edited by J. Tusell et al., vol. 1, bk. 1, 399–407. Madrid: UNED.

———. 1991. "Don Javier de Borbón-Parma en el exilio. El Carlismo contra el Fascismo." Paper presented at the conference, El exilio durante el Franquismo, Salamanca, May.

Daniel, E. Valentine. 1987. *Fluid Signs: Being a Person the Tamil Way.* Berkeley: University of California Press.

Davant, Jean Louis. 1987. "Boceto para una historia del pueblo vasco." In *Euskadi en Guerra,* edited by Jean Louis Davant et al., 13–59. Bayonne: Ekin.

Davant, Jean Louis, Jokin Apalategui, José-Luis Cereceda, Miguel Castells, and El Movimiento Vasco de Liberación Nacional. 1987. *Euskadi en Guerra.* Bayonne: Ekin.

Diccionario de la lengua española. 1980. Madrid: Espasa Calpa.

Domenech Puig, R. 1956. *Diario de campana de un Requeté.* Barcelona: Selección.

Donézar, José María. 1975. *La desamortización de Mendizabal en Navarra, 1836–1851*. Madrid: Consejo Superior de Investigaciones Científicas.

Eade, John, and Michael J. Sallnow, eds. 1991. *Contesting the Sacred: The Anthropology of Christian Pilgrimage*. London: Routledge.

Echevarría, Tomas. 1986. *Franco ¿No era normal? Uno de sus hechos injustificables. La persecución de los carlistas*. Madrid.

Echeverría Zabalza, Javier. 1994. "Antecedentes de la Navarra actual. Algunos elementos sobre la estructura social de Navarra de los dos primeros tercios del siglo XX." *Gerónimo de Ustariz*, no. 9/10: 31–54.

Ellwood, Sheelagh M. 1987. *Spanish Fascism in the Franco Era*. London: Macmillan.

Elorza, Antonio. 1978. *Ideologias del nacionalismo vasco*. San Sebastián: Txertoa.

Enciclopedia general ilustrada del País Vasco. 1976. Vol. 7 of *Diccionario enciclopedico vasco*. San Sebastián: Auñamendi.

Equipo Mundo (E. Alvarez Puga, J. C. Clemente, and J. M. Girones). 1970. *Los 90 ministros de Franco*. Barcelona: Dopesa.

Eriz, Juan Felix. 1986. *Yo he sido mediador de ETA. Mi larga andadura por un diálogo*. Madrid: Arnao.

Esparza Zabalegui, José María. 1988. *Jotas heréticas de Navarra*. Tafalla: Altaffayalla Kultur Taldea.

Etayo, Carlos. 1990. *Glorias del Requeté. La Defensa de los Montes Torozos*. Pamplona: Sancho el Fuerte.

Extramiana, José. 1983. *La guerra de los Vascos en la narrativa del 98. Unamuno, Valle-Inclan, Baroja*. San Sebastián: Haranburu.

Fernández, Silvia, and Paco Roda. 1998. *Las mujeres en la historia de Pamplona*. Pamplona: Gobierno de Navarra.

Fernández, Vicente. 1988. *Carlismo y rebeldía campesina. Un estudio sobre la conflictividad social en Cantabria durante la crisis-final del Antiguo Régimen*. Madrid: Siglo XXI and Ayuntamiento de Torrelavega.

———. 1990. "Moviments populars. Pagesis i carlisme a les regions del Cantabric (Asturies i Cantabria)." In *Carlisme i moviments absolutistes*, edited by Josep María Fradera, Jesus Millán, and Ramón Garrabou, 227–44. Vic (Osuna): Eumo.

Fernández Sebastian, Javier. 1991. *La genesis del fuerismo. Prensa y ideas politicas en la crisis del Antiguo Régimen (País Vasco, 1750–1840)*. Madrid: Siglo XXI.

Ferrer, Melchor. 1941–1960. *Historia de Tradicionalismo Español*. 37 vols. Seville: Catolica Española.

———. 1946. *Observaciones de un viejo Carlista a unas cartas del Conde de Rodezno*. N.p.

Ferrer Muñoz, Manuel. 1990. "Organización y actividad del Requeté en Navarra entre 1931 y 1936." *Aportes* 14: 11–18.

Flandes Aldeyturriaga, Gloria. 1988. "'Aquel julio de 1936 . . . .' La vida cotidiana en Pamplona antes y después del levantamiento militar." *Principe de Viana* XLIX, anejo 10, Congreso General de Historia de Navarra, 5: Comunicaciones. Historia Contemporánea, 139–46.

Floristán Imízcoz, Alfredo. 1982. *La Merindad de Estella en la Edad Moderna. Los hombres y la tierra.* Pamplona: Institución Principe de Viana.

———. 1986. "Población, siglos XVI–XIX." In *La gran atlas de Navarra,* vol. 2, edited by A. J. Martín Duque, 155–60. Pamplona: Caja de Ahorros de Navarra.

———. 1993. "Desamortización y organización del espacio agrario en Navarra a mediados del siglo XIX." *Principe de Viana* LIV, anejo 15, Segundo Congreso de Historia de Navarra 3: Historia Moderna y Contemporánea, 285–98.

Fonseca, Juan. 1972. "Progresismo y tradicionalismo." *Esfuerzo Común,* no. 140 (1 March): 32–33.

Fraga Iribarne, Manuel. 1980. *Memoria breve de una vida publica.* Espejo de España, no. 54. Barcelona: Planeta.

———. 1987. *En busca del tiempo servido.* Barcelona: Planeta.

Fraser, Ronald. 1979. *Blood of Spain: The Experience of Civil War, 1936–39.* Harmondsworth: Allen Lane.

Fuente Langas, Jesús María. 1994. "Los tradicionalistas navarros bajo la dictadura de Primo de Rivera (1923–1930)." *Principe de Viana* 55, no. 202: 417–26.

Furley, J. 1876. *Among the Carlists.* London: Trinity.

Fusi, Juan Pablo. 1987. *Franco: A Biography.* London: Unwin Hyman.

Fussell, Paul. 1975. *The Great War and Modern Memory.* Oxford: Oxford University Press.

———. 1988. *Thank God for the Atom Bomb.* New York: Summit.

———. 1989. *Wartime: Understanding and Behaviour in the Second World War.* Oxford: Oxford University Press.

Gambra, Rafael. 1983. *El lenguaje y los mitos.* Madrid: Speiro.

García de Cortazar, F., and J. M. Lorenzo Espinosa. 1988. *Historia del País Vasco,* San Sebastián: Txertoa.

García Escudero, José María. 1975. *Historia política de las dos Españas.* 4 vols. Madrid: Nacional.

García Sanchiz, Federico. 1943. *Navarra.* Madrid: Aspas.

García-Sanz Marcotegui, Angel. 1984. *Navarra. Conflictividad social a comienzos del siglo XX y noticia del anarcosindicalista Gregorio Suberviola Baigorri (1896–1924).* Pamplona: Pamiela.

———. 1985. *Republicanos Navarros.* Pamplona: Pamiela.

———. 1990a. "Las elecciones de diputados forales en el distrito de Estella–Los Arcos (1877–1915)." *Principe de Viana* 51: 441–82.

———. 1990b. *Las elecciones municipales de Pamplona en la Restauración (1891–1923).* Pamplona: Gobierno de Navarra.

———. 1992. *Caciques y políticos forales. Las elecciones a la diputación de Navarra (1877–1923).* Pamplona: I. G. Castuera.

———. 1994. *Intransigencia, exaltación y populismo. La política navarra en tres semanarios criptocarlistas (1913–1915).* Donostia: Txertoa.

———. 1995. *Daniel Irujo Urra (1862–1911). El carlo-nacionalismo imposible del defensor de Sabino Arana.* Pamplona: Pamiela.

García Serrano, Rafael. 1964. *Diccionario para un macuto*. Madrid: Nacional.

―――. 1992. *Cantatas de mi molchila*. Madrid: Movierecord.

Garmendia, Vicente, ed. 1975. *El Carlismo*. Paris: Masson.

―――. 1984. *La ideología Carlista (1868–1876). En los orígenes del nacionalismo vasco*. San Sebastián: Diputacíon Foral de Guipuzcoa.

Garralda Arizcun, José Fermin. 1986. "Los carlistas expulsados de la Diputación del Reino de Navarra y del ayuntamiento de Pamplona en 1834." *Principe de Viana* XLVII, Primer Congreso de Historia de Navarra siglos XVIII–XX, 2: 287–312.

Geertz, Clifford. 1983. *Local Knowledge: Further Essays in Interpretive Anthropology*. New York: Basic Books.

Gerónimo de Uztariz-en Lur Lantaldea. 1991. "Cambio económico y distribución social de la propiedad en Navarra entre finales del S.XIX y mediados del S.XX." *Gerónimo de Uztariz* 5: 57–84.

Gil, Miguel L. 1990. *La epopeya en Valle-Inclan. Triologia de la desilusion*. Madrid: Pliegos.

Gil Bera, Eduardo. 1996. *Sobre la marcha*. Valencia: Pre-textos.

Gilmour, David. 1985. *The Transformation of Spain: From Franco to the Constitutional Monarchy*. London: Quartet Books.

Gobierno de Navarra. 1977. *Elecciones generales 1977*. Pamplona: Centro de Información y Documentación de Navarra.

―――. 1979a. *Elecciones generales 1979*. Pamplona: Centro de Información y Documentación de Navarra.

―――. 1979b. *Elecciones al Parlamento Foral 1979*. Pamplona: Centro de Información y Documentación de Navarra.

―――. 1982. *Elecciones Generales 1982*. Pamplona: Centro de Información y Documentación de Navarra.

―――. 1983. *Elecciones al Parlamento de Navarra 1983*. Pamplona: Centro de Información y Documentación de Navarra.

―――. 1987. *Elecciones al Parlamento de Navarra 1987*. Pamplona: Centro de Información y Documentación de Navarra.

Golubovic, Z. 1991. "Characteristics, Limits and Perspectives of Self-Government: A Critical Assessment." In *Yugoslavia in Turmoil: After Self-Management?* edited by James Simmie and José Dekleva, 33–44. London: Pinter.

Graburn, Nelson. 1983. *To Pray, Pay and Play: The Cultural Structure of Japanese Domestic Tourism*. Centre des Hautes Études serie B, no. 26. Aix-en-Provence: Université de Droit, d'Economie et des Sciences.

Gurko, Leo. 1962. *Joseph Conrad: Giant in Exile*. New York: Collier.

Gurmendez, C. 1978. "La autogestión, un equivoco." *El País*, 28 June.

Gurpide Beope, J. 1943. *Geografía e historia de Navarra*. Pamplona: Aramburu.

Gurruchaga, Ander. 1985. *El código nacionalista Vasco durante el Franquismo*. Barcelona: Anthropos.

Gurrutxaga, Ildefonso. 1990. "Las guerras carlistas en el siglo XIX y su significacion en la historia vasca." In *150 años del convenio de Bergara y de la ley del 25-X-1839*, edited by Joseba Agirreazkuenaga and José Ramon Urquijo Goitia, 137–76. Vitoria: Parlamento Vasco.

Haranburu, Luis, ed. 1983. *Enciclopedia histórico-geográfico de Navarra*. 6 vols. San Sebastián: Haranburu.

Heine, Hartmut. 1983. *La oposición politica al Franquismo. De 1939–1952*. Barcelona: Critica.

Hermet, Guy. 1986. *Los católicos en la España franquista*. Vol. II, *Crónica de una dictadura*. Madrid: Centro de Investigaciones Científicas.

Hertz, Robert. 1983. "Saint Besse: A Study of an Alpine Cult." In *Saints and Their Cults: Studies in Religious Sociology, Folklore and History*, edited by Stephen Wilson, 55–100. Cambridge: Cambridge University Press. First published as "Saint Besse, Étude d'un culte alpestre." *Revue de l'Histoire des Religions* 67 (1913): 115–80. Republished in R. Hertz, *Sociologie religieuse et folklore*, 110–60. Paris: PUF, 1928. Reprint 1970.

Herzberger, David K. 1995. *Narrating the Past: Fiction and Historiography in Postwar Spain*. Durham, N.C.: Duke University Press.

Hobsbawm, Eric, and Terence O. Ranger, eds. 1982. *The Invention of Tradition*. Cambridge: Cambridge University Press.

Holt, Edgar. 1967. *The Carlist Wars in Spain*. London: Putnam.

Huici Urmeneta, Vicente, José María Jimeno Jurío, Javier Monzon, and Alfonso Estevez. 1984. *Historia de Navarra*. San Sebastián: Txertoa.

Huici Urmeneta, Vicente, Mikel Sorauren, and José María Jimeno Jurío. 1982. *Historia contemporánea de Navarra*. Askatasun Haizea no. 51. San Sebastián: Txertoa.

Idoate, Florencio. 1966. *Rincones de la historia de Navarra*, vol. III. Pamplona: Diputación Foral de Navarra.

Imbuluzqueta Alcasena, Gloria. 1988. " 'El Fuerista Navarro'. Periodico pamplonés en el bloqueo carlista de 1874." *Principe de Viana* XLIX, anejo 9, Primer Congreso General de la Historia de Navarra, 4: Communicaciones, 363–74.

Informe Montejurra '76. 1976. Pamplona.

Iriarte, E., and R. Chocarro. 1990. *Informacion. NN SS de Planeamiento*. Ayuntamiento de Cirauqui.

Iriarte, José Vicente. 1995. *Movimiento obrero en Navarra (1967–1977). Organización y conflictividad*. Pamplona: Gobierno de Navarra.

Iribarren, José María. 1946. *De Pascuas a Romas*. Pamplona: Gómez.

Iztueta, P. 1981. *Sociología del fenomeno contestatario del clero Vasco, 1940–1975*. Zarautz: Elkar.

Jauregui, F., and P. Vega. 1984. *Crónicas del antifranquismo (2). 1963–1970. El nacimiento de una nueva clase política*. Barcelona: Argos Vergara.

Jimeno Jurío, José María. 1988. "Alcance de la represion en Navarra." *Gerónimo de Ustariz* 2: 108–16.

———. 1990. *Calendario festivo. Primavera*. Pamplona: Panorama.

Jordan, Barry. 1990. *Writing and Politics in Franco's Spain*. London: Routledge.

Juaristi, Jon. 1989. "Un cadáver en el jardin. ETA, 20 años después." *El Correo Español–El Pueblo Vasco*, 26 February, 85–87.

———. 1997. *El Bucle Melancólico. Historias de Nacionalistas Vascos*. Madrid: Espasa.

———. 1999. *Sacra némesis. Nueva historias de nacionalistas vascos*. Madrid: Espasa Calpe.

Kemp, Peter. 1957. *Mine Were of Trouble*. London: Cassell.

———. 1990. *The Thorns of Memory*. London: Sinclair-Stevenson.

Kenny, Michael. 1960. "Patterns of Patronage in Spain." *Anthropological Quarterly* 33: 14–24.

———. 1962. *A Spanish Tapestry: Town and Country in Castile*. Bloomington: Indiana University Press.

Kertzer, David I. 1988. *Ritual, Politics, and Power*. New Haven, Conn.: Yale University Press.

Lane, Christel. 1981. *The Rites of Rulers: Ritual in Industrial Society — The Soviet Case*. Cambridge: Cambridge University Press.

Lannon, Francis. 1986. "Un desafio vasco a la iglesia española de la pre–Guerra Civil." *Revista Internacional de los Estudios Vascos* 31, no. 1: 77–96.

———. 1987. *Privilege, Persecution, and Prophecy: The Catholic Church in Spain*. Oxford: Clarendon Press.

La Parra López, Emilio. 1991. "El Carlismo en el País Valenciano (1833–1883)." In *Los Carlistas, 1800–1876*, edited by Francisco Rodríguez de Coro, 247–59. Vitoria: Fundación Sancho el Sabio.

Lapeskera, Ramón. 1993. *Navarra Insólita*. Vol. 2. Pamplona: Pamiela.

Lapuente Martínez, L. 1971. "Estudio etnográfico de Amescoa (2)." *Cuadernos de etnología y etnografía de Navarra* 3, no. 8 (Mayo–Agosto): 113–70.

Larrañaga, C., and C. Pérez. 1988. "La Religión en la vida de la mujer, 1939–1987." In *La mujer y la palabra*, edited by Teresa Del Valle. San Sebastián: Baroja.

Larrion, José Luis. n.d. *Romerias*. Temas de Cultura Popular no. 42. Pamplona: Diputación Foral de Navarra.

Larronde, Jean-Claude. 1977. *El nacionalismo vasco. Su origen y ideología en la obra de Sabino Arana-Goiri*. San Sebastián: Txertoa.

La Torre, Joseba de. 1991. *Los campesinos navarros ante la guerra napoleónica. Financiación bélica y desamortización civil*. Serie Estudios. Madrid: Ministerio de Agricultura, Pesca y Alimentación.

———. 1992. *Lucha antifeudal y conflictos de clases en Navarra, 1808–1820*. Bilbao: Universidad del País Vasco.

Lauzurica, Javier. 1939. "Circular sobre el Domund y la fiesta de Cristo-Rey." *Boletín Oficial del Obispado de Vitoria*, 1 October, 399.

Lavardín, J. 1976. *Historia del ultimo pretendiente a la corona de España*. Paris: Ruedo Iberico.

Lázaro Torres, Rosa María. 1991. *La otra cara del Carlismo. Vizcaya bajo los Carlistas, 1833–1839*. Zaragoza: Librería General.

Leatherbarrow, David. 1987. "The Image and Its Setting: A Study of the Sacro Monte at Varallo." *Res* 14 (autumn): 107–22.

Lee, Laurie. 1991. *A Moment of War.* London: Viking.

Lhande Heguy, Pierre. 1975 (1907). *En torno al hogar vasco.* Donosti: Auñamendi.

Lisón Tolosana, Carmelo. 1966. *Belmonte de los Caballeros: Anthropology and History in an Aragonese Community.* Oxford: Oxford University Press.

———. 1980. *Invitación a la antropología cultural de España.* Madrid: Akal.

———. 1983. *Antropología social y hermenéutica.* Madrid: Fondo de Cultura Económica.

Lizarza Iribarren, Antonio. 1953. *Memorias de la conspiración. Como se preparó en Navarra la Cruzada, 1931–1936.* Pamplona.

London, John. 1995. "The Ideology and Practice of Sport." In *Spanish Cultural Studies: An Introduction,* edited by H. Graham and J. Labanyi, 204–7. Oxford: Oxford University Press.

López Andono, J. 1990. *Soy de la ilustre villa de Cirauqui.* Madrid.

López Anton, J. J. 1990. "Trayectoria ideológica del carlismo bajo Don Jaime (1909–1931). Aproximación y estudio de los postulados regionalistas del Jaimismo navarro (1918–1931)." *Aportes* 15: 36–50.

López Atxurra, Rafael. 1990. "La I Guerra Carlista y la Ley del 25 de octubre de 1839 en los textos escolares (1876–1979). Un ensayo sobre la reproducción de las ideologias." *Gerónimo de Uztariz* 4: 59–80.

López Rodó, Laureano. 1977. *La larga marcha hacia la Monarquía.* Barcelona: Noguer.

———. 1990. *Memorias.* Barcelona: Plaza & Janés.

———. 1991. *Años decisivos.* Barcelona: Plaza & Janés.

———. 1992. *El principio del fin.* Barcelona: Plaza & Janés.

———. 1993. *Claves de la Transición. Memorias IV. Diálogos con el Rey y con las principales figures de una etapa histórica.* Barcelona: Plaza & Janés.

López-Sanz, Francisco. 1963. *¿Un million de muertos? . . . pero con ¡Heroes y Martires!* Pamplona: Gómez.

———. 1966. *¡Llevaban su sangre!* Pamplona: Gómez.

Luengo Teixidor, Félix. 1990. "La formación del poder local franquista en Guipúzcoa (1937–1945)." *Gerónomio de Uztariz* 4: 83–95.

———. 1991. *La crisis de la Restauración. Partidos, elecciones y conflictividad social en Guipuzcoa, 1917–1923.* Bilbao: Universidad del País Vasco.

MacClancy, Jeremy. 1989. "GAC: Militant Carlist Activism under the Ageing Franco." In *Essays in Basque Social Anthropology and History,* edited by William Douglass, 140–54. Reno: University of Nevada Press.

———. 1991. "Diferenciación regional dentro de Navarra." *Revista de Antropología Social,* 1991, no. 0: 115–30. Reprinted in *Los pueblos del norte de España,* edited by C. Lisón-Tolosana, 115–30. Madrid: Universidad Complutense, 1992.

———. 1993. "At Play with Identity in the Basque Arena." In *Inside European Identities,* edited by Sharon Macdonald, 84–97. Oxford: Berg.

————. 1996. "Nationalism at Play: The Basques of Vizcaya and Athletic Bilbao." In *Sport, Identity and Ethnicity*, edited by Jeremy MacClancy, 181–99. Oxford: Berg.

————. n.d. "Basque Nationalism versus *Navarrismo* in the Transition." Unpublished manuscript.

Majuelo Gil, Emilio. 1986. *La Segunda Republica en Navarra. Conflictividad agraria en la Ribera Tudelana.* Pamplona: Pamiela.

————. 1989. *Luchas de clases en Navarra (1931–1936).* Pamplona: Gobierno de Navarra.

Mañas Leache, José Luis, and Juan Pedro Urabayen Mihura. 1988. "Las últimas elecciones de la II República en Navarra (Elecciones a compromisarios para la elección de Presidente de la República, 26-IV-1936)." *Principe de Viana*, XLIX, anejo 10, Primer Congreso General de Historia de Navarra, 5: Communicaciones. Historia Contemporánea, 243–64.

Marquine Barrio, Antonio. 1982. "El atentado de Begoña." *Historia 16*, no. 76: 11–19.

Martín Duque, Angel J., ed. 1986. *Gran atlas de Navarra.* 2 vols. Pamplona: Caja de Ahorros de Navarra.

Martinena Ruíz, Juan José. 1989. *Cartografía navarra en los Archivos Militares de Madrid.* Pamplona: Departamento de Educación y Cultura, Gobierno de Navarra.

Martín Gaite, Carmen. 1987. *Usos amorosos de la postguerra española.* Barcelona: Anagrama.

Martín Villa, Rodolfo. 1984. *Al servicio del Estado.* Barcelona: Planeta.

Marx, Karl. 1929. *La revolución Española.* Madrid: Cenit.

Marx, Karl, and Friedrich Engels. 1939. *The Revolution in Spain.* London: Lawrence and Wishart.

Mate, R. 1978. *La autogestión.* Madrid: Manana.

Melgar, Francisco. 1964. *El noble final de la escisión dinástica.* Madrid.

Mendaza Clemente, David. 1994. "Cambio en la estructura de clases y procesos históricos en Navarra y Zaragoza." *Gerónimo de Ustariz*, no. 9/10: 55–74.

Miguel, Francisco de. 1978. *Sociología del Franquismo.* Barcelona: Exito.

Miguel, Raimundo de. 1969. "Tradición." *Montejurra*, no. 48 (September–October): 24–25.

Miguel Sanz, J. de. 1986. "La Organización Revolucionaria de Trabajadores en Navarra, 1964–1977." Unpublished memoria de licenciatura, UNED, Pamplona.

Millán, Jesús. 1990. "La resistencia a la revolución en el País Valenciano. Oligarquias y capas populares en el movimiento carlista." In *150 años del convenio de Bergara y de la ley del 25-X-1839*, edited by Joseba Agirreazkuenaga and José Ramón Urquijo Goitia, 441–71. Vitoria: Parlamento Vasco.

Mina Apat, María Cruz. 1985. "Elecciones y partidos en Navarra (1891–1923)." In *La España de la Restauración. Política, economía, legislación y cultura.* I Coloquio de Segovia sobre Historia Contemporánea, dirigido por Manuel Tuñon de Lara, ed. M. Artola. Madrid: Siglo XXI.

Ministerio de Cultura. 1989. *Las mujeres en la Guerra Civil.* Salamanca.

Miranda, Francisco, et al. 1990. "La oposición dentro del regimen. El carlismo en Navarra." In *La oposición al régimen de Franco. Estado de la cuestion y metodología de la investigación.* Vol. 1, tome 2, edited by Javier Tusell et al., 469–80. Madrid: UNED.

Miranda Rubio, Francisco. 1994. "Los procuradores de representación familiar en la novena legislatura franquista (1967–1971)." *Principe de Viana* XLV, no. 203: 615–37.

Mitchell, Timothy J. 1988. *Violence and Piety in Spanish Folklore.* Philadelphia: University of Pennsylvania Press.

Montoya, J. 1874. *Estella y los Carlistas. Defensas del fuerte de Estella y consideraciones sobre la Guerra Carlista en Navarra.* Madrid.

Monzón, Telesforo. n.d. *Herri baten oihua.* Mesa nacional de Herri Batasuna.

Morinis, E. Alan. 1984. *Pilgrimage in the Hindu Tradition: A Case Study of West Bengal.* Delhi: Oxford University Press.

———. 1992. Introduction to *Sacred Journeys: The Anthropology of Pilgrimage,* edited by E. A. Morinis, 1–28. Westport, Conn.: Greenwood.

Mundet i Gifre, Josep M. 1991. "El Carlismo Catalan." In *Los Carlistas, 1800–1876,* edited by Francisco Rodríguez de Coro, 211–28. Vitoria: Fundación Sancho el Sabio.

Nagore Yarnoz, J. 1982. *En la Primera de Navarra. Memorias de un voluntario navarro en Radio Requeté de Compana.* Madrid.

Nairn, Tom. 1988. *The Enchanted Glass: Britain and Its Monarchy.* London: Radius.

Needham, Rodney. 1987. *Counterpoints.* Berkeley: University of California Press.

Neville, Gwen Kennedy. 1987. *Kinship and Pilgrimage: Rituals of Reunion in Protestant American Culture.* New York: Oxford University Press.

Nicholls, David. 1989. *Deity and Domination: Images of God and the State in the Nineteenth and Twentieth Centuries.* London: Routledge.

Nolan, Mary Lee, and Sidney Nolan. 1989. *Christian Pilgrimage in Modern Western Europe.* Chapel Hill: University of North Carolina Press.

Nonell Brú, Salvador. 1965. *Así eran nuestros muertos del laureado Tercio de Requetés de Ntra. Sra. de Montserrat.* Barcelona: Casulleras.

"Ortzi" [Francisco Letamendia]. 1978. *La Historia de Euskadi. El nacionalismo vasco y ETA.* Barcelona: Ibérica.

Osorio, Alfonso. 1980. *Trayectoria política de un ministro de la Corona.* Barcelona: Planeta.

Oteiza, Jorge. 1984. *Ejercicios espirituales en un tunel.* 2d ed. N.p.

Pablo, Santiago de. 1995. *Trabajo, diversión y vida cotidiana. El País Vasco en los años treinta.* Vitoria: Papeles de Zabalanda.

Pablo Contreras, S. de. 1989. *La Segunda Republica en Álava. Elecciones, partidos y vida politica.* Bilbao: Universidad del País Vasco.

Pan-Montojo, Juan L. 1990. *Carlistas y liberales en Navarra (1833–1839).* Pamplona: Gobierno de Navarra.

Pascual, Angel. 1986. "Del Frente Popular a la insurrección militar de julio de 1936 en Navarra." In *Navarra 1936. "De la esperanza al terror,"* edited by Altaffaylla Kultur Taldea, 37–53. Tafalla: Altaffaylla Kultur Taldea.

———. 1988. "Le soulevement militaire de 1936 et la participation de la Navarre dans la Guerre Civile. La genese du conflit." Diss., Universite du Pau et des Pays de l'Adour.

Payne, Stanley G. 1977. "Carlism—Basque or 'Spanish' Nationalism?" In *Anglo-American Contributions to Basque Studies: Essays in Honor of Jon Bilbao*, edited by W. A. Douglass, R. W. Etulain, and W. H. Jacobsen, Jr. Reno: Desert Research Institute Publications on the Social Sciences.

———. 1987. *The Franco Regime, 1936–1975.* Madison: University of Wisconsin Press.

Pazos, Anton M. 1990. *El clero Navarro (1900–1936). Origen social, procedencia geográfica y formación sacerdotal.* Pamplona: Ediciones Universidad de Navarra.

Pereda de la Reguera, Manuel. 1964. *Carlos y Irene.* Santander: Instituto de la Información.

Pérez-Agote, Alfonso. 1989. "Cambio social e ideológico en Navarra (1936–1982). Algunas claves para su comprensión." *Revista Española de Investigaciones Sociológicas* 46: 7–21.

Pérez de la Dehesa, Rafael. 1966. *Política y sociedad en el primer Unamuno, 1894–1904.* Madrid.

Pérez de Olaguer, A. 1937. *Los de siempre. Hechos y anécdotas del Requeté.* Pamplona: Requeté.

Pérez Goyena, Antonio. 1954–1964. *Ensayo de bibliografía Navarra.* 9 vols. Pamplona: Diputación Foral de Navarra.

Perry, Nicholas, and Loreto Echevarria. 1988. *Under the Heel of Mary.* London: Routledge.

Picaud, Aimerico. 1951. *Liber de Sancti Jacobi* (Codex Calixtinus). Santiago de Compostela: Consejo Superior de Investigaciones Científicas.

Pirala, Antonio. 1877. *Historia contemporánea de España.* Madrid.

Pitt-Rivers, Julian. [1954] 1972. *The People of the Sierra.* Chicago: University of Chicago Press.

Plata Parga, G. 1991. *La derecha vasca y la crisis de la democracia española (1931–1936).* Bilbao: Diputación Foral de Bizkaia.

Powell, Charles. 1990. *El piloto del cambio. El Rey, la Monarquía y la transición a la democracia.* Barcelona: Planeta.

Prats i Salas, Joan. 1990. *El Carlisme sota la Restauracio. El partit carlí a la provincia de Tarragona (1885–1907).* Tarragona: Diputacio de Tarragona.

Preciado, Nativel. 1975. "Un 'principe' azul mahon." *Historia* (June): 10–13.

Preston, Paul. 1986. *The Triumph of Democracy in Spain.* London: Methuen.

———. 1990. *The Politics of Revenge: Fascism and the Military in 20th Century Spain.* London: Unwin Hyman.

———. 1993. *Franco: A Biography.* London: Harper Collins.

Real Cuesta, Javier. 1985. *El Carlismo Vasco, 1876–1900*. Madrid: Siglo XXI.

———. 1991. *Partidos, elecciones y bloques de poder en el País Vasco, 1876–1923*. Bilbao: Universidad de Deusto.

Rebollo Torio, Miguel A. 1978. *Lenguaje y politica. Vocabulario Político, Republicano y Franquista*. Interdisciplinar, 2nd ser., 39. Valencia: Torres.

———. 1980. "Historia y lenguaje." In *Historiografía española contemporanea. X Coloquio de Pau. Balance y resumen*, edited by M. Tuñon de Lara. Madrid: Siglo XXI.

Redondo, Luis, and Juan de Zavala. 1957. *El Requeté (La Tradición no muere)*. Barcelona: AHR.

Rego Nieto, M. 1985. *El Carlismo Orensano, 1936–1980*. Vigo.

Reig Tapia, A. 1988. "La justificación ideológica del 'Alzamiento' de 1936." In *La Segunda Republica. Bienio rectificador y Frente Popular, 1934–1936*, edited by J. L. García Delgado, 211–33. Madrid: Siglo XXI.

Resa, José María. 1968. *Memorias de un Requeté*. Barcelona.

Revilla Cebrecos, C. 1975. *Tercio de Lacar*. Madrid: G. Del Toro.

Rincón, Luciano. 1985. ETA (1974–1984). Barcelona: Plaza & Janés.

Río Aldaz, Ramón del. 1987. *Orígenes de la Guerra Carlista en Navarra, 1820–1824*. Pamplona: Institución Principe de Viana.

———. 1991. "Los antecedentes de la reforma fiscal burguesa en Navarra. Los ultimos años del donativo (1817–1834)." *Gerónimo de Uztariz* 5: 5–27.

Rodríguez de Coro, Francisco. 1986. *San Sebastián. Revolución Liberal y la Segunda Guerra Carlista (1868–1876)*. San Sebastián/Donostia: Grupo Doctor Camino de Historia Donostiarra.

———. 1991a. "La 'Edad Clasica' del Carlismo (1833–1876)." In *Los Carlistas, 1800–1876*, edited by Francisco Rodríguez de Coro, 67–117. Vitoria: Fundación Sancho el Sabio.

———, ed. 1991b. *Los Carlistas, 1800–1876*. Vitoria: Fundación Sancho el Sabio.

Rodríguez Ranz, J. A. 1988. "El tradicionalismo en Guipúzcoa durante la Segunda Republica. Elites y bases. Análisis de una dualidad politico-estructural." In *Segundo Congreso Mundial Vasco*. Vol. V, 367–75. Vitoria: Parlamento Vasco.

Romero Raizábal, Ignacio. 1936. *Boinas Rojas en Asturias*. San Sebastián.

———. 1938. *Cancionero Carlista*. San Sebastián: Española.

———. 1965. *El principe requeté (una historia con sabor de novela)*. Santander: Aldus.

———. 1968. *El Carlismo en el Vaticano (Historia en miniatura del trato entre los Papas y los Reyes Carlistas)*. Santander: Aldus Velarde.

———. 1952. *Heroes de romance (Cosas de Requetés)*. Santander: Aldus.

———. 1972. *El prisionero de Dachau 156.270*. Zaragoza.

Rubio Ruiz, Daniel. 1992. "Aproprament a la base social dels conflictes precarlins al Corregiment de Cervera." In *El carlisme i la seva base social*, edited by Josep María Sole i Sabate, 103–16. Barcelona: Llibres de l'Index.

Rújula López, Pedro. 1995. *Rebeldía campesina y primer carlismo. Los orígenes de la Guerra Civil en Aragón*. Zaragoza: Departamento de Educación y Cultura, Gobierno de Aragón.

Rutherford, Andrew. 1978. *The Literature of War: Five Studies in Heroic Virtue.* London: Macmillan.

Sahlins, Marshall. 1985. *Islands of History.* Chicago: Chicago University Press.

Salgado-Araujo, Francisco Franco. 1976. *Mis conversaciones privadas con Franco.* Barcelona: Planeta.

Sallnow, Michael J. 1981. "Communitas Reconsidered: The Sociology of Andean Pilgrimage." *Man,* (n.s.), 16: 163–83.

———. 1987. *Pilgrims of the Andes: Regional Cults in Cusco.* Washington, D.C.: Smithsonian.

Sánchez, José Mariano. 1987. *The Spanish Civil War as a Religious Tragedy.* Notre Dame, Ind.: University of Notre Dame Press.

Sánchez Carracedo, H. 1940. *Un mártir de Cristo Rey. Antonio Molle Lazo.* Barcelona.

Sánchez Erauskin, Javier. 1994. *Por Dios hacía el imperio. Nacionalcatolicismo en las Vascongadas del primer Franquismo 1936–1945.* Donostia/San Sebastián: R & B Ediciones.

Sánchez Gómez, M. A. 1985. *El primer carlismo montañés. Aspectos sociales y localización geográfica.* Santander: Tantin

Santa Cruz, Manuel [A. Ruiz de Galarreta]. 1979–1992. *Apuntes y documentos para la historia del Tradicionalismo Español 1939–1966.* 29 vols. Madrid.

Santamaría Blasco, E. 1988. "Iglesia y Movimiento Obrero Navarro en los Años Sesenta." Memoria de licenciatura (Diss.), Universidad de Zaragoza.

Santamaría Recarte, Fernando, José Mari Oreja Reta, and Carlos Maiza Oxcoidi. 1992. "Fuentes para el estudio de la propiedad de la tierra en Navarra (siglos XIX–XX)." *Principe de Viana* LIII, anejo 16, Segundo Congreso de Historia de Navarra de los siglos XVII–XIX y XX, 337–45.

Sanz, José Miguel. 1986. "La Organización Revolucionaria de Trabajadores. Sus orígenes y desarollo en Navarra, 1964–1977." Memoria de licenciatura (unpublished undergraduate diss.), Universidad Nacional de la Educación a la Distancia, Pamplona.

Sarabia, R. 1940. *Un mártir de Cristo Rey. Antonio Molle Lazo.* Madrid: El Perpetuo Socorro.

Saralegui Lorea, Casmirio. 1991. *Vivencias y recuerdos de un cripto.* Tafalla: Altaffaylla Kultur Taldea.

Saz Campos, Ismael. 1986. *Mussolini contra la IIa Republica.* Valencia: Alfons El Magnanim.

Serrano Moreno, A. M. 1989. "Las elecciones a Cortes Constituyentes de 1931 en Navarra." *Principe de Viana* L: 687–776.

Sesmero Cutanda, Enriqueta. 1991. "Partidas paralelas." In *Los Carlistas, 1800–1876,* edited by Francisco Rodríguez de Coro, 353–69. Vitoria: Fundación Sancho el Sabio.

Sherzer, Joel. 1987. "Language, Culture, and Discourse." *American Anthropologist* 89: 295–309.

Shubert, Adrian. 1990. *A Social History of Modern Spain*. London: Unwin Hyman.

Simmie, James. 1991. "Self-Management in Yugoslavia." In *Yugoslavia in Turmoil: After Self-Management?* edited by James Simmie and José Dekleva, 3–9. London: Pinter.

Smidovik, J. 1991. "Disfunctions of the System of Self-Management in the Economy, in Local Territorial Communities and in Public Administration." In *Yugoslavia in Turmoil: After Self-Management?* edited by James Simmie and José Dekleva, 17–32. London: Pinter.

Smith, Anthony D. 1991. *National Identity*. Harmondsworth: Penguin.

Sole i Sabate, Josep María, ed. 1992. *El carlisme i la seva base social*. Barcelona: Llibres de l'Index.

Soriano, Manuel. 1995. *La sombra del rey*. Madrid: Temas de Hoy.

Sperber, Murray A. 1974. Introduction to *And I Remember: A Spanish Civil War Anthology*, edited by M. A. Sperber, v–xxiv. London: Hart-Davis, MacGibbon.

Thomas, Gareth. 1990. *The Novel of the Spanish Civil War*. Cambridge: Cambridge University Press.

Toquero, José María. 1988. "El Carlimso Vasconavarro y Don Juan de Borbón. La influencia del Conde de Rodezno." In *Congreso de Historia del Euskal-Herria. Seccion II: Edad Moderna y Contemporánea*. Vol. VII. Vitoria: Gobierno Vasco.

———. 1989. *Franco y Don Juan. La oposición monárquica al franquismo*. Barcelona: Plaza & Janeś.

Turner, Victor. 1967. *The Forest of Symbols: Aspects of Ndembu Ritual*. Chicago: University of Chicago Press.

———. 1969. *The Ritual Process: Structure and Anti-Structure*. London: Routledge & Kegan Paul.

———. 1974. *Dramas, Fields, and Metaphors: Symbolic Action in Human Society*. Ithaca: Cornell University Press.

———. 1975. "Death and the Dead in the Pilgrimage Process." In *Religion and Social Change in Southern Africa: Anthropological Essays in Honour of Monica Wilson*, edited by M. G. Whisson and M. West, 107–28. Cape Town: D. Philip.

———. 1978. "Encounter with Freud: The Making of a Comparative Symbologist." In *The Making of Psychological Anthropology*, edited by G. D. Spindler, 558–83. Berkeley: University of California Press.

Udalaren Euskara Zerbitzua. 1995. *El Euskera en Valdizarbe. Testimonios escritos y orales*. N.p.

Unamuno, Miguel de. 1916. "En torno al casticismo." Ensayos I. Madrid: Residencia de Estudiantes.

———. 1917. "La crisis actual del patriotismo español." In *Ensayos VI*, 145–60. Madrid: Residencia de Estudiantes.

———. [1897] 1940. *Paz en la Guerra*. Madrid: Espasa-Calpe.

———. 1966. "El porvenir de España." *Obras Completas*. Vol. IV, 973–92. Madrid: Escelicer.

Urabayen, Félix. [1924] 1988. *El barrio maldito*. Pamplona: Pamiela.

Urla, Jacqueline. 1993. "Contesting Modernities: Language Standardization and the Production of an Ancient/Modern Culture." *Critique of Anthropology* 13: 101–18.

Urquijo Goitia, José Ramón. 1998. "La Primera Guerra Carlista desde la ideología nacionalista vasca." *Vasconia. Cuadernos de Historia–Geografía* 26: 65–110.

Urra Lusarreta, J. 1957. *En las trincheras del frente de Madrid.* Pamplona.

Valle, Teresa del, ed. 1985. *Mujer Vasca. Imagen y realidad.* Barcelona: Anthropos.

Vallverdu i Marti, Robert. 1992. "La batalla 'sorpresa' de l'Aleixar. Analisi sociologica dels guerrillers carlins." In *El carlisme i la seva base social,* edited by Josep María Sole i Sabate, 165–85. Barcelona: Llibres de l'Index.

Vázquez de Prada Tiffe, Mercedes, and Rosario Ruíz Garrido. 1995. "Los contrafueros de 1952–54 y la oposición Carlista al Franquismo en Navarra." *II Encuentro de Investigadores del Franquismo.* Vol. II, 235–46. Institut de Cultura "Juan Gil Albert." FEIS: Alicante.

Vázquez de Prado, Mercedes, and Francisco J. Caspistegui. 1991. "Tradicionalismo y politica. Orígenes y evolución hasta el régimen de Franco (1808–1975)." Paper presented at symposium, La Política Conservadora en la España Contemporánea (1868–1982), UNED, Madrid.

Vidal-Abarca López, Juan. 1991. "Álava y el Carlismo. La Familia Varona." In *Los Carlistas, 1800–1876,* edited by Francisco Rodríguez de Coro, 161–207. Vitoria: Fundación Sancho el Sabio.

Vilarrubias, Felio A. 1975. *El Carlismo en el ser de España. Una ideología popular y heroica en el contexto de la crisis universal de las ideologías.* Barcelona: Casulleras.

Vila San Juan, José Luis. 1993. *Los reyes carlistas. Los otros Borbones.* Barcelona: Planeta.

Villanueva, Aurora. 1997. "Los incidentes del 3 de diciembre de 1945 en la Plaza del Castillo de Pamplona." *Principe de Viana* LVIII (September–December): 629–49.

Virto Ibañez, Juan Jesús. 1987. *Las elecciones municipales de 1931 en Navarra.* Pamplona: Gobierno de Navarra.

Warner, Marina. 1976. *Alone of All Her Sex: The Myth and Cult of the Virgin Mary.* London: Weidenfeld & Nicolson.

Wilhelmsen, Alexandra. 1995. *La formación del pensamiento político del Carlismo (1810–1875).* Madrid: Fundación Hernando de Larramendi & ACTAS.

Williamson, Judith. 1986. *Consuming Passions: The Dynamics of Popular Culture.* London: Boyars.

Winston, Colin M. 1985. *Workers and the Right in Spain, 1900–1936.* Princeton, N.J.: Princeton University Press.

Zaratiegui Labiano, Jesús María. 1996. "Efectos de la aplicación del sufragio universal en Navarra. Las elecciones generales de 1886 y 1891." *Principe de Viana* LVII: 177–224.

Zavala, José María. 1976. *Partido Carlista.* Barcelona: Arance.

———. 1977. *Partido Carlista.* Bilbao: Albia.

Zubiaur, Francisco Javier, and José Angel Zubiaur. 1980. *Estudio etnográfico de San Martín de Unx (Navarra).* Pamplona: Institución Principe de Viana.

Zubiaur, José Angel. n.d. "Elecciones a Procuradores Familiares en Navarra en 1971." Unpublished ms.

Zulaika, Joseba. 1987. *Tratado estético-ritual Vasco*. San Sebastián: Baroja.

————. 1988. *Basque Violence: Metaphor and Sacrament*. Reno: University of Nevada Press.

Index

Abarzuza, 133
"Abrazo de Vergara," 233
Acción Carlista, 202
Les Accords secrets Franco-Anglais de décembre de 1940 (Don Javier), 77–78
agriculture, 35–36, 37, 38–39, 208–9
Agrupación de Agricultores, 218
Agrupación de Asociaciones Tradicionalistas (Group of Traditional Associations), 170
Agrupación Electoral Montejurra, 216, 217
Agrupación Independiente, 219–20
Agrupación Tierra Estella, 218
Aitzibita (bulletin-magazine), 227
El Alcázar (newspaper), 179
Alfonso Carlos, 77, 78
Alfonso XII, 10, 13
Alfonso XIII, 69, 74
Alianza Foral Navarra, 216, 217
Alsina, José, 120
Anderson, Benedict, 154
anti-Carlists: caricatures of Carlists, 63–64. *See also* liberals
Antoñana, Pablo, 30, 241
Aplec, 135–36
Araluce, José María, 180
Arbeloa, Victor Manuel, 238
Areilza, José María de, 180–81, 182
Arellano, Luis, 76
Aronson, Theo, 245
Arraiza, Asunción, 127
arson, 47, 49
Artajona, 68–69
Arteche, José de, 235

Arzalluz, Xabier, 234
Asamblea Democrática de Gernika (Democratic Assembly of Gernika), 168
Así eran nuestros muertos del Laureado Tercio de Requetés de Ntra. Sra. De Montserrat (Brú), 17
Asociación de Adoración Nocturna (Association of Nocturnal Adoration), 59
Asociación de las Hijas de María (Association of Daughters of Mary), 59
Asociación Estudiantil Tradicionalista (Carlist student association; AET), 81, 94, 117, 147, 166–67, 171
Astrain, Javier, 238
atrocities: committed by liberals, 63; massacre of liberals in Cirauqui, 42–44, 63
Atxaga, Bernardo, 241
autogestión, 158–61
Ayegui, 127

Baroja, Pío, 16, 241
barracas, 215
Basque Autonomous Police, 237
Basque Country: Carlism in, 4, 5–6; Carlist family values and, 110–11; Navarrese politics and, 193–94; Partido Nacionalista Vasco and, 12; progressive Carlism and, 192
Basque culture, 228–30
Basque flag, 231
Basque nationalism: Carlism and, 233–41; Cirauqui elections, 54, 55; Repub-

lican forces and, 23; rise of, 225–26;
village politics and, 226–28
batasuneros, 237, 238, 239
batua, 229
Baudoin I, 97
berets, 32–33, 67, 68
Berruezo, Reyes, 238
Bilbao, Esteban, 93, 153, 175
blood, 31–32, 142–43
Boletín de Orientación Tradicionalista
(newssheet), 81
Don Boniface (parish priest), 206–7,
211–14, 216, 217
Borbón, Carlos María Isidro de. *See*
Don Carlos
Borbón-Parma, Cecilia de, 90–91, 96,
162
Borbón-Parma, Francisca de, 90–91
Borbón-Parma, François Xavier de. *See*
Don Javier
Borbón-Parma, Isabel de, 90
Borbón-Parma, María-Teresa de, 90–
91, 117, 120–21, 130, 160–61, 164,
172, 175, 199 ·
Borbón-Parmas: Carlist portrayals of,
102–9; imagery of the royal family
and, 110–11; progressive Montejurra
and, 173; reformation of traditional-
ists and, 170. *See also* Carlos Hugo;
Don Javier
Brigadas de Paisanos Armadoes (Bri-
gades of Armed Peasants), 5
Brú, S. Nonell, 17
El Bucle Melancólico (Juaristi), 234
Burgo, Jaime del, 138

Campos de España (periodical), 100
Cánovas del Castillo, Antonio, 11–12
Carlism: between 1875 and 1936, 10–
14; anti-Carlist caricatures, 63–64;
Basque nationalism and, 233–41; in
the Basque Provinces, 4, 5–6, 12; in
Cataluña, 81–82; Catholicism and, 3,
7–8, 10, 18–22, 114, 122; demonizing

of Republicans, 22–24; DIOS, PA-
TRIA, REY, FUEROS slogan, 72–73,
162–63; early social composition, 2–
3; electoral politics and, 11, 54–55,
194–98, 216–20; the family and, 28–
31, 64–72, 73, 110–11; Franco and,
75–76, 164–66; guerrilla warfare
and, 6; ideologies of, 6–9; integrists
and, 7, 8, 10–11, 12, 13; under Isabella II, 10; Junta of Regional and
Provincial Chiefs, 81; literature of the
Civil War, 16–18; Karl Marx on, 116;
masculine orientation, 27; metaphor
of blood and, 31–32, 142–43; military forces and organization, 4, 11,
13–14, 26–27; military traditions,
24–27; Montejurra and, 244–45; in
Navarre, 4, 5, 12, 13–14, 55–56; origins of, 1–2; portrayals of the Borbón-Parmas, 102–9; post–Civil War
succession issues, 77–81, 82–83, 84–
88; postelectoral history, 201–2; postwar camps, 76–77; during Primo de
Rivera's dictatorship, 13; progressive
definition of, 122; progressive historiography and, 116–26; progressives
and, 94–95, 102, 111–15 (*see also* progressive Carlism); public rituals,
134–35 (*see also* Montejurra); red berets and, 32–33, 67, 68; reformation
of traditionalists, 169–72; rhetoric of
rural life and, 5; rural/urban geography and, 5–6; socialists and, 123–24;
social nature and geography, 1–6;
traditionalism and, 8–9; Unamuno
on, 120; viewed as dead, 241–42;
women and, 27–28. *See also* Cirauqui
Carlists; progressive Carlism
Carlist Circles, 13; in Cirauqui, 45–46;
in Pamplona, closing of, 81; post–
Civil War fate, 74; at Zaragoza, closing of, 84
Carlist journalism: on Montejurra, 128,
129, 137, 144–45, 155–56; portrayals

of Don Javier and Carlos Hugo, 102–9; repression of, 164, 165; supporting Carlos VIII, 80; traditionalist revival and, 176

Carlist rituals, 134–36. *See also* Montejurra

Carlist Wars: battles at Montejurra, 132–33; in progressive historiography, 120, 122; sale of common lands and, 38. *See also* First Carlist War; Second Carlist War

carlofranquistas, 76, 92

Don Carlos (Carlos María Isidro de Borbón), 2, 123, 125

Carlos Hugo (Hugues), 86, 188; attempts at revitalization, 191; bid for the throne, 96–98; Carlist portrayals of, 104–9; the Comunión and, 95, 104; consolidation of progressive hegemony, 163; divorce of, 199, 200; exile of, 157; Franco and, 95, 96, 97–98, 157; imagery of the royal family and, 110–11; Montejurra and, 90–91, 95, 96, 130, 147–48, 152, 175, 178, 179; popular mystique of, 105–6; Princess Irene and, 97, 106, 109, 199, 200; progressive ideology and, 157, 158; progressive reform and, 93–95; public image and political power, 106–8; reformation of traditionalists and, 169, 170; "rescue" of Don Javier, 184; resignation of, 198–201; return from exile, 186, 190; royal imagery and, 108–9; Don Sixto and, 183; socialist self-management and, 159–60; Spanish nationality and, 96, 97; Unión de Centro Democrático and, 195; on use of arms, 192; Zamanillo's conflict with, 98–99

carlosoctavistas, 80, 85, 98, 152

Carlos V, 121

Carlos VI, 120

Carlos VII, 10, 30, 103, 119, 133, 138, 157

Carlos VIII (Karl Pius of Habsburg), 79–81, 85

Carnicero, Carlos, 197

Caro Baroja, Julio, 21–22

Carrero Blanco, Luis, 97–98

Carrillo, Santiago, 168, 175

Casa del Pueblo, 46, 50

Cataluña, 6, 81–82

Catholic Church/Catholicism: Carlism and, 3, 7–8, 10, 18–22, 114, 122; Cirauqui Carlists and, 57–61, 72–73; mass ceremonies of, 133–34; in "organic traditionalism," 9; progressives on, 114; protective religious objects, 68–69; Republican reform and, 61; *requetés* and, 18–22; during the Second Republic, 13; Second Vatican Council and, 89–90, 109; Thomistic rigidity in, 8. *See also* priests

Don Cayetano, 103

Cerralbo, Marqués de, 11, 12

chaqueta vuelta, 70–71

chaquetero, 70–71

children: Carlist family and, 65

church-based associations, 59

Cia Navascués, Polycarpo, 19, 21, 22

Cirauqui: agriculture in, 35–36, 37, 38–39; arson and vandalism in, 47–48, 49; Basque culture and, 228–30; Basque nationalism and, 225–30, 237; Don Boniface and, 206–7, 211–14, 216, 217; cadastral survey, 36–37, 38; demise of Carlism in, 220–25; electoral politics in, 54–55; emigration, 39; feast days, 205; fiestas, 214–16; First Carlist war and, 40; fragmentation and disunity in, 56; under Franco, 203–7; la guerra de las banderas, 230–32; industrial development and, 208; intergenerational change in, 223–24; mayoral activities, 205–6; mechanization of agriculture and, 208–9; physical description of, 34–35; politicomilitary history, 39–40; politics of village nationalism, 226–28; population trends, 208, 209; public education and, 208; *requeté* culture and, 56–72; Second Carlist War and, 40–45, 52; Second Republic and, 45–50, 55; socioeconomic history, 34–39; sociopolitical composition, 51–56; Spanish Civil War and, 50–51; town council meetings, 219; transition to democracy, 216–2; village projects, 205–7, 227

Cirauqui Carlists: Basque nationalism and, 237; Catholic religiosity and, 57–61, 72–73; challenging Don Boniface, 211–14; Circles, 45–46; conscription and, 44; criticism of progressives, 224; demise of Carlism and, 220–25; denial of association with, 221–22; DIOS, PATRIA, REY, FUEROS slogan and, 72–73; electoral politics and, 54–55, 216–20; family and, 64–72, 73; fiestas, 214–16; under Franco, 204–5; genealogical notions of Carlism in, 70–72, 73, 220–21, 223, 224; la guerra de las banderas, 230–32; intergenerational change and, 223–24; massacre of liberals, 42–44, 63; perceptions of history, 62–64; politicomilitary history, 39–40; progressives and, 209–20; *requeté* culture and, 56–72; Second Carlist War and, 40–45; Second Republic and, 45–46, 47, 49–50; sociopolitical composition, 51, 52, 54–55; Spanish Civil War and, 50–51; village projects and, 227

Cirauqui liberals: family political tradition and, 71; massacre of, 42–44, 63; Second Carlist war and, 40–41, 42, 43–44, 45; sociopolitical composition, 51, 52

Circles, Carlist. *See* Carlist Circles

Civil Guards, 48, 49, 136, 152, 157, 178, 181, 182, 214

Clemente, Josep Carles, 117–20, 121, 122, 124–25, 126

Codón Fernández, José María, 28–29, 149

Comisiones Obreras (Workers' Commission), 167

common lands, 38, 47, 48, 49

communes, 159

Communist Party, 167–68, 201

community: Carlist notions of Catholicism and, 57–58

Compañia de Emigrados, 52

Comunión Carlista Legitimista, 202

Comunión Católico-Monarquica Española, 202

Comunión Tradicionalista, 13, 28, 46, 202; Carlos Hugo (Hugues) and, 91, 99, 100, 101, 104; Fal Conde and, 86–87; Franco and, 86–87, 92–93, 100, 101; Franco's reforms following World War II and, 84; Don Javier and, 82–83, 86–88, 89, 92–93, 99, 100–101, 104; Junta of Regional and Provincial Chiefs and, 81; legalization of, 186; Ley de Sucesión and, 85; post–Civil War fate, 74, 75; post-electoral reformation, 202; postwar camps, 76–77; in progressive historiography, 120, 125–26; progressives and, 90, 95, 99, 100, 101, 109, 162; reorganization of, 92–93; Don Sixto and, 184; succession issue and, 77, 78, 79, 82–83, 85, 86–87, 88, 91–92; traditionalist reformation and, 170; Zamanillo and, 99

Comunión Tradicionalista Carlista, 202, 245

Confraternidad de la Cruz Verdadera (Confraternity of the True Cross), 59

Confraternidad del Rosario Sagrado (Confraternity of the Sacred Rosary), 59

conscription, 44
Conservatives: in Cirauqui elections, 54
Coordinación Democrática (Democratic Coordination), 168
Council of Trent, 114
Cross of Saint Andrew, 25, 68, 69
cursillos, 157, 158, 163, 187, 188, 210

Day of Carlist Struggle, The, 172
Day of the Holy Cross, 46
death, 19–20
Decree of Unification, 74, 99
Delegación Nacional de Requetés, 99
Democratic party: in Cirauqui elections, 54
detentes, 25, 68, 69
El Dia de la Lucha Carlista, 172
El Dia del Pueblo, 215
El Diario de Barcelona (newspaper), 96
El Diario de Navarra (newspaper), 128, 243
DIOS, PATRIA, REY, FUEROS slogan, 72–73, 162–63
Domínguez Arévalo, Tomás, 13
Dorregaray, Antonio, 40, 42–43

education, 18
Egin (newspaper), 236, 237
Esfuerzo Común (journal), 165
Espoz y Mina, Francisco, 40
Estella, 14, 35, 42, 44, 129–30, 131, 132, 133, 138, 184, 201
estorilinos, 152, 179
etarras, 235
Euskadiko Karlista Alderdia (Basque Carlist Party; EKA), 192, 193, 194, 201, 217
Euskadi ta Askatasuna (The Basque Country and Freedom; ETA), 165, 166, 179, 192, 193, 195, 210, 225, 236, 241
Euskera, 131, 229, 230
Eusko Alkartasuna, 228
Evaristo Casariego, Jesús, 25

Fagoaga, Miguel, 170
Falange, 18, 50, 74, 80, 84, 92–93
Falange Española Tradicionalista y de las Juntas de Ofensiva Nacional-Sindicalista (FET), 74
Fal Conde, Manuel: Carlos Hugo and, 99; Carlos VIII and, 80; dismissal of, 87, 88; *falcondismo* and, 76–77; Franco and, 79; Irache monastery and, 138; Montejurra and, 148; at Montserrat, 84; opposition to, 86–87; *requeté* motto of, 20; as secretary-general of the Comunión, 13; stubborn traditionalism of, 76–77, 80, 82
falcondismo, 77, 80, 81
family: Carlist notions of, 28–31, 64–70; changing values and, 109–10; Montejurra and, 143–44; political tradition and, 70–72, 73; royal family and, 110–11
fathers, 66–68
feast days, 58–59, 205
Federación de Naciones Ibericas (Federation of Iberian Nations), 120
federalism, 191–92
Ferdinand VII, 2, 4
Ferrer, Melchor, 42, 43–44, 139
Fiesta de Solidaridad de los Pueblos (Festival of Solidarity of the Pueblos), 191
fiestas, 214–16
First Carlist War, 6; battles at Montejurra, 132–33; Cirauqui Carlists and, 40; modern Carlists and, 62; origins of, 2
First National Carlist Congress, 163
Foral Guard, 52
Forcadell, Ramón, 170
Fraga Iribarne, Manuel, 97, 180, 181
Doña Francisca, 111, 184
Franco, Francisco, 1, 15, 33; Carlism under, 75–76; Carlist regency proposals and, 79; Carlos Hugos (Hugues) and, 95, 96, 97–98, 157; the Co-

munión and, 86–87, 92–93, 100, 101; Conde de Rodezno and, 76; consolidation of power, 74; death of, 169; FET and, 74, 75; Don Javier and, 83; Don Juan and, 85, 86; Juan Carlos and, 101; Ley de Sucesión, 84–85; modern reforms and, 89, 90; reforms following World War II, 83–84; Spanish monarchy and, 96–97

Freemasons, 120

Frente Obrero Sindicalista (Syndicalist Workers' Front), 197

Frente Popular de Navarra (Navarrese Popular Front), 50, 176

Frente Revolucionario Democrático (Revolutionary Democratic Front), 167

fueros, 4, 7, 10, 76, 83, 118, 125, 202

funerals, 65

García Sanchiz, Federico, 25, 28

García Valiño, Rafael, 153

Gil Bera, Eduardo, 241

Gironella, José María, 18

González, Felipe, 217

Gordoa, José Ruiz de, 181

Gorriti (Carlist chronicler), 41, 42, 44

Grupos de Acción Carlista (GAC), 165–66

gudaris, 235

Guembe, Vicente, 38

Guerra, Alfonso, 234

"La Guerra de las Banderas," 230–32

guerrilla warfare, 6

hearth traditions, 65

Hermandad de los Caballeros Voluntarios de la Cruz (Brotherhood of the Gentlemen Volunteers of the Cross), 133

Hermandad de Maestrazgo (Brotherhood of Maestrazgo), 171

Hermandad Nacional de Antiguos Combatientes de Tercios de Reque-

tés (National Brotherhood of Veterans of the Requeté Regiments), 171

Hermandad Nacional de Requetés Veteranos (National Brotherhood of Veteran Requetés), 179

Hermandad Penitencial Canónica (Canonical Penitential Brotherhood) de la Vía Crucis de Montejurra, 136, 141, 153

Herri Batasuna (HB), 217, 218, 228, 234, 237, 238, 239

La historia triste de Fernando y Belisa (Evaristo Casariego), 25

Holy Family, 29, 30

Hugues. *See* Carlos Hugo

huguistas, 93–95, 167, 178–79, 188. *See also* progressive Carlism

Ideario Tradicionalista, 99

Idoy (Carlist leader in Cirauqui), 42–43

ikastola, 230

ikurriña, 231

Información Mensual, 157, 161

Informe Montejurra '76, 180

Integrist party, 54

integrists, 8, 10–11, 12, 137

Irache monastery, 138

Doña Irene (Princess of the Netherlands), 97, 106, 109, 164, 165, 178, 180, 184, 199, 200

Isabella II, 2, 10, 119

Iturmendi, Antonio, 86, 93

Izquierda Unida (United Left), 201, 202, 228

Don Jaime, 12, 26

Jaime III, 120

javierista, 102

Javierada, 133

Don Javier (François Xavier de Borbón-Parma): abdication, 170; appointed regent, 77; Carlist portrayals of, 102–3; Carlos VIII and, 80; the Comunión and, 82–83, 86–88, 89, 92–93, 99, 100–101, 104; death of, 184; Fal Conde and, 87; Franco and, 96; Hugues and, 89; imagery of the royal family and, 110–11; issue of being the pretender, 82–83, 85–86, 91; Don Juan and, 86, 87–88; "kidnapping" and "rescue" of, 184; leadership qualities, 78, 104; Ley de Sucesión and, 85; Montejurra and, 148, 149, 175; multiple loyalties of, 77–78, 103–4; in progressive historiography, 119–20, 125–26; Zamanillo and, 98

javieristas, 83, 86, 91, 92, 93, 97, 135–36, 152, 153

John XXIII, 89

journalism. *See* Carlist journalism

Don Juan, 79, 80, 84, 85, 86, 87–88, 91–92, 97, 168

Juan Carlos, 85, 86, 95, 96, 101, 168, 186

juanistas, 91, 93, 97, 98, 152

Juaristi, Jon, 234

Junta Democrática, 168

La Junta Depuradora Carlista, 170, 176

Junta Nacional de Requetés, 165

Junta Regional de Navarre, 14

Juntas Defensa del Carlismo, 98

Karl Pius of Habsburg. *See* Carlos VIII

Kemp, Peter, 21, 33

kingship: Carlist notions of, 30

kutxas, 68

Lacalle Yabar, Tirso, 43

Lácar, Battle of, 45

Lee, Laurie, 26

Lerín, Conde de, 35

Ley de Referéndum, 84

Ley de Sucesión, 84–85

Lhande Heguy, Pierre, 67

liberals/liberalism: in Carlist ideology, 7, 8; in the early nineteenth century, 1–2. *See also* Cirauqui liberals

Liga Comunista Revolucionaria (Revolutionary Communist League), 167

¡Llevaban su sangre! (López-Sanz), 17, 24, 31–32

Lombardia, Pedro, 148

López Rodó, Laureano, 97

López-Sanz, Francisco, 17–18, 19, 24, 31–32, 114

Doña Magdalena, 110, 130, 184

Mañeru, 130

Marcha de la Libertad, 224

Marchelina, Marqués de, 171

Doña Margarita, 28, 138

Margaritas, 28, 151

Doña María de las Nieves, 80, 178

Marianism, 109

Maroto, Rafael, 6, 118

Marquéz de Prado, José Arturo, 179, 180

Martín Villa, Rodolfa, 181, 182

Mártires de la Tradición, 171, 176

martyrs, 112–13

Marx, Karl, 116, 120, 125

Massó, Raymond, 94–95, 100, 148, 152

Memorias de un requeté (Resa), 24

Mendigorría, 68

Mendizabal, Eustakio, 237

Miguel, Raimundo de, 107, 111, 149

La Mina (periodical), 100

Misión (journal), 84

Molle Lazo, Antonio, 33

El momento actual español cargado de utopia (María-Teresa de Borbón-Parma), 160–61

Monjardin, 138

Montejurra: of 1939, 127; of 1966, 100, 149; of 1976, 177–84; of 1977, 184–85; of 1986, 243–44; as active process, 154–56; banning of, 164, 184; battles at, 132–33; Carlist journalists and, 128, 129, 137, 144–45, 155–56; Carlos Hugo (Hugues) and, 90–91, 95, 96, 130, 147–48, 152, 175, 178,

179; contemporary national context
of, 133–34; current status of, 244–45;
heterogeneous appeal of, 153–54;
historical geography and, 137–
40; Don Javier and, 148, 149, 175;
notions of emotion, spirit, and
blood, 141–43; notions of family
and, 143–44; notions of reenactment
and sacrifice, 140–41; opposition
groups and, 167; organizers of, 136;
origins and history of, 127–31, 132–
33, 134, 244; other Carlist rituals and,
134–36; Partido Carlista and, 244–
45; as political stage, 100, 136, 146–
50; progressive Carlism and, 191;
progressive version of, 172–76; *requetés* and, 130, 132–33, 137–38,
139–41, 144, 145–46, 154; ritual contexts of, 131–34; solidarity and, 150–
54; traditionalist development of,
128–31; in traditionalist discourse,
137–45; traditionalist revival and,
176; veteran's views of, 145–46;
women and, 151
Montejurra 1976: confrontation in,
177–79; demise of the *sixtinos* and,
182–84; national politics and, 179–82
Montejurra (magazine), 96, 101, 137,
165, 175, 184
Montserrat, 81, 83, 84, 135, 171
Monzón, Telesforo, 236
mothers, 68
Movimiento. *See* Falange Española
Tradicionalista y de las Juntas de
Ofensiva Nacional-Sindicalista
Movimiento Obrero Tradicionalista
(MOT), 100, 149, 171
Multhiko Alaiak, 210
Muñoz Grandes, Agustín, 153

Nacionalistas Vascos, 217
National Carlist Congress, 100
National Junta, 81, 82, 86, 93, 95
Navarre: Basque nationalism in, 225–

26; Carlism in, 4, 5, 12, 13–14, 55–56;
Carlist Catholicism and, 60; Carlist
education in, 18; conscription in, 44;
electoral politics in, 53–54; Franco
and, 15, 76; general elections of 1977
in, 189; Montejurra and, 128–31, 136;
nationalist-*navarrista* divide in, 193–
94; Partido Carlista in, 197–98; political violence during the Second Republic, 49; progressives in, 192–94;
requetés and, 15; Spanish Civil War
and, 14; structural inequality in, 38.
See also Cirauqui
navarristas, 193
Nostros (bulletin), 241
Núcleo de Lealtad, 79

Olaechea, Don Marcelino, 133
Olazábal, Rafael, 86, 88
olentzero, 229
"Operación Maestrazgo," 164
Operación Reconquista, 180
opposition politics, 166–68
Opus Dei, 89
Ordinance of the Requeté, 24
"organic traditionalism," 9
Organización Revolucionaria de Tra-
bajadores (Workers' Revolutionary
Organization), 167
Organización Sindical (Syndical Orga-
nization), 167
Oriamendi, 197
Oriol, Antonio María de, 180
Oriol, José María de, 170
Oroquieta, Battle of, 40
Osorio, Alfonso, 181
Oteiza, Jorge, 235

Pamplona, 14, 43, 51, 52, 81, 210
Partido Carlista: attempts to revitalize,
190–91; ban from 1977 elections, 1;
Basque nationalism and, 226, 240; in
Cirauqui, 217, 218; criticism of na-
tional leadership, 189–90; federalism

and, 191–92; founding of, 162; general elections of 1977, 188–89; general elections of 1979, 194–95; lack of financial support and, 197; legalization and, 1, 186; loss of members, 195–96; Montejurra and, 177–79, 184–85, 244–45; in Navarre, 193–94; opposition politics and, 166–68; popular views of, 196–97; postelectoral history, 201–2; in progressive historiography, 120; reformation of traditionalists and, 169; resignation of Carlos Hugo, 198–201; resignation of Zavala, 198. *See also* progressive Carlism

Partido Comunista Español (Spanish Communist Party; PCE), 167–68, 186

Partido Nacionalista Vasco (Basque Nationalist Party; PNV), 12, 180, 193, 233, 234, 240

Partido Socialista Obrero Español (Spanish Workers Socialist Party; PSOE), 168, 192, 193, 195, 217, 218, 219, 233, 237

Paz en la guerra (Unamuno), 70, 108, 139

El Pensamiento Navarro (newspaper), 54, 101, 128, 129, 137, 145, 151, 164, 165–66, 174, 175–76, 178, 180

Pétain, Philippe, 78

Pidal, Alejandro, 12

pilgrimages, 131–32, 133. *See also* Montejurra

Piñar, Blas, 148, 152

Pirala, Antonio, 42, 43

Plataforma de Convergencia Democrática (Platform of Democratic Convergence), 168

Plaza de los Fueros, 131, 138, 164

Pragmatic Sanction, 2

press. *See* Carlist journalism

priests: Carlist Catholicism and, 60–61; Carlist notions of family and, 29–30;

in Navarre, 4, 60; progressive challenges to, 211–14; in *requetés*, 21–22; village projects and, 206–7

Prieto, Indalecio, 19

Primo de Rivera, José Antonio, 18

Primo de Rivera, Miguel de, 13, 45

progressive Carlism: attempts to revitalize, 190–91; Basque nationalism and, 240; Carlist reactions to, 98–99; Carlos Hugo (Hugues) and, 94–95, 157, 158, 163, 198–201; Catholicism and, 114; in Cirauqui, 209–20; clarifying Carlist discourse, 111–15; communists and, 167–68; the Comunión and, 109; conceptions of Carlist membership and, 161; criticism of national leadership, 189–90; *cursillos* and, 187, 188; definition of Carlism, 122; DIOS, PATRIA, REY, FUEROS slogan and, 162–63; disorganization of, 186–90; electoral failure of, 194–98; Franco and, 164–66; general elections of 1977, 188–89; general elections of 1979, 194–95; ideological evolution, 157–61; imagery of the royal family and, 110–11; lack of financial support and, 188; lack of militants, 188; on martyrs, 112–13; Montejurra and, 172–76, 177, 178–79, 183, 184–85, 191; national congresses, 158; opposition politics and, 166–68; ousting of conservatives, 163–64; popular views of, 196–97; portrayals of Don Javier and Carlos Hugo, 102–9; prose of, 114–15; on *pueblos*, 112; redefinition Carlism, 161–63; reform and, 94, 95, 102; revisionist history and, 116–26; rise of, 93–94; socialist self-management and, 158–61, 195; social revolution and, 158; on traditionalism, 113–14; traditionalists' revival and, 169–70, 171–72; weaknesses of, 187–88. *See also* Partido Carlista

progressive historiography: assessment of, 121–26; nature of, 116–21
public education, 208
pueblos, 112, 173, 238

Quintillo, 135

red berets, 32–33, 67, 68
Reds. *See* Republicans
Regency of Estella, 91, 107, 202
Rego Nieto, Manuel, 107
Relato cruento (Antoñana), 241
religion. *See* Catholic Church/ Catholicism
religious objects, 25, 68–69
religious rites, 58–59
Republicans: in Cirauqui elections, 54, 55; *requeté* demonization of, 22–24; women and, 27
Requeté, 13–14, 27, 171
requetés: the Aplec and, 135; Catholic religiosity and, 18–22, 57–61, 72–73; from Cirauqui, 50–51; demonizing of Red forces, 22–24; family and, 28–31, 64–72, 73; Franco's honoring of, 15; incorporation into the Nationalist army, 33; literature of, 16–18; metaphor of blood and, 31–32; military traditions, 24–27; Montejurra and, 130, 137–38, 139–41, 144, 145–46, 154, 176; notions of death and, 19–20; perceptions of history, 62–64; post–Civil War fate, 74–75; priests in, 21–22; protective religious objects and, 25, 68–69; red berets and, 32–33, 67, 68; revival of, 14; rhetoric of crusade and, 22–23; Spanish Civil War and, 14; traditionalist reformation and, 171
Resa, José María, 24, 29, 31, 32
Rincón, Luciano, 238
Rodezno, Conde de, 76, 77, 79, 86
romerías, 131–32, 133
Rosón, Juan José, 236

Royal Division of Navarre, 40
royal family, 110–11
Ruiz Hernández, Luis, 107

Sábado Gráfico, 165
Sacred Heart, 68, 69
Salic Law, 2
San Cristóbal hermitage, 58
San Isidro, 40, 45
Santa Cruz, Manuel de, 75, 236–37
scapulars, 68
Second Carlist War, 6, 10; battle at Montejurra, 132; Cirauqui and, 40–45, 52; modern Carlist perceptions of, 62; protective religious objects and, 69; red berets and, 32
Second Republic: Cirauqui Carlists during, 45–50, 55; electoral politics and, 55; establishment of, 13; religious reform and, 61
Second Vatican Council, 89–90, 109, 114
self-management, socialist, 158–61, 195
Seville, Duke of, 79
Sindicato Estudiantil Universitario, 94
Sindicatos Libres (Free Syndicate), 120, 124
Sivatte, Mauricio de, 81, 82
sivattistas, 91, 98, 135, 152
sixtinos: demise of, 182–84; Montejurra 1976 and, 178–79, 180, 181–82
Don Sixto, 111, 178–79, 182, 183, 184
Sobre la marcha (Gil Bera), 241
socialists, 123–24
socialist self-management, 158–61, 195
social revolution, 158
Sociedad de Trabajadores sin Tierra (Society of Landless Workers; STT), 49, 50
Sociedad de Trabajadores (Society of Workers), 120
Sorlada, 58
Spanish Civil War: anti-Carlist caricatures, 64; Carlist literature of, 16–18;

Cirauqui and, 50–51; in Navarre, 14; *requetés* and, 15, 33 (*see also* requetés)
Suárez, Adolfo, 181, 182, 183–84

Tercio de Montejurra, 139
Tiempos Críticos (journal), 81
trade unions, 124
traditionalism/traditionalists: in Carlism, 8–9; Montejurra and, 176, 177–79, 180, 181–82; progressives on, 113–14; reformation and revival of, 169–72
turncoats, 70–71
Turner, Victor, 150

Unamuno, Miguel de, 16, 70, 108, 120, 125, 138, 139
Un espía llamado Sara (Atxaga), 241
uniforms: protective religious objects and, 68–69
Unión Carlista, 202
Unión de Centro Democrático (UCD), 195, 216–17, 218
Unión del Pueblo Navarro (UPN), 217, 218, 237
Unión General de Trabajadores (Workers' General Union), 46
Unión Nacional Española (Spanish National Union), 180
Unión Navarra de Izquierdas, 217
United Nations, 83
Un millon de muertos (Gironella), 18
¿Un millón de muertos? . . . pero con ¡Heroes y Martires! (López-Sanz), 17–18
Urabayen, Felix, 64
Urra, Don N., 51

Valcarlos, 157, 187
Valencia, Juan María, 212, 213–14
Valiente, José María, 92, 93, 95, 97, 98, 101, 148, 149, 171

Valle-Inclán, Ramón del, 16
Valvanera, 157
Vázquez de Mella, Juan, 9, 11, 12–13, 113, 119, 164
La vía Carlista al socialismo autogestionario (Carlos Hugo), 160, 191
village Carlism. *See* Cirauqui Carlists
Virgin Mary, 68, 109
Virgin of Andion, 68
Virgin of Jerusalem, 68
Vitriain, Don Joaquin, 130, 141, 142
Los Voluntarios de la Libertad (Volunteers of Liberty), 41–44

War of the Early Risers, 6
widows, 65
women: Montejurra and, 151; protective religious objects and, 68–69; Republicans and, 27; *requeté* Carlism and, 27–28

Xavier, 133
Xavier, Saint Francis, 185

youth movement, 187
Yugoslavia, 158, 160

Zamanillo, José Luis, 92–93, 95, 98–99, 148, 170, 178
Zaragoza, 84
Zavala, José María de: attempts at revitalization, 190–91; the Comunión and, 100, 101; *cursillos* and, 157; Grupos de Acción Carlista and, 166; Montejurra and, 149, 164–65; ousting of conservatives and, 163; progressive revisionist history and, 117, 121; resignation of, 198
Zufia, Mariano, 192, 201
Zumalacárregui, Tomás de, 14, 40, 236–37

DATE DUE